Empires of Ancient Eurasia

The Silk Roads are *the* symbol of the interconnectedness of ancient Eurasian civilizations. Using challenging land and maritime routes, merchants and adventurers, diplomats and missionaries, sailors and soldiers, and camels, horses and ships carried their commodities, ideas, languages and pathogens enormous distances across Eurasia. The result was an underlying unity that traveled the length of the routes and that is preserved to this day, expressed in common technologies, artistic styles, cultures and religions, even disease and immunity patterns. In words and images, Craig Benjamin explores the processes that allowed for the comingling of so many goods, ideas and diseases around a geographical hub deep in central Eurasia. He argues that the First Silk Roads Era was the catalyst for an extraordinary increase in the complexity of human relationships and collective learning, a complexity that helped drive our species inexorably along a path toward modernity.

Craig Benjamin is Professor of history at Grand Valley State University in Michigan. He is the author of several books and numerous chapters and articles on ancient history, including Volume 4 of the *Cambridge History of the World* (Cambridge 2015). Craig has filmed programs and courses for the History Channel and The Great Courses. He is a past President of the World History Association and Vice President of the International Big History Association.

New Approaches to Asian History

This dynamic new series publishes books on the milestones in Asian history, those that have come to define particular periods or to mark turning points in the political, cultural and social evolution of the region. The books in this series are intended as introductions for students to be used in the classroom. They are written by scholars whose credentials are well established in their particular fields and who have, in many cases, taught the subject across a number of years.

Books in the series

1. Judith M. Brown, *Global South Asians: Introducing the Modern Diaspora*
2. Diana Lary, *China's Republic*
3. Peter A. Lorge, *The Asian Military Revolution: From Gunpowder to the Bomb*
4. Ian Talbot and Gurharpal Singh, *The Partition of India*
5. Stephen F. Dale, *The Muslim Empires of the Ottomans, Safavids, and Mughals*
6. Diana Lary, *The Chinese People at War: Human Suffering and Social Transformation, 1937–1945*
7. Sunil S. Amrith, *Migration and Diaspora in Modern Asia*
8. Thomas David DuBois, *Religion and the Making of Modern East Asia*
9. Susan L. Mann, *Gender and Sexuality in Modern Chinese History*
10. Tirthankar Roy, *India in the World Economy: From Antiquity to the Present*
11. Robin R. Wang, *Yinyang: The Way of Heaven and Earth in Chinese Thought and Culture*
12. Li Feng, *Early China: A Social and Cultural History*
13. Diana Lary, *China's Civil War: A Social History, 1945–1949*
14. Kiri Paramore, *Japanese Confucianism: A Cultural History*
15. Robert Peckham, *Epidemics in Modern Asia*

Empires of Ancient Eurasia

The First Silk Roads Era, 100 BCE–250 CE

Craig Benjamin

Grand Valley State University

CAMBRIDGE
UNIVERSITY PRESS

CAMBRIDGE
UNIVERSITY PRESS

University Printing House, Cambridge CB2 8BS, United Kingdom

One Liberty Plaza, 20th Floor, New York, NY 10006, USA

477 Williamstown Road, Port Melbourne, VIC 3207, Australia

314–321, 3rd Floor, Plot 3, Splendor Forum, Jasola District Centre, New Delhi – 110025, India

79 Anson Road, #06–04/06, Singapore 079906

Cambridge University Press is part of the University of Cambridge.

It furthers the University's mission by disseminating knowledge in the pursuit of education, learning, and research at the highest international levels of excellence.

www.cambridge.org
Information on this title: www.cambridge.org/9781107114968
DOI: 10.1017/9781316335567

First published 2018

Printed in the United Kingdom by Clays, St Ives plc

A catalogue record for this publication is available from the British Library.

ISBN 978-1-107-11496-8 Hardback
ISBN 978-1-107-53543-5 Paperback

Contents

Figures and Maps

Figures

Maps

Introduction

During a period of roughly three and a half centuries, between the late second century before the Common Era (BCE) and the mid-third century of the Common Era (CE), many of the human communities dwelling within the vast Afro-Eurasian world zone became linked together into an interconnected system of exchanges via a network of routes known today as the Silk Roads. This "First Silk Roads Era" resulted in the most significant transregional commercial and cultural interactions experienced by humans to this point in history. Although silk was certainly one of the most important material commodities that was moved along this network of land and maritime routes, what made this first iteration of the Silk Roads so significant was the exchange of non-material "commodities" that occurred as a consequence of commerce. Because of the trade in silk and other luxury goods, different crop species and agricultural technologies, religions, philosophies and languages, ideas about art and music and devastating epidemic diseases also spread rapidly across Eurasia, with profound consequences for subsequent human and environmental history.

It is this extraordinary cultural and biological diffusion that marks the First Silk Roads Era as one of the most crucial periods in ancient world history. After tens of thousands of years of small-scale regional interactions, it was during the First Silk Roads Era that millions of humans dwelling in diverse communities across a vast expanse of geographical space were connected in an exchange network so dynamic and diverse that, in retrospect, it now seems to be the quintessential example of an ancient globalization (more on this later). It was because of the operation of this network of diplomatic and commercial routes that many of the core ideas of ancient Afro-Eurasian states and civilizations were able to diffuse widely for the first time. This was the moment, for example, when both Chinese and Greek philosophical and political ideas spread into Central Asia; when musical instruments and concepts of harmony that had been developed within Central Asian pastoral nomadic societies were diffused to the east, south and west; and when all regions of Eurasia began to share their unique ideas about spirituality and meaning, which now flowed and often synthesized with each other via the trade routes. Arguably the most significant consequence of this sharing of spiritual concepts was the spread of the South Asian ideology of Buddhism into East and Southeast Asia, a diffusion of tremendous consequence to untold millions of humans ever since.

While this book attempts to dispel many of the myths that have grown up around the popular conception of the ancient Silk Roads, it is nonetheless reasonable to argue that this extraordinary cultural diffusion occurred, at least in part, because wealthy aristocrats in Rome (mostly women but also men) decided that to be truly fashionable they had to be seen in the streets of the city wearing the "latest thing" in fashion, a sensuous, translucent material that came from somewhere exotic far away across the deserts, a material called silk. The patricians of Rome, along with many other elites of Inner Eurasia, created a substantial demand for high-quality Chinese silk, which the Han Dynasty was able to meet by manufacturing the textile on an almost industrial scale. But it was the work of a diverse group of diplomats, merchants, sailors, pastoral nomads, and their horses, camels and ships, mostly operating within and around the fringes of two powerful Inner Eurasian imperial states, that made the exchanges possible. Each of these complex states, and the various groups that connected them, was crucial in facilitating the exchanges that occurred during the First Silk Roads Era, and their contributions are all explored in the pages that follow.

Although a myriad of individuals and smaller cultures contributed to the First Silk Roads Era, such as the Sogdians and smaller states and consortiums of South Asia, trade and cultural exchange on such an unprecedented scale was predicated on the political and economic stability created by the four large imperial states that controlled much of Eurasia during the First Silk Roads Era – those of the Han Dynasty in China, the Kushan and Parthian Empires of Inner Eurasia and the Roman Empire. This meant that at any time during the first two centuries of the Common Era just four men and their imperial courts, bureaucracies and armies controlled enormous regions of Afro-Eurasia. These powerful administrations established law and order over enormous areas; they created political and military stability (although there were also intermittent periods of instability, particularly between the Romans and Parthians); they minted and used coinage; and they constructed sophisticated roads and maritime infrastructure. It was because of the successful operation of these four great empires that commercial and cultural exchanges on such an unprecedented scale could occur. Because of this geopolitical reality, any attempt to analyze the operation of the Silk Roads during this crucial period requires an understanding of the historical processes that led to the establishment and successful operation of these empires, and this also is one of the major aims of this book.

However, despite the crucial role played by these four "great powers" of their age, the Silk Roads were always something more than a trans-civilizational exchange network. As historian David Christian has pointed out, the Silk Roads were also trans-ecological in that they brought pastoral nomads, small-scale subsistence farmers and even hunter-gatherers into contact with each other and with the great imperial states.[1] To a certain extent the trans-ecological nature of the network was inevitable, given that the trade routes passed along the edges of mountainous and arid zones occupied by the pastoral nomads. This meant that even the most powerful of the agrarian civilizations active during the First Silk Roads Era never controlled the full extent of the network, and it was communities of pastoralists and other commercial intermediaries that played a critical role in facilitating both the material and nonmaterial exchanges. The histories and activities of these various intermediaries, including the great pastoral nomadic confederations that formed and thrived during the First Silk Roads Era, also play a crucial role in the pages that follow.

Naming the Silk Roads

The term *Silk Roads* is a relatively new one, not a label that was used by the ancient sedentary and nomadic peoples who interacted along these transregional routes 2,000 years ago. The name comes from the German term *die Seidenstrassen*, which was coined in the late nineteenth century by German geographer and explorer Baron Ferdinand von Richthofen. In the first of five volumes on the geography of China, von Richthofen used the term both in the singular, *die Seidenstrasse*, and also in the plural, *die Seidenstrassen*.[2] Von Richthofen used the singular form to label a specific stretch of the network of routes that linked China and the Mediterranean through Central Asia, a section that had been described by one Marinus of Tyre, an important ancient source noted by the Roman geographer Ptolemy. For von Richthofen this single route was thus "die

[1] D. Christian, "Silk Roads or Steppe Roads? The Silk Roads in World History," *Journal of World History* 11, No. 1 (2000), pp. 1–26.

[2] See particularly F. von Richthofen, *China. Ergebnisse eigener Reisen und darauf gegründeter Studien*. 5 vols. Berlin: Reimer, 1877–1912, vol. 1; and F. von Richthofen, "Über die zentralasiatischen Seiden- strassen bis zum 2. Jh. n. Chr." *Verhandlungen der Gesellschaft für Erdkunde zu Berlin*, 1877, pp. 96–122.

Seienstrasse des Marinus."[3] We have much more to say about the route described by Marinus of Tyre in Chapter 5.

Despite his use of the singular term when naming that part of the network described by Marinus, von Richthofen knew there was never a single road, but rather a complicated network of paths whose use was often influenced by environmental or political factors. He wrote that "it would be a mistake to consider that it [Marinus' route] was the only one at any given moment or even the most important one."[4] This meant that for von Richthofen the plural form of the term he had coined was much more accurate: *Die Seidenstrassen*, or "the Silk Roads." In a fascinating historiographic study of von Richthofen, Daniel Waugh reminds us that the influential German geographer also used other terms to describe these exchange routes, including *Verkehr Strassen* (Communication Roads), *Handelsstrassen* (Trade Roads) and *Hauptstrassen* (Main Roads), which he used in reference to the principal or most important of these trade and exchange routes. Von Richthofen limited his use of the term *Silk Roads* to the Han-Roman period, when he knew that silk was the most important commodity being transported along the routes. These careful uses of different terms to label the ancient trade network represent an early recognition by von Richthofen that, not only were the routes that connected Han China and the Roman Empire diverse and complicated, divided into "Main Roads" and a myriad of subsidiary branches, but they were equally important for both commercial and cultural exchanges.

In the late nineteenth and early twentieth centuries, other Europeans began to take an interest in Central Asia, such as Swedish adventurer Sven Hedin and Hungarian-British explorer Marc Aurel Stein. Initially Hedin, who had been a student of von Richthofen at the University of Berlin and who regarded him as something of a mentor, was reluctant to use the term *die Seidenstrassen*. As Waugh points out, it was another German scholar, Albert Herrmann, who in his 1910 book on connections between Han China and the Mediterranean actually used *Seidenstrasse* in the title.[5] Decades later, after leading several successful expeditions into Central Asia and publishing his exploits in best-selling books, Sven Hedin became very comfortable with using the term *Silk Roads*, although his

[3] D. Waugh, "Richthofen's 'Silk Roads': Towards the Archaeology of a Concept," *The Silk Road* 5, No. 1 (Summer 2007), p. 4, fig. 3.

[4] Quoted in Waugh 2007, p. 4.

[5] A. Herrmann, *Die alten Seidenstrassen zwischen China und Syrien. Beiträge zur alten Geographie Asiens. I. Abteilung. Einleitung. Die chinesischen Quellen. Zentralasien nach Ssema Ts'ien und den Annalen der Han-Dynastie.* Quellen und Forschungen zur alten Geschichte und Geographie. Heft 21. Berlin: Weidmannsche Buchhandlung, 1910.

1936 book *The Silk Road* actually had little to say about the historical trade routes and much to say about Hedin's own dramatic exploits.[6]

Since these early uses of the term coined by Baron Ferdinand von Richthofen, recognition of both the term and the "idea" of the Silk Roads has expanded dramatically in the public and academic consciousness. It now conjures up images of long caravans of Bactrian camels with bales of raw Chinese silk strapped to their flanks, transporting these precious cargoes all the way from the Han capitals of Chang'an or Luoyang deep into the deserts of Central Asia. Here the textiles were passed onto middlemen who transported them all the way to Rome, where they were turned by "wretched flocks of maidens" into magnificent gowns to be worn by the elite women of the Roman Empire. While this vision contains many historically realistic elements, this romantic idea of the Silk Roads has also become somewhat hackneyed, to the extent that some historians now question the veracity and usefulness of the term *Silk Roads*.

One of the first to do so was Warwick Ball, who argued in 1998 that the term was now meaningless and created a totally false impression of the realities of ancient trade through Central Asia.[7] In a thoughtful 2010 article partly titled "The Road that Never Was," Khodadad Rezakhani contended that "the concept of a continuous, purpose-driven road or even 'routes' is counterproductive in the study of world history," and that it has "no basis in historical reality or records."[8] With this in mind, Rezakhani concludes, doing away with "the whole concept of the 'Silk Road' might do us, at least as historians, a world of good and let us study what in reality was going on in the region."[9] Warwick Ball followed up his initial concerns about the usefulness of the term *Silk Roads* with the following observation in his 2007 book on the monuments of Afghanistan: "The 'Silk road' has now become both band wagon and gravy train, with an endless stream of books, journals, conferences and international exhibitions devoted to it, reaching virtual mania proportions that is almost unstoppable."[10]

6 S. Hedin, *Sidenvägen. En bilfärd genom Centralasien.* Stockholm: Bonniers, 1936 (English translation: *The Silk Road.* New York: E. P. Dutton, 1938; German translation: *Die Seidenstrasse.* 10. Aufl. Leipzig: Brockhaus, 1942; Japanese translation: *Chûô Ajia: Tanken kikô zenshû.* Tokyo, 1966).

7 W. Ball, "Following the Mythical Road," *Geographical Magazine* 70, No. 3 (1998), pp. 18–23.

8 K. Rezakhani, "The Road That Never Was: The Silk Road and Trans-Eurasian Exchange," *Project Muse* 30, No. 3. (2010), pp. 420ff.

9 Rezakhani 2010, p. 420.

10 W. Ball, *The Monuments of Afghanistan: History, Archaeology, and Architecture.* London: I. B. Tauris, 2007, p. 80.

Empires of Ancient Eurasia and the First Silk Roads Era might thus be regarded as yet another contribution to this seemingly endless stream of books and other materials on the Silk Roads. But this volume tries to ground the study of the ancient Silk Roads firmly upon the historical, geographical and environmental reality of the region and period, rather than upon some clichéd falsehood. Through our careful treatment of primary sources, coins and other forms of evidence in the pages that follow, we attempt to counter the argument that the Silk Roads have "no basis in historical reality or records." We also believe that the English translation of Ferdinand von Richthofen's term *die Seidenstrassen* is now so deeply embedded in both the popular and historical consciousness that it remains an extraordinarily useful and relevant term for students of ancient Eurasian history. *Empires of Ancient Eurasia and the First Silk Roads Era* thus offers a summary of the histories of all the imperial states, commercial cultures, pastoral nomads and ancient mariners that facilitated Silk Roads exchanges, based on an analysis of all the available evidence for the practical mechanisms whereby these exchanges actually occurred, in order to ground this period and these processes firmly in historical reality.

Conceptualizing the First Silk Roads Era

Although historians, unlike their colleagues in the social sciences, often prefer to avoid theoretical constructs in their analyses of the past, it might be useful here to consider some different ways of conceptualizing the First Silk Roads Era, from the perspectives of big history, world systems theory and globalization theory. Each of these theoretical constructs has influenced the way we have approached our analysis of the First Silk Roads Era in this book.

The Silk Roads from the Perspective of Big History

One of the most important influences on Ferdinand von Richthofen's ideas about the geography of Asia were the accounts written by Prussian geographer, naturalist and explorer Alexander von Humboldt concerning his travels in Central Asia in 1929. An extraordinary traveler and visionary "big thinker," von Humboldt worked to bring various disciplinary branches of science and social science together into a unified conception of the forces that shaped the earth and indeed the cosmos.[11] Alexander

[11] On Alexander von Humboldt, see, for example, L. D. Walls, "Introducing Humboldt's Cosmos," *Minding Nature* (August 2009), pp. 3–15.

von Humboldt is also regarded as one of the founding influences on the modern field of big history, which similarly combines science, social science and history into a tool for analyzing processes on the macro scale.[12]

A big history analysis of human history demonstrates that, unlike the history of every other species on the planet, which are essentially captive to slow processes of biological evolutionary change, human history is characterized by a number of key moments of remarkable cultural and technological change. Big historians identify a handful of these "cultural revolutions," each of which, like changing gears in a car, has profoundly affected the pace of subsequent change in the human condition. One such major cultural revolution in the history of our species was the appearance of agriculture, a process that began around 10,000 years ago, driven partly by the waning of the last ice age, and partly by demographic pressure caused by the adoption of affluent foraging lifeways. As a result, some human communities became sedentary and dependent upon a small number of domesticated animals and plants for survival, a fundamental alteration of our previous nomadic, foraging lifeways. The transition to agriculture led eventually to a third cultural revolution, the appearance in some regions of the first cities and states around 5,000 years ago. Where the appropriate "goldilocks conditions" (i.e., conditions that were "just right") were in place, such as in the valleys of the Tigris, Euphrates, Nile, Indus, Huang He and Yellow Rivers, large numbers of humans who had been living in small villages now settled in huge, densely populated cities.

It is this handful of profound cultural and technological revolutions that fundamentally separates human history from the history of all other life on earth. Big historians attempt to identify the major causal factors, or "prime movers," that triggered these revolutions, including particularly the role of climate change and of demographic pressure. But all the evidence also indicates that, for the most part, those regions in which these changes first occurred were also characterized by high levels of cultural exchange. This means that contacts between different groups have also been an important prime mover in instigating change on this sort of scale, and the more diverse the participants in these exchanges, the more profound the change has been. The late pioneering world historian William McNeill had no doubt that intercultural contacts had indeed been "the main drive wheel of history."[13] The most significant

[12] For an introduction to the approach of big history, see D. Christian, C. Brown and C. Benjamin, *Big History: Between Nothing and Everything*. New York: McGraw Hill, 2014.

[13] W. McNeill, *The Rise of the West*. Chicago: University of Chicago Press, 1961, p. xv.

transregional exchange network of the premodern world was undoubtedly that created by the Silk Roads, a network that resulted in unparalleled levels of diverse intercultural communication and exchange. For big historians, this is precisely why the First Silk Roads Era was so important. Silk Roads exchanges created a revolutionary "goldilocks" moment that helped shape the future course of global history. As we unfold the story of the Silk Roads, then, we also explore one of the great revolutionary episodes in the history of humanity, an episode that helped facilitate a gear shift that led eventually toward modernity.

The First Silk Roads Era also powerfully magnified the unique human capacity of collective learning, a term that describes the ability of our species to store, exchange and share information collectively. From the very beginning of human history some 200,000 years ago, and certainly throughout the long Era of Agrarian Civilizations (roughly 3200 BCE to 1750 CE), few human communities ever existed in complete isolation. As various groups of pastoralists, complex states and often enormous agrarian civilizations expanded their boundaries, they tended to bump together and become smaller parts of much larger systems. Sometimes they connected with each other because their borders met and merged along contested military frontiers, such as that between the Romans and Parthians, or that between the Han Dynasty and the Xiongnu nomadic confederation. But more often they came together in a looser sense as people from one region traded with or traveled into other regions beyond the boundaries of their own civilization. Both of these mechanisms of expansion and contact were greatly in evidence during the First Silk Roads Era.

This regular comingling of states and cultures means that any attempt to consider agrarian civilizations as discrete entities contained between the sort of modern borders we see on maps just doesn't work. The borders between these various communities were really just vague regions where the control of imperial leaders was regularly contested by the claims of local rulers. These processes were complex and the borders between civilizations were always fluid. But the gradual linking up of different civilizations into much larger organisms was immensely important because it led to a huge increase in the size, diversity and intensity of opportunities for collective learning, this capacity to exchange and store information that appears to be unique to human beings.

Ever since the Paleolithic Era of human history (which began around 200,000 years ago), the exchange of ideas between diverse peoples and cultures has been a prime mover in promoting historical change through enhanced collective learning. But during the Paleolithic and subsequent Early Agrarian Eras (which began around 10,000 years ago), exchanges were limited by the small size of the groups involved. Only when exchanges began to dramatically expand in scope during the Era of Agrarian Civilizations do we start to see a significant impact on collective learning. The expansion of exchange networks magnified the power of collective learning, intensifying our capacity for finding new ways of relating to the natural world and to each other. During the First Silk Roads Era, millions of humans living within the vast Afro-Eurasian world zone were connected through vibrant trade and cultural exchange. This was true only within individual world zones, however.[14] Significant exchange networks were also constructed during the era in the Americas, Australasia, and the Pacific. But the four world zones were so isolated from each other that humans living in each remained largely ignorant of events in the others until the late fifteenth century.

Within the Afro-Eurasian world zone, the expansion in size and reach of imperial states and the appearance of the lifeway of pastoral nomadism led to a significant increase in opportunities for exchanges of goods and ideas between different regions. Eventually, these imperial states, along with a myriad of groups following different lifeways outside of the empires, found themselves linked into a vast interconnected network. Not only were trade goods exchanged in these networks, but also social, religious and philosophical ideas, languages, new technologies and diseases. While significant smaller exchange networks developed much earlier between many of the foundational civilizations of Afro-Eurasia, a big history perspective demonstrates that the most important exchange network that existed anywhere during the Era of Agrarian Civilizations was that which operated during the First Silk Roads Era.

The Silk Roads as a World System or Human Web

Because of these early connections that developed between ancient civilizations, many historians now argue that from the moment they appeared these civilizations were always embedded in much larger geopolitical structures again, something like a "world system." This way of thinking about the historical past is a fairly recent development; before world systems theory appeared in the 1970s, most historians still thought of "the civilization" as the basic unit for analyzing history on the macro scale. Civilizationists were heavily influenced by the work of early twentieth-century European historians Oswald Spengler and Arnold

[14] The term *world zones* refers to four unconnected geographic zones that emerged as sea levels rose at the end of the last ice age. The zones were Afro-Eurasia, the Americas, Australasia and the Pacific. See Christian et al., 2014, p. 313.

Toynbee, who in seminal publications offered superb analyses of dozens of civilizations. Their intention was comparative, and thus they needed to study civilizations as distinct and separate entities, but this meant they had little to say on the *relationship* between these apparently discrete worlds. Even today, many world history books are still written from this "civilizationist" perspective, with blocks of information on the various civilizations of the Afro-Eurasian and American world zones, but little on how they *interacted* with each other within those zones. However, with the emergence of world systems theorists like Immanuel Wallerstein that emphasis was reversed, and the focus was shifted to the interactions and connections *between* civilizations.

A world system is essentially a self-contained relationship (usually unequal) between two or more societies. The term *world system* can sound misleading, because it was only in the twentieth century that the entire world did actually become connected in a vast globalized system. But the term has also been applied to other periods in history when societies over large areas engaged in some sort of relationship, be it through trade, war or cultural exchange. In this sense, to paraphrase Immanuel Wallerstein, a world system is not of the world or in the world; rather it is a system that *is* a world unto itself.[15] Wallerstein identified three different types of world systems. The first of these was a "world economy," essentially a world system composed of two or more states that trade with and often fight with each other periodically. In the context of the First Silk Roads Era, the commercial and military relationship between the Roman and Parthian Empires might be considered a kind of world economy. The second type is a "world empire," which occurs if one of the states in a world economy comes to dominate the others under its hegemony. This seems less relevant to Afro-Eurasia during the First Silk Roads Era, because none of the four major imperial states ever came to dominate the others. The third type Wallerstein identified is a minisystem, a group of interacting societies that are not actually states. The relationship between various pastoral nomadic confederations during the First Silk Roads Era might be considered a minisystem.[16]

It is arguable whether the Silk Roads ever constituted a world system the way Wallerstein conceived of it. But there is no doubt that the central

[15] I. Wallerstein, "The Timespace of World-Systems Analysis: A Philosophical Essay," *Historical Geography* 23, No. 172 (1993), pp. 5–22.

[16] I. Wallerstein, *The Modern World System I: Capitalist Agriculture and the Origins of the European World-Economy in the Sixteenth Century*, New Edition. Berkeley and Los Angeles: University of California Press, 2001. Previously published in 1974 by Academic Press, Inc.

argument of world systems theorists – that the relationship between civilizations and other groups within the system are so pervasive that something like "a world system" should replace the civilization as the basic unit for historical analysis on the macro scale – is highly relevant to the study of the Silk Roads. In that sense, even as we offer in the pages that follow individual chapters on the history of four "great powers" of ancient Eurasia, the focus is equally on the connections that developed between them. Wallerstein's theory shared some similarities with the ideas advanced by another significant and quite revolutionary school of historians that emerged in France in the 1960s and 1970s. This so-called *Annales* group included Marc Bloch, Immanuel le Roy Ladurie and Fernand Braudel. The *Annales* historians took the idea of breaking down barriers between discrete entities further by arguing that it was time to dismantle not only the idea that civilizations could be studied as discrete entities, but also the artificial barriers that existed between the various social science and humanities disciplines. By seeking explanations for historical events and processes through a variety of disciplinary lenses, both world systems theorists and members of the *Annales* group were highly influential in the emergence of the transdisciplinary field of big history.

Although Wallerstein originally maintained that the first world system did not appear until the fifteenth century CE, others have argued that, virtually from the moment agrarian civilizations appeared on the planet, they established relationships that led quickly to the emergence of small but genuine world systems. In her 1989 work *Before European Hegemony: The World System AD 1250–1350*, Janet Abu-Lughod argued that the roots of the modern world system need to be sought somewhere between the twelfth and fourteenth centuries. This was followed by the 1993 publication of *The World System: Five Hundred Years or Five Thousand?* by Andre Gunder Frank and Barry Gills, in which they claimed that the vast Afro-Eurasian world zone had actually constituted a genuine world system from the emergence of the first agrarian civilization in Mesopotamia in c. 3200 BCE, a system that became increasingly interconnected through exchange networks like the Silk Roads.[17]

Building on some of the ideas proposed by world systems theorists, in 2003 John McNeill and his father, William McNeill, both extremely influential proponents of the field of world history, published a book in which they argued for the reconceptualizing of networks of human interconnections into an entity that they call the "human web." The McNeills

[17] A. G. Frank and D. K. Gills, eds., *The World System: Five Hundred Years or Five Thousand?* New York: Routledge, 1992.

pointed out that from the very beginning of human history, individuals and communities have been forming connecting webs, large and small, rigid and flexible. By studying these webs historians can reveal patterns of interaction and exchange, and of cooperation or competition, that have driven history relentlessly into the modern age. By analyzing everything from the "thin localized" webs of the Early Agrarian Era, through the "denser, more interactive, metropolitan webs" of the great agrarian civilizations such as the Silk Roads and eventually the "electrified global web" of today, the McNeills have also created a mechanism for deeper world historical understanding by focusing on these larger structures of connectivity.[18] From our perspective this is undoubtedly correct. The analysis of the Silk Roads contained within this volume borrows much from world systems theory, and also from the idea of an eternal web of connections that has bound societies together from the very beginning of human history, but that intensified during certain periods such as the First Silk Roads Era.

The Silk Roads as an Ancient Globalization

Another way of conceptualizing the First Silk Roads Era might be to consider it as an example of an ancient globalization. Most theorists think of globalization as very much a modern process whose origins can be traced to the construction of European colonial empires around the globe beginning in the sixteenth century. Recently, however, other scholars have been arguing that globalizations (with an emphasis on the plural) actually occurred multiple times in the ancient world.[19] This conclusion is based on an influential definition of globalization offered by John Tomlinson in 1999. At the heart of globalization, Tomlinson argued, is the establishment of a "complex connectivity," essentially a dense web of interactions between different communities created by trade and cultural exchange.[20] For a network to achieve the level of complex connectivity, it needs to intensify until it triggers a wide range of social changes that, to a certain extent, brings all its participants into an amalgamation that is somewhat homogenous, but also fractured and hybrid.[21]

[18] J. McNeill and W. McNeill, *The Human Web: A Bird's-Eye View of World History*. New York: W. W. Norton and Company, 2003.

[19] See, for example, J. Jennings, *Globalizations and the Ancient World*. Cambridge: Cambridge University Press, 2011.

[20] J. Tomlinson, *Globalization and Culture*. Chicago: University of Chicago Press, 1999, p. 2.

[21] Jennings 2011, pp. 2–3.

Historian Justin Jennings has argued that many periods and places in the ancient world meet Tomlinson's definition of a globalization. He articulates eight key trends that are the hallmark of globalization, and we would argue that some of these were clearly visible in Eurasia during the First Silk Roads Era.[22] For example, the trend of "time-space" compression, where long-distance exchanges and the social processes that follow make the world feel like a smaller and more connected place, must undoubtedly have been experienced by merchants and diplomats of Afro-Eurasia during the first two centuries CE. Another trend is "standardization." When diverse groups come together to participate in a common purpose, such as transregional commerce, they can only do so successfully if they achieve some common mechanisms such as shared languages and an agreed upon understanding of how the economics of this commerce should operate. Although we lack many of the details of these mechanisms in the ancient world, it is clear that commerce on the scale of the Silk Roads must have been predicated on common languages (or at least the use of skilled interpreters), as well as common understandings of tariffs and taxes and the value of various luxury commodities as measured in currencies, particularly Roman gold and silver coinage.

Another defining trend of ancient globalization is "homogenization," the process whereby "foreign" ideas are adopted by other groups. The Silk Roads clearly facilitated processes of homogenization as religions, ideologies and technologies that evolved in one region were adopted by communities living in far distant regions. A final trend is "vulnerability." Communities engaged in processes of globalization can become so interdependent that if something goes badly wrong in one place, everyone is adversely affected. Vulnerability is the very essence of what occurred in the third century CE, as the near simultaneous collapse of the Han, Kushan and Parthian Empires, political and military crisis in the Roman Empire and outbreaks of disease epidemics essentially led to the disintegration of the Silk Roads globalized network and to hardship for millions of its participants. Most globalization theorists would agree that all eight of Jennings's trends have occurred in the past couple of centuries, but there is less agreement that these trends also appeared in the ancient world at different periods. However, from our point of view there can be no doubt that the First Silk Roads Era is as clear an example of ancient globalization as one can find anywhere in the long annals of history. As Jennings concludes, if we find "(a) a surge in long-distance connections during an earlier period that (b) caused an array of cultural

[22] Jennings 2011, pp. 30–32.

changes that are associated with the creation of a global culture," we have "strong evidence for an earlier globalization era."[23]

Conclusion

The story that unfolds in the pages that follow owes much to the perspectives provided by big history, world systems theory, the human web and ancient globalizations theory. Whichever approach we use to conceptualize the First Silk Roads Era, there is no doubt that during a period of some 350 years between the late second century BCE and the mid-third century CE, material and intellectual exchanges facilitated by commercial hubs within Inner Eurasia and the Indian Ocean Basin brought the Afro-Eurasian world zone together into a thriving, vibrant, connected web of exchanges that had profound political, economic, social and cultural consequences for all those involved. The demise of the Parthian, Kushan and Han Chinese Empires, along with a troubled half century in the Roman Empire, brought an end to the First Silk Roads Era and a significant decline in levels of transregional trade and cultural exchange. A Second Silk Roads Era subsequently thrived between roughly 600 and 1000 CE, connecting China, India, Southeast Asia, the Dar al-Islam and the Byzantine Empire into another vast web based on overland and maritime trade, but that period belongs to another study.

There is no doubt that the primary function of the Silk Roads during both periods was to facilitate trade, but the transmission of intellectual and artistic ideas and of diseases had an even more significant impact on subsequent human history. Perhaps the most important cultural consequence of commercial exchange was the spread of religions across Afro-Eurasia, particularly Buddhism, which moved from India through Central Asia and on to China and East Asia. Associated with the diffusion of Buddhism was the eastward spread of artistic ideas and techniques, such as the syncretic sculptural styles that developed in the second century CE in the Kushan-controlled workshops of Gandhara (in Pakistan) and Mathura (in India), where the first ever representation of the Buddha was conceived. An important biological consequence of Silk Roads trade was the spread of disease and plague, which occurred late in the era. The passing of disease bacteria along the Silk Roads by traders played a significant role in the depopulation and subsequent decline of both the Han and Roman Empires. These are just a handful of examples, each of which is explored in greater detail in the chapters that follow, that support

[23] Jennings 2011, pp. 31–32.

the claim that the First Silk Roads Era profoundly affected the subsequent shape and direction of all human history.

Empires of Eurasia and the First Silk Roads Era explores the environmental, ecological, political, economic and cultural conditions that made these and so many other exchanges possible. It considers the establishment, early history and expansion of four great imperial states and the role pastoral nomads played in connecting them. It explores the challenging geography of the routes, including the major land connections between East, Central, South and West Asia, and the maritime routes of the Indian Ocean Basin. It considers the many diverse individuals, cultures, ecologies and biological organisms that were brought together by these various routes, and analyzes the costs and profits generated by this explosion of commerce. Finally, it unfolds a cavalcade of events and conditions that brought a rapid end to this extraordinary moment in ancient history, and the demise of three of the four major imperial states that had been responsible for its success. As Warwick Ball pointed out, many books are now available in "the endless stream" on the history of the Silk Roads, but this book focuses exclusively on the *First* Silk Roads Era, arguably one of the most important and influential periods in the history of humanity.

Selected Further Reading

Benjamin, C., "Collective Learning and the Silk Roads," in L. Grinin and A. Korotayev, eds., *Evolution 2015: From Big Bang to Nanorobots*. Volgograd, Russia: Uchitel, 2015, pp. 101–111.

Christian, D., "Silk Roads or Steppe Roads? The Silk Roads in World History," *Journal of World History* 11, No. 1 (2000).

Christian, D., C. Brown and C. Benjamin, *Big History: Between Nothing and Everything*. New York: McGraw Hill, 2014.

Frank, A. G. and D. K. Gills, eds., *The World System: Five Hundred Years or Five Thousand?* New York: Routledge, 1992.

Jennings, J., *Globalizations and the Ancient World*. Cambridge: Cambridge University Press, 2011.

McNeill, J. and W. McNeill, *The Human Web: A Bird's-Eye View of World History*. New York: W.W. Norton and Company, 2003.

Rezakhani, K., "The Road That Never Was: The Silk Road and Trans-Eurasian Exchange," *Project Muse* 30, No. 3. (2010), pp. 420ff.

Waugh, D., "Richthofen's 'Silk Roads': Towards the Archaeology of a Concept." *The Silk Road* 5, No. 1 (Summer 2007), pp. 1ff.

1 Pastoral Nomads and the Empires of the Steppe

This chapter addresses several topics related to the lifeway of pastoral nomadism. The types of exchanges that occurred along the Silk Roads were greatly facilitated by the mobility and range of nomads and the confederations nomads established. With this in mind we consider a series of questions about the role of nomads in the First Silk Roads Era. What evidence do we have about the origins of pastoral nomadism in Afro-Eurasia? When and why did pastoralists begin to spread out across that vast world zone in a series of large-scale migrations? Why did some pastoral nomadic communities evolve into militarized nomadic confederations? And what do we know about the evolution and domestication of the horse, the animal that helped militarized nomads become so effective? In the final part of this chapter we turn to two particularly powerful and substantial militarized nomadic confederations that were destined to play a critical role in the story of the Silk Roads – the Yuezhi and the Xiongnu. Is it going too far to argue that it was the dramatic defeat of the Yuezhi by the Xiongnu in c. 166 CE that was ultimately responsible for the establishment of the First Silk Roads Era?

Origins of Pastoral Nomadism

The linking of large agrarian civilizations like the Han Dynasty in China to other Eurasian sedentary states and civilizations was partly facilitated by pastoral nomads. Pastoralism emerged as a viable lifeway several thousand years ago when some human communities learned that it was possible to survive and even live well by using the products of domesticated animals such as sheep, cattle, goats, camels and horses. Pastoralists can thus be defined as "those who are dependent chiefly on their herds of domestic stock for subsistence."[1] Because the lifeway of pastoralism was based on livestock herding and grazing, it was generally

[1] L. Krader, "The Ecology of Nomadic Pastoralism," *International Social Science Journal* 11 (1959), p. 499.

seminomadic and often fully nomadic, which meant that pastoralists never established agrarian civilizations with their large cities and complex hierarchical societies. Yet the interactions of pastoralists with virtually every complex state and agrarian civilization across Eurasia over thousands of years were crucial to the way history unfolded within that enormous world zone.

Following the initial transition some human communities made from foraging to farming, a process that in Eurasia began around 8000 BCE, many groups eventually embraced farming and became dependent upon agriculture for their survival, a lifeway that required full-time sedentism. We know that not all human communities adopted farming, however. In each of the planet's four world zones (Afro-Eurasia, the Americas, Australasia and Oceania), some groups preferred to continue as nomadic hunter-foragers, operating in areas outside of the agrarian regions, while other communities, those who would become known as pastoralists, embraced a hybrid lifeway that incorporated elements of both farming and foraging. Although pastoralists also practiced agriculture when environmental conditions favored it, they generally followed a seminomadic existence that was dependent upon the grazing and utilization of a handful of animal species. Pastoralism was thus a specific and intentional survival choice that some communities made within the broad framework of the transition to agriculture. The emergence of pastoralism was both a product of human cultural evolution and an intentional economic choice.[2]

Pastoralism did not appear 10,000 years ago with the transition to agriculture, however. Archaeologists including Andrew Sherratt have argued that pastoralism only became a viable lifeway sometime early in the fifth millennium BCE after humans had come up with new ways of using animal products. Sherratt named this discovery the "secondary products revolution."[3] These secondary products were foods and other resources (including energy) that pastoralists acquired from animals while they were still alive, including their wool, milk and blood, their traction power to haul carts and plows and, later, their ability to exploit the strength and endurance of horses to rapidly mobilize. It was through experimenting with the most effective ways to use these secondary products of animals that this new human hybrid lifeway of pastoralism

[2] As argued by M. Tosi, "Theoretical Considerations on the Origin of Pastoral Nomadism," in G. Seaman, ed., *Foundations of Empire: Archaeology and Art of the Eurasian Steppes*. Los Angeles and Berkeley: University of California Press, 1992, p. 27.

[3] A. Sherratt, "Plough and Pastoralism: Aspects of the Secondary Products Revolution," in I. Hodder, G. Isaac and N. Hammond, eds., *Patterns of the Past*. Cambridge: Cambridge University Press, 1981, pp. 261–305.

emerged. Although many of these animals, including sheep, goats and cattle, had all been domesticated much earlier during the original agricultural revolution, it was only after humans had learned to exploit the secondary products of these and other herd species that some communities began to use them to greatly extend their range and colonize large areas of Eurasian grassland that were largely unsuitable for farming.

Andrew Sherratt has estimated the emergence of pastoral nomadism sometime after 5000 BCE, but the precise chronology of its origins and diffusion is difficult to determine. Archaeologists have discovered evidence of farming communities that seemed to have become particularly dependent on domesticated animals such as the horse within early cultures that appeared in the Ukraine and parts of southern Russia. The site of Dereivka on the right bank of the Dnieper River in Ukraine is particularly interesting in this context. Some archaeologists have argued that large herds of domesticated horses were kept there, based on the high percentage of horse bones and horse-riding material discovered.[4] Not all archaeologists are convinced of the primacy of Dereivka, however. Marsha Levine has called the idea that the horse was first domesticated at Dereivka a "myth," arguing that the Dereivka people were hunter-foragers and subsistence farmers, not horse-riding pastoralists. However, no alternative site for the initial appearance of horse-riding pastoralists has so far been discovered.[5]

The Steppe and Pastoral Nomadic Lifeways

The specific environment in which Eurasian pastoralist communities dwelt – the steppe – was critical for the lifeway of pastoralism, because, although the steppe cannot support sustained agriculture, it does sustain extensive seasonal pastures of grasslands. Humans cannot eat the grass that grows on the steppe, but they can eat and use the products of animals that graze on it. This allows the human species to tap into an otherwise unusable energy source. The Eurasian steppe is an expansive zone of grassland that extends more than 8,000 kilometers (5,000 miles) from the Alföld Plain in Hungary and Romania in the west, through the Ukraine and Central Asia, all the way to Manchuria in the east.

[4] On Dereivka, see, for example, J. P. Mallory, "Dereivka," *Encyclopedia of Indo-European Culture*. Dearborn, MI: Fitzroy, 1997; and R. Drews, *Early Riders: The Beginning of Mounted Warriors in Asia and Europe*. New York and London: Routledge, Taylor and Francis Group, 2004.

[5] M. Levine, "The Origins of Horse Husbandry on the Eurasian Steppe," in M. Levine, Y. Rassamakin, A. Kislenko and N. Tatarintseva, *Late Prehistoric Exploitation of the Eurasian Steppe*. Cambridge: McDonald Institute for Archaeological Research, 1999, p. 17.

The steppe is not a uniformly flat expanse of grassy plains, but varies considerably in its geography. At various places the grasslands are interrupted by rivers, hills, high mountains and arid deserts, which divide the vast ocean of grass into different regions. These sometimes geographically forbidding dividing features were never a real barrier to the pastoral nomads, however, which meant that various groups could and often did interact with each other, and with sedentary societies, across the entire length and breadth of the Eurasian steppe. Rather than barriers, these intervening geographical features more often served as places of refuge for nomads fleeing pursuing armies sent by the farming societies that the nomads had probably just finished raiding.

The steppe environment, including the grasslands, deserts, rivers and mountains, strongly influenced the lifeway of the nomads. To prevent overgrazing on the steppe, pastoralist families often lived by themselves or in small clusters with their flocks and herds, and rotated their pastures seasonally. Because they were critically dependent on the products of their animals as they migrated, the pastoralist diet consisted mostly of dairy products such as cheese, yogurt and an alcoholic drink made from fermented mare's milk called *kumis*, supplemented with meat from their animals and from hunting. The slaughtering of the pastoralists' herds and flocks for meat had to be managed very carefully. Not only did the very survival of pastoralist communities depend upon maintaining their animals but their herds and flocks also functioned as the nomad's wealth. In addition to providing most of their food, animal by-products such as wool, hair, horns and leather also provided the nomads with materials for most, but not all, of their needs. This lack of complete self-sufficiency meant that trading or raiding with sedentary societies was necessary, and this led to the development of a symbiotic relationship between pastoralists and their sedentary neighbors. The nomads would trade their animal products and some of their animals, horses in particular, in exchange for silk, grains, weapons, tools and other luxury items not provided by the steppe environment.[6]

Within their small clusters of household groups, everyone – men, women and children – had specific and important roles in maintaining the lifeway, particularly food production, which meant that a relatively egalitarian social structure emerged. Their portable dwellings, which could be set up or packed quickly, were mostly round, tent-like shelters known commonly as *yurts* or *gers*, constructed usually of wooden lattice walls covered by

[6] On the question of pastoral nomadic self-sufficiency, or lack thereof, see A. M. Khazanov, *Nomads and the Outside World*, 2nd edn., trans. J. Crookenden. Madison: University of Wisconsin Press, 1994.

Figure 1.1 Mongolian steppe nomads scene: *gers* (*yurts*) and grazing animals
http://media.gettyimages.com/photos/get-camp-in-gobi-desert-mongolia-picture-id545846568?s=170667a
Credit: Chalermkiat Seedokmai

sheets of felt. Pastoral nomads could pack up their camps rapidly when necessary. Large-scale migrations could occur when large numbers of camps moved at the same time, perhaps because of sustainability pressure in the grazing grounds, or because one community or "tribe" had been forced to move by the arrival of a more powerful neighbor.

The word *tribe* remains a difficult term for historians and anthropologists to define, particularly in the context of pastoral nomads. In general, a tribe is a sociopolitical group based on familial ties to a real or imagined ancestor.[7] The identity of the tribe is taken from the dominant group to whom the tracing of this kinship relationship was important. Members of the tribe might come and go, but as long as the dominant group maintained its position of authority over the subgroups, the identity of the tribe remained that of the ruling hegemonic group. The ruling group seldom had complete dominance in a pastoral nomadic tribe, however, and members would regularly consult subgroup leaders to maintain tribal harmony. Even the highest leaders of powerful militarized

[7] For further discussion of this definition, see R. Lindner, "What Was a Nomadic Tribe?" *Comparative Studies in Society and History* 24 (1982), pp. 689–711.

confederations, such as the famous Mongol leader Chinggis Khan, were more like semi-elected officials who undoubtedly possessed superb military skills, but also the diplomatic and negotiating skills necessary to manage the complex social relations required to maintain cohesion and harmony within the larger group or tribe.

Bronze Age Pastoralist Migrations

By the time the first cities and states started appearing in Afro-Eurasia late in the fourth millennium BCE, pastoralist lifeways had already become so productive that large communities were living well by surviving almost exclusively on the products of their animals. But again, because they were not completely self-sufficient even the most successful of these communities still had to trade or raid periodically with sedentary societies. These pastoral nomadic communities exploited both the steppe grasslands and the arid lands that ran in horizontal belts from northwest Africa through Central Asia to Mongolia. In order to survive in these marginal ecological zones pastoralists needed to become increasingly nomadic so that they could graze their animals over large areas. The discovery of burial mounds scattered across the Eurasian steppe, which the Soviet archaeologists named *kurgany*, provides clear evidence of increasing nomadism in some of these communities, and of a gradual spread of pastoralist communities from west to east.

By mapping the placement of kurgans and associated artifacts, archaeologists have been able to trace cycles of expansion across the steppe, with periods of semi-sedentism in between, cycles probably motivated by climate change and demographic pressures. In periods of warmer and wetter weather, agriculture would have been a more viable alternative in regions once suited only to nomadism, and in time large, sedentary communities developed around the camps of regional leaders, as rooms added on to tents converted them into houses. Once environmental conditions changed, however, and became less favorable to farming, the pastoralists returned to nomadism, often migrating vast distances across Eurasia in search of grazing land and other resources.

Two important Chinese Early Han Dynasty sources that are crucial to our understanding of the First Silk Roads Era, the *Shiji* by Sima Qian and the *Han Shu* by Ban Gu, both include descriptions of the lifeways of various pastoral nomadic groups dwelling in the border regions to the north and west of the Huang He (Yellow River) during the final centuries BCE. These accounts, in conjunction with archaeological evidence, have helped historians identify periods of increased pastoral nomadic mobility in the eastern steppes during this time frame, perhaps focused on an epicenter in Kazakhstan or southern Siberia, from which these movements may have emanated. The most likely cause of this increased activity was climate change. As weather patterns became cooler and drier, this made both agriculture and pastoralism more difficult in certain steppe regions. The pastoralists responded by grazing their herds over more extensive regions, and also by migrating in search of new pasturelands further to the south and east, leading to increased crowding and pressure among the pastoralist groups already dwelling along the borders of ancient China.[8]

Because fluctuating weather and changing climate patterns are the most likely explanation for periods of increased pastoral nomadic migration, some archaeologists have argued for a correlation between temperature and rainfall records in the steppe, and archaeological evidence of intensified periods of migration. Russian archaeologists have identified three cycles of large-scale Bronze Age migration eastward across the steppe: c. 3400–3200 BCE; c. 2600–2400 BCE; and c. 2000–1800 BCE.[9] These migration cycles essentially represent the invasion of large regions of eastern Eurasia by different confederations of pastoral nomads who probably spoke various Indo-European languages, and who had journeyed eastward from a homeland probably located somewhere in the Caucasus region and southern Russia.[10]

The term "Indo-European" (or I-E) is used to describe a very successful group of languages that can all be traced back to an ancient common ancestor language, but that have become differentiated over thousands of years. Because specialists can trace the diffusion of different I-E languages, they are incredibly important to historians. The various branches of the family and the timing of their diffusion have been located widely across Eurasia, which means that historians can use this information to outline the migrations of many ancient peoples, particularly pastoral nomads. The spread of I-E languages often came at the expense of other non-Indo-European languages, which essentially disappeared once

[8] On evidence for these migrations, see Khazanov 1994, p. 95; and L. T. Yablonsky, "Some Ethnogenetical Hypotheses," in J. Davis-Kimball, V. A. Bashilov and L. T. Yablonsky, eds., *Nomads of the Eurasian Steppes in the Early Iron Age*. Los Angeles and Berkeley: University of California Press, 1995, pp. 241–252.

[9] Considerable disagreement remains between archaeologists on the dates of these migrations. On this see J. P. Mallory, *In Search of the Indo-Europeans*. London: Thames and Hudson, 1989; and M. Gimbutas, "Proto-Indo-European Culture," in G. Cardona et al., *Indo-European and Indo-Europeans: Papers Presented at the Third Indo-European Conference at the University of Pennsylvania*. Philadelphia: University of Pennsylvania, 1970, pp. 155ff.

[10] On the correlation between the migration of pastoral nomads and the spread of Indo-European languages, see, for example, D. W. Anthony, *The Horse, the Wheel and Language: How Bronze-Age Riders from the Eurasian Steppes Shaped the Modern World*. Princeton, NJ: Princeton University Press, 2010.

the I-E speakers arrived, allowing I-E languages to become the largest and most widely diffused linguistic family in the world.[11]

The origin of the first Indo-European speakers has been tentatively located by language specialists in the Caucasus region, somewhere between the Black and Caspian Seas. It is generally assumed that the original I-E languages were spoken by pastoral nomads from that region who eventually spread out in a series of migrations across Eurasia, taking their language with them. Indo-European languages are classified into various branches, including Aryan or Indo-Iranian, Thraco-Phrygian, Illyrian, Venetic, Anatolian, Hellenic, Italic, Celtic, Germanic, Balto-Slavic, Tocharian and Albanian. Today the Indo-European family includes more than 440 different languages and dialects, spoken by roughly 50 percent of the people on the planet. Indo-European languages still spoken widely today include English, French, German, Hindi, Persian, Portuguese, Russian and Spanish (each with more than 100 million native speakers), as well as many smaller national or minority languages.

With each wave of migration by Indo-European-speaking pastoralists, the pattern of kurgan and language diffusion shows a relentless spread to the east, through southern Siberia and Central Asia, extending eventually into Mongolia and western China. Archaeological evidence for the Early Bronze Age cycle of expansion is strongest in the western steppes, particularly the pit-grave *Yamnaya* pastoral nomadic culture that was located in the region between the Bug and Dniester Rivers in the west and the Ural River in the east. Artifacts from Yamnaya pit-graves provide evidence of horse riding, and also the use of wheeled vehicles that were probably pulled by oxen and that may have facilitated large-scale migration across the flatter regions of steppe.[12] A large number of the metal goods discovered in Yamnaya sites, particularly weapons such as daggers, axes and maces, had been manufactured elsewhere and obtained by the nomads from sedentary metalworking farming societies, which suggests that even by the late fourth millennium BCE, exchanges between pastoralists, farmers and metalworkers of the western steppe were already occurring.

During the second cycle of expansion, I-E-speaking pastoral nomads migrated further to the east and settled in regions of southern Siberia and

[11] For an excellent introduction to Indo-European languages and their relationship with pastoral nomadic migrations, see Mallory 1989.

[12] See Mallory 1989; and V. P. Shilov, "The Origins of Migration and Animal Husbandry in the Steppes of Eastern Europe," in J. Clutton-Brock, ed., *The Walking Larder*, London: One Word Archaeology, 1989, pp. 120–123; S. Piggott, *The Earliest Wheeled Transport*, London: Thames and Hudson, 1983, pp. 54–60.

the Central Asian steppe, migrations that were again most probably driven by overpopulation and climate pressure in the western steppe. The most important pastoralist culture to appear in the central and southern steppe is that of the *Afanasevo*, a culture named after the site of Afanaseva Gora in southern Siberia that was first excavated by Soviet archaeologists in 1920. Artifacts unearthed in Afanasevo tombs are strikingly similar to those of Yamnaya and other pit-grave cultures.[13] This suggests that the Afanasevo was an extension of pastoral nomadic migrant communities from the west, combined perhaps with the assimilation of local indigenous populations. Quite possibly it was groups of the Afanasevo culture that subsequently migrated further south again, relocating along the northern and western borders of early dynastic China, as is discussed later in this chapter.

By the late Bronze Age (between c. 2000 and c. 1500 BCE), evidence suggests the incidence of a new wave of large-scale pastoral nomadic migration, which seems to have caused widespread disruption across many regions of the steppe. The steppe-bronze culture that emerged as a product of this invasion is known as *Andronovo*, which probably consisted of groups who spoke an Indo-Iranian variant of the I-E languages family. The Andronovo built fortified villages and dwelt in large, partly subterranean houses. They survived by breeding cattle, sheep, goats, pigs and horses, and their lifeway varied between mobile pastoralism and occasional periods of semisedentary agriculture when the environment and climate allowed for it. Some Andronovon settlements became quite large, essentially fortified towns; archaeologists have excavated royal tombs and discovered chariots, an indication that the Andronovons may have fought local communities as they expanded, seeking grazing territory.

Although the chariot played a crucial role in military operations and state building in many parts of ancient Afro-Eurasia, including the valleys and surrounding regions of the Tigris, Euphrates, Nile, Ganges and Yellow Rivers, it was not destined to play a significant role in the military history of Central Asia. The chariot radically transformed warfare in Mesopotamia, Egypt, India and China, but it was less practical in the steppe, mountain and desert environments of Central Asia, and it was replaced during the first millennium BCE by the much more practical and effective horse-riding archer warriors, with their composite bows and arrows. Eventually, even the military forces of sedentary societies like

[13] On the Afanasevo, see A. P. Okladnikov, "Inner Asia at the Dawn of History," in D. Sinor, ed., *The Cambridge History of Early Inner Asia.* Cambridge: Cambridge University Press, 1990, reprint. 1994, pp. 79ff.

Han China were forced to adopt similar technologies and strategies in order to compete with militarized nomads. Evidence of the emergence of militarized nomads, with the skills and technologies, and the endurance and mobility, to raid at will and even dominate their sedentary agrarian neighbors, appears in the early first millennium BCE, as discussed in what follows. Some of the more powerful of these militarized groups, like the Xiongnu, Yuezhi and Saka, went on to form large and powerful state-like confederations that have sometimes been called the "Empires of the Steppe."

However, as we noted earlier in this chapter, not even the largest and most powerful political confederations formed by pastoralists, whether militarized or not, can be considered agrarian civilizations, such as those established early in the First Silk Roads Era by the Han Chinese, Kushans, Parthians and Romans. Nomadic confederations were certainly impressive in size, organization and military power, but they lacked many of the defining features of civilizations. They had no cities, no large, dense populations, little monumental architecture (with the exception of the tombs of particularly important leaders) and, in most cases, no writing. Nonetheless, the establishment and longevity of many powerful confederations demonstrated the ability of pastoral nomads to prosper in large, well-organized structures that controlled the vast interior of Inner Eurasia. These mobile communities helped link together all of the different lifeways, cultures and states of Eurasia, including the agrarian civilizations. The political structure and military skills of the larger confederations allowed many of them to dominate the steppe by developing huge military horse-riding contingents that became formidable opponents of the armies of all sedentary civilizations. Fundamental to all these historical developments, which played a crucial role in the First Silk Roads Era, was the domestication of the animal that made the lifeway of militarized nomadism possible in the first place, the horse.

Evolution and Domestication of the Horse

Any analysis of human historical processes that includes a big history perspective will occasionally be as intently focused on the biological and geological contexts in which human affairs have played out, as it is on the events themselves. Given the critical role of the environment in providing the natural "stage" for the First Silk Roads Era, this book includes at various points information about the geological processes that created this particular environmental context, and also about the biological processes that allowed for the evolution of species that played a critical role in the operation of the Silk Roads, including the silkworm, the Bactrian camel and the horse. The next section of this chapter focuses on the evolution and domestication of the horse.

Pastoralists actually depend on a relatively small number of grazing animals for their success, including cattle, sheep and goats, animals that had all been domesticated quite early in the agricultural revolution. The domestication of the camel was also important for groups dwelling in desert environments like the Sahara, the Arabian Peninsula and the various arid regions of Inner Eurasia. Dromedary (or one-humped) camels may have first been domesticated in Arabia during the third millennium BCE, while Bactrian camels are thought to have first been domesticated independently of the dromedary in modern Afghanistan or Turkmenistan sometime in the mid-third millennium BCE.[14] Fully nomadic lifeways based on domesticated camels probably did not appear before the first millennium BCE, however. We say more about the crucial role of the two-humped Bactrian camel in the First Silk Roads Era in a later chapter.

As important as each of these species was to the practice of pastoralism in Afro-Eurasia, it was the domestication of the horse that was critical in the prowess of the militarized nomads, so it is important to understand how this extraordinary animal came to be available for their use in the otherwise largely deserted landscape of the steppes.[15] The modern horse is derived from an incredibly ancient lineage. The ancestor of all horses appeared during the early Eocene Epoch some 55 million years ago, a small, hoofed browsing mammal known as Eohippus. This "dawn horse" was less than 45 centimeters (18 inches) high, with an arched back and raised hindquarters. Fossils of Eohippus have been found in Europe and North America, but it was in the latter continent that the subsequent evolution of the horse unfolded.

The fossils of Mesohippus, which appear in the fossil record after 33 million years ago, are found exclusively in North America. Mesohippus was more horse-like in appearance than the dawn horse. It was a little taller at 60 centimeters (2 feet), and it had a larger brain, a snout more like a muzzle, and longer and more slender legs than Eohippus. The fossil record shows that by around 23 million years ago, a new descendant species, Miohippus, had divided into various evolutionary branches, one of which would lead to the modern horse. The first

[14] For more on early camel domestication, see D. Christian, *A History of Russia, Central Asia and Mongolia* vol. 1. *Inner Eurasia from Prehistory to the Mongol Empire*. Oxford: Blackwell, 1998, p. 82.

[15] For a comprehensive overview of the domestication of the horse told through fossil evidence, see B. J. MacFadden, *Fossil Horses: Systematics, Paleobiology, and Evolution of the Family Equidae*. Cambridge: Cambridge University Press, 1994.

representatives of this line, Parahippus and its descendants, evolved teeth adapted to eating grass. This was a specific genetic adaptation to the spread of grasslands across North American plains, providing Parahippus with a more sustainable food supply. This also meant that the horse was now exquisitely pre-adapted to eventually flourish on the vast steppe grasslands of Eurasia.

The coarseness of grass compared to the succulent shrub leaves that earlier horse ancestors had been eating demanded a different kind of tooth structure, and this adaptation was essentially completed in the species Merychippus, which looked much more like a modern pony. Merychippus stood about 1 meter (3 feet, 3 inches), and had a skull shape similar to that of the modern horse. Another evolutionary change in Merychippus was that the long bones of the lower leg had become fused, an adaptation to fast running that has been preserved ever since in all modern horses. Eventually, by about 2.6 million years ago, Equus – the genus to which all modern equines, including horses, asses and zebras, belong – appeared on the North American plains. Equus stood about 1.2 meters (4 feet) tall, and it was so well adapted to the environment that by 2 million years ago it had spread from the plains of North America to South America, as well as to extensive regions of Eurasia, continents that still had connections between them until quite recently in geological time. Equus flourished in its North American homeland throughout the Pleistocene Era, but then it disappears quite suddenly from the North American fossil record by around 10,000 years ago, probably as a result of climate change and of overhunting by early human migrants to the Americas. This disappearance led to one of the great ironies of world ecological history. The animal that had evolved and flourished in the Americas was apparently hunted to extinction in that world zone by about 10,000 years ago, and was only reintroduced to the Americas in the early sixteenth century by Spanish conquistadores. It was this reintroduction that eventually facilitated the rise of the superb horse-riding plains cultures like the Comanche and Apache.

Despite becoming extinct in the Americas, herds of wild horses flourished in Eurasia and, as we have seen, the animal was eventually domesticated during the fifth millennium BCE, possibly somewhere in the steppe lands of the Ukraine, perhaps even at Dereivka. The actual process of domestication remains unclear, however, and several key questions about this process are still awaiting definitive answers. Was there a single place of domestication, or multiple places? That is, did early domesticated horses spread throughout Eurasia, or was it the practice of horse domestication that spread to new areas? And if it was the domestication practice, did local breeders simply capture their own wild horses and

Figure 1.2 Horses grazing on the Mongolian steppe
http://media.gettyimages.com/photos/mongolian-horses-picture-id640153774?s=170667a
Credit: Kelly Cheng

introduce them into the domesticated horse gene pool? Modern genetic techniques have been helpful in trying to answer these questions, but in different regions the horse genome has yielded different results. Studies of mitochondrial DNA show considerable diversity among individuals, supporting the idea that there were multiple sites of domestication, and that horses from different geographical areas contributed to the domestic horse. This supports the theory that humans spread domestic horses from western Eurasia and that domestic populations were supplemented with wild individuals, increasing the genetic diversity of domestic horses, and also the widespread practice of interbreeding within the species.[16]

It is difficult to imagine any animal that has had a more extraordinary impact upon human history than the horse, a product of evolutionary processes that began 55 million years ago in the woodlands of ancient North America. The domestication of the horse was also an energy revolution for our species; even today humans still measure the strength

[16] For more on this, see V. Warmuth et al., "Reconstructing the Origin and Spread of Horse Domestication in the Eurasian Steppe," in *Proceedings from the National Academy of Sciences* (PNAS) 2012, 109 (21), pp. 8202–8206.

of automobiles in "horsepower." It was horse domestication that allowed militarized pastoral nomads like the Yuezhi, Saka (Scythians) and Xiongnu to become strong enough to challenge and often dominate the agrarian civilizations of ancient Eurasia. It is no surprise, then, that all the great militarized nomadic confederations held their horses in the highest regard, both physically and spiritually. The Mongols, for example, would scatter mares' milk on the ground before setting out on their campaigns of conquest; and their horses were sometimes sacrificed to provide transport to heaven for Mongol commanders.[17] There is a widely quoted traditional saying about the relationship between the Mongols and their horses, which is equally applicable to all of the militarized nomadic confederations in Eurasian history: "A Mongol without his horse is like a bird without its wings." We have more to say about the horses of the steppe in a later chapter, including an almost obsessive fascination with the "heavenly horses of Dayuan" that Chinese Han Dynasty emperor Wudi developed, an obsession that played a crucial role in China's early engagement with Central Asia.

Flourishing of Militarized Nomads

Both the steppe environment and the availability of the domesticated horse facilitated the formidable military skills of the nomads, and helped give them several distinct advantages over even the most powerful forces of sedentary civilizations. The highly mobile, militarized horse-riding pastoralists of the Eurasian steppe probably did not emerge until early in the first millennium BCE.[18] Two well-known later examples of the extraordinary reach of militarized pastoral nomads are the Huns, who proved so problematic for Germanic tribes and Romans in the late Roman Empire, and the Mongols, who in the thirteenth century carved out the largest contiguous empire the world had ever seen. But the Huns and Mongols are simply the most widely known of numerous militarized nomadic confederations that proved incredibly difficult for even the most powerful agrarian civilizations to deal with, even as they also ultimately proved beneficial to these same civilizations by helping link them together into enormous exchange networks.

To answer our question about why some pastoral nomadic communities developed powerful militarized contingents, we need to take into account environmental factors such as ongoing climate change, overpopulation and pressure for more grazing land; an intensification of

[17] See, for example, M. Rossabi, "All the Khan's Horses," *Natural History*, October 1994.
[18] Anthony 2010, p. 412.

trade between nomadic and sedentary societies; and an increased military technological capacity through the development of a more powerful weapon, the composite bow. E. G. Pulleyblank has argued that the development of the composite bow was the most significant factor in explaining enhanced nomadic militarized activity in the mid-first millennium BCE.[19] It was the development of this bow that led directly to the appearance of large contingents of mounted archers in Inner Eurasia that became the principal distinguishing characteristic of the classic militarized nomadism of the era. This in turn allowed for, as David Christian puts it, "the formation of steppe empires as powerful as the agrarian empires that had emerged on the fringes of the steppes in Outer Eurasia."[20]

Traditionally, the composite bow was made from wood, animal horn and sinew laminated together into a single powerful bow. Wood formed the core of the bow, with a thin layer of horn attached to the inner side and the sinew to the outer. Goat and sheep horn were most commonly used by Eurasian nomads, with the sinew obtained from the back and legs of wild deer. The glue that bound these materials together was obtained by boiling the hides of domestic or wild animals. When the bow was drawn back prior to firing, the horn and sinew between them stored far more energy than was available in an all-wooden bow of similar size. A significant disadvantage of the composite bow, however, was that the glue lost its binding strength in rain or humid conditions. Because of this, military contingents living in wet or humid environments generally used all-wood bows, but in the dry and arid conditions of the Eurasian steppe, the composite bow was ideal.

The origins and chronology of the composite bow are not clear, because it was invented by pastoral nomads who of course left no written records. Centuries later it was also adopted by sedentary states who came into contact with the nomads. Arrowheads have been discovered by archaeologists in chariot burials at Krivoe Lake in the Ural Mountains in Russia, associated with the *Sintashta* culture, which flourished between 2100 and 1700 BCE, but the bows that fired them have not survived.[21] Whatever its origin, by the mid-first millennium BCE the widespread use

[19] E. G. Pulleyblank, "The Chinese and Their Neighbours in Prehistoric and Early Historic Times," in D. N. Keightley, ed., *The Origins of Chinese Civilization*. Berkeley and Los Angeles: University of California Press, 1983, pp. 451–452.

[20] Christian 1998, p. 125.

[21] On these discoveries, see N. I. Shishlina, "O slozhnom luke srubnoikul'tury," in S. V. Studzitzkaya, ed., *Problemyarheologii Evrazii. Trudy Gosudarstven-nogo istoricheskogo muzeya*, Vyp. 74. Moscow: Gosudarstvennyi istoricheskii mu-zei, 1990, pp. 23–37; cited by A. Bersenev, A. Epimakhov and D. Zdanovich in "The Sintashta Bow of the Bronze Age of the South Trans-Urals, Russia," in M. Mödlinger, M. Uckelmann and

Figure 1.3 Modern Mongolian archer with composite bow and arrow
http://media.gettyimages.com/photos/mongolian-archer-picture-id108348615?s=170667a
Credit: hadynyah

of the composite bow by militarized mounted nomads allowed for a major, technologically facilitated redistribution in the balance of power between pastoralists and sedentary agrarian civilizations, most of which also possessed formidable militaries.

However, the success of pastoral nomads against the military contingents of various states was not only a product of the domestication of the horse and the invention of the composite bow. Horse-riding archers were also incredibly well disciplined, having undergone rigorous training from a young age, and often having perfected their skills through regular long

S. Matthews, eds., *Bronze Age Warfare: Manufacture and Use of Weaponry*. Oxford: Archaeopress, 2001, pp. 175–186.

and demanding animal hunts across the steppe. Thirteenth-century Persian historian Ata-Malik Juvaini discussed the Mongols' use of hunts as military training in his often eyewitness account of Mongol expansion, *The History of the World Conqueror*. Juvaini noted that often the entire army was dispatched over extensive areas of the steppe to round up large numbers of animals, including wolves and snow leopards, that could be slaughtered and their meat dried before the onset of winter, although some animals were spared for breeding. Mongol leader Chinggis Khan turned this survival activity into a military training exercise to instill discipline, meting out corporal punishment to individuals or groups who allowed any animals to escape. Once rounded up the animals were ruthlessly slaughtered in the order of seniority within the military – first the Khan, then other elites, and finally the entire army, but only after being given explicit permission.[22]

Juvaini and other sources, particularly those that focus on the Mongols, also note that militarized nomadic contingents were superbly tailored for mobility and speed. Because members of the cavalry were lightly armored and had been trained to live off the land through the hunts, each unit was able to function independently of supply lines. In addition, not only were militarized nomads superbly skilled with the composite bow and arrow, which they used with incredible accuracy because of years of practice in hunts and in battle, but warriors also used axes, swords, and maces to great effect. The commanders of nomadic forces carried out carefully planned campaigns that relied upon reconnaissance and accurate intelligence about the strength and deployment of their enemies. Militarized nomads were also adept at the use of various terror tactics, both to control conquered peoples and to send brutal messages to would-be enemies, as the Mongols so effectively demonstrated.

Yet, as we have been arguing, despite their well-deserved reputation as formidable warriors, pastoral nomads were also crucial in facilitating long-distance exchanges between states and civilizations, making networks such as the Silk Roads viable. Before the appearance of pastoralists in the more marginal steppe, desert and mountain environments of Eurasia, many agrarian cultures and states were quite isolated from each other. But once pastoral nomadic communities emerged, they used their strength, their mobility and their need to access, through commerce or raiding, materials not available on the steppe to effectively link up many of the different structures, lifeways and communities of Inner Eurasia. Ultimately then, even as we acknowledge the military

[22] Ala Ad Din Ata Malik Juvaini, *History of the World Conqueror*, trans. J. A. Boyle, Harvard, MA: Harvard University Press, 1958.

prowess of the pastoralists, it is their role as facilitators and often protectors of trade that helps explain their immense historical importance over thousands of years. This is particularly true of the two most important pastoral nomadic neighbors of ancient China, and two of the key players in the story of the First Silk Roads Era, the Xiongnu and the Yuezhi.

Ancient China's Powerful Nomadic Neighbors: The Xiongnu and the Yuezhi

To conclude this chapter we turn to our final question on the role of the Xiongnu and Yuezhi pastoralists, and of their interactions with the Han Dynasty of ancient China, in helping establish the Silk Roads network. Both these powerful confederations were neighbors of the Han and several earlier Chinese dynasties, and both were destined to play a role in world history almost as important as their later and much better-known successors such as the Huns and the Mongols. The Xiongnu make their first appearance in written history in a superb account in Early Han Dynasty historian Sima Qian's great work, the *Shiji.* He describes a lifeway that seems purely nomadic: the Xiongnu move about with their herds of horses, cattle, sheep, goats and camels in migrations ranging from short excursions among hilly pastures to longer trips into the Gobi.[23] In battle the highly skilled Xiongnu mounted archers used composite bows that could fire arrows with sufficient force to penetrate armor; they were also adept with swords and spears.[24]

Despite Sima Qian's account, other types of evidence indicate that, like all pastoral nomadic groups, the Xiongnu were not always nomadic. At archaeological sites such as Noin-Ula in Mongolia, evidence has been uncovered of farming activity, of permanent dwellings and fortified settlements, of advanced craftsmanship including rug-weaving and leather-making and of the creation of superb art objects made of fine gold, iron and bronze.[25] At the Xiongnu site of Zhukaigou in Inner Mongolia, archaeologists have unearthed distinctive bronze vessels including some clearly imported from the Shang Dynasty in China, an indication that the ancestors of the Xiongnu may have dwelt in the region and interacted with Chinese sedentary states from at least

[23] SJ 123. See B. Watson, *Records of the Grand Historian by Sima Qian – Han Dynasty II*, revised edn. New York: Columbia University Press, 1993, p. 136.

[24] SJ 110, Watson 1993, p. 129.

[25] The Xiongnu tombs at Noin-Ula were excavated by Soviet archaeologist Pyotr Kozlov in 1924–1925. See D. I. Rudenko and L. M. Gumilev, "Archaeological Studies of P. K. Kozlov from the Standpoint of Historical Geography," *Communications of the All-Union Geographical Society*, No. 3, 1966.

1200 BCE.[26] These discoveries have altered our previous impression of the lifeway of not only the Xiongnu, but pastoral nomads in general, who clearly followed a far more sedentary lifeway than that outlined in the histories of the Early Han Dynasty.

The Xiongnu reached the peak of their power during the reign of their most formidable leader, the *shanyu*, Modu, who reigned from 209–174 BCE. Modu eventually amassed a force, according to the probably inflated Han sources, of more than 300,000 skilled archer warriors, allowing the Xiongnu to treat the Han military almost with contempt. Under Modu the Xiongnu became a potent and dangerous force. They grew superbly adept at warfare, using feigned retreats, sudden surprise attacks, constant harassment of weakened enemies and exceptional discipline to defeat their enemies. Modu's rise to power is a compelling story that begins with an attempt by his father, Touman, to get rid of his oldest son, in order to promote as his successor a younger son from a more favored consort. To do this, Touman first sent Modu as a hostage to the Xiongnus' great rivals, the Yuezhi. After Modu had been accepted as a hostage by the Yuezhi, Touman suddenly attacked them, assuming that the Yuezhi would kill his son in retaliation and thus rid him of his succession problem. But the resourceful Modu managed to steal one of the Yuezhi's best horses and escape. His father was so struck by his bravery that he put Modu in command of a force of 10,000 mounted archer warriors.[27]

Despite this reward, Modu was now determined to kill and replace his father. Sima Qian writes that Modu had some arrows made that whistled in flight, and he used them to drill his troops in shooting from horseback. He ordered his men, under pain of death should they disobey, to shoot wherever they saw and heard Modu's whistling arrows strike. While accompanying his father, Shanyu Touman, on a hunting expedition, Modu suddenly turned and shot a whistling arrow at his father. Every one of his men turned without hesitation and fired their arrows in the same direction, shooting the *shanyu* dead. Then Modu executed his stepmother, his younger brother and all the high officials of the nation who refused to take orders from him, and set himself up as the new *shanyu*. During thirty-five years of superb if brutal rule as *shanyu*, Modu extended Xiongnu power far beyond its traditional heartland, conquering his pastoral neighbors and incorporating them into the confederation, before turning to confront his only remaining regional rivals, the Yuezhi

[26] See K. M. Linduff, "Zhukaigou, Steppe Culture and the Rise of Chinese Civilization," *Antiquity* 69 (1995), pp. 133–145.

[27] SJ 110, Watson 1993, p. 134.

confederation and the Han Dynasty itself. As Sima Qian describes it: "When Modu came to power the Xiongnu reached the peak of their strength and size, subjugating all of the other barbarian tribes of the north and turning south to confront China as a rival nation."[28]

The most powerful of all the nomadic neighbors of the Xiongnu was the rival confederation of the Yuezhi. The ancestors of the Yuezhi were pastoral nomads that had been part of the waves of Bronze Age migration that had brought Indo-European-speaking pastoralists long distances across Inner Asia, from the Caucasus to the western border of early dynastic China, as discussed earlier in this chapter. Here they dwelt for many centuries, growing wealthy and powerful through trade in jade and horses, and through their formidable military strength. Their prowess was such that they became well known to many ancient Eurasian peoples who mention them in various texts – the Chinese certainly, but also Tibetans and Persians, and even Greeks and Romans. This means that, even though they left no written records of their own, it has been possible for historians to piece together their history because of this range of references in various contiguous sources.

The main settlement location of the Yuezhi was in the Gansu Corridor of western China, where melting snows from the high mountains sustain a variety of oasis settlements. We learn from Sima Qian, and also from the annals of the Early Han Dynasty, the *Han Shu*, that the Yuezhi had a force of 100,000 trained mounted archers, and before the rise of Shanyu Modu, they had been powerful enough to treat the Xiongnu "with disdain."[29] This enormous force of horseback archers was made up of contingents from subordinate groups that may have followed a range of different lifestyles, from farmers to full-time nomads and everything in between. This reminds us that, when we use names like Xiongnu or Yuezhi, we are really referring to the ruling family or clan that gave its name to these stable confederations of different tribes, which would have contained groups that varied substantially in their cultural practices and perhaps even their languages.

Before the rise of Modu, the Yuezhi were justified in their dismissive attitude toward the Xiongnu; but from the moment the great *shanyu* appeared, the Yuezhi were in trouble. Modu began to authorize or personally lead damaging raids upon the Yuezhi from 207 BCE onward, while at the same time also launching attacks against Chinese Han forces, which for several decades were hard-pressed to keep the Xiongnu out. As is explored in the chapters that follow, during the early decades of the Han Dynasty the emperors decided to adopt a strategy of negotiated

[28] SJ 123, Watson 1993, p. 136. [29] HS 96A 15A; SJ 123, Watson 1993, p. 234.

peace treaties with Modu and his successors, who accepted valuable Chinese tributes (including huge quantities of Chinese silk and even Han princesses), while still sending disdainful letters to the emperors demanding even more.[30]

It was through such letters that the Han court heard of the devastating attacks upon the Yuezhi, which culminated in a final disastrous defeat probably in the year 166 BCE. The ruler of the Yuezhi was killed and his skull turned into a drinking cup for the Xiongnu ruler.[31] The Yuezhi leadership felt they had no alternative other than to migrate far away from their homeland and the dangerous Xiongnu. This migration of the Yuezhi was destined to take them far from western China, but in the process of relocating they were able to carve out for themselves a new and even more significant role in the history of the ancient world, including in the story of the First Silk Roads Era.

Migration of the Yuezhi

The migration of the Yuezhi was significant for a number of reasons, perhaps most importantly because it led to the establishment of the Kushan Empire, one of the four great imperial powers that dominated much of Eurasia during the First Silk Roads Era.[32] But the migration itself also had a major impact on the geopolitics of Inner Eurasia through the various interactions that the Yuezhi had with different communities and groups living along their migration route. As they moved into regions already occupied by pastoralists or agriculturists, the migrating horde created a domino effect that forced various groups of Saka pastoral nomads in particular to uproot and undertake their own substantial migrations. Some Saka headed south through the western Tarim Basin, crossed the so-called Hanging Pass through the Karakorum Mountains, and settled in Kashmir. Others were forced into Bactria (the northern part of modern Afghanistan), where they settled for a while in Sakastan (present-day Seistan Province), before later being forced, probably as a result of the expansion of early Kushan power, to move to the southeast into the Upper Indus Valley and the Punjab. Here they established a series of powerful Saka or *Shaka* kingdoms that remain important enough to early

[30] On the subject of a Han princess being sent to the Xiongnu, see, for example, C. S. Chang, "War and Peace with the Hsiungnu in Early Han China," in *Essays in Commemoration of the Eightieth Birthday of Professor T'ao Hsi-sheng*. Ann Arbor: University of Michigan Press, 1979, p. 684.

[31] SJ 123, Watson 1993, pp. 231 and 234; HS 96 A 15A; HS 61 2A.

[32] On this migration, see C. Benjamin, *The Yuezhi. Origin, Migration and the Conquest of Northern Bactria*. Turnhout: Brepols Silk Roads Studies XIV, 2007.

Indian history that an entire era is dated from their formation; this *Shaka* era commences in 78 CE.

The Yuezhi left their homeland in c. 166 BCE and initially traveled around 1,900 kilometers (1,200 miles) northwest into the fertile Ili River Valley, where they settled somewhere north of Lake Issyk Kul, near the site of the capital of modern Kazakhstan, Almaty. Today this region is cultivated with purple lavender, wheat, maize, hops, vegetables and sunflowers, and more than 2,000 years ago this must have been an equally desirable resettlement site for the Yuezhi. For the next three decades they occupied the valley and surrounding regions, some groups probably taking up farming, others practicing seasonal pastoralism, while the ruling dynasty no doubt extracted tribute from other sedentary farmers in the region. Enjoying this peaceful existence, perhaps they even started to forget about their old enemies the Xiongnu, and also another nomadic confederation that they had once treated with disdain, the Wusun. But their enemies had not forgotten them, and sometime around 133 BCE a powerful contingent of mounted Wusun and Xiongnu archer warriors suddenly appeared in the Issyk Kul region, routing the Yuezhi and forcing them to resume their migration.[33]

This second stage of the migration of the Yuezhi was longer; they traveled westward deep into the heart of Central Asia. They passed through the fertile Ferghana Valley and an adjacent region called Kangju in the Han sources, both located mostly in modern Uzbekistan. Sometime around the year 130 BCE, the Yuezhi ended this second stage of their migration and settled in fertile river valleys that drained southward into the Amu Darya. The Amu Darya is one of the great rivers of Central Asia; today it forms the northern border of Afghanistan, separating that nation from Uzbekistan. The river has been important for thousands of years; the ancient Greeks knew it as the Oxus, while the Han Chinese called it the Gui.

Soon after their arrival the Yuezhi were forced to fight a battle against a powerful group of resident Saka, who they defeated and evicted. This victory gave them control over the kingdom of Greco-Bactria to the south of the Amu Darya, a region that, as we see in a later chapter, had previously been incorporated into several earlier empires including those of the Persians, of Alexander of Macedon and of his successors, the Seleucids. Bactrian military resistance to the Yuezhi conquest is treated dismissively by the Han historians, but few sedentary kingdoms would have been able to withstand an invasion by a powerful militarized nomadic confederation still possessing, so the sources inform us, up to

[33] HS 61 4B.

Figure 1.4 The Amu Darya flowing through the Wakhan Corridor in modern Afghanistan
http://media.gettyimages.com/photos/woman-crossing-the-oxus-with-her-goats-picture-id454130115
Credit: MEP

100,000 highly skilled archer warriors, particularly as the kingdom had also been attacked by Saka forces just a few years earlier.[34] The Yuezhi conquest of Bactria is a clear example of the conquest of a wealthy agrarian society by militarized pastoralists. But this particular invasion also needs to be recognized as a milestone in the historiography of history writing, because it was the very first incident ever in world history that was commented upon by both Western (as in Greco-Roman) and Eastern (as in Chinese) historians.[35]

In the years immediately following their conquest of Bactria, the Yuezhi consolidated their position in the region. The Bactrians were allowed to keep their own local rulers, because pastoralists generally preferred to rule through subordinate chiefs of the regions they had conquered. The same would be true of the Mongols 1,300 years later. The Bactrians also continued to conduct their lucrative markets in the great capital city of Bactra, which helped the Yuezhi to further appreciate the value of trade and commerce. By the third decade of the second century BCE, then, the Yuezhi were occupying a strongly fortified

[34] HS 96A 15A; SJ 123, Watson 1993, p. 235.

[35] Along with the Early Han histories already considered, Western sources that also comment upon the conquest of Greco-Bactria include Strabo, *The Geography of Strabo*, Jones, HL translated & ed., 8 volumes. London: The Loeb Classical Library, volume 11 chapter 8, lines 2 and 4; Pompeius Trogus, *Prologues*, chapters 41 and 42; and Ptolemy, *Natural History*, volume 6, chapter 2, p. 6. See also J. W. McCrindle, *Ancient India as Described by Ptolemy*. London, 1885, p. 268.

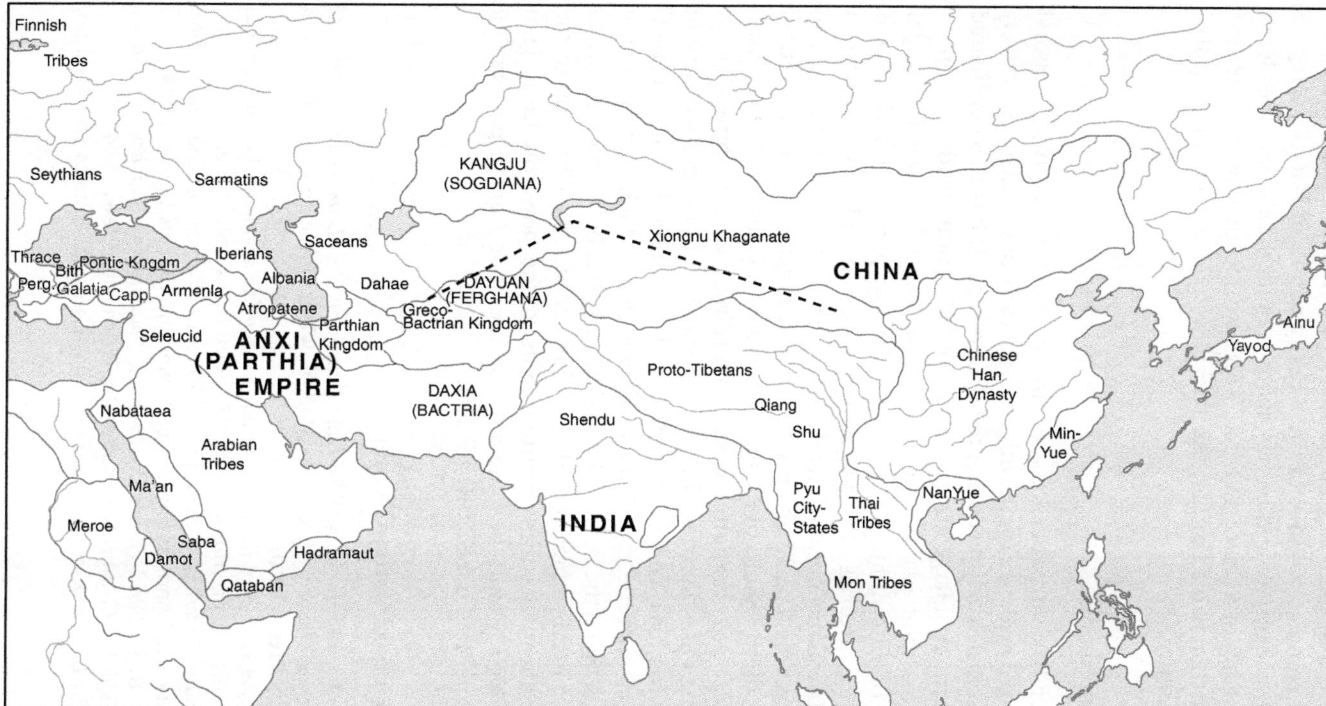

Map 1.1 General Direction of the Migration of the Yuezhi
https://upload.wikimedia.org/wikipedia/commons/thumb/b/bd/ZhangQianTravel.jpg/350px-ZhangQianTravel.jpg
https://qph.ec.quoracdn.net/main-qimg-ad45168b84a045f62b79639fa346cfa6-c

position, were well established as farmers, pastoralists and tribute takers and were in complete control of the wealthy region of Bactria, a region that through geography and earlier history could already be considered the "crossroads" of ancient Eurasia. This also meant that, for the first time in more than half a century, the Yuezhi were once more in control of their own destiny.

Conclusion

This chapter has introduced the environment and lifeway of pastoral nomadism, and evidence for the migration of early pastoralists extensively across the Eurasian steppe during the Bronze Age. It has also considered the establishment of large and powerful confederations made up of militarized pastoral nomads, skilled horseback-riding archer warriors under the control of elite military strategists. The last part of this chapter is focused on the histories of two such militarized confederations, those of the Xiongnu and the Yuezhi. The defeat of the Yuezhi by the Xiongnu in c. 166 BCE set the Yuezhi off on a thirty-year migration, until they settled finally in southern regions of the modern nation of Uzbekistan, in Central Asia. This was the situation that an extraordinary young Chinese envoy named Zhang Qian discovered when he turned up in Bactria a couple of years later, after his own epic journey from Han China. It is no exaggeration to suggest that the expedition of Zhang Qian, which we return to in Chapter 3, changed the course of world history. But before we can unfold that story we need to first consider the history of early China up to the emergence late in the third century BCE of the powerful Early Han Dynasty, which would become one of the four "great powers" of Eurasia during the First Silk Roads Era.

Selected Further Reading

Anthony, D. W., *The Horse, the Wheel and Language: How Bronze-Age Riders from the Eurasian Steppes Shaped the Modern World*. Princeton, NJ: Princeton University Press, 2010.

Christian, D., *A History of Russia, Central Asia and Mongolia* vol. 1. *Inner Eurasia from Prehistory to the Mongol Empire*. Oxford: Blackwells, 1998.

Drews, R., *Early Riders: The Beginning of Mounted Warriors in Asia and Europe*. New York and London: Routledge, Taylor and Francis Group, 2004.

MacFadden, B. J., *Fossil Horses: Systematics, Paleobiology, and Evolution of the Family Equidae*. Cambridge: Cambridge University Press, 1994.

Mallory, J. P., *In Search of the Indo-Europeans*. London: Thames and Hudson, 1989.

Okladnikov, A. P., "Inner Asia at the Dawn of History," in D. Sinor, ed., *The Cambridge History of Early Inner Asia.* Cambridge: Cambridge University Press, 1990, reprint. 1994, pp. 79ff.

Pulleyblank, E. G., "The Chinese and Their Neighbours in Prehistoric and Early Historic Times," in D. N. Keightley, ed., *The Origins of Chinese Civilization.* Berkeley and Los Angeles: University of California Press, 1983.

Sherratt, A., "Plough and Pastoralism: Aspects of the Secondary Products Revolution," in I. Hodder, G. Isaac and N. Hammond, eds., *Patterns of the Past.* Cambridge: Cambridge University Press, 1981, pp. 261–305.

2 Early China

Prelude to the Silk Roads

In the first chapter we introduced the lifeway of pastoral nomadism, and argued that for millennia the large state-like confederations that some groups of nomads formed – the Empires of the Steppe – played a crucial role in facilitating material and cultural exchanges across Eurasia. During the First Silk Roads Era it was confederations formed by the Xiongnu, Yuezhi and Saka in particular that helped link the many complex states and agrarian civilizations that existed throughout that period. As important as the pastoralists were to this process, trade and exchange on the scale of the Silk Roads only became possible late in the first millennium BCE because of the appearance of the huge agrarian civilizations of the Han, Kushans, Parthians and Romans. These states established law and order over enormous areas of Afro-Eurasia; they created political and military stability; they minted and used coinage; and they constructed sophisticated roads and maritime infrastructure that directly aided material and cultural exchange across enormous distances.

As the title of this book suggests, in addition to considering the role of pastoral nomads in the operation of ancient exchange networks, *Empires of Ancient Eurasia and the First Silk Roads Era* is also of necessity focused on the origins and historical evolution of the four great imperial structures that made the Silk Roads possible. In later chapters we consider the history and role of the Roman, Parthian and Kushan Empires during the First Silk Roads Era, as well as other key players such as the Sogdians, Arabs, and merchants and mariners of South Asia. But the early chapters of this book are focused on the development of the Silk Roads from the East Asian end, and as part of that focus this chapter provides an overview of the early history of China leading up to the establishment of the powerful Early Han Dynasty. In the next chapter we focus more tightly on the circumstances whereby the Han became directly and intentionally engaged in material and cultural exchanges with the other states and cultures of Eurasia for the first time, thereby instituting the First Silk Roads Era. But here we attempt to answer three central questions about the early development of Chinese civilization. How did the geography and environment of mainland East Asia influence the development of complex cultures in that region? How did some of these early states evolve into powerful dynasties that learned to control millions of humans? And how did the early dynastic history of China pave the way for the emergence of the first genuine imperial agrarian civilizations in East Asian history, those of the Qin and Han Dynasties?

Pre-dynastic China

To our first question, then, the role of geography and environment in influencing the development of complex states in East Asia. The process whereby agrarian civilizations emerged and evolved there was actually very similar to the way this occurred in other parts of Eurasia. However, because of its relative geographical isolation from other early complex states, East Asian civilization developed its own distinctive ideas about government, social structure and the relationship between the individual and communities within the state. The geographical term *East Asia* refers to a huge mainland area dominated by the modern nation of China, and also the Korean Peninsula, the long archipelago of Japan and the thousands of other islands that populate the Yellow and South China Seas, including Taiwan. Because of its enormous size, China has a tremendous variety of topography, climate and vegetation. This can be most easily grasped by dividing the country into four key regions: the eastern plains, the northern grasslands, the southern hill regions and the mountainous and arid west.

The eastern region consists of alluvial plains that have been built up by China's two great river systems, those of the Yellow River (or Huang He) and Yangtze (or Chang Jian). It is within these densely populated eastern plains that much of China's long history has played out, where the earliest farming cultures and cities in East Asia appeared and where the heartland of all of China's ancient dynasties was located. To the north of these plains, along the edges of the Mongolian Plateau, lie extensive steppe grasslands, an environment particularly suited to pastoral nomadism. As we have seen, powerful nomadic confederations such as the Xiongnu and Yuezhi prospered in this environment, and, as was the case in many other regions of Afro-Eurasia, the interaction between nomads and sedentary farming cultures added considerable dynamism to early Chinese history.

The southern regions of China consist mostly of hill country and mountain ranges that receive extensive rainfall, up to 2 meters (60 inches) a year in some places. This area is particularly suitable for rice cultivation, which grew naturally in the wild in the shallow tributaries and estuaries of the Yangtze River Valley catchment before it was domesticated by early farmers. The domestication of rice was so successful that it has been the staple food for millions of East and Southeast Asian people ever since. In the southwest, the tropical forests of today's Yunnan Province tended to isolate this region from central and northern China until the Qin and Han periods, although contacts were established through the forests between these regions and South and Southeast Asia.

The fourth major geographical region of China is the mountainous and generally arid west, a place where the tectonic collision of the Indian and Eurasian Plates has produced tremendous mountain ranges like the Himalaya, Karakoram and Tien Shan. These mountains were a formidable barrier to communication between China and the rest of Eurasia, partly because there are very few "easy" passes through these ranges, and also because the mountains are interspersed with some particularly harsh deserts including the Gobi and Taklimakan. This combination of geographical barriers, along with the vast distances between early Chinese states and the complex states that first emerged in Mesopotamia, Egypt and the Indus Valley, meant that for much of its ancient history China was protected from competing civilizations in the West. Unlike much of the rest of Eurasia, China was never incorporated into anyone else's empire until the nineteenth century. But this also meant that China experienced little cultural influence from the early civilizations of the Indus, Mesopotamia or Egypt, a very different situation to the high levels of trade and cultural exchange that occurred between these other ancient states almost from the beginning of their history. It was only late in the first millennium BCE that the mountain and desert barriers to the west were effectively breached by Chinese adventurers, diplomats, merchants and soldiers. It was their endeavors that led directly to the tremendous levels of cultural and mercantile exchange between East Asia and the rest of Eurasia that so characterized the First Silk Roads Era.

The relative geographical isolation of East Asia prior to the end of the first millennium BCE also meant that the earliest East Asian states were focused more on internal integration than on external expansion, and this in turn helped shape the distinctive quality of some of the ideas that emerged in the region about political and social organization. This is not to suggest that early complex societies in East Asia existed in a vacuum, however. Although the steppe grasslands of the north, the tropical forests of the south and the mountains and deserts of the west did limit contact between early Chinese dynasties and other Eurasian agrarian civilizations, early contacts were established with other mainland and island regions of East Asia, and the ongoing relationship with pastoral nomads along the northern and western borders acted as something of a cultural conduit throughout much of China's long history.

One example of interaction between early Chinese sedentary farming cultures and pastoral nomads can be seen in the *Qijia* culture, evidence of which archaeologists have discovered in the Gansu Corridor in northwestern China. In this arid region, sustaining agriculture was and is a constant challenge, and the discovery of various metal (mostly copper) implements of nomadic origin in Qijia tombs suggests that a type of symbiotic relationship might have developed between the farmers and the pastoral nomads who dwelt on the adjacent steppe.[1] Further evidence of some sort of a relationship between early Chinese farming communities and pastoral nomads can be found in the discovery of desiccated Europoid mummies in the eastern Tarim Basin to the west of Gansu, the so-called Tarim Mummies.[2] The oldest group of Tarim Mummies, which have been dated to c. 1800 BCE, might be seen to represent the arrival of Indo-European pastoral nomadic peoples in the region, nomads that are potentially identifiable with the ancestors of the Yuezhi discussed in the previous chapter. The different types of burials and grave goods discovered with the mummies, and indeed the fact that in cemeteries such as Yanbulaq both Europoid and Mongoloid mummies have been found together, also indicates some degree of interaction between existing farming populations and newly arrived nomadic migrants from the West.

It was in the valley of the Huang He, rich with fertile soil and abundant river water, that the earliest settled communities and cultures of East Asia appeared. Archaeological evidence shows that by roughly 6500 BCE farmers had learned to domesticate a drought-resistant and very nutritious wild grass called millet.[3] This led to an increase in sedentary populations until, by c. 5000 BCE, hundreds of villages were flourishing in the middle Huang He Valley, growing millet, soybeans, mung beans and hemp (to make clothing), and exploiting domesticated pigs, cattle, sheep and ducks. The complex farming culture that operated in these villages in the Yellow River Valley between roughly 5000 and 3000 BCE is known to archaeologists as the *Yangshao* culture, identified through its very fine painted pottery. As populations continued to increase and

[1] On the Qijia, see K. C. Chang, *The Archaeology of Ancient China*, 4th edn. New Haven, CT, and London, 1986, pp. 198–199.

[2] On the Tarim Mummies, see J. P. Mallory and V. H. Mair, *The Tarim Mummies: Ancient China and the Mystery of the Earliest Peoples from the West*. London: Thames and Hudson, 2000.

[3] Two excellent books on the early stages of Chinese history are K. C. Chang and X. Pingfang, eds., *The Formation of Chinese Civilization: An Archaeological Perspective*. New Haven, CT: Yale University Press, 2005; and L. Li, *The Chinese Neolithic: Trajectories to Early States*. Cambridge: Cambridge University Press, 2004.

society became more complex, a new and more sophisticated agrarian culture emerged in the Huang He Valley by about 3000 BCE, which archaeologists call the *Longshan* culture. The Longshan may have been responsible for the domestication of a new species that was destined to have a significant impact on world history – the silk worm. Evidence suggests that by at least 2700 BCE, and probably much earlier, the Longshan people had learned to unwind silk from the cocoon of a very special species of silk moth caterpillar and to spin this into fiber they could use for weaving cloth.

Early Dynastic China: Xia and Shang (c. 2100–1046 BCE)

Early in the second millennium a new state-like structure appeared in the Huang He Valley, the *Erlitou* culture, which has been tentatively identified with a dynasty named the Xia in certain ancient Chinese texts, including the *Shiji* compiled by Early Han Dynasty historian Sima Qian in the second century BCE. For centuries, Chinese scholars had assumed the Xia Dynasty to have been only a fictitious creation of ancient authors like Sima Qian, but archaeological discoveries that began in 1959 at the site of Erlitou, near Luoyang, have given considerable material support to the legendary stories.[4] Radiocarbon dating indicates that the Xia/Erlitou culture flourished for several centuries between c. 2100 and c. 1800 BCE, and that they built substantial towns and mastered the use of bronze metallurgy.

The Xia/Erlitou culture was eventually succeeded by the Shang Dynasty, which ruled for about 500 years between 1554 and 1046 BCE.[5] We should point out here that the term *dynasty* can have two separate but related meanings. Politically it refers to a succession of rulers who all belong to the same family (or clan), and this line of succession can last for many generations. But *dynasty* is also used to describe the entire chronological period during which the family or clan reigned, along with all of the events, developments and material culture such as art and technology that appeared during that period. This means we can talk about Zhou Dynasty philosophies, or Han Dynasty ironworking, or

4 Considerable debate remains among historians and archaeologists on whether the Erlitou culture should be identified as the Xia Dynasty. See L. Liu, "Academic Freedom, Political Correctness, and Early Civilization in Chinese Archaeology: The Debate on Xia–Erlitou Relations," *Antiquity* 83 (2009), pp. 831–843.

5 On the Shang Dynasty, see D. N. Keightley, "The Shang: China's First Historical Dynasty," in M. Loewe and E. L. Shaughnessy, eds., *The Cambridge History of Ancient China: From the Origins of Civilization to 221 BC*. Cambridge: Cambridge University Press, 1999; and R. Thorp, *China in the Early Bronze Age: Shang Civilization*. Philadelphia: University of Pennsylvania Press, 2006.

Figure 2.1 Shang Dynasty bronze wine container (*pou*)
http://images.metmuseum.org/CRDImages/as/web-large/DP140829.jpg
Credit: Gift of J. Pierpont Morgan, 1917

a Ming Dynasty vase, and so on. The Shang Dynasty controlled a large territory (much larger than that of the Xia/Erlitou) and was responsible for many significant advances in governance, technology, writing and urbanization. The powerful Shang kings claimed divine descent and communicated with their dead ancestors for guidance. The kings also instituted a hereditary succession structure, issued binding decrees and practiced human sacrifice at the time of their burials in lavish underground tombs.

Along with the continuing development of sophisticated bronze metallurgy, exquisite jade working and careful urban planning, as demonstrated strikingly in the archaeological discoveries at Anyang, perhaps the most important contribution of the Shang to Chinese civilization was the invention of the first writing system in East Asia. The earliest evidence we have of writing in China comes from the Shang Dynasty. Uniquely, unlike the earliest writing in ancient Mesopotamia, Egypt or the Mediterranean region, this first East Asian writing system was not used for accounting, but rather as a means whereby the kings and their elites could communicate with their dead ancestor spirits by writing questions on animal bones and shells, the so-called oracle bones.

Oracle bones are the shoulder blades of oxen or sheep, or the under shells of turtles. For centuries peasant farmers working in fields near

Anyang had been digging these "magical" bones up in their fields. Naming them "dragon bones," Chinese apothecaries assumed them to have some sort of medicinal power, so they had been ground into powder and used to treat a variety of ailments, including open wounds and stomach complaints. Eventually, early in the twentieth century, they came to the attention of scholars who began to collect the bones and publish the inscriptions. To date more than 100,000 oracle bones have been discovered, providing historians with an extraordinary record of the Shang Dynasty.[6]

Shang oracle bones were inscribed with questions that the court wanted to ask their ancestor spirits: Will we have successful harvests this season? Should the king attack his enemies on a particular day? Will there be natural disasters in the weeks ahead? After inscribing the questions on the bone or shell, a religious official would heat it until it split into a network of cracks, which would then be interpreted as the response from the ancestor spirits. Often the response was then inscribed beside the original question, on the same bone or shell. Of the more than 2,000 characters that have been identified on oracle bones, most of them have a modern recognizable counterpart, which means that, unlike Mesopotamian cuneiform or Egyptian hieroglyphics for example, the Chinese writing system that emerged under the Shang has essentially been in continual use for more than 3,000 years. This "logographic"[7] script that emerged, seemingly fully developed during the Shang period, was extremely difficult and required many years of study to master. The challenging nature of Chinese writing partly explains the later emergence of a highly educated literary elite that went on to become the scholar-bureaucrat class that would dominate Chinese and East Asian government and culture in the millennia that followed, including during the First Silk Roads Era.

The Shang kings used their well-armed military to suppress other regional powers and to demand tribute and slaves from rival states, but ultimately they were unable to deal with an increasingly powerful group named in the Shang oracle bones as the Zhou, a tribe that probably came initially from the Fen River Valley before settling in the Wei River Valley, both tributaries of the Huang He to the west of the heartland of the

[6] See R. Bagley, "Anyang Writing and the Origin of the Chinese Writing System," in S. D. Houston, ed., *The First Writing*. Cambridge: Cambridge University Press, 2004, pp. 190–249.

[7] Logographs are symbols formed to two elements. The semantic element suggests the meaning of the word, while the phonetic element indicates how the word should be pronounced.

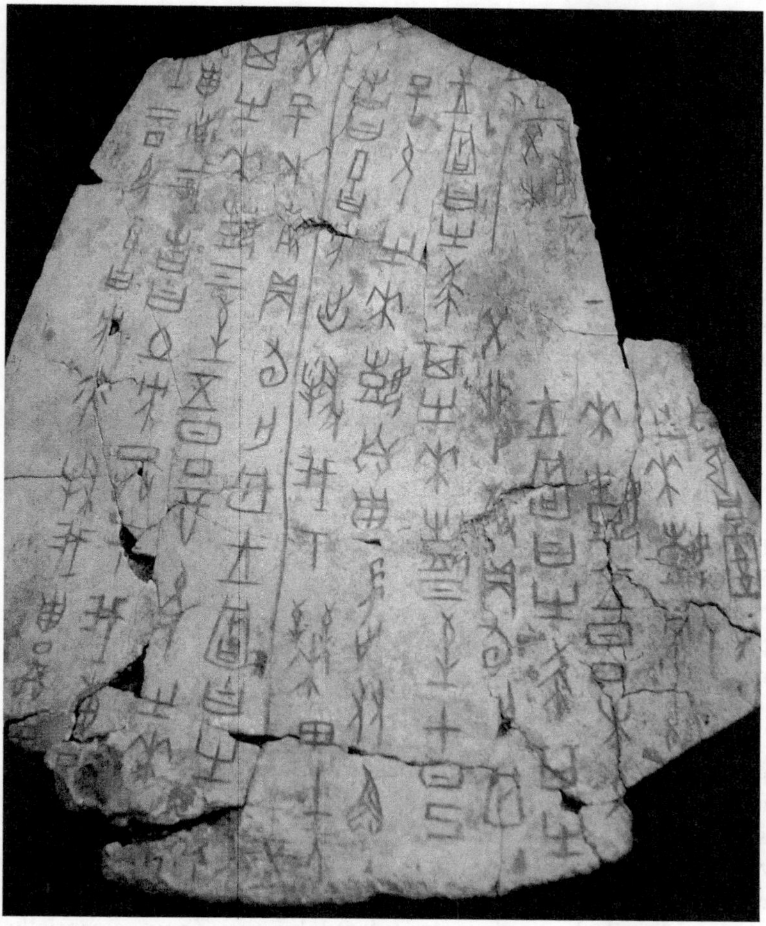

Figure 2.2 Shang Dynasty oracle bone inscription
http://media.gettyimages.com/photos/oracle-chinese-ancient-words-in-shang-dynasty-picture-id520017655?s=170667a
Credit: Zens photo

Shang state. After a long period of conflict with the Shang, the Zhou military eventually came sweeping out of the west and destroyed the Shang, after accusing the last Shang king of being a criminal obsessed with women, wine and tyranny. The beheading of the Shang king in 1046 marks the end of the Shang and the beginning of the Zhou Dynasty, which would go on to rule substantial regions of China for the next 800 years.

Zhou Dynasty (1045–221 BCE)

The advent of the Zhou marked a new stage in the way Chinese elites were able to justify their violent seizure of power, and provides part of the answer to our second question about how early states were able to evolve into powerful dynasties that learned to control millions of humans. The Zhou promoted the idea that there was a parallel between affairs on earth and affairs in heaven, and that the gods in heaven had the ability to bestow power upon earthly political regimes. Two centuries after the destruction of the Shang, statements began appearing in literary works such as the *Book of Odes* justifying Zhou seizure of power by arguing that they had been granted the "Mandate of Heaven." This new political theory claimed that heavenly support for earthly rulers was bestowed or withdrawn as a direct result of the quality of leadership. As long as leaders ruled conscientiously and ethically, and observed all rites and rituals necessary for the maintenance of order, they would continue to enjoy the mandate. Ineffective leadership would unsettle not just the earthly realm but indeed the entire cosmos, and the divine powers in heaven who sit in impartial judgment over the affairs of the world would have to withdraw their support.

King Wen of the Zhou, who later scholars claimed had received the Mandate of Heaven, may have been inspired by a very rare astronomical occurrence. Modern astronomers have pointed out that in the fifth month of the year 1059 BCE, the planets of Jupiter, Saturn, Mars, Venus and Mercury all essentially lined up in a narrow band between 7 and 2 degrees in the northwestern sky, a remarkable phenomenon that would have been easily seen from the Zhou capital.[8] To King Wen and his advisors, this rare event (which only occurs every 516 years) would surely have been interpreted as a sign from heaven. Whatever its inspiration, this Mandate of Heaven political theory first articulated by the Zhou, essentially a mechanism for validating the power of successful dynasties, even those formed by a violent overthrow of the state, would go on to dominate Chinese imperial politics for the next 3,000 years, until the abdication of the last emperor in 1912.

The Zhou Dynasty is divided into two distinct periods. During the Western Zhou (1045–771 BCE), royal power was focused in a network of royal cities based in the western Feng River Valley, with a capital known as Fengfao, the ruins of which lie in a suburb of the modern city of Xian. During the Eastern Zhou (770–221 BCE), the court relocated to the eastern city of Luoyang after the chaotic rule of King You. Because the

[8] See D. W. Pankenier, "The Cosmo-Political Background of Heaven's Mandate," *Early China* 20 (1995), pp. 121–176.

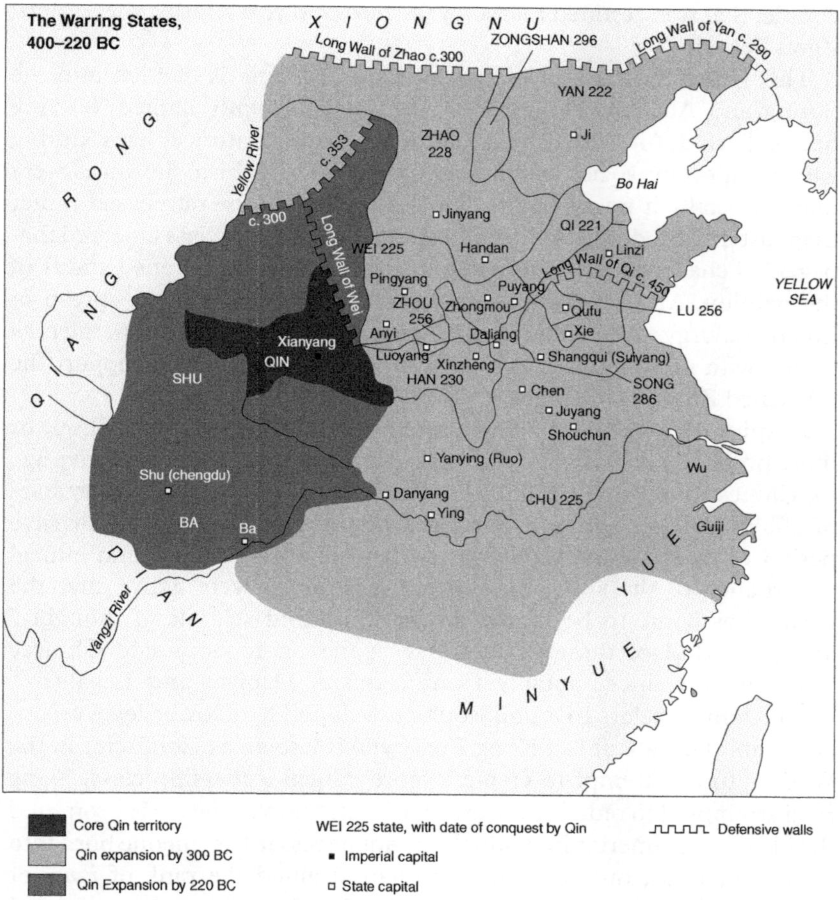

Map 2.1 Map of Warring States Era (400–220 BCE), Late Zhou Dynasty

Western Zhou state was much larger than that of the Shang, the Zhou put in place a decentralized administrative structure in which local leaders were allowed to rule their own kingdoms so long as they supported the Zhou with tribute and troops. For several centuries this structure worked surprisingly well. Eventually, however, regional leaders amassed so much power that they established their own bureaucracies and military forces, until by the mid-eighth century BCE, any sense of unity had disappeared and widespread conflict broke out between the regional kingdoms, conflict that was destined to last for the next 550 years during the Eastern Zhou Period.

This half a millennium of civil warfare in China is divided into the Spring and Autumn Period (770–481) and the aptly named Warring States Period (480–221), tumultuous, violent historical eras during which important social, technological and philosophical advances were made. Socially it now became possible for land to be purchased rather than just inherited, which meant that a wealthy middle class emerged that began to challenge the inherited and previously unquestioned status of the nobility. An important technological innovation was the spread of iron metallurgy within China, which meant that regional armies were now armed with more lethal weapons, and also less inclined to support the weakened Zhou royal family.

Despite the violent and fragmented nature of the Eastern Zhou, or more probably because of it, this was also an extraordinarily creative age for Chinese philosophy. Numerous intellectuals lamented the sorry state of affairs in the Zhou and pondered how to end this bitterly divisive period of almost continuous warfare and restore effective and ethical governance to the state. So many philosophers were active that the period has come to be known as the "hundred schools of thought," and a handful of these schools have gone on to dominate Chinese thinking ever since, notably Confucianism, Daoism and Legalism.[9] Confucianism refers to a philosophy developed by a lower-level aristocrat from the state of Lu, Kong Fuzi, who is known as Confucius in the West.[10] In an attempt to create a more ethical leadership class, Kong Fuzi attempted to redefine the criteria for status in society. He promoted the idea that a superior individual was not necessarily someone born into a superior class, but someone who had attained the rank of *junzi* or "princeling" through pursuing high levels of intellectual and ethical cultivation. The precise meaning of Confucian philosophy has proven very difficult to pin down, despite the best efforts of scholars for the past 2,500 years. Confucianism is ambiguous and not clearly articulated in the key Confucian text, the *Analects*. On the one hand the great philosopher does seem to be offering an argument in favor of the maintenance of a hierarchical society headed by a "noble class," and seems dismissive of anyone engaged in business or seeking profit. But on the other hand, Confucius also appears to be advocating for a radical redefinition of

[9] An excellent and now classic introduction to each of these philosophies is Y.-l. Feng, *A Short History of Chinese Philosophy*, trans. D. Bodde. New York: The Free Press, 1966.

[10] On the relationship between Confucianism and government, see X. Yao, "Regional Study: Confucianism and the State," in C. Benjamin, ed., *Cambridge History of the World Vol. IV*. Cambridge: Cambridge University Press, 2015, pp. 435ff.

status by pointing out that the noble man need not necessarily have been born into the aristocracy, but might attain his position through advanced levels of education and the cultivation of higher moral standards. Men who had attained the rank of *junzi* would, Confucius believed, have the intellectual and ethical capacity to lead by example and restore order and harmony to chaotic Zhou society.

An alternative to the educational activism of the Confucians was the ideology proposed by the Daoists, who were more pessimistic about the ability of humans to construct harmonious, ordered societies. Distrustful of governments, the Daoists argued that humans needed to modify and tailor their behavior to live in harmony with the "Way," a mysterious, nameless, creative force at the heart of the universe. Daoists argued that we need to detach ourselves from our immediate concern with the tedious and ultimately trivial aspects of everyday life, and learn to live in harmony with the cosmos and with other humans in civil society by retreating from engagement with the world of politics and complex social interactions. It was human striving, ambition and activism that had brought the world into the chaotic Warring States Period in the first place, the Daoists felt, so the only way out of chaos was to cease striving and live as simply as possible. Attractive as both Confucianism and Daoism have been to East Asian people ever since they first emerged, in the end it was a very different philosophy that ultimately succeeded in reuniting China at the end of the Warring States Period. The application of this philosophy of Legalism provides part of the answer to the third question this chapter addresses, how the early dynastic history of China paved the way for the emergence of the first genuine imperial states in East Asian history, those of the Qin and Han Dynasties.

Qin Dynasty (221–206 BCE)

One of the warring states, the powerful Qin from northwestern China, adopted the ideology of Legalism, which insisted that social cohesion could only be achieved through the application of strict laws and harsh, collective punishments. Using often brutal, legalist tactics, it was the Qin who finally succeeded in defeating their warring states rivals and reuniting China under their own short-lived but highly effective Qin Dynasty. Although the reign of the Qin was brief, only fifteen years, their achievements in unifying and strengthening the state made it possible for their successors, the Han, to establish a truly enormous Chinese empire that would last for 400 years, utterly transforming East Asian civilization and profoundly influencing much of Eurasia as well. In 221, the victorious Qin king Ying Zheng, having survived an assassination attempt that, had it succeeded, would have radically altered the course of Chinese and indeed world history, proclaimed himself *Shi Huangdi*, a title he coined from the words *huang* (which means "august") and *di* (which means "lord"). This conjunction of "august lord" now became the title for "emperor." The word *shi* is the number one in Chinese, so *Shi Huangdi* means "First August Lord," or, in reality, First Emperor. Having created his own title, the First Emperor, in a reign of just eleven years, undertook a series of stunning reforms that few rulers in history have matched in reigns many times as long.

To unite the divided kingdoms and peoples of China he needed to first weaken the power of the feudal nobility, which he did by moving its leading members to the Qin capital at Xianyang (just west of modern Xian) and keeping them as virtual hostages. In place of the Zhou feudal structure, China was now divided into thirty-six provinces, each under the control of administrative bureaucracies rather than noble lords.[11] To guard against future rebellions, he ordered the civilian populations to surrender all the weapons they had amassed after centuries of warfare, and private possession of arms now joined the prohibited list in the new Qin law codes. This rigidly Legalist code was promulgated throughout the empire and it regulated all aspects of society; lawbreakers were subject to harsh punishments including hard labor, amputations and death.

Shi Huangdi next passed a series of linguistic and economic reforms aimed at further unifying the Qin state. The writing system was reformed by the introduction of a new style called *xiaozhuan* (small seal script), which was now mandated throughout the state. All weights, currency and measurements were also standardized; any attempt to maintain local measurement or writing systems was decreed to be an act of treason by the law. The First Emperor also introduced reforms that allowed for private ownership of land by the peasants, although in reality the lives of the peasants remained little better than those of serfs. Their lot was made worse by the massive building projects started by the emperor, which required huge drafts of conscripted labor. The most impressive of these projects resulted in the construction of two of the great wonders of the world – the emperor's own tomb, and the Great Wall of China.

The structure that later became the Great Wall had originated during the Warring States Period when several of the northern states had built their own stamped earth walls for defense from militarized nomads on the steppe and from each other. Even as the Warring States Period played itself out with the success of the Qin, militarized nomads remained

11 On this, see R. D. S. Yates, "State Control of Bureaucrats under the Qin: Techniques and Procedures," *Early China* 20 (1995), pp. 331–365.

a constant threat in the north. Later Han sources note that Qin general Meng Tan led a massive force of some 300,000 Chinese soldiers to attack the Xiongnu and try and evict them from the steppe grasslands north of the great bend in the Huang He.[12] In the aftermath of this campaign, the emperor ordered that the preexisting regional walls should now be connected to form a single defensive system along the entire northern border, a massive undertaking that took ten years to complete using the labor of hundreds of thousands of soldiers and conscripted workers.

To try and deal with the logistics of having to transport the huge quantities of materials required for construction, the builders used local resources wherever possible. Where the wall was constructed across mountain ranges, for example, the builders used local stone quarried from the mountains; but where it traversed the flat northern plains, rammed earth was used for construction. No historical records have survived to indicate the exact length or course of the Qin Dynasty walls, and much of this initial ancient wall has long since crumbled away, but it seems to have stretched from Liadong in the east (in modern Jilin Province) to Linzhao in the west (in the eastern part of Gansu Province). During the subsequent Han Dynasty, as Chinese diplomats and military officials began to interact with Central Asian states and also launch aggressive campaigns against the Xiongnu, the wall was extended further to the west to protect the caravans, troops and guard posts that were established there, developments discussed in the next chapter.

The second of Shi Huangdi's monumental building projects was his own tomb, a vast mausoleum just east of the modern city of Xian that was lost to history for almost 2,000 years, and was rediscovered by accident in 1974 by a group of local farmers who were digging wells. Once Chinese archaeologists began to investigate the discovery, the vast underground mausoleum was revealed. In the east vault, archaeologists discovered royal chariots with bronze horses and an extraordinary terracotta army of thousands of life-sized soldiers created from a series of mix-and-match clay molds. Each terracotta soldier was then individualized by artists so that no two soldiers are identical. Each man was built with solid legs and a hollow torso, and each was sculpted wearing the uniform and carrying the weapons of his particular branch of the military: infantry, cavalry, charioteers with life-sized chariots and clay horses, standing and kneeling archers and officers occupying their own headquarters building. Finally, all the standing warriors were attached to clay plinths that rested on the tiled floor, which still resembles a modern parade ground today; here the

[12] On this campaign, see C. Beckwith, *Empires of the Silk Road: A History of Central Asia from the Bronze Age to the Present*. Princeton, NJ: Princeton University Press, 2009, pp. 71–73.

Figure 2.3 Terracotta warriors in the tomb of the first Qin Dynasty emperor, Shi Huangdi (reigned 220–210 BCE)
http://media.gettyimages.com/photos/terracotta-warriors-in-xian-china-picture-id503638562?s=170667a
Credit: Nikada

massive army was lined up in perfect formation, ready to march out upon some ghostly campaign.[13]

Sima Qian, the Han Dynasty historian who wrote a little over a century after the death of the First Emperor, included a description of the tomb in the *Shiji*.[14] He informs us that the tomb was under construction from 245 to 210 (that is, from when the teenage King Ying became king of the Qin state right up until his death); that many thousands of laborers were conscripted to work on the mausoleum, most of whom were worked to death; and that all surviving laborers were killed and buried with the emperor to keep the tomb's location a secret. Sima Qian also provided a description of the emperor's personal tomb within the vast complex. It consisted of a huge central chamber topped by a ceiling studded with pearls and precious stones to represent the moon, sun and stars, and with

[13] See J. Portal, ed., *The First Emperor: China's Terracotta Army*. Cambridge, MA: Harvard University Press, 2006.

[14] Sima Qian, *The Records of the Grand Historian*, trans. Y. Hsien-yi and G. Yang, Beijing, China: Foreign Language Press, 1979, chapter 6.

exact representations of the Huang He and Yangtze running across the floor in rivers of mercury before flowing into a mercury ocean. Lamps containing whale oil, the longest-burning substance known at the time, were used to light the scene and the doors were sealed with molten copper. Finally, armed and primed crossbows were set up as booby traps for any who dared to enter the tomb of Qin Shi Huangdi.

The charismatic First Emperor was succeeded by a relatively inept son who could not control the nobility nor feed the peasants, so rebel armies arose across China, leading quite quickly to the collapse of Qin authority. The most formidable of these rebel armies was led by a peasant named Liu Bang, and by 206 BCE, Liu Bang had defeated his rivals and established the Han Dynasty, which was destined to rule China for the next 400 years.

Early Han Dynasty (206 BCE–9 CE)

The advent of the Han Dynasty radically changed the political and administrative structure of Chinese government, and through its military and cultural prowess, also influenced the psyche and even the legitimacy of the Chinese people. One example of the significance of the Han Dynasty to subsequent Chinese history is the fact that ethnic Chinese still call themselves "Han" to this day. The Han were able to build upon the achievements of the First Emperor, Shi Huangdi, to create one of the great empires in world history, the equivalent of what the Romans were able to achieve at the opposite end of Eurasia at more or less the same time. The Han essentially instigated a second stage in the creation of a more durable political structure that had begun under the Qin. They did this so successfully that the Han Dynasty went on to rule China for most of the next four centuries, from 206 BCE to 220 CE, as one of the great powers of ancient Eurasia.

The Han Dynasty began when rebel leader Liu Bang emerged as the eventual victor in the power struggle between rival forces competing to bring down the Qin Dynasty. Liu Bang was born into an otherwise insignificant family in a village in present-day Jiangsu Province. His birth was so lowly that his parents' names have not been recorded by history. Legend has it that one night before Liu Bang was born, his mother was forced to shelter from a fierce storm under a bridge. Her husband went out to find her, but in a flash of lightning he looked up and saw a huge dragon towering above the bridge and the frightened woman. Soon after this incident, Liu Bang's mother gave birth to him; as he grew to manhood, his high nose and thick whiskers gave him something of the appearance of a dragon, and the legend of his conception was also said to explain the seventy-two strange dark spots on his left leg!

Liu Bang was later put in charge of escorting convicts to work on the great tomb of the first Qin emperor, but during the journey many prisoners escaped, which meant that Liu Bang would have faced the mandatory death penalty according to the Legalist code. Because of this he was forced to become a fugitive, and then a successful rebel leader who was the first to lead his army into the Qin capital at Xianyang. After defeating his rivals in a long and complex military and diplomatic struggle, Liu Bang (whose posthumous imperial reign name is Gaozu) declared himself emperor. He immediately began construction of a new capital in the Wei River Valley named "Chang'an" (Perpetual Peace), and proclaimed the beginning of the Han Dynasty in 206 BCE.

The Han presided over a four-century-long period of political consolidation under strong central government with a well-organized and highly educated bureaucracy. This was also a great age of imperial expansion; under the Han, China grew into a huge empire that stretched eventually from Vietnam in the south to Korea in the north, and from the China Sea in the east deep into the heart of Central Asia in the west. This dramatic expansion of the Chinese state had major world historical implications, because, as we see in the next chapter, it was under the Han that East Asia began to seriously engage with the rest of Eurasia for the first time, essentially instigating the First Silk Roads Era.

Like the Zhou, the Han Dynasty is divided into two distinct periods, separated by a break in its dynastic rule. During the first period, the Early Han ruled from their capital at Chang'an, located within the modern Chinese city of Xian. Because the Early Han ruled from the western capital of Chang'an, historians also refer to them as the "Western Han." The Later Han Dynasty was forced to relocate its capital to the eastern city of Luoyang, and therefore the Later Han Dynasty is also known as the "Eastern Han." Politically the Early Han succeeded where the Qin failed because they were more moderate in their approach to government, which depended less on the charisma and power of the emperor, and more on establishing an effective and sustainable bureaucratic administrative structure.[15] The Han reduced taxes on the peasants and set out to enlist the support of Confucian scholars and Daoist philosophers, essentially replacing harsh Qin Legalist rule by reviving intellectual life. In general, throughout both the Early and Later Han, the government attempted to keep taxes on the land as light as possible. The tax on

[15] On Qin and Han administration, see M. E. Lewis, *The Early Chinese Empire: Qin and Han*. Cambridge, MA: Belknap Press of Harvard University Press, 2007.

agricultural production was only about one-thirtieth of the autumn harvest, which was a benefit to both peasants and landed nobility.

The Han created a large bureaucracy staffed by skilled and well-paid administrators to rule their empire. During the first century of Han rule, the decision was made to employ men to staff this bureaucracy on the basis of an examination system that demanded a deep knowledge of Confucian philosophy. This was a masterstroke because of the Confucian insistence on ethical behavior and loyalty to one's superiors and to the state. Not that all these political innovations happened at once; they were introduced by different emperors during the first century of the dynasty. Indeed, during the first stage of the Han, the state inherited by Liu Bang actually retained much of the administrative structure put in place by the first emperor of the preceding Qin Dynasty. But the new Han emperor retreated somewhat from the Qin experiment in strong centralized rule by establishing vassal kingdoms in some areas. Because of the alliances he had been forced to build in order to claim the throne, Liu Bang had little choice in this. Immediately after proclaiming the Han Dynasty he had little alternative other than to divide the country into several quasi "feudal states" to satisfy some of his wartime allies. However, ever conscious of the ambition of the nobility and the potential for the country to slip back into a warring states mentality, as his reign progressed Liu Bang attempted to regain control of much of the land he had "given away" by reincorporating it back into the empire, and also by appointing members of his own family to rule the kingdoms. Yet throughout his reign Liu Bang was forced to retain a much more decentralized administrative structure than the Qin had done, and this proved a constant source of concern when ambitious nobles and Liu family members competed with each other to gain more power.

Liu Bang's successors intensified the process of creating a more centralized government by introducing a provincial form of administration in which the country was divided into commanderies and kingdoms. Historians have available a complete list of these provincial units from a census taken in 2 CE, by which time there were eighty-three commanderies and ten kingdoms.[16] The commanderies were each governed by a Grand Administrator appointed by the central government. The kingdoms were governed by kings who were usually close relatives of the emperor, but these kingdoms theoretically had more autonomy

[16] See M. Loewe, *The Government of the Qin and Han Empires 221 BCE–220 CE*. Indianapolis, IN, and Cambridge: Hackett Publishing Company, Inc., 2006, chapter 3, pp. 37–55. See also maps and accompanying data on pp. 197, 198 and 200.

than the commanderies. We know from historical documents, however, that the central government was often able to manipulate the succession of kings. This, along with the fact that the government appointed the senior political advisors to the kings, meant that in reality the kingdoms were almost as directly controlled by the Han government as were the commanderies. In this sophisticated administrative structure, the commanderies were further divided into prefectures, of which there were 1,587 in the year 2 CE. The prefectures in turn were divided into districts, and the districts into much smaller units that we might think of as wards today. This was without doubt the most sophisticated and best-organized imperial administrative structure in world history to this point, and it required a vast and equally well-organized bureaucracy to administer it.

Wudi and the "Triumph of Confucianism" (141–87 BCE)

After the death of Liu Bang, his successors from Emperor Hui to Emperor Jing tried to rule this complex Chinese state by combining Legalist methods with Daoist principles. Some of the early emperors were not particularly enamored with Confucianism, and Emperor Wendi in particular, who ruled from 179 to 159, was actually a devout Daoist. During what is often called the "pseudo-Daoist era," a stable centralized government was established through revival of the agriculture sector and the gradual erosion of the power of the former "feudal states." It was during the reign of the competent and vigorous Emperor Wudi, the "Martial Emperor" who ruled from 141 to 87 BCE, that the Han government made the decision to adopt Confucianism as the official philosophy of the state. This policy shift has often been described as the "triumph of Confucianism," and is a key reason why Confucianism remained at the core of Chinese government for much of the next 2,000 years. Wudi and his successors recognized the advantages to government of core Confucian values such as self-restraint and loyalty to the state, and they supported and promoted Confucian scholars in government.

Wudi also established a state educational system based on the Confucian classics, topped by an imperial Confucian academy in Chang'an to train future officials. Particular policy initiatives aimed at promoting the core Confucian value of "filial piety" were advanced by the state, and Emperor Wu and his successors made frequent calls to recruit filial sons into the bureaucracy. Filial piety essentially meant being loving, respectful and dutiful to the needs of family elders, which to Confucius had meant mostly parents and grandparents. Under the Han this notion

Figure 2.4 Modern statue of Early Han Dynasty emperor Wudi (reigned 141–87 BCE)
www.gettyimages.co.uk/license/136247606
Credit: Eastimages

was extended politically and socially. Because men could be promoted partly on their reputation for filial piety, some resorted to greatly exaggerated acts of piety, such as mourning the death of one's parents or grandparents for an inordinately long period of time. Nonetheless, numerous sources (including government edicts issued between 186 and 165 BCE, early in the history of the Western Han)[17] attest that senior administrators of regional provinces were expected to send young men known to be "filial and incorruptible" to the capital each year, where they would be appointed to administrative positions.[18]

Along with Wudi, the Confucian scholars themselves deserve considerable credit for this "triumph of Confucianism," in that they were able to adapt this flexible philosophy to the specific mood and need of the times. Confucians began to see the world around them as a self-sustaining organism in which the balance of the cosmic forces of yin and yang and the associated five elements were used to interpret and predict political cycles and dynastic successions. The cosmology that emerged legitimized the Han Dynasty and elevated the status of the emperor as the only person capable of linking heaven, earth and humanity into a harmonious whole. In reality, elements of both Daoism and Confucianism can be discerned in the concept of the power and role of the emperor that emerged in the Early Han Dynasty, particularly in the work of philosopher Dong Zhongshu, who lived from 179 to 104 BCE and rose to high office under Wudi.[19] The Daoist influence is seen in the argument that the ruler ruled best through inaction, by keeping out of and above the tedious affairs of everyday government. The Confucian influence was more moral, arguing that a ruler who did not do his job properly would disturb the balance between heaven and earth, thus opening up the state to a range of natural disasters because of the loss of the Mandate of Heaven. The historical evidence of Han political rule does suggest that most Han emperors from Wudi on did genuinely support the Confucian ideal that the highest officials of the state should be men of intellectual and ethical ability – "filial and incorrupt" – rather than noble born.

The official adoption of Confucianism by Wudi seventy years after the establishment of the Han Dynasty enhanced the civil service nomination system, and also strengthened the examination by basing it squarely on the knowledge candidates possessed of the Confucian classics and

[17] Loewe 2006, p. 74.

[18] For further discussion of this, see L. Feng, *Early China: A Social and Cultural History*. Cambridge: Cambridge University Press, 2013, pp. 287–288.

[19] On Dong Zhongshu, see S. A. Queen, *From Chronicle to Canon: The Hermeneutics of the Spring and Autumn Annals According to Tung Chung-shu*. Cambridge: Cambridge University Press, 1996.

commentaries. This meant that candidates for high office needed to have had considerable training as scholars in a wide range of academic disciplines before they could take up an administrative position, and these Confucian scholar-bureaucrats now gained prominent status as the new elite in Han society. Although they were well rewarded for their service, Confucian bureaucrats rarely became "yes men" for the government. They remained committed to a type of principled loyalty that demanded that they be prepared to criticize government policy if they thought it was warranted. We know that some scholars opposed government monopolies of commercial products, for example, while others criticized aggressive and expansionist foreign policy if it placed great demands on the people. They were also fierce watchdogs against unnecessary expenditure and imperial extravagance.

The Confucian scholar-bureaucrats were also aggressively active in resisting the increasing power of the eunuchs, particularly during the Later Han Dynasty. Eunuchs were men who had been castrated at an early age so that they could fulfill specific roles in Chinese society. Because eunuchs could be trusted with concubines, and also because they could never start a rival family, many rose to positions of great power in several Chinese dynasties, against the better wishes of the Confucian bureaucrats. The result of this coupling of Confucian bureaucracy with Chinese imperial government was, to paraphrase noted Chinese scholar Patricia Buckley Ebrey, a sort of balance of power between the "inner court" of the emperor (including the emperor's family and eunuchs) and the "outer court" of the Confucian-trained and highly educated bureaucracy.[20] The important role played by Confucian scholars in government lasted, with some interruptions, until the establishment of the Republic of China in 1911, making it one of the core political foundations of Chinese civilization for almost 2,000 years.

Yet we need to remember that in the real world of politics and government, Emperor Wudi, like his predecessors, still combined Legalist methods with these increasingly orthodox Confucian ideals. Although traditionally Liu Bang has been credited by historians with abolishing the Qin law code, official government documents discovered by archaeologists in Han Dynasty tombs have revealed that the Han also had harsh laws and punishments in place, including public execution.[21] Like the Qin, the Han government demanded conscripted labor service from its population. Every man, woman and child had to register with local

[20] P. B. Ebrey, *Cambridge Illustrated History of China*. Cambridge: Cambridge University Press, 1996, reprint 2000, p. 80.

[21] See Y. Liu, *Origins of Chinese Law: Penal and Administrative Law in Its Early Development*. Hong Kong: Oxford University Press, 1998.

authorities; failure to do so, or any refusal to perform conscripted labor, was severely punished. The duties of the conscripted labor force also included increased levels of military service, particularly after Wudi instigated a period of aggressive imperial expansion late in the second century BCE.

During the latter second and much of the first centuries BCE, the Han engaged in a long and exhausting struggle with the Xiongnu for control of the oasis states in the Tarim Basin, a tense and complex military conflict examined in the next chapter. During that same period, Han armies were also active in other regions as Wudi sought to aggressively expand the empire. In the south, Wudi dispatched a large Han naval force to the region of Nanyue in 111 BCE, which brought the modern regions of Guangdong, Guanxi and northern Vietnam into the Han realm. This helped facilitate increased maritime commercial links between China and Southeast Asia, connections discussed in a later chapter on maritime trade during the First Silk Roads Era. Once Han military garrisons had been established in Nanyue and other southern regions, merchants and settlers followed. If we compare figures in the 2 CE census with another taken in 140 CE, we see that as many as 10 million people had migrated from northern China into the Yangtze Valley and further south during the period.[22]

Two years later, Han forces conquered the Dian kingdom in present-day Yunnan Province; by the following year, 108 BCE, the Han had also conquered the northern region of the Korean Peninsula and established a commandery at Lelang to rule this new Han imperial province. Some idea of the vast size of the Han Empire can be seen in the fact that the census taken in the year 2 CE recorded the population of the empire as 57,671,400 individuals, an astonishingly large population.[23] It was under Martial Emperor Wudi, then, that the Han Empire reached the heights of its power and size. Wudi justified his expansionist policies to the west in terms of self-defense against the most dangerous of China's foes, the militarized Xiongnu confederation. As we see in the next chapter, it was by seeking an alliance with the Yuezhi pastoral nomadic confederation against the Xiongnu that China essentially established the first Silk Roads exchange network.

To finance these military and colonization campaigns, Wudi was forced to find new sources of revenue, including minting coins, monopolizing trade in lucrative goods such as salt, iron and liquor, confiscating

[22] Ebrey 2000, p. 82.

[23] See S. Nishijima, "The Economic and Social History of Former Han," in D. Twitchett and M. Loewe, *Cambridge History of China: Volume I – The Ch'in and Han Empires, 221 BC–AD 220*. Cambridge: Cambridge University Press, 1986, pp. 545–607.

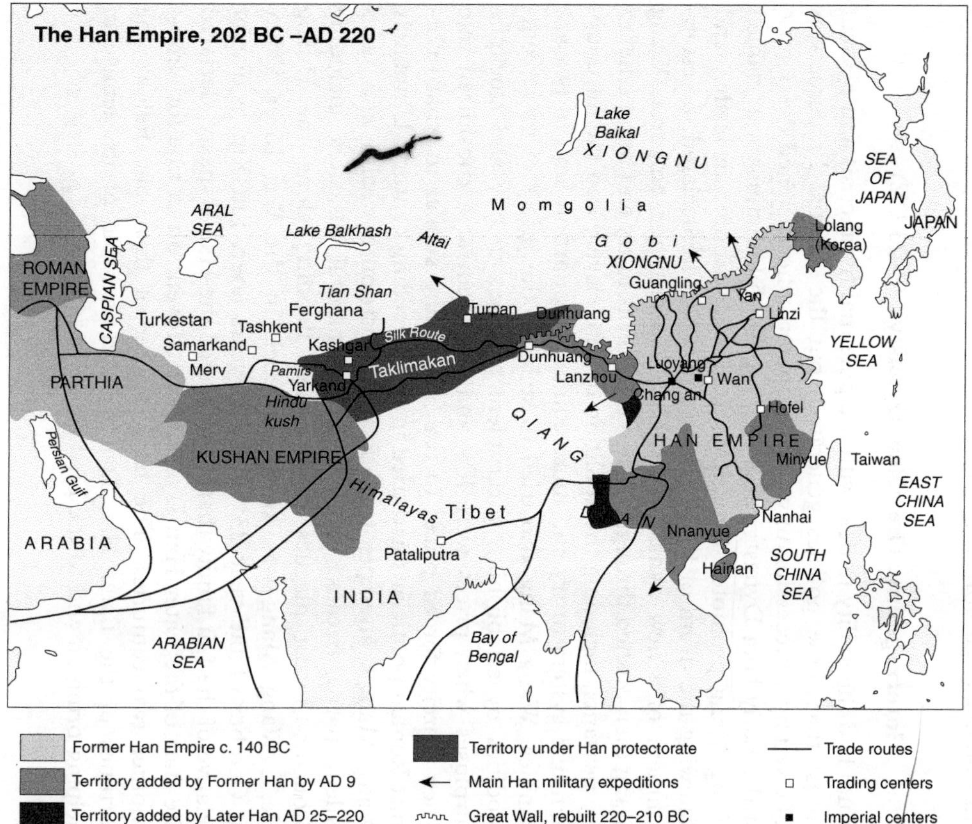

Map 2.2 Han Dynasty empire

some land from the nobles, selling titles and high offices and increasing taxes on business activity and on the peasants. Documents from the period include reports on intense debates among scholar-bureaucrats concerning the ethics of these government fundraising initiatives. On one side of the debate were officials who defended Wudi's policies as necessary because of the high cost of safeguarding the state from the Xiongnu. On the other were scholar-officials who in the best Confucian style argued that the pursuit of material profit should never be an acceptable motive of government.[24]

Interregnum: The "New Dynasty" (9–23 CE)

Wudi had the ability to deal with the potential fiscal crisis and peasant unrest that these policies generated, but the Martial Emperor was followed by a succession of weaker emperors who hastened the demise of the Early Han Dynasty. In 8 CE, a powerful administrator named Wang Mang promoted himself as a superior Confucian leader, and following the death of Emperor Ping in 9 CE, he declared the establishment of a new dynasty with himself as its first emperor. Wang Mang then pushed through a series of reforms to try and bring relief to the peasants, including the abolition of debt slavery and the introduction of a system to try and more equitably apportion land to peasant families. Wang Mang also tried to stabilize the prices of basic commodities by establishing government agencies to buy and stockpile surpluses when prices were low and sell them at a subsidized rate when scarcity forced prices to rise, something similar to what reformist Roman politicians had tried in the preceding century. Ultimately Wang Mang's attempts to radically redistribute wealth and taxes failed, partly because of a series of natural disasters including droughts, locust plagues and massive flooding along the Huang He.[25] Wang Mang was killed by rebels in the Wei River Valley in October of the year 23 CE. Two years later, Liu Xiu, a distant relative of the Liu family that had founded the Han Dynasty, declared the start of the Later Han Dynasty, which went on to rule for almost another two centuries. The final chapter of this book follows the fortunes of the Later Han Dynasty and the role of its demise in helping bring an end to the First Silk Roads Era.

[24] See E. M. Gale, ed. and trans., *Discourses on Salt and Iron*. Leiden: E. J. Brill, 1931, pp. 1–7 and 9–11.

[25] See H. Bielenstein, *The Restoration of the Han Dynasty*. Stockholm: Elanders Boktryckeri Aktiebolag, 1953, pp. 154–156.

Conclusion

This chapter has traced the history of early China from the emergence of the earliest agrarian communities through to the appearance of the first complex cultures of the Yangshao and Longshan. The second part of this chapter outlines the history of the first dynasties of China, from the semi-legendary Xia, through the Shang and Zhou, to the first Chinese imperial states of the Qin and Han Dynasties. We have also considered the emergence of many of the foundational philosophies of ancient China, including Confucianism, Daoism, Legalism and the Mandate of Heaven, and the way these ideas were used to legitimize government and organize society, through to the so-called triumph of Confucianism in the Early Han Dynasty. In the next chapter we consider in greater detail the expansion of Han power and influence into Central Asia, and the impact this had on ultimately connecting East Asia to much of the rest of the Afro-Eurasian world zone via the Silk Roads network.

Selected Further Reading

Beckwith, C., *Empires of the Silk Road: A History of Central Asia from the Bronze Age to the Present*. Princeton, NJ: Princeton University Press, 2009.

Chang, K. C. and X. Pingfang, eds., *The Formation of Chinese Civilization: An Archaeological Perspective*. New Haven, CT: Yale University Press, 2005.

Ebrey, P. B., *Cambridge Illustrated History of China*. Cambridge: Cambridge University Press, 1996, reprint 2000.

Feng, L., *Early China: A Social and Cultural History*. Cambridge: Cambridge University Press, 2013.

Feng, Y.-l., *A Short History of Chinese Philosophy*, trans. Derk Bodde, New York: The Free Press, 1966.

Lewis, M. E., *The Early Chinese Empire: Qin and Han*. Cambridge, MA: Belknap Press of Harvard University Press, 2007.

Liu, L., *The Chinese Neolithic: Trajectories to Early States*. Cambridge: Cambridge University Press, 2004.

Loewe, M., *The Government of the Qin and Han Empires 221 BCE – 220 CE*. Indianapolis, IN, and Cambridge: Hackett Publishing Company, Inc., 2006.

Mallory, J. P. and V. H. Mair, *The Tarim Mummies: Ancient China and the Mystery of the Earliest Peoples from the West*. London: Thames and Hudson, 2000.

Thorp, R., *China in the Early Bronze Age: Shang Civilization*. Philadelphia: University of Pennsylvania Press, 2006.

3 Zhang Qian and Han Expansion into Central Asia

In Chapter 1 we introduced the Xiongnu and Yuezhi pastoral nomadic confederations, which both occupied extensive regions along the western and northern borders of ancient China. After being defeated by the Xiongnu in or about the year 166 BCE, the Yuezhi were essentially evicted from their homeland in the Gansu Corridor and forced to undertake what turned out to be a thirty-year-long migration to the northern border of the Central Asian kingdom of Greco-Bactria, part of the modern nation of Afghanistan. We left the Yuezhi around the year 130 BCE dwelling in a strongly fortified position north of the fabled Oxus River (the modern Amu Darya) and apparently in complete control of Greco-Bactria to the south. This was the situation a Chinese envoy named Zhang Qian found when he reached Bactria a couple of years later, after his own epic decade-long journey from the Early Han Dynasty capital of Chang'an.

This chapter picks up the story of the First Silk Roads Era with the exploits of this courageous Han envoy, who during an expedition of a dozen years' duration demonstrated extraordinary perseverance in the face of hardships and setbacks. In unfolding his exploits we also address a challenging question in the field of big history. When viewed on the macro scale, historical processes often appear subject to almost inevitable forces of political and cultural evolution that seem beyond the influence of mere individuals. But does an analysis of the exploits of an individual like Zhang Qian suggest that, on some quite rare occasions the course of human history can be changed by the personal endeavors of a single human? A second question this chapter considers is related to the bitter conflict between the Han and Xiongnu. Why did the already tense relationship between them deteriorate so dramatically during the reign of Han Wudi? The long and bloody steppe war that followed had profound implications for ancient Eurasian history in general, and for the development of the Silk Roads in particular.

Expedition of Zhang Qian

Zhang Qian was sent by Emperor Wudi to seek out the migrating Yuezhi, partly in the hope of convincing them to return to China and join the Han in an alliance against their common enemy, the Xiongnu.[1] The expedition that followed turned out to be an epic tale of adventure. Zhang Qian had to breach both the formidable geographical barriers of western China that we discussed in the previous chapter and the military and intelligence barriers imposed by the Xiongnu. He had to cross thousands of miles of desert, steppe and mountain ranges, visiting places that, as far as we know, no Chinese traveler had ever heard of before, let alone seen. When he finally returned to the Han court and presented his report to Wudi, the Han became seriously aware for the first time of the complex world beyond their western borders, of the diverse cultures and belief systems that existed there and of the opportunities for imperial Han expansion the western regions presented. Indeed, Zhang Qian's report explicitly introduced Wudi and the Han court to the diplomatic and strategic opportunities available were they to expand their diplomatic interests into Central Asia, opportunities that as we shall see, Wudi was quick to exploit. It was as a direct result of the expedition of Zhang Qian, then, that material and nonmaterial exchanges began to flourish along the Silk Roads. The envoy's report, along with Wudi's own expansionist mind-set, enticed the Chinese out of millennia of relative cultural and geographic isolation from the West, and into active engagement with the rest of Eurasia, including indirectly the Greco-Roman world, for the first time. Historian Sima Qian, an eyewitness to many of these events, was in no doubt about the crucial significance of the expedition of Zhang Qian when he wrote: "For the first time, relations were established between the lands of the northwest and the Han. It was Zhang Qian ... who opened the way for this move."[2]

The expedition of Zhang Qian was one part of a significant policy shift in the Hans' relationship with the Xiongnu that was instituted by the vigorous Wudi. Following a disastrous attempt early in the Han Dynasty to confront the Xiongnu in 201 BCE, an attempt in which Han founder Liu Bang almost lost his life, successive Han emperors had adopted the policy of *heqin* (which means "peace and affinity"), sending substantial quantities of tribute and even Han princesses to the various Xiongnu *shanyu* in the hope of limiting Xiongnu military incursions into Han

[1] On the expedition of Zhang Qian, see C. Benjamin, *The Yuezhi: Origins, Migration and the Conquest of Northern Bactria*. Turnhout: Brepols Silk Roads Studies XIV, 2007.

[2] Sima Qian, *Shi Ji*, trans. B. Watson, *Records of the Grand Historian by Sima Qian – Han Dynasty II*, revised edn. New York: Columbia University Press, 1993, chapter 123, p. 240.

territory. This had effectively reduced the Han to the status of a tributary vassal of the Xiongnu. After the reign of Shanyu Modu and the subsequent defeat and eviction of the Yuezhi, the Xiongnu were powerful enough to control a vast steppe empire that functioned not only as a source of constant military concern for the Han, but also as an effective barrier between China and much of the rest of Eurasia.

Even while they continued the *heqin* policy, various Early Han emperors had considered the possibility of renewing a military strategy against the Xiongnu. During the reign of Wendi (r. 180–157 BCE), a government minister named Chao Cuo had written a memorandum to the emperor titled *Guard the Frontiers and Protect the Borders*.[3] Chao Cuo argued that the Han military should be transformed from an essentially infantry-focused force to one based on a strong cavalry, to try and counter the effectiveness of the mounted archers of the Xiongnu. He also suggested that the Han should enlist surrendered and disaffected nomadic cavalry into its ranks, essentially "using barbarians to fight barbarians," in a way that the Roman military would later do with its legions stationed along the Germanic borders. Chao Cuo acknowledged that the Xiongnu horsemen had better endurance, superior horses and much better archery skills, but he also suggested that if the Han were to develop a better-equipped cavalry force of its own, with its superior discipline they could counter these Xiongnu advantages.[4] Partly as a consequence of Chao Cuo's report, during the reign of Wendi's successor, Jingdi (r. 157–141 BCE), the Han instituted a breeding program for horses in preparation for creating the large cavalry contingents the strategist had envisioned. Thirty-six government pastures were established along the border regions to build up the military's stock of tough, maneuverable horses. Naturally, these pastures were frequently raided by the Xiongnu, both to obtain some of the horses for themselves and to disrupt the program, but by the time Wudi came to the throne in 141 BCE, some 450,000 horses were available for military use.[5]

From the beginning of his reign in 141 BCE Wudi was determined to end the *heqin* strategy and confront the Xiongnu militarily. The *Han Shu* (*Annals of the Early Han*), in the context of explaining the motives behind the expedition of Zhang Qian, explicitly states that "as it happened, the Han was wishing to start operations to eliminate the nomads";[6] Sima

[3] N. Di Cosmo, *Ancient China and Its Enemies: The Rise of Nomadic Power in East Asian History*. Cambridge: Cambridge University Press, 2002, pp. 203–204.

[4] Di Cosmo 2002, 203.

[5] C.-s. Chang, *The Rise of the Chinese Empire, Volume 1: Nation, State and Imperialism in Early China ca. 1600 BC–AD 8*. Ann Arbor: University of Michigan Press, 2007, pp. 151–152.

[6] HS 61 1A.

Qian bluntly states that "the Han at this time was engaged in a concerted effort to try to destroy the Xiongnu."[7] But before Han armies could be dispatched into Xiongnu territory, the emperor and his advisors badly needed intelligence about the geopolitical situation in the regions to the west of the Han. So, one of the motives of this mission called for by Wudi must surely have been to simply obtain more information about the world beyond the northwestern borderlands and beyond the Xiongnu Empire. At the same time, Wudi may also have genuinely hoped to forge an alliance with the Yuezhi against their common Xiongnu foes, after he became aware of their defeat and eviction, although it is doubtful the Chinese had any real idea of where the Yuezhi had gone.

Both these motives required the recruitment of an envoy who would attempt to overcome these physical and military barriers and pursue the migrating Yuezhi. In 139 BCE, just two years into his reign, the teenage emperor Wudi moved to put his plan into action by recruiting the appropriate man for the job. The Han histories provide very limited biographical information on the early career of Zhang Qian, who, according to the sources, appears to have been an obscure member of the lower nobility who served as a palace attendant. But we do have a few details about his recruitment. Sima Qian informs us that Wudi sent a summons throughout Han China for men capable of undertaking such a mission. Zhang Qian answered the summons and was ultimately appointed by Wudi as "envoy to the Yuezhi."[8]

Both the *Shiji* and the *Han Shu* recount the subsequent journey of Zhang Qian into uncharted territory. The expedition departed the Han capital of Chang'an in probably 138 BCE and headed west through the Gansu Corridor and into the Gobi Desert, regions then firmly under the control of the Xiongnu. Not surprisingly, Zhang Qian and his party were almost immediately captured by Xiongnu forces. Most of the party were killed, and Zhang Qian and his closest retinue were transported far to the north to the headquarters of the *shanyu*. The Xiongnu ruler was singularly unimpressed by Zhang Qian's attempt to pass through his territory, declaring, as Sima Qian puts it: "The Yuezhi people live to the north of me. What does the Han mean by trying to send an envoy to them!"[9] The Xiongnu decided to retain Zhang Qian as a hostage, keeping him in what might be described as "gentlemanly detention," but Zhang Qian was not to be deterred from his mission. The Han Shu explains what happened next: "For over ten years he (the *Shanyu*) detained Zhang Qian, giving him a wife to whom he had children. However, Zhang

[7] SJ 123, Watson 1993, p. 231. [8] SJ 123, Watson 1993, p. 231.
[9] SJ 123, Watson 1993, p. 231.

Qian constantly retained the Han emblems of authority without loss. Living in the western part of the Xiongnu he found an opportunity to escape with his followers in the direction of the Yuezhi."[10]

For the next several weeks, Zhang Qian traveled westward, passing across the northern Gobi Desert and into a region the Han sources called Dayuan, which is the rich Ferghana Valley of modern Uzbekistan. Because of his ten years in detention, by the time Zhang Qian arrived in Ferghana, the Yuezhi had already passed through the region some years earlier, as they had continued their migration further west following their eviction from the Ili Valley by the Wusun and Xiongnu. According to the report Zhang Qian later delivered to Wudi, the people of Dayuan had apparently heard of the wealth and power of the Han, which is more than could be said about the Hans' knowledge of Ferghana; as far as we know, Zhang Qian was the first Chinese individual to ever see the valley. Upon arriving there Zhang Qian was taken to the king of Dayuan. After explaining the importance of his mission, he promised the king rich rewards from the Han if he would help him on his way. The exact enticement he made, or so we read in the *Han Shu*, is that "the wealth and goods which the Han will present to you will be beyond description."[11] According to the sources, the king of Dayuan apparently knew exactly where the Yuezhi had gone after they had so recently passed through his territory, and he happily provided guides to Zhang Qian to help him on his way.

The Heavenly Horses of Dayuan

As Zhang Qian and his small party moved through Dayuan, they noticed herds of unusual horses grazing freely upon the rich grasslands of the region. These horses had short legs, powerful chests and round, barrel-shaped bodies, but it was not these features that so surprised the Chinese envoy. As he watched them gallop, the horses appeared to sweat a red liquid that appeared as thin strips parallel to the horses' ribs and necks; to Zhang Qian, this appeared quite extraordinary, even magical. Modern scientists have proposed two different ideas about these ancient "blood-sweating" horses of Ferghana, which most horse geneticists believe have since gone extinct. One is that small subcutaneous blood vessels between the ribs may have burst as the horses pushed themselves on a hard gallop. The second and more widely accepted theory is that a parasitic nematode still common on the Central Asian steppe today – the *Parafilaria multipapillosal* – probably burrowed into the subcutaneous tissues of the horses' ribs and necks, causing the skin nodules to bleed and

[10] HS 61 2A. [11] HS 61 2A.

the blood to mix with sweat on the horses' bodies, creating strips of vivid pink foam.[12]

When Zhang Qian eventually made it back to the Han court, he included an account of these blood-sweating horses in his report to Wudi, who was enthralled. By coincidence, the emperor had recently divined through reading the *I Ching* (*Book of Changes*), a Zhou Dynasty divination classic text, a prophesy that "divine horses will soon appear from the northwest." When he heard of the blood-sweating horses from Ferghana, he immediately made the connection and named them the

Figure 3.1 Han Dynasty horses, carriages and riders (stone inscription)
www.gettyimages.co.uk/license/478237654
Credit: cl2004lhy

[12] For more on the heavenly horses, and on humans' uses of the horse in military campaigns in the ancient world more generally, see B. Davis, "Timeline of the Development of the Horse," *Sino-Platonic Papers* 177, August 2007.

"heavenly horses of Dayuan." It was partly in an attempt to acquire some of these horses that Wudi launched two ambitious military campaigns to Ferghana in 104 and 103 BCE, campaigns discussed later in this chapter.

Zhang Qian in Bactria

With the help of the guides provided by the king of Dayuan, Zhang Qian was led to the neighboring state of Kangju, also located in modern Uzbekistan. In his report, Zhang Qian described Kangju as powerful enough to be "not easily defeated by Han forces."[13] At the same time it was "constrained to serve the Xiongnu in the east," and also to acknowledge "nominal sovereignty to the Yuezhi in the south."[14] Despite their apparent military strength, then, the residents of Kangju found themselves as the meat in a militarized nomadic sandwich, and had wisely adopted a conciliatory position toward both the Xiongnu who controlled the steppes to their north and east and the Yuezhi who were now in control of Bactria to the south. The ruler of Kangju was apparently also happy to assist Zhang Qian's passage through the country, and led him south to the new stronghold of the Yuezhi.

Zhang Qian probably arrived at the court of the Yuezhi ruling dynasty in or about 128 BCE, a full ten years after he had set out from Changan. He immediately sought an audience with the Yuezhi king in the hope of persuading the Yuezhi to return with him and join the Han in the coming military campaign against the Xiongnu. Sima Qian, probably paraphrasing from the report Zhang Qian delivered to the Han court following his return to Chang'an, provides almost an eyewitness account of the interview and of the attitude of the Yuezhi king:

> "Since the king of the Yuezhi had been killed by the Xiongnu, his son had succeeded him as ruler and had forced the kingdom of Bactria to recognize his sovereignty. The region he ruled was rich and fertile and seldom troubled by invaders, and the king thought only of his own enjoyment. He considered the Han too far away to bother with and had no particular intention of avenging his father's death by attacking the Xiongnu."[15]

To Zhang Qian's undoubted disappointment, then, the ruler of the Yuezhi rejected out of hand the envoy's request to enter into an alliance with the Han, and had no interest in returning to confront the Yuezhis' former enemies. This is hardly surprising of course, considering the devastating defeat the Xiongnu had inflicted upon the Yuezhi in the Gansu three decades earlier, not to mention the challenges of the thirty-

[13] HS 61 3A. [14] HS 96A 15B. [15] SJ 123, Watson 1993, p. 232.

year-long migration the Yuezhi confederation had so recently and successfully concluded. Now settled in a wealthy and fertile region, and having apparently established hegemony over the former Greco-Bactrian state as well as concluding some sort of a strategic alliance with Kangju, it is no wonder that the Yuezhi ruler had set his mind on a life of ease and given up all thoughts of taking revenge upon the Xiongnu for the death of his father.

Undaunted, Zhang Qian decided to remain in the region for the following year and accumulate as much information as he could about Bactria and other nearby regions as part of the "intelligence-gathering" component of his mission. The information he collected and the reports he compiled are of great importance to historians of ancient Eurasia. These are the first Chinese reports ever made on any region to the west of China; they essentially represent the discovery of a whole new world that until this moment the Han apparently had no idea even existed. The information Zhang Qian assembled and later reported to the Han court was surprisingly detailed. For example, he describes Bactria as a large state with a population numbering more than 1,000,000 persons, and its inhabitants were only too happy to provide supplies for the Han envoy.[16] The population consisted of farmers who cultivated the land, but also urban dwellers, including many "clever" merchants.

In the great market in the capital city of Bactra he was astonished to find goods on sale from southern regions of what would later become part of China, including bamboo canes and cloth from the southwestern regions of modern China. When Zhang Qian asked where the Bactrians had obtained these materials, he was told, "our merchants go to buy them in the markets in Shendu (India)," far to the south and east.[17] This demonstrates that even before the more northerly Silk Roads had begun to operate, some quantities of trade goods from the southern regions of mainland East Asia, areas outside of Han control during this period, had already made their way into India, probably by way of what Edward Rtveladze named the "Great Indian Road."[18] This overland route began in southern China in the provinces of Sichuan and Chongqing, headed initially southwest through modern Burma and Bangladesh, then westward along the valley of the Ganges River in India, before turning north and crossing mountain passes into modern Afghanistan and other regions of Central Asia. Long before the Silk Roads network began to operate in

[16] SJ 123, Watson 1993, pp. 235–236. [17] SJ 123, Watson 1993, p. 235; HS 61 3A.

[18] See particularly E. V. Rtveladze, "The Great Indian Road: India-Central Asia-Transcaucasia," *Anabasis* 1 (2010), pp. 80–96; and J. D. Lerner's review of Rtveladze's Russian-language book on the subject, which is summarized in English in the shorter *Anabasis* 1 article, in *Anabasis* 5 (2014), pp. 209–214.

earnest, then, merchants had already established a long-distance trade route from China to Central Asia. What Wudi and the Han government would essentially do following the expedition of Zhang Qian and subsequent campaigns against the Xiongnu, would be to open up new northern routes from China to Central Asia, via the Tarim Basin, routes that ultimately proved more sustainable and capable of transporting larger volumes of trade goods.

Zhang Qian sought more information on India, which the Chinese called Shendu. He was informed that the kingdom is located well to the southeast of Bactria along a great river, and that the soldiers ride elephants into battle.[19] The river was most probably the Indus, but might even have been the Ganges; both must have been known to merchants who traveled on the Great Indian Road. The river environment was described as "hot and damp," and most of the residents of Shendu as farmers. The Han envoy also found out something about the powerful Iranian empire of the Parthians to the west, which within a decade of his visit would come under the control of perhaps the greatest of all Parthian kings, Mithridates II (123–88 BCE), events discussed in Chapter 6. Zhang Qian reported that Parthia (which he named Anxi) was large and urbanized, with what he described as "several hundred cities of various sizes" in which merchants were extremely active, and with a splendid silver coinage.[20] He learned that Parthian farmers grew rice and wheat, and also an extraordinary vine called "grape" from which they made wine.[21] The Chinese already knew about wine; they had been consuming the sort that was made from rice for millennia. But this reference by Zhang Qian was apparently the first knowledge the Chinese had of a plant that would become one of the most important Silk Roads imports into China – the grapevine.

Return to Han China

After his year-long intelligence-gathering sojourn in Bactria, Zhang Qian returned to the Yuezhi "capital" north of the Amu Darya to make one last attempt to persuade the king to return with him to China. But as Sima Qian tells us, "In the end Zhang Qian was never able to interest the Yuezhi in his proposals."[22] The envoy had no option now other than to try and return to Chang'an with all the valuable information he had acquired. Given the experiences of his outward journey, he decided to try and return to the Han capital by a more southerly route, in an attempt

19 SJ 123, Watson 1993, p. 236; HS 61 3A. 20 HS 96A 14A.
21 SJ 123, Watson 1993, p. 233–236. 22 SJ 123, Watson 1993, p. 232.

to circumvent Xiongnu-controlled territory. He headed due east from Bactria, then southeast through the Kunlun Massif, the "Southern Mountains" that separate the Tarim Basin from the Tibetan Plateau. But even though he had chosen this return route in the express hope of avoiding his enemies, Zhang Qian was once again captured by the Xiongnu. This time he was detained for more than a year, but then fortuitously the reigning *shanyu* died, plunging the Xiongnu confederation into turmoil. He made the most of this window of opportunity, and probably in 126 or 125 BCE he arrived back at the *no doubt* astonished Han court in Chang'an accompanied only by his Xiongnu wife and child and his slave, Ganfu.

Immediately upon his return Zhang Qian was promoted to the position of "supreme counselor of the palace" by Wudi. The envoy then delivered his report in person to the emperor, an event possibly personally witnessed by the Han historian Sima Qian, who remains a key source for this entire story. The most important part of the report was Zhang Qian's descriptions of all the places he had visited or heard about that had previously been completely unknown to the Chinese: the Ferghana Valley with its heavenly horses; the powerful yet "diplomatic" kingdom of Kangju; the great mercantile state of Bactria; Parthia with its hundreds of large cities, coinage and grapevines; India, where the soldiers ride elephants into battle; and many others. He described them, to paraphrase Sima Qian, as large states with many rare goods, but that were militarily weak and that prized Han wealth and goods. If they could be won over, either through alliances or conquest, Wudi could "extend his domain by 10,000 li ... and his might would become known to all the lands within the four seas."[23] This was an argument no emperor could refuse. Zhang Qian had eloquently articulated two of the key motivations for all empire builders in world history, from the first Sumerian imperial ruler Sargon of Akkad through to the European global empires of the twentieth century – commercial gain and imperial glory for the ruler and his state!

Subsequent Missions of Zhang Qian and Outbreak of Hostilities with the Xiongnu

In the years following his return, Zhang Qian was dispatched on several subsequent diplomatic and military missions by Wudi. In probably 124 BCE, just a year or two after returning from his epic journey to Bactria, the envoy was sent to southern China, regions at that time beyond the control of the Han, to try and discover how the cane and cloth goods he

[23] SJ 123, Watson 1993, p. 236.

had seen in the markets at Bactra were being sent to India. After traveling thousands of *li* to the south, Zhang Qian and his party were confronted by violent Kunming tribes who "devote themselves to plunder and robbery."[24] The Kunming captured and murdered as many of the Han party as they could, preventing the mission from getting through. The attempt was abandoned, but what a difference it would have made to subsequent Silk Roads history had a southern route indeed been discovered, allowing Chinese trade goods to be exported westward along this southern route and thus circumventing the Xiongnu far to the north.

Having survived the murderous attack by the Kunming, a year or so later Zhang Qian was appointed as a subordinate military commander and employed as special envoy and guide for senior Han general Wei Qing in an aggressive campaign against the Xiongnu, part of Wudi's strategy to confront the confederation head on. General Wei Qing had already led two successful campaigns against the Xiongnu, one of which had crushed Xiongnu forces north of the Huang He and recaptured the Ordos region, a desert and steppe plateau encircled by the great bend of the Huang He. As a result of Wei Qing's success, the Xiongnu had been driven from the Ordos and thousands of Han farmers had been moved into the region in an attempt to repopulate it, and by the practice of irrigation agriculture turned it into a secure base for further operations against the Xiongnu.[25] Now, in this new campaign of (probably) 123 BCE, Zhang Qian's knowledge of the region north and west of the Ordos was vital to the campaign. Sima Qian informs us that, because he knew where water and grazing pasture for the Han army's horses were to be found in Xiongnu territory, he was able to "save the army from hardship."[26] The campaign was successful, and as a result Zhang Qian was promoted again by Wudi to the title of *Bowang* or "Broad Vision Marquis," thus making him a member of the highest nobility of Han China.

What had now become open war between the Han and Xiongnu continued the following year, when in 122 BCE a force of 10,000 Xiongnu cavalry raided the northern Shanggu region of Han territory. In the spring of 121, the Han retaliated by sending General Huo Qibing and a force of 10,000 "swift cavalry" out of Longxi, which rode 1,000 *li* deep into Xiongnu territory, killing or capturing 18,000 enemy troops.[27] Later that same year, Huo Qibing led a second large cavalry force some 2,000 *li* to the Heavenly Mountains in the west, this time capturing or

[24] SJ 123, Watson 1993, pp. 236–237. [25] Feng 2013, p. 273.
[26] SJ 123, Watson 1993, p. 237. [27] SJ 110, Watson 1993, p. 152.

killing 30,000 Xiongnu troops.[28] In retaliation the Xiongnu attacked and invaded Yanmen in Dai, and in response Wudi sent Zhang Qian and General Li Guang to attack the Xiongnu. The Xiongnu trapped and surrounded Li Guang's forces, but Zhang Qian and his troops arrived in time to save them. However, in the aftermath Zhang Qian was accused of having arrived late at a crucial rendezvous with Li Guang, and the Broad Vision Marquis was sentenced by the tempestuous Wudi to execution. But after purchasing a pardon, Zhang Qian was reduced to the rank of commoner instead.

By the following year (121 BCE), Zhang Qian's reputation had been restored, probably because the emperor realized how much he needed the advice and eyewitness experience of his well-traveled envoy. During his capture by the Xiongnu, Zhang Qian had gathered detailed information about the Wusun, another powerful militarized nomadic confederation that fifteen years earlier had been responsible for driving the Yuezhi out of the Ili Valley and ultimately on to Bactria. Zhang Qian now proposed a diplomatic mission to the Wusun leadership, persuading Wudi that if the Han could establish "an alliance with the Wusun, Daxia and the other countries to the west could all be persuaded to come to court and acknowledge themselves as foreign vassals."[29] The emperor agreed and appointed Zhang Qian as leader of a party of 300 men, 600 horses and, as potential tribute to be paid to the Wusun should they agree with the proposal, tens of thousands of cattle and sheep and an enormous treasury of cash, silk and gold. Zhang Qian's mission to the Wusun was part of a much wider diplomatic initiative that the Han had decided to pursue. Other officials traveling with Zhang Qian's expedition were also given imperial credentials and material resources so that "they could be sent to neighboring states along the way" to try and persuade them to also join in the Han tributary network. These initiatives are the first evidence we have of the dispatch of large quantities of silk out of Han China and into Central Asia, not as part of a commercial enterprise but rather as diplomatic tribute, an important distinction discussed in the next chapter.

Once Zhang Qian reached the headquarters of the Wusun *kunmo*, he found himself in the midst of a complex political climate among the Wusun, who were split into several factions. The *kunmo* had ten sons, and because the question of succession was dominating Wusun politics, no one seemed to have the authority to make a decision concerning the possibility of entering into a formal tributary relationship with the Han. While Zhang Qian negotiated, with the assistance of Wusun guides he

[28] SJ 109, Watson 1993, p. 125, and 110, pp. 152 and 171.
[29] SJ 123, Watson 1993, p. 238.

also sent some of his deputies on follow-up missions to regions he had visited on his initial expedition to the Yuezhi, including Ferghana, Kangju and Bactria.[30] While these envoys were traveling further west in Central Asia, in 120 BCE Zhang Qian was able to convince a party of Wusun envoys to return with him to the Han court in Chang'an, where they were apparently impressed with "the breadth and greatness of the Han Empire."[31] According to Sima Qian, this visit helped stabilize relations between the Wusun and Han, and a grateful Wudi honored Zhang Qian for this and so many other contributions to the Han state by appointing him to the position of Grand Messenger, thus "ranking him among the nine highest ministers of the government."[32] Zhang Qian did not live long to enjoy his illustrious status; within a year or two, in either 119 or 118 BCE, the great envoy was dead. But in those final years, his life's work was further vindicated when the same deputies he had dispatched to the states of the western regions returned to Chang'an. They were accompanied by envoys from many of the same Inner Eurasian states that Zhang Qian had first visited a decade or so earlier, which further consolidated Han relations with the city-states of the Tarim Basin and helped the Han expand its burgeoning tributary network.

Continued Han Military and Diplomatic Expansion into Central Asia

With these alliances in place, during the dozen or so years following the death of Zhang Qian, the Han extended their fortifications and their imperial domains further to the west, establishing agricultural and military "provinces" deeper and deeper into Central Asia. To the south, renewed attempts were also made by various Han parties to discover a southern route through to India and Bactria, but each time these were forestalled by the Kunming.[33] This meant that the northern route through the Tarim Basin to Central Asia had to be stabilized, and this in turn required renewing military operations against the Xiongnu.

Campaigns of 119–105 BCE

Accordingly, in 119 BCE a major campaign was launched against the Xiongnu. Strategists believed that the Xiongnu *shanyu* was convinced that if he moved his headquarters to the northern regions of the Gobi Desert he would be safe from Han military forces. Determined to prove

[30] SJ 123, Watson 1993, pp. 238ff. [31] SJ 123, Watson 1993, p. 240.
[32] SJ 123, Watson 1993, p. 240. [33] SJ 123, Watson 1993, p. 241.

Figure 3.2 Remains of the Han Dynasty Great Wall extension in Gansu Province, Western China
http://media.gettyimages.com/photos/remnants-of-wall-in-xinjiang-picture-id119991785?s=170667a
Credit: James D. Rogers

the *shanyu* wrong, the Han fattened their horses on grain and sent out a massive force of 100,000 cavalrymen with 140,000 horses. The force then split into three: the swift cavalry under Huo Qubing advanced from Dai, the bulk of the cavalry under Wei Qing moved north from Dingxiang and General Li Guang led the vanguard.[34]

The *shanyu* received word of the approach of these dangerous contingents of Han cavalry, so withdrew his baggage trains and waited with his best troops on the northern edge of the desert. Once Wei Qing's forces arrived the Xiongnu closed battle, but the *shanyu* was surrounded and forced to abandon his army. With a small group of his finest horsemen he broke out and fled to the northwest. Han forces pursued him, capturing or killing 19,000 enemy troops, but not the *shanyu*. The bulk of the Xiongnu cavalry also escaped from the Han and followed the *shanyu* north. While all this was unfolding, Han general Huo Qubing had also advanced 2,000 *li* to the north from Dai, and in an incredibly successful campaign, according to Sima Qian, he captured or killed

[34] SJ 109, Watson 1993, p. 125, and 110, pp. 171ff.

Figure 3.3 Remains of the Han Dynasty fortified gate at Yumen Pass, Gansu Province, China
http://media.gettyimages.com/photos/yumen-pass-gate-near-dunhuang-china-picture-id698506960
Credit: Copyright Xinzheng. All Rights Reserved

70,000 enemy troops. Because of these twin military disasters, the Xiongnu now reestablished their court far to the north, a very long way away from the Han border.

With the northern route through the Gansu Corridor and Tarim Basin now more secure from Xiongnu attacks, the Han established the new province of Jiuquan, in order, again according to Sima Qian, "to provide a safe route to the lands of the north west."[35] Han agricultural garrisons, complete with new irrigation infrastructure, were established in territory well beyond the Huang He, from Shuofang west to Longju. Some 50,000–60,000 colonists and soldiers took up residency in these garrisons, and their farms gradually expanded further to the north, claiming more and more former Xiongnu Gobi territory for the Han. Further Han military campaigns were launched in 119, which resulted in the killing or capturing of large numbers of Xiongnu horsemen, although this time at considerable cost to Han forces. The Han then sent an envoy to try and persuade the Xiongnu to enter into a vassal relationship with the Chinese,

[35] SJ 123, Watson 1993, p. 240.

but according to Sima Qian, the *shanyu* flew into a rage and detained the Han party instead.[36]

Nonetheless, the Xiongnu were now far less inclined to engage the Han militarily. In 111 BCE, a year in which large Han cavalry contingents were regularly dispatched thousands of *li* into Xiongnu territory, Wudi made a grand tour of the northern border. At the military garrison of Shuofang he held an inspection of 180,000 Han cavalry troops, having first sent an envoy to provocatively inform the Xiongnu court of the event. Through the envoy Wudi informed the Xiongnu leadership that he was waiting at the border with his troops: advance and attack if you dare, or acknowledge yourself a vassal of the Han. The *shanyu* was enraged and again detained the envoy, but later withdrew much further to the north, perhaps as far as the shores of Lake Baikal in southern Siberia. Although personally refusing to talk with the Han, he did send envoys to continue negotiations.[37]

In consort with these military operations, and with the Xiongnu now at least temporarily tamed, Wudi took the opportunity to dispatch more and more missions to the west, including, according to the sources, to Parthia, India and even Mesopotamia.[38] These diplomatic missions were huge, the largest comprising several hundred members and enormous quantities of tributary goods including silk; even the smallest mission contained at least 100 members. They were also sent with such frequency that, according to the *Han Shu*, the "envoys were in sight of each other on the roads."[39] Despite their apparent frequency and enormous size, these diplomatic journeys were always challenging, and envoys were on the road for years. Sima Qian notes that even those parties traveling to closer Tarim Basin states would be away for a few years, while "those travelling to distant lands required eight or nine years to complete their journey."[40]

The missions dispatched toward the end of Zhang Qian's life, or in the years immediately following his death, were led by various officials and soldiers, some of whom had served with Zhang Qian on one of his journeys. But they were also often staffed by volunteers whose ethical quality and honesty was somewhat suspect. According to the sources, because of the corrupt behavior of many of these "worthless men," some of "the men of foreign lands soon became disgusted (and) refused to supply the envoys with food and provisions."[41] The state of Bactria was apparently an exception, and continued to provide

[36] SJ 123, Watson 1993, pp. 154–155. [37] SJ 123, Watson 1993, p. 156.
[38] SJ 123, Watson 1993, pp. 154–155. [39] HS 61 6A.
[40] SJ 123, Watson 1993, p. 241. [41] SJ 123, Watson 1993, p. 242.

supplies for large Han parties, further evidence of the continuing wealth of Bactria, even after Yuezhi subjugation. This meant that Bactria, and presumably the principal commercial city of Bactra, had positioned itself well as a major diplomatic and mercantile center at the very crossroads of Inner Eurasia, a role it would continue to play in the centuries that followed after it was incorporated into the Kushan Empire.

The massive military operations Han Wudi launched against the Xiongnu, some of the largest campaigns ever seen in world history to this point, continued throughout the reign of the emperor. Between 110 and 108 BCE, the Han continued to reinforce and expand the western province of Jiuquan to drive a wedge between the Xiongnu and their allies the Qiang pastoral nomads, making communication between them much more difficult. The Han also sent an imperial princess to marry the *kunmo* of the Wusun, bringing the Wusun more firmly into the Han tributary network and away from their former allies the Xiongnu.[42] Diplomatic overtures were also regularly made to the Xiongnu themselves, asking them to submit to the Han and acknowledge themselves as vassals, but the *shanyu* remained unimpressed.[43]

Indeed, rather than acknowledging themselves as vassals of the Han, between 108 and 105 the Xiongnu instead launched a series of regular raids along the new Han western border regions and newly created provinces. In response, the Han appointed Guo Chang as "Barbarian Quelling General," and sent General Zhao Ponu to strengthen the garrisons of the western provinces. In new campaigns against the Xiongnu, the two generals extended Han operations even further west, capturing major Tarim Basin town-states such as Loulan and Turfan, thus blocking Xiongnu access to the Tarim Basin. In 105 BCE, Shanyu Wuwei died and was succeeded by his young son, the "Boy Shanyu."[44] The young *shanyu* had to deal with a crisis in the severe winter of 105/104, but despite the loss of many animals and ongoing Han diplomatic efforts to forge an alliance, the *shanyu* continued to have, as Sima Qian put it, "a great fondness for warfare."[45] Indeed, in 104 BCE, Han general Zhao Ponu and his force of 20,000 cavalry were trapped and forced to surrender by the Boy Shanyu, who was said to be delighted. His brief reign ended a year or so later when he died unexpectedly, and his own son was so young that the Xiongnu proclaimed his uncle Goulihu as the new *shanyu*.

[42] SJ 123, Watson 1993, p. 234. [43] SJ 110, Watson 1993, p. 157.
[44] SJ 110, Watson 1993, pp. 158–159. [45] SJ 110, Watson 1993, pp. 158–159.

Campaigns to Dayuan: 104–102 BCE

In 105 BCE, word reached the Han court that the Chinese envoy sent to Dayuan (the Ferghana Valley) had been assassinated. In response, and also partly in an attempt to acquire some of the heavenly horses of Dayuan that Zhang Qian had described to the emperor, in 104 BCE, Wudi dispatched a Han army of 40,000 cavalrymen under General Li Guangli on a 3,000-mile campaign to Ferghana, the deepest military incursion into Central Asia that the Han had thus far attempted. But stretched to the limit of their supplies after months on the road, and a very long way from home, the army was defeated by the forces of Dayuan and forced to return empty-handed.[46]

Undaunted, and apparently now absolutely determined to obtain some of the heavenly horses, Wudi sent another army of 60,000 men back to Ferghana in 102 BCE, again under the command of Li Guangli. After another epic campaign, the general managed to defeat the forces of the kingdom of Dayuan, cut off the head of its ruler and acquire 3,000 of the heavenly horses, although only 1,000 survived the journey back to China, and only a dozen or so of these were of the highest quality necessary for breeding. The Xiongnu tried to block the return of the Han army from Ferghana, but were unable to reach them in time, and Li Guangli was able to lead his forces triumphantly back to Han China after one of the most ambitious campaigns in the history of Han engagement with Central Asia.[47] The campaign had ramifications far beyond that of acquiring horses. According to the *Han Shu*, this dramatic geographic extension of Han power "shocked and frightened" all the other states of the western regions, and most now sent gifts and envoys to the Han to declare themselves vassal states.[48] Sima Qian also insists that the Han were riding high after defeating Dayuan: "Its might filled the neighboring states with terror."[49]

Campaigns of 99–59 BCE

Despite the Hans' successful campaign to Dayuan and the diplomatic advantages that ensued, the war against the Xiongnu continued well into the next century. Li Guangli was in action again in 99 BCE, leading 30,000 Han cavalrymen north from the military commandery at Jiuquan. Despite initial success, he was surrounded by the Xiongnu and suffered major losses. During the same season, General Li Ling also engaged with the Xiongnu *shanyu*, but after killing and wounding

[46] SJ 110, Watson 1993, pp. 158–159. [47] SJ 110, Watson 1993, p. 160. [48] HS 96A.
[49] SJ 110, Watson 1993, p. 160.

10,000 enemy soldiers, Li Ling's provisions ran out and he was captured by the *shanyu*, who apparently treated him with honor and gave his own daughter as a wife to the Han general.[50] Wudi launched another multi-pronged campaign against the Xiongnu in 97 BCE, but the results were again patchy and Li Guangli was also forced to surrender to the *shanyu*. Sima Qian makes a point of noting that no honors were awarded to any of the Han generals that year because of their lack of success.[51]

Even as these military efforts against the Xiongnu continued, some successful, others not, all the evidence indicates that the diplomatic relationship that had been established between the Han and their Tarim Basin vassal states remained strong. Despite the fact that the northern Tarim city-state of Turfan was constantly threatened by the Xiongnu, it made formal vassal submission to the Han during the last years of Wudi's reign. Even after the death of the great Martial Emperor in 87 BCE, the military and diplomatic initiatives he had initiated continued unabated in the decades that followed. Sometime after 81 BCE, early in the reign of Wudi's successor, Zhaodi, a new Han garrisoned agricultural commandery was established at Wuwei.[52] In 77 BCE, the Han attempted to kill the king of Loulan and replace him with a puppet of his own, an indication of just how much the Han now regarded the Tarim Basin as "our territory."[53]

Indeed, the Han were now so deeply invested in Central Asia that, in either 60 or 59 BCE, during the reign of Xuandi, the court made a decision to establish a permanent presence deep in the Tarim Basin to protect its various garrisons, commanderies and allied states from the Xiongnu and to reinforce its hegemonic status among the various tributary town-states of the region. Accordingly, the Office of the Protector General of the Western Regions was established, and General Cheng Chi was appointed the first protector general. This decision meant that the Han now had a powerful, permanent military presence in the Tarim Basin, which allowed it to establish durable control over both the northern and southern routes around the Taklimakan Desert and the town-states located along them.[54] Cheng Chi had immediate success in 59 BCE when a Xiongnu prince renounced his allegiance to the *shanyu*

[50] SJ 110, Watson 1993, pp. 127–128 and 161. [51] SJ 110, Watson 1993, p. 161.

[52] A. F. P. Hulsewe and M. A. N. Loewe, *China in Central Asia. The Early Stage: 125 B.C.–A.D. 23*. An Annotated Translation of Chapters 61 and 96 of the History of the Former Han Dynasty, Leiden: Brill, 1979, p. 40 n.

[53] Hulsewe and Loewe 1979, p. 89.

[54] For an early but still convincing assessment of the broader world historical importance of the establishment of the Office of the Protector General of the Western Regions, see F. J. Teggart's classic *Rome and China: A Study of Correlations in Historical Events*. Berkeley: University of California Press, 1939, p. 106.

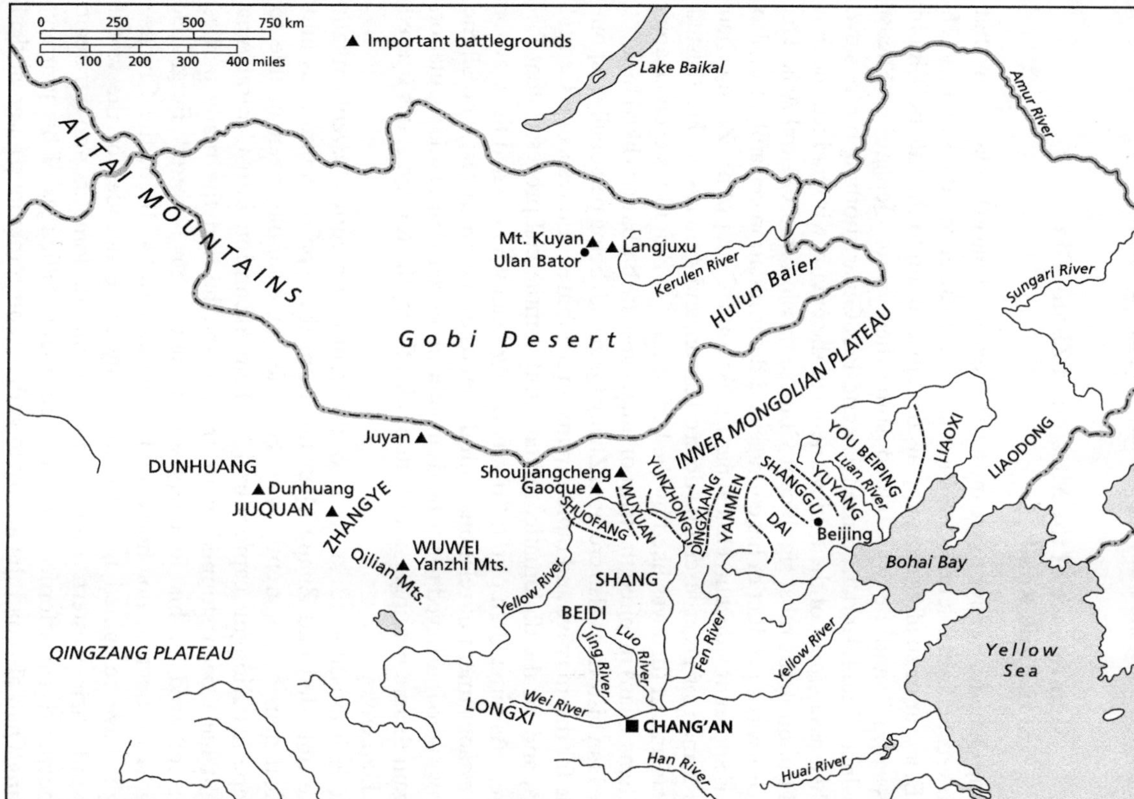

Map 3.1 Map of Han campaigns against the Xiongnu

himself in the hands of the protector general.[55] Later protec- were to play an important role in relations between the Han ..erful Kushan Empire, and thus in the operation of trade and exchange during the First Silk Roads Era, as we see in a later chapter.

Significance of the Mission of Zhang Qian to the Silk Roads

Zhang Qian did not live to see most of the extraordinary developments that followed his initial journey to Bactria. The great envoy died in 119/118 BCE, a year or so after receiving his final promotion to the title of "Grand Messenger," and he was buried somewhere near Qenggu in Shensi Province. Han historians Sima Qian and Ban Gu are nothing but positive in their assessment of the achievements of the envoy, who had led the first and undoubtedly most significant Chinese mission into Central Asia. His success was a product of his courage and determination certainly, but also of his apparently decent, ethical nature. As Sima Qian put it: "Zhang Qian was a man of great strength, determination and generosity. He trusted others and in turn was liked by the barbarians."[56] Ban Gu is even clearer: "(Zhang Qian) inspired the trust of others and the barbarians liked him."[57] The Han historians also credited Zhang Qian with being personally responsible for this massive and rapid expansion of Chinese interests into Central Asia, and for the diplomatic, military and commercial processes that followed. As Sima Qian put it: "It was Zhang Qian who opened the way for the establishment of relations with the lands of the northwest, and all the envoys who journeyed to the lands in later times relied upon his reputation to gain them a hearing. As a result of his efforts, the foreign states trusted the Han envoys."[58]

It is impossible to know how differently subsequent events might have unfolded had Zhang Qian not been the type of courageous and ethical man he apparently was. Had he, for example, been unable to escape his Xiongnu captors in 128, Han expansion into Central Asia might have been stopped in its tracks, and he and the many parties that followed in his footsteps might never have visited Ferghana, Sogdia or Bactria, nor heard of Parthia and India. If so, the Chinese might have remained ignorant for many more decades of the world beyond their western borders and of the diplomatic and strategic opportunities it afforded. Despite the many challenges of his journey, Zhang Qian also had the ability to gather (and remember!) a great deal

[55] Teggart 1939, p. 106. [56] SJ 123, Watson 1993, p. 233. [57] HS 61 2B.
[58] SJ 123, Watson 1993, p. 240.

of detailed information, which he later delivered in the compelling report that so beguiled Emperor Wudi with the possibilities of imperial expansion to the west. Essentially it was this report that was largely responsible for enticing China out of millennia of relative isolation and into active engagement with the rest of Inner Eurasia for the first time, including eventually with the Greco-Roman world.

We should also perhaps be grateful that Zhang Qian was less persuasive in his interviews with the king of the Yuezhi, because if the Yuezhi had agreed to return to China and form an alliance with the Han, there would have been no Kushan Empire. This would have made a huge difference to the history of ancient Eurasia, because the extraordinary levels of trans-Eurasian cultural exchange that occurred during the First Silk Roads Era were very much facilitated by the powerful Kushan Empire that was founded by the Yuezhi, as we shall see. In considering one of the questions we posed in the introduction, the exploits of Zhang Qian do indeed remind historians who work on the macro scale that, despite being largely subject to inevitable forces and processes of political, economic, social and cultural evolution often beyond the influence of any mere individuals, history does on occasion still seem to hinge upon a series of serendipitous decisions, coincidences and chances, and on the astonishing personal endeavors of individuals like Zhang Qian.

Conclusion

This chapter has followed the epic journey of Han envoy Zhang Qian from the Han capital of Chang'an deep into Central Asia and back. It has also sketched the main campaigns in the long and bloody war between the Han and Xiongnu, which was the larger geopolitical context in which Zhang Qian's expedition occurred. As a result of Emperor Wudi's decision to end the *heqin* policy of his predecessors and adopt a more aggressive military approach to the relationship with the Xiongnu, by the mid-first century BCE, the Han military had pushed the Xiongnu back to the northern steppe. The Han government had also established a series of military garrisons along the northwestern borders of the state to safeguard its growing tributary empire in Central Asia. In the next chapter we see how the endeavors of Zhang Qian and the Han military bore extraordinary fruit, as continuing Han diplomatic and military activities facilitated the movement of large quantities of silk and other Chinese goods deep into Central Asia and eventually on toward the Mediterranean Basin.

Selected Further Reading

Benjamin, C., *The Yuezhi: Origins, Migration and the Conquest of Northern Bactria.* Turnhout: Brepols, *Silk Roads Studies* XIV, 2007.

Chang, C.-s., *The Rise of the Chinese Empire, Volume 1: Nation, State and Imperialism in Early China ca. 1600 BC–AD 8*, Ann Arbor: University of Michigan Press, 2007.

Di Cosmo, N., *Ancient China and Its Enemies: The Rise of Nomadic Power in East Asian History*. Cambridge: Cambridge University Press, 2002.

Hulsewe, A. F. P. and M. A. N. Loewe, *China in Central Asia. The Early Stage: 125 B.C.–A.D. 23.* An Annotated Translation of Chapters 61 and 96 of the History of the Former Han Dynasty. Leiden: Brill, 1979.

Sima Qian, *Shi Ji, Records of the Grand Historian by Sima Qian – Han Dynasty II*, trans. B. Watson, revised edn. New York: Columbia University Press, 1993.

Teggart, F. J., *Rome and China: A Study of Correlations in Historical Events.* Berkeley: University of California Press, 1939.

4 The Early Han Dynasty and the Eastern Silk Roads

As we have noted several times already, for thousands of years before the start of the First Silk Roads Era, most of the agrarian civilizations of ancient Afro-Eurasia – those of Mesopotamia, Egypt and the Mediterranean, and of Central Asia, the Iranian Plateau and the Indus Valley – had been interacting with each other for millennia through regular trade and occasional warfare. The one great civilization that had been missing from this early world system was located in East Asia, sealed off from the beginning of its history behind formidable geographical barriers, and in regular contact only with other East Asian communities, and with groups of pastoral nomads to the north and west. Some of these nomadic groups formed powerful confederations, particularly the Xiongnu, whose vast "Empire of the Steppe" created an additional military and intelligence barrier between East and Central Asia. As far as we know, it was the expedition of Han envoy Zhang Qian that first breached these geographic and military barriers, and it was his subsequent report to Emperor Wudi that led to the dispatching of many subsequent Chinese diplomatic and military missions into Central Asia, events unfolded in the previous chapter.

It was at this moment, late in the second century BCE, that exchanges between Han China and other Inner Eurasian states began to intensify, with profound ramifications for Eurasian and world history. Before the advent of the Qin and Han there had been no Chinese "empire," just a series of relatively small states ruled by a variety of impressive though localized dynasties. This all changed with the short-lived Qin, and particularly during the Han Dynasty, which under Wudi expanded to become a huge imperial state that stretched from Vietnam to Korea, and from the Yellow Sea deep into Central Asia. It was during this period of dynamic imperial expansion that East Asian civilization joined the existing Afro-Eurasian trading and exchange system for the first time. Although we know that small quantities of trade goods from southern regions of China had previously made their way into markets in Central Asia by way of what has been called the "Great Indian Road," following the expansion of the Han Empire and the extensive campaigns against the Xiongnu, much larger volumes of Chinese material goods, technologies and ideas about the world began to spread across Inner Eurasia. At the same time, foreign ideas about religion, food, music, philosophy and art also began to make their way eastward and to influence the material and intellectual culture of East Asian civilization.

In the previous chapter, we saw that, immediately following the return of Zhang Qian, Chinese military and diplomatic activity in Inner Eurasia dramatically increased. One result of this was the dispatching of valuable treasuries of Chinese tribute gifts into Central Asia, including enormous quantities of raw Chinese silk. Substantial quantities of this silk, sent originally as tribute to both sedentary states and nomadic confederations, was eventually transported further west along the various land and maritime routes that would constitute the Silk Roads network, to be transformed ultimately into gorgeous garments worn by patrician women in faraway cities like Palmyra and Rome. But the question of exactly how silk and other Chinese commodities traveled from China to the Mediterranean during this First Silk Roads Era continues to challenge historians. The traditional image of enormous caravans of Bactrian camels under the control of Chinese merchants, carrying cargoes of commercial silk out of Chang'an and on to Sogdian or Kushan middlemen has increasingly been called into question.[1] In addition, the idea that Chinese merchants had been completely uninvolved in commercial exchanges beyond their region before the advent of the First Silk Roads Era is also no longer tenable, because we know that, as well as the operation of the Great Indian Road, for centuries before the Early Han Dynasty considerable trade and exchange had also been taking place along the northern and western borders of China, with the Xiongnu, the Yuezhi and other pastoral nomadic groups.

With this background in mind, this chapter attempts to answer a series of questions related to the early engagement of the Han with the Silk Roads network. The first of these is one of the most challenging: what were the specific circumstances and mechanisms whereby large quantities of Chinese silk and other luxury goods made their way into Central Asia during the Early Han Dynasty? Related to this is the question of how commodities dispatched as tribute were monetized by Han diplomats and Inner Eurasian nomadic and sedentary elites. In the middle part of this chapter, we focus on the particular geographical constraints and challenges facing travelers on what now became the eastern routes of the

[1] See, for example, K. Rezakhani, "The Road That Never Was: The Silk Road and Trans-Eurasian Exchange," *Project Muse* 30, No. 3. (2010), pp. 420ff.

developing Silk Roads network. How did diplomats and merchants make their way from the capital of Chang'an to the far western edge of the Han tributary empire? What role did the Bactrian camel and Central Asian merchant communities such as the Sogdians play in making travel and trade on the eastern part of the Silk Roads possible? The final part of this chapter examines the development of a flourishing sericulture in Han China. How were the Chinese able to produce enough high-quality silk to satisfy a growing market, not just in Central Asia, but also in Southwest Asia and the Mediterranean Basin, including the Roman Empire?

Early Chinese Material Exchanges with Pastoral Nomads

Textual evidence indicates that, at least by the Zhou Dynasty and perhaps even earlier, several ancient Chinese dynasties had been involved in material exchanges with nomads dwelling along their western and northern borders. One such nomadic confederation was the Yuezhi, the same group that centuries later Zhang Qian was sent to find in an attempt to form an alliance against the Xiongnu. We have clear evidence that the Yuezhi engaged in substantial trade in goods such as camels, white jade, composite bows and particularly horses with the Zhou Dynasty. Numerous references in the *Yi Zhou Shu* and *Guanzi*, both of which date to the seventh century BCE, attest to the value the Zhou ascribed to these highly valuable commodities, and name the Yuezhi as one of the key suppliers.[2]

The Xiongnu are also mentioned in these same Zhou Dynasty sources, although their commercial relationship with the Chinese seemed less important than that between the Zhou and the Yuezhi. However, as we saw in the previous chapter, following the rise to power of Shanyu Modu and his successors, which occurred during the first century of the Early Han Dynasty, Han emperors had adopted the policy of *heqin*, which stipulated the transfer of substantial amounts of tribute to the Xiongnu from the Han court in return for the Xiongnu not attacking Han territory. In most cases, the precise amount of tribute the Han paid to the Xiongnu is not specified in the *Shiji* or *Han Shu*. But we do have some figures from the early first century BCE reign of Shanyu Hulugu (r. 95–85 BCE), who demanded that the following tribute be paid to him: 10,000 *dan* of wine (about 400,000 liters), 5,000 *hu* of grain (about 100,000 liters) and

[2] A comprehensive list of the references to the Yuezhi in the *Yi Zhou Shu* can be found in A. K. Narain, *The Tokharians*. Shillong, India, 2000, pp. 4–5. Full text in Li Mian, commentator: Guan Zhong, *Guanzi Jinzhu Jinyi*. 2 vols. Taipei: Taiwan Commercial Press, 1988. See also C. Benjamin, *The Yuezhi: Origins, Migration and the Conquest of Northern Bactria*. Turnhout: Brepols, 2007, pp. 31ff.

a staggering 10,000 bales of raw silk.[3] We also know that, with the Yuezhi now dwelling far away in Bactria, the Han and Xiongnu regularly engaged in the trading of steppe horses and furs for Han agricultural products and luxury goods, particularly silk, and also that the Xiongnu were able to obtain Han iron weapons via a black market.[4]

We have more data for the year 51 BCE, during which a Xiongnu leader named Huhanye (r. 58–31 BCE), who was a rival to Shanyu Zhizhi (r. 56–36 BCE), made a personal tributary submission to the Han court. After agreeing to become a vassal of the Han and paying some form of tribute to the court, Huhanye received lavish gifts from the Han in return. This included a large quantity of gold, 200,000 coins, seventy-seven suits of clothes, fifteen horses, 19,000 *hu* of grain (about 680,000 liters), 8,000 bales of silk fabric and 1,500 kilograms of silk floss.[5] The sources also note that after 51 BCE, all gifts to Xiongnu leaders were in the form of silk, and political submission was guaranteed only as long as the Han could keep providing ever-larger quantities of silk to the *shanyu.*[6] This silk was transported either as silk floss or bales of silk fabric, and the quantities were staggering. In the year 1 BCE, for example, the Han court sent 7,500 catties of floss and 30,000 bales of silk to the Xiongnu *shanyu*. What happened to this silk after it reached the Xiongnu is unknown, but the most obvious inference is that much of it must have been transported on further to the west by means of commercial intermediaries, destined for markets along the Silk Roads, and eventually also in Rome.

Han Diplomatic Missions and the Export of Silk

Despite the payment of these enormous quantities of silk to the Xiongnu as a part of the *heqin* agreement and the ongoing "black market" trade in potential Silk Roads export goods between the Xiongnu and Han along the borders, perhaps the most important mechanism for the transport of silk and other Chinese products into Central Asia was the diplomatic caravans dispatched by Wudi and his successors to the various states of the Tarim Basin and other Inner Eurasian regions following the initial expedition of Zhang Qian. These valuable materials, particularly silk and gold, were used in diplomatic exchanges with the leaders of the "western states," and also to

3 HS 96A; see Yu Ying-Shi, "Han Foreign Relations," in D. Twitchett and M. Loewe, eds., *The Cambridge History of China Volume 1: The Ch'in and Han Empires 221 BC–AD 220*. Cambridge: Cambridge University Press, 1986, p. 387.

4 X. Liu, *Ancient India and Ancient China: Trade and Religious Exchanges AD 1–600*. Oxford: Oxford University Press, 1988, p. 14.

5 Yu Ying-Shi 1986, pp. 395–396.

6 Yu Ying-Shi 1986, pp. 396–397.

Figure 4.1 Bactrian camels and religious figures, depicted on the walls of a cave at Mogao, near Dunhuang, Gansu Province, western China http://media.gettyimages.com/photos/mogao-caves-picture-id125983260?s=170667a
Credit: Top Photo Corporation

pay for food and lodging in the town-states of Central Asia. After the Office of the Protector General was established in 59/60 CE, however, Han envoys were no longer expected to pay for their lodgings when visiting vassal states. Instead they collected tribute from the states of the Tarim Basin, including agricultural products such as raisins, along with precious stones and furs, to be dispatched back to Chang'an.[7] The sources might also be interpreted as implying that Han diplomatic missions into Central Asia were often accompanied by commercial caravans carrying large quantities of silk, which were apparently sold for substantial profits along the way.

As we saw in the previous chapter, these Chinese diplomatic missions were dispatched with great frequency and were often very large in size. During the late second century BCE, these missions traveled extensively between Chang'an and numerous Central Asian states, both in the Tarim Basin and further afield. Sima Qian offers a comprehensive description of the size and frequency of these parties:

[7] As discussed by Liu 1988.

"The largest of these embassies to foreign states numbered several hundred persons, while even the smaller parties included over one hundred members, though later, as the envoys became more accustomed to the route, the number was gradually reduced. The credentials and gifts which the envoys bore with them were much like those supplied to the envoys in Zhang Qian's time. In the course of one year anywhere from five or six to over ten parties would be sent out."[8]

Sima Qian also comments on the size of Zhang Qian's mission to the Wusun, which was accompanied by 10,000 cattle and sheep and carried a fortune in gold and silk.[9]

We also noted in the previous chapter that the authors of both the *Shiji* and *Han Shu* were less than impressed with the motives and behavior of many of the envoys who followed in the footsteps of Zhang Qian. Sima Qian, describing the situation either late in the second or early in the first century BCE, is particularly scathing in the following illuminating passage:

When the envoys returned from a mission, it invariably happened that they had plundered or stolen goods on their way ... The officials and soldiers who had accompanied them on a mission would in turn start at once enthusiastically describing the wealth to be found in the foreign nations. Those who told the most impressive tales were granted the seals of an envoy, while those who spoke more modestly were made assistants. As a result, all sorts of worthless men hurried forward with wild tales to imitate their example. The envoys were all sons of poor families who handled the government gifts and goods that were entrusted to them as though they were private property and looked for opportunities to buy goods at a cheap price in the foreign countries and make a profit on their return to China. The men of the foreign lands soon became disgusted when they found that each of the Han envoys told some different story and, considering that the Han armies were too far away to worry about, refused to supply the envoys with food and provisions, making things very difficult for them.[10]

Sima Qian also contrasts the attitude of the rulers of various Central Asian states toward these "worthless men" with that of the apparently more formidable Xiongnu envoys:

Whenever a Xiongnu envoy appeared in the region carrying credentials from the Shanyu, he was escorted from state to state and provided with food, and no one dared to detain him or cause him any difficulty. In the case of the Han envoys, however, if they did not hand out silks or other goods they were given no food, and unless they purchased animals in the markets they could get no mounts for their riders. This was because the people considered the Han too far away to bother about. They also believed that the Han had plenty of goods and money and it was therefore proper to make the envoys pay for whatever they wanted. As may be seen, they were much more afraid of the Xiongnu envoys than of those from the Han.[11]

[8] SJ 123, Watson 1993, pp. 240–241. [9] SJ 123, Watson 1993, p. 238.
[10] SJ 123, Watson 1993, p. 242. [11] SJ 123, Watson 1993, p. 244.

As Etienne de la Vaissière has persuasively argued in his study of the role of the Sogdians in Silk Roads trade, this very different attitude of the elites and merchants of Central Asian states toward Han and Xiongnu envoys provides striking evidence of another mechanism, beyond the payment of silk tribute to the Xiongnu, whereby large quantities of Han silk made their way deep into Inner Eurasia.[12] Clearly many Chinese envoys were helping themselves to valuable tributary resources that had been intended for the elites of these western states; and the practice must have been lucrative because, as Sima Qian noted, "all sorts of worthless men hurried forward," indicating the scale of the practice of using official goods for personal commercial gain. This meant that, as de la Vaissière puts it:

> A real commercial circuit was established at the margins of the official diplomatic circuit, and was maintained at its expense: the populations of Central Asia intended to be remunerated for their services, and the Chinese envoys wished to buy in the West, in exchange for the silk of their government, those precious products whose resale would make them rich in China. That which the official Chinese texts call plunder or want of respect was in reality a form of commercial organization. At the margins of the far-reaching diplomatic exchanges between the nomadic military elites and the Chinese state, these commercial contacts brought profit to the Central Asian merchants and to the Chinese gentlemen of fortune.[13]

It was surely by this complicated and unofficial arrangement, and not by the coordinated operations of large private commercial export consortiums in Han China, that large quantities of silk began to flow westward from the Han capital at Chang'an. Chinese silk that had begun its journey as diplomatic tribute now found its way into the hands of commercial groups in Central Asia who were intent to use it to gain a profit. Of course, the huge quantities of silk paid to the Xiongnu under the *heqin* agreement also probably found their way into this evolving commercial network, although evidence for this is sparse at best. But the sources certainly provide evidence of a flourishing trade in Chinese goods, including silk, in many of the town-states in the Tarim Basin by late in the second century BCE. As de la Vaissière concludes, "we are dealing here with the first attested commerce, which owed its structure to the means available to Chinese diplomacy."[14]

[12] E. de la Vaissière, *Sogdian Traders. A History*, trans. James Ward, Handbook of Oriental Studies, Vol. X. Leiden: Brill, 2005, chapter 1, pp. 30–32.

[13] De la Vaissière 2005, p. 31.

[14] De la Vaissière 2005, p. 32.

Geographical Challenges of the Eastern Silk Roads Routes from China

To our second question now, concerning the geography of the routes followed by diplomats and merchants westward from the Han heartland into Central Asia. Evidence suggests that the geographical challenges of the routes were daunting to say the least, despite the fact that migrations and local trade had probably been taking place along all the major trans-Inner Eurasian routes for millennia. The geography of Central Asia makes only a few paths through the high mountains and deserts of the region viable, so the bands of *homo erectus* that first migrated out of Africa and eventually on to China almost 2 million years ago, and subsequent waves of human migration from 90,000 years ago, probably followed similar paths to those diplomatic and commercial routes that eventually developed into the Silk Roads network.

The key geographic considerations for travelers along the Silk Roads was access to water, and also dealing with significant fluctuations in temperature, including those caused by the major variations in elevation they encountered making their way across the high mountains and desert basins of Inner Eurasia. Diplomatic and commercial parties also needed access to supplies of food on the journey, which meant that places in which successful agriculture was being carried out would have been critically important stops along the way. This limited the routes to regions where irrigation or stream-fed farming was practiced, or areas where crops were grown around oases on the edge of the great deserts that were scattered along the length of the eastern Silk Roads, or to lowland river deltas, or to locations that were irrigated by the storage of water deposits from melting snow and ice.

Examples of the sort of regions that probably flourished through effective irrigation control during the First Silk Roads Era were identified in the 1950s by Soviet archaeologists S. P. Tolstov and B. V. Andrianov, who published a study of reconstructed water systems that probably operated in the Amu Darya and Syr Darya deltas during the period. They identified a period of maximum development between the fourth century BCE and the second century CE during which some 2 million hectares was being irrigated by small basin schemes and large permanent reservoirs. This was four times the area under cultivation in those regions today, and it allowed for the support and growth of key Silk Roads cities such as Samarkand and Bukhara.[15]

[15] S. P Tolstov and B. V. Andrianov, "Novie materiali po istorii razvitia Khorezm," *Isnt Ethnografii Kratkiie Soobschenia* 26, 1957, discussed in T. Williams on behalf of ICOMOS, *The Silk Roads: An ICOMOS Thematic Study*. Charenton-le-Pont: International Council of Monuments and Sites, 2014, p. 17.

The oases that sprang up around the edges of the Taklamakan Desert in the Tarim Basin also developed complex irrigation systems that depended on successful underground distribution. Farmers used a system later known as a *qanat*, a Persian word that describes an underground channel to store and distribute water. The *qanats* are connected to aquifers or to other sources of water (such as streams regularly swollen by melting snow), and use a series of shafts to channel the water to agricultural fields. A similar system is known to have operated in the Turfan Hollow of the Tarim Basin during the First Silk Roads Era, where it is known as a *karez* in the Uyghur language. The *karez* in Turfan consists of a series of vertical shaft wells that are connected by underground canals to collect water from the surface that has come down from the nearby Tian Shan and Flaming Mountains. Because Turfan is in a basin, the underground canals use gravity to bring the water into dams closer to the community, and being underground they also protect from water loss by evaporation. Even today some 1,100 *karez* are in operation in the Turfan Basin, and the modern city of Turfan has built a water museum to celebrate the extraordinary technology that made living in this harsh desert environment possible. The availability of large supplies of water also meant that these

Figure 4.2 Underground *qanat* irrigation system, Kerman Province, Iran
www.gettyimages.co.uk/license/639731210
Credit: Andrea Ricordi, Italy

communities in the Turfan Basin, and indeed right across the Tarim Basin, were able to accommodate the large numbers of Han diplomats and merchants, along with their agents, camels and camel drivers, for days and weeks at a time, thus making the evolving Silk Roads network viable.[16]

When the Han Dynasty started constructing agricultural military garrisons along the western frontier and into the Hexi Corridor, Chinese soldiers labored to construct similar sophisticated irrigation systems to make these settlements tenable.[17] Thousands of wooden documents have been found discarded at several of these Han outposts and at watchtowers between them, and among the bureaucratic records are frequent allusions to the type of irrigation being used to grow crops to sustain the population of mostly soldiers.[18] As well as establishing these military outposts and larger garrison towns, Han soldiers and conscripted laborers were employed to extend the Great Wall of China as far west as the Yunmen Pass, also known as the Jade Gate, named for one of the many valuable tributary and commercial products that passed through it. This was a frontier pass located to the west of Dunhuang in the modern province of Gansu. Emperor Wudi arranged to have the first Jade Gate constructed around 121 BCE, not long after the return of Zhang Qian from Bactria.[19] Its remains can still be seen today about 80 kilometers northwest of Dunhuang, as a reminder of the extraordinary reach of the Han Dynasty and the lengths it went to in order to establish and maintain a powerful presence in Central Asia. These various Han agricultural and infrastructure initiatives, coupled with ongoing diplomatic missions to the states of the Tarim Basin and military operations to keep driving the Xiongnu back to the northern steppe and away from the exchange routes, made the first section of the eastern Silk Roads from Chang'an feasible and relatively safe.

Departure from Chang'an, the Imperial Capital

During the second and first centuries BCE, Han envoys carrying tribute, and any merchants that may have traveled with them, would mostly have

[16] On the *karez* system of Turfan, see A. Bertrand, "The Hydraulic Systems in Turfan (Xinjian)," *The Silk Road* 8 (2010), pp. 27ff.

[17] X. Liu, "Exchanges within the Silk Roads World System," in C. Benjamin, ed., *Cambridge History of the World Vol. IV.* Cambridge: Cambridge University Press, 2015, pp. 457–458.

[18] Liu 2015, p. 458; see also Chen Zhi, *Juyan Hanjian Yanjiu* [*Study of Documents on Wooden Slips from Juyan Gate*]. Tianjin: Gujichubanshe, 1986.

[19] J. Hill, *Through the Jade Gate to Rome: A Study of the Silk Roads during the Later Han Dynasty, 1st to 2nd Centuries CE.* Charlestown: BookSurge, 2009, p. vi.

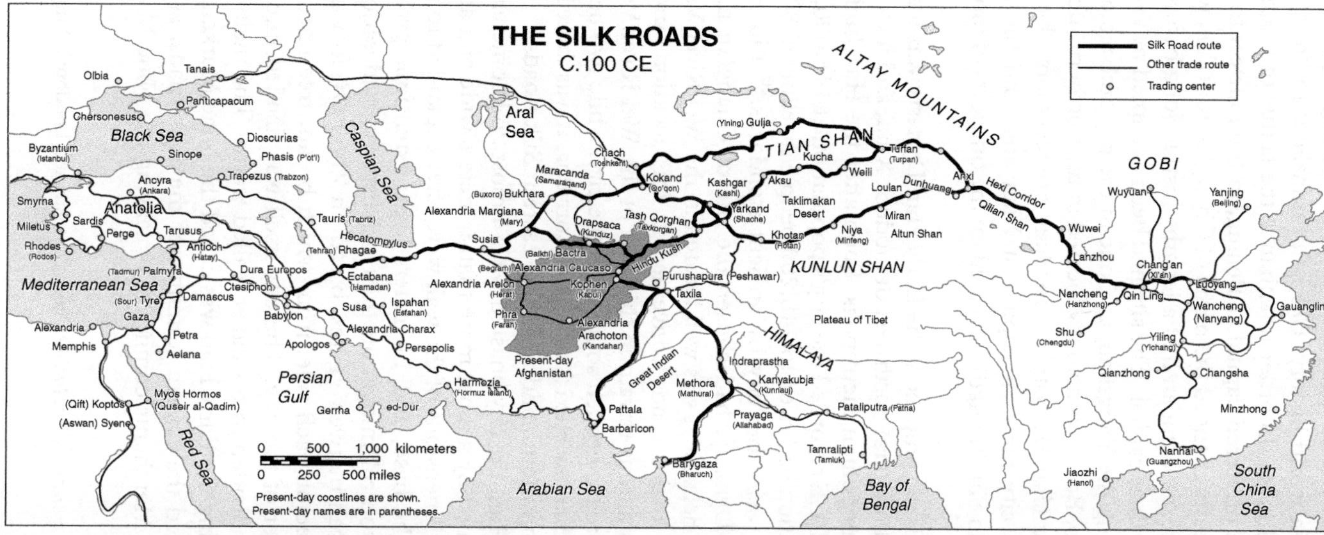

Map 4.1 Map of major Silk Roads land routes
www.chinadiscovery.com/assets/images/silk-road/maps/China-Silk-Road-Map-full.jpg

commenced their journey at the Early Han capital of Chang'an, one of the great imperial cities in world history. *Chang'an* translates to "perpetual peace" in classical Chinese. In order to enhance the status of the much later Ming Dynasty's preferred capital at Beijing, in the fourteenth century Ming administrators changed the name of Chang'an to *Xi'an*, which means "western peace." Chang'an had a lengthy history long before the Early Han chose it as their capital. The site had been occupied by various early cultures including the Yangshao, and one of the key archaeological sites for the Yangshao, Banpo, is actually located in the northern suburbs of modern Xian. The Han Dynasty's immediate predecessors, the Qin, had also chosen the city for their capital of Xianyang, and the great terracotta tomb of Qin Shi Huangdi is located on the outskirts of modern Xian.

The capital city/palace complex of the Early Han Dynasty was located about 2 miles (3.2 kilometers) northwest of modern Xian, and it evolved into a splendid, cosmopolitan metropolis. Soon after the Han built the city, a census of 195 BCE recorded the city's population at 146,000; by 2 CE, the city's population had risen to 246,200 people dwelling in 80,000 households, so this was a big city by ancient standards.[20] Liu Bang, founder of the Han Dynasty, had chosen the site of Chang'an mostly for strategic reasons, because it was well located in the Wei River Valley, and because several major roads converged at this location. Indeed, because of the mountainous terrain in this part of the Wei River Valley, only two practicable roads headed south from the city, while two headed westward toward the narrow Hexi (or Gansu) Corridor. It was these latter roads that became important conduits of the eastern Silk Roads.

During the Early Han, the city boasted walls almost 26 kilometers (42 miles) long, surrounded by a moat more than 6 meters wide and almost 5 meters deep. The dimensions of the wall were later expanded to up to 16 meters thick at the base, and 12 meters high, extensions probably due more to flood control mitigation than defensive considerations.[21] The walls were pierced by twelve gates, based on Zhou Dynasty urban planning rituals, three on each side, from which broad, tree-lined avenues led to the center of the city. The city itself was divided into nine distinct districts, subdivided into smaller walled wards. The main market of Chang'an during the Early Han was called the Nine Markets, and this essentially marked the eastern terminus of the Silk Roads, at least during this first era. Merchants coming to or leaving the Nine Markets

[20] A. Schinz, *The Magic Square: Cities in Ancient China*, Stuttgart and London: Edition Axel Menges, 1996, p. 428.

[21] Schinz 1996, p. 428.

did so via the avenues that led to the Northeast and Northwest Gates, the most frequently used approaches by both farmers and merchants.

From Chang'an to Dunhuang

Han diplomatic missions bearing large quantities of silk and other valuable tributary goods would have probably passed out of the Northwest Gate and crossed a major bridge over the Wei River, before continuing westward across the northern plains and through the narrow Hexi Corridor toward Dunhuang, some 1,600 kilometers distant.[22] Much of this region had been taken from the Xiongnu during the reign of Wudi, following the major military campaigns of 122 and 121 BCE discussed in the preceding chapter. This added substantial new territory to the Han Empire, from the Hexi Corridor itself and on to Lop Nur in the Tarim Basin. As we noted earlier, to try and maintain control of the corridor the Great Wall was extended as far as the Jade Gate, and four new agricultural garrisons were established at Wuwei, Zhangyi, Jiuquan and Dunhuang, settled by Han soldiers and colonists.

Each of these agricultural military settlements must have functioned as important and secure resting and staging posts for Han envoys and merchants, although arguably Dunhuang was always the most important. Even today the sand dune-fringed town of Dunhuang still has the feel and excitement of a frontier settlement, although the herds of Bactrian camels that would have been tied up in the main streets 2,000 years ago have been replaced by hundreds of parked mopeds! Throughout the First Silk Roads Era Dunhuang was a key military and diplomatic garrison town, a lush and comfortable oasis in an otherwise hostile desert environment, providing security, water, fresh food and accommodation for envoys, merchants and soldiers.

Dunhuang was strategically very well located, at the crossroads of the major southern Tarim Basin Silk Roads route and another important route that led from India northward through Tibet, then on through Dunhuang to Mongolia and southern Siberia. Dunhuang was also the key to control of the narrow Hexi Corridor, the natural conduit that connects the northern plains of China with the Tarim Basin. Archaeological evidence demonstrates that the Dunhuang oasis was occupied from at least 2000 BCE, and it was probably also a key region under the control of the Yuezhi for many centuries before they were pushed out by the Xiongnu. As one of the four garrison towns established by Wudi, Dunhuang was fortified and occupied by Han colonists and soldiers. The name *Dunhuang* translates to "blazing

[22] Williams 2014, p. 87.

beacon," a reference to lighting of beacons by colonists when facing attack from the Xiongnu.[23]

Dunhuang thus provided welcome security and resources for envoys and merchants heading westward into Central Asia, and also those returning eastward following lengthy journeys. It also became a major center for religious pilgrims, and late in the First Silk Roads Era, Buddhist monks established an important Buddhist community there. The monks carved caves for themselves in the soft rock of the region, particularly at Mogao and Yulin, and these developed into places for meditation and worship. Many of these caves were later decorated with superb religious art, particularly in the troubled centuries that followed the decline of the First Silk Roads Era. This magnificent cave art is striking evidence of the role Dunhuang and the Hexi Corridor played, not just in the transport of material goods, but in the dissemination of religious and intellectual ideas. The caves constitute some of the greatest religious art galleries of the ancient world, featuring hundreds of magnificently realized and vividly colored Buddhist and Daoist wall paintings, and they have also yielded Manichaean, Jewish and even Christian artifacts, evidence of the wide variety of faiths practiced by the merchants and pilgrims who traveled along the Silk Roads.

From Dunhuang to Kashgar

From Dunhuang the caravans were faced with two alternative routes, both long and challenging, and both circumventing the formidable Taklimakan Desert. Central Asia contains some of the most inhospitable deserts in the world, with little water, vegetation or wildlife. The Taklimakan Desert, one of the largest sandy deserts on the planet, was and is prone to frequent sandstorms that whip the fragile surface into a frenzy, burying anything in their path. Windborne sand deposits cover some parts of the desert in layers up to 350 meters thick, often in the form of spectacular sand dunes. The climate of the Taklimakan is continental, meaning it is subject to high temperatures in summer (up to 38 degrees Celsius in the eastern regions of the desert) and cold winters (−10 to −20 degrees Celsius). The desert area stretches almost 1,000 kilometers from east to west, and at its widest more than 400 kilometers from north to south, giving it a total area of 320,000 square kilometers.

The origin of the name *Taklimakan* is obscure. It might be a Uyghur name based on the Arabic words *tark*, meaning "to leave alone, to

[23] A. F. P. Hulsewe and M. A. N. Loewe, *China in Central Asia. The Early Stage: 125 B.C.–A.D. 23.* An Annotated Translation of Chapters 61 and 96 of the History of the Former Han Dynasty. Leiden: Brill, 1979, pp. 75–76.

abandon," and *makan*, which means "place"; so the "place to leave alone."[24] Alternatively, it might be derived from the Turkic words *taqlar makan*, meaning "the place of ruins."[25] Either of these definitions provides some sense of the forbidding nature of this the sixteenth largest desert on earth, and helps explain why the Taklimakan functioned for so long as a natural barrier between East and West. Venturing into the interior of the desert was virtually impossible; even today it is only feasible with the proper equipment and supplies, particularly water. But traders did have a viable way around this barrier, and that was to follow ancient pathways around the northern and southern edges of the desert.

The Taklimakan is surrounded by enormous snow-covered mountain ranges: the Kunlun Massif to the south, the Pamirs to the west and the Tien Shan to the north. The desert lies within the internal-draining Tarim Basin, and so the entire runoff from the surrounding mountains remains in the basin itself. Because of the heat and rate of evaporation generated by the desert, none of this runoff water penetrates very far into the Taklimakan. But melting snows and rainfall from the surrounding mountains do produce piedmont streams, and as we have just seen, by using effective storage and distributions systems such as the Turfan *karez*, the water from these streams can be stored in underground storage facilities to help sustain fringe oasis towns. These include Aksu, Kucha and Turfan in the northern Taklimakan, and Yarkand, Miran and Khotan along the southern fringes of the desert. It was these oasis towns that provided resources and accommodation for the Silk Roads caravans, making large-scale diplomatic and commercial activity possible.

A caravan, having set off from Dunhuang and chosen either the northern or southern route around the desert, would rest each night in one of these oasis towns as it skirted the desert. Eventually both these routes came back together again more than 2,000 kilometers on at the town of Kashgar, at the far western end of the Taklimakan. Kashgar is located in a fertile oasis watered by the Kashgar River and local springs. The mix of loess and alluvial soils surrounding the town allows for the cultivation today of corn, rice, wheat, melons, grapes, apricots, cherries and peaches. The town and its well-watered and abundant fields must have been a particularly welcome sight at the end of a journey around the Taklimakan Desert. At Kashgar, or at some point just to the west, Chinese diplomatic and merchant travelers would probably have concluded their outward journey. Goods that had been distributed at towns along the way, or at Kashgar itself, would now find themselves in the

[24] E. M. Pospelov, *Geograficheskiye nazvaniya mira*, Moscow, 1998, p. 408.
[25] G. Jarring, "The Toponym Takla-makan," Turkic Languages col. 1, 1997, pp. 227–240.

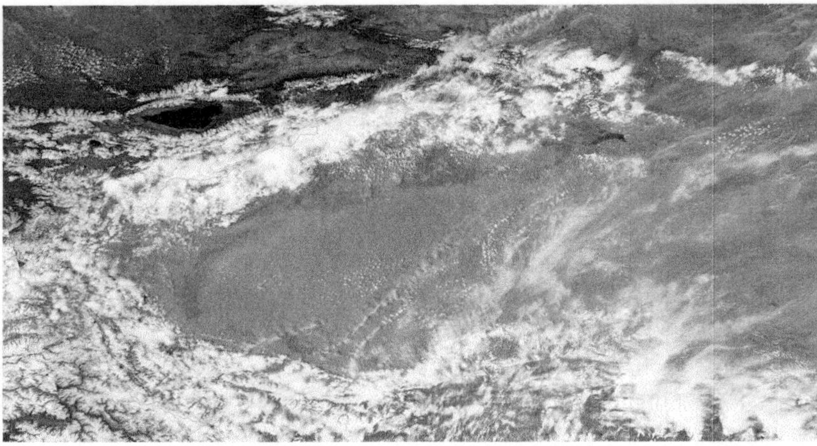

Figure 4.3 The Tarim Basin and Taklimakan Desert from space, with the snow-covered Tien Shan Mountains to the north, the Kunlun Massif to the south and the Pamirs to the west
http://media.gettyimages.com/photos/dust-and-clouds-hovered-over-the-taklimakan-desert-picture-id98185216?s=170667a
Credit: Stocktrek Images

hands of other Central Asian peoples, who would pass them on to Kushan, Sogdian or South Asian merchants. We can assume that for a substantial fee these intermediaries would then move the Han goods further west or south, many of them to be transported eventually by land or sea toward their ultimate destination of the Mediterranean Basin. We can also assume that Chinese diplomatic or commercial caravans would have picked up a range of valuable Western and Central Asian goods at Kashgar, and taken these back to Chang'an to be sold for a substantial profit.

At each of the oasis towns along the land routes, traders would have stayed in what later became known as *caravanserais*. *Caravanserai* is a Persian compound word describing a home or shelter for caravans. The word *caravan* means a group of travelers on a long journey, and *sarai* means a building with an enclosed courtyard. These were roadside inns where travelers could rest and recover from the day's journey, the ancient equivalent of the modern motel. The ruins of thousands of Central Asian caravanserais from later Silk Roads periods have been excavated and studied. These were sturdily built and apparently well run, typically large, single buildings with a square walled exterior, and a single portal wide enough to permit large or heavily laden beasts such as camels to enter. The courtyard was generally open to the sky, and along

Figure 4.4 Remains of the ancient Silk Roads town of Jiaohe, located on the northern route through the Tarim Basin, Xinjiang Province, China http://media.gettyimages.com/photos/panorama-of-jiaohe-ancient-ruinschina-picture-id689673188?s=170667a
Credit: xia yuan

the inside walls were stalls, bays, niches or chambers to accommodate merchants and their servants, their animals and their merchandise. Here the traders and their animals would rest and recover from the rigors of the day, before setting out next morning on a new stage of the journey – this is the infrastructure that made the Silk Roads possible.

We can almost imagine the atmosphere in an ancient caravanserai during the First Silk Roads Era: the babble of different languages; discussions around the fires on the potential profit to be made from the cargo, or the different ideological beliefs of the diplomats and merchants; and the exchange of all sorts of practical information about the routes. These ancient inns made possible not only the transmission of huge quantities of valuable material goods, but also the dissemination of many of the great ideas produced in the civilizations and nomadic cultures that now found themselves connected into a vast world system through material exchanges. But the most frequent topic of conversation must surely have been the physical challenges of the routes in any given season, what is the best way around the deserts this year, which mountain passes were still snow-covered and which were open, and so on. Surrounding the Taklamakan Desert in all directions is equally hostile terrain, including the Gobi Desert and the highest mountain ranges on earth. These Inner Eurasian mountains are all products of plate tectonics, driven skyward by the slow-motion and ongoing collision between the Indo-Australian and Eurasian Plates. It is the Great Himalaya and her outliers – the Karakorum, the Hindu Kush, the Pamirs, the Kunlun and the Tien Shan – that helped to isolate East Asia from West, Central and South Asia for so many millennia.

Routes beyond Kashgar

As this list of formidable mountain barriers suggests, the middlemen who moved Chinese goods further on from Kashgar also had a limited range of route options available. One way headed west via the Ferghana Valley and Samarkand, and then southwest, crossing the Amu Darya at Termez and on to the Bactrian commercial city of Bactra that Zhang Qian had visited during his first mission to the west. An alternative more northerly route also passed through the fertile valleys of Ferghana and the Zerafshan River, then continued west through Samarkand to Merv.[26] From here the route would have led across the Iranian Plateau, where the goods would be passed on to Parthian, Syrian or Greek merchants for transportation down to the valleys of the Tigris and Euphrates, and eventually via the Syrian desert on to the shores of the Mediterranean. An alternative path went south from Kashgar, more or less following the route of the modern Karakoram Highway, and then down the valley of the Indus River, ending up in port cities in northwest India like Barbaricum and Barygaza, from where goods were sent by ship to Roman Egypt via the Indian Ocean and Red Sea. We have more to say about these land and maritime routes in subsequent chapters.

One particularly challenging barrier that separates far western China from Bactria is the so-called Pamir Knot, a conglomeration of several mountain ranges that have been forced by plate tectonic movements into a twisted knot of blind valleys and high passes. The word *knot* describes the convergence of these high mountain ranges, including the Tien Shan, Karakorum, Kunlun, Hindu Kush and Pamirs, in a single geographic region. Even today the heavily glaciated Pamir Mountains at the heart of the knot are one of the least accessible regions in the world. The Pamir Knot is penetrated by only a few geographic corridors, including the narrow Wakhan Corridor running through the Pamirs between Tajikistan and Pakistan, and the Karakorum Highway that links Kashgar with Gilgit in Pakistan.

Silk Roads merchants and diplomats heading south to the port cities of India would have had to make their way through the formidable Karakorum Range. The distance from the town of Tashkurgan in far southwest China through the Karakorum and on to Taxila, one of the capitals of the Kushan Empire, is about 700 kilometers. Ancient travelers

[26] Williams 2014, p. 82.

Figure 4.5 The M41 ("Pamir Highway") just below the 4,655-meter-high Ak-Baital Pass in the Pamir Mountains, modern Tajikistan
http://media.gettyimages.com/photos/pamir-highway-between-akbaital-pass-and-karakul-picture-id530293993?s=170667a
Credit: Jean-Philippe Tournut

would have followed a mix of narrow river valley or high mountain paths that required the crossing of two major passes, the Khunjerab and Wakhir.[27] The modern Karakorum Highway, which since 1986 has joined China and Pakistan along the highest paved road in the world, essentially follows this southern branch route of the Silk Roads. The road was jointly constructed by Pakistani and Chinese engineers between 1959 and 1986, at the cost of some 900 workers' lives. As travelers on the highway today negotiate the 4,693 meter-high (15,397 feet) Khunjerab Pass, they get some sense of the challenges that merchants on the Silk Roads 2,000 years before must have faced, as they also tried to cross this mighty mountain barrier.

We actually have a unique textual glimpse of the challenging environment of the Khunjerab Pass, or some other nearby Karakorum pass, as it was during the First Silk Roads Era in the form of 2,000-year-old references in the *Han Shu* to what was then called the "Hanging Pass" or the "Suspended Crossing." The *Han Shu* first tells us something about the

[27] Williams 2014, p. 85.

inhabitants of the region, who "live in the mountains, and work the land that lies between the rocks ... they pile up stones on one another to make dwellings. The inhabitants drink by joining their hands together."[28] This is clearly a description of a small settlement located high up in the mountains, where the inhabitants live in stone huts and eke out a precarious agricultural existence on terraces built up by stone walls upon the steep hillsides. The intriguing reference to "joining hands together" to drink might suggest the necessity of linking arms into a human chain to even reach a water supply in the steep rocky gorges of the region.

Later in the *Han Shu*, a Han envoy named Tuzhin gives an eyewitness account of his crossing of the Hanging Pass, providing compelling evidence of just one of the challenges Silk Roads merchants faced:

> "(There is) a path that is (40 cm) wide, but leads forward for a length of thirty li, overlooking a precipice whose depth is unfathomed. Travelers passing on horse or foot hold on to one another and pull each other along with ropes ... When animals fall, before they have dropped half-way down the chasm they are shattered in pieces, and when men fall, the situation is such that they are unable to rescue one another. The danger of these precipices defies description."[29]

Of course, we can't be certain precisely which pass Envoy Tuzhin was discussing, but it was most probably one of the key passes that crossed the Karakoram and connected the Tarim Basin with the Gilgit Valley of northern Pakistan. It was across passes just like this that modern Chinese and Pakistani engineers laid the highest paved highway in the world. No wonder that some travelers today refer to the Karakoram Highway as "the eighth wonder of the world."[30]

Role of the Sogdians

In later chapters we consider the various commercial intermediaries who operated in the Kushan and Parthian Empires, and in South Asia and the Eastern Mediterranean, who were responsible for moving Chinese goods on beyond Kashgar, by land and by sea. But it is worth noting here the role of another group destined to become, during subsequent Silk Roads eras, the greatest Inner Eurasian merchants of all, the Sogdians. Thanks to a detailed study by Etienne de la Vaissière we now know a great deal about the critical role Sogdians played in all periods of the history of the Silk Roads, although this was limited during the First Silk Roads Era.[31]

[28] HS 96A 8B/9A. [29] HS 96A 12A/12B.
[30] M. Z. Ispahani, *Roads and Rivals: The Political Uses of Access in the Borderlands of Asia*. Ithaca, NY: Cornell University Press, 1989, p. 191.
[31] De la Vaissière 2005.

Figure 4.6 A high pass through the Karakorum, Khunjerab National Park, Pakistan
www.gettyimages.co.uk/license/683941040
Credit: Punnawit Suwuttananun

The Sogdians were probably the same people that Zhang Qian had observed dwelling in the Central Asian regions which the Early Han sources name as Kangju and Dayuan. In the *Shiji*, Sima Qian describes the occupants of Dayuan as being skillful at commerce and haggling "over a fraction of a cent";[32] the *Han Shu* (*Annals of the Early Han*) also notes that the residents of Kangju were commercially minded.[33] *Han Shu* references also describe a group of Sogdian merchants who may have undertaken a journey to Han China under diplomatic cover late in the first century BCE. De la Vaissière speculates that this mission might actually mark the beginning of Sogdian involvement in long-range transregional commerce, which now began to flourish in conjunction with Han diplomatic missions into Central Asia.[34] All of this means that it was commercially minded Central Asian groups like the Sogdians who regularly crossed the high passes that led into and out of the Tarim Basin, transporting goods south across the Karakorum passes and down the Indus River toward India, west through the Pamir Knot to Bactria, or northwest toward Sogdia and the Syr Darya Valley. During the First Silk Roads Era, the bulk of commercial trade

[32] SJ 123, Watson 1993, p. 245. [33] HS 96 A. [34] De la Vaissière 2005, p. 70.

probably followed either the southern or western routes toward the northwest Indian coast, but, as de la Vaissière notes, "if the Sogdians controlled only a secondary route, at least they participated, even from a distance, in the development of commerce in the first centuries of our era."[35] From these modest beginnings during the First Silk Roads Era, the Sogdians would go on to become some of the greatest traders in all the long history of ancient Eurasia during subsequent periods of Silk Roads exchanges.

Role of the Bactrian Camel

Envoy Tuzhin's description in the *Han Shu* of the fate of animals that happened to fall from the precipitous Hanging Pass reminds us that, as well as the tenacious envoys and merchants who made their way repeatedly through this inhospitable terrain, another key player in the story of the First Silk Roads Era needs to be considered, and that is the Bactrian camel. The two-humped Bactrian camel (*Camelus bactrianus*) is native to the steppes of Central Asia, and is named after the region of Bactria, the same region Han envoy Zhang Qian visited on his first journey to the west. The Bactrian is of the same *Camelus* genus as the single-humped dromedary, but because of the Bactrian's ability to survive at high altitudes and cope with extremes of temperature, it quickly became the preferred beast of burden for Silk Roads travelers because it was so perfectly adapted to this unforgiving environment.

The Bactrian was probably domesticated independently of the dromedary sometime in the third millennium BCE, in northern Bactria (northeast Afghanistan or southwest Turkmenistan), while the dromedary was probably domesticated more than 1,000 years earlier in Arabia.[36] The two humps on the Bactrian camel are composed of fat, not water. When water is available, the Bactrian can drink more than 50 liters at one time, but when it is not, the Bactrian can survive for months without water. Although the Bactrian camel can weigh up to 680 kilograms (1,500 pounds), it can also move fast when required, up to 65 kilometers an hour (40 miles per hour). Its ability to carry heavy loads long distances is virtually unsurpassed in the animal world. Bactrians can carry loads of up to 450 kilograms (1,000 pounds) at a rate of 47 kilometers (30 miles) for four days straight. Bales of ancient Chinese silk might have weighed around 60 kilograms each (around 130 pounds), which means that each Bactrian could carry six or seven bales of the precious fabric.[37] After

[35] De la Vaissière 2005, p. 41. [36] "Camel," Encyclopedia Britannica Online, 2007.
[37] See *National Geographic: Bactrian Camel* at www.nationalgeographic.com/animals/mammals/b/bactrian-camel/.

a rest day, the camel could move the same loads on at the same rate for the next four days. It is hard to imagine an animal more physically suited to transport bales of silk and other high-value commercial goods across Inner Eurasia.

Other aspects of the Bactrian camel's physiology help make it supremely well adapted to the region. The face is long and triangular, with a split upper lip, long eyelashes and sealable nostrils, evolutionary adaptations that help to keep out the dust and debris that fly at ferocious speed in the frequent sandstorms that occur in the region. The camel has a long, woolly winter coat, dark brown to sandy beige in color, but it sheds this rapidly once the freezing cold winters give way to the spring, with huge sections peeling off at once. Perhaps the most significant environmental adaptation of all, however, is the two broad toes that the Bactrian camel has on each foot, with an undivided sole between. The camel spreads its toes widely and uses the webbing between as a perfect adaptation to walking on sand and to climbing the huge sand dunes of the region. The Bactrian camel's existence in the wild is seriously threatened today; fewer than 1,000 or so of these animals

Figure 4.7 Close-up of the head and shoulders of a Bactrian camel
www.gettyimages.co.uk/license/649142533
Credit: Erica Stoianov/EyeEm

remain in the wilds of northwest China and Mongolia, and these have been placed on the critically endangered species list. However, in many places in the world, Bactrian camels are thriving in captivity; an estimated global population of 2 million exists in domesticated form.[38] It is no exaggeration to suggest that if there had been no Bactrian camel, Silk Roads trade would probably have been on a much smaller and less sustainable scale.

Silk: The Major Han Export Commodity

Finally, in this chapter about the conduct of Silk Roads trade from the Chinese end of the network, we turn to the key exports that traveled out of Han China on the backs of the hardy Bactrian camel, particularly silk. Other Chinese export goods such as iron, lacquerware and ceramics were also in demand in markets across Eurasia, but there is no doubt that the major Chinese export commodity was raw silk, an elegant, translucent, sensual material that easily took vivid natural dyes and that came to be regarded as the last word in fashion by elite women and men in Rome and other wealthy Silk Roads cities such as Palmyra, which has yielded valuable archaeological evidence of Han silk exports (discussed in the next chapter). It was this highly valuable textile that was carried in bales on the flanks of Bactrian camels from Chang'an deep onto Central Asia and beyond, and that justifiably gives its name to the entire trading network. Just how were the Chinese able to produce enough high-quality silk to satisfy the range of diplomatic and commercial markets that developed across Eurasia?

The origins of the silk industry, or sericulture, are somewhat mysterious. According to Chinese legend, it was Empress Leizu, wife of the mythical Yellow Emperor, who first discovered the secret of silk sometime around 2700 BCE when a silkworm cocoon fell into her teacup and unraveled. But the historical origins of silkworm domestication revealed by archaeology suggest that this began much earlier within the Yangshao culture. The discovery by archaeologists of an ivory cup decorated with the image of a silkworm has been dated to around 4000 BCE, and discoveries of parts of ancient looms that might have been used for silk production have been found at the site of Hemudu in Zhejiang Province, dating to around 5000 BCE.[39] The oldest surviving example of silk fabric, which was used to wrap

[38] "Bactrian Camel," EdgeofExistence.org. EDGE, 2010; and J. Hare, *Camelus ferus*, in IUCN Red List of Threatened Species, 2008.

[39] See C. Clunas and J. Harrison-Hall, eds., *Ming: 50 Years that Changed China*. London: British Museum Exhibition Catalogue, 2014.

the body of a deceased child, has been found at a Yangshao site in Qingtaicun, and dates to 3630 BCE.[40]

These discoveries suggest that silkworms must have been domesticated early during the transition to agriculture in China. Fragments of silk have been found in Shang Dynasty tombs, indicating the status and high value the fabric had attained by the early dynastic era in China, and several of the Zhou Dynasty classic texts contain practical information about sericulture, particularly the *Book of History* and the *Book of Rites*. The texts demonstrate that the reeling and spinning of silk were household duties for women, who carried out these tasks in specialized workshops and in their homes. In silk-producing regions, the women of extended families worked long hours each day for as many as six months a year feeding, tending and supervising silkworms, and unraveling, spinning, weaving, dyeing and embroidering silk. Sericulture became so deeply engrained in Chinese women's culture that each spring, the empress herself symbolically inaugurated the silk-raising season.

The key to the development of large-scale silk production in China is the *Bombyx mori* moth, which lays up to 500 eggs before dying soon afterward. The eggs hatch into silkworms that live by consuming large quantities of mulberry leaves. The *Bombyx mori* is a domesticated moth, but its wild ancestor the *Bombyx mandrina Moore* lived naturally on white mulberry trees that are unique to China. Through thousands of years of artificial selection by humans, the domesticated *Bombyx mori* has evolved into a blind and flightless moth that is only capable of eating, mating and producing eggs. Eventually the silkworms spin their silken cocoons on the twigs of mulberry trees. The silk in a cocoon consists of a continuous filament made of a protein and gum secreted from the worms' salivary glands. The gum is removed by placing the cocoons in boiling water, which also destroys the silkworm pupae inside. The filament is then unwound and drawn tightly onto reels that are then packed according to the quality of the thread and are ready for spinning or plying. A single cocoon produces a filament a staggering one mile long, but only a small percentage of this is usable, which means that approximately 2,500 silkworms are needed to produce a pound of silk. Given the quantities of silk that were dispatched to the Xiongnu as tribute or transported into Central Asia by envoys, the size of the sericulture industry in China during the Han Dynasty was astonishing.

Indeed, even by the Early Han silk production had become an industry. Silk thread was not only being used to make clothing, but also to make

[40] S. Vainker, *Chinese Silk: A Cultural History*. New York: Rutgers University Press, 2004, pp. 17–20.

Figure 4.8 The silk moth, or *Bombyx mori*
www.gettyimages.co.uk/license/109902521
Credit: Meighan Makarchuk

fishing lines, bowstrings, strings for musical instruments and, later, even paper, after its invention in China late in the first century CE. Silk clothing gradually evolved from something reserved strictly for elites to everyday garments worn by all sectors of society. Yet silk also became a commodity of absolute value, used to pay employees, particularly government officials, and also by farmers who paid their taxes in grain and silk. As we have seen, the Han court also used large quantities of silk as tribute paid to the Xiongnu under the *heqin* policy, and Han envoys to Central Asia transported large quantities of silk to use as gifts and tribute in the town-states of the western regions.

Despite all these widespread uses of silk within China, Han envoys, merchants and indeed the government soon came to realize that they possessed the secrets to the production of a commodity that was equally highly valued outside of China, and a commodity that merchants and consumers were prepared to pay a great deal of money to obtain. This meant that the technique of sericulture needed to be kept a closely guarded secret controlled by the authorities so that the exporters (and the government) did not lose their monopoly. We don't want to exaggerate this monopoly, however, or to suggest that silk was completely unknown outside of China; even the ancient Greek philosopher Aristotle mentions it. But the Han Chinese, with the *Bombyx mori*, white mulberry trees and well-developed sericulture industry, were the ancient Eurasian masters of high-volume, high-quality silk production, and as the market for the fabric increased throughout Inner Eurasia and eventually the Mediterranean Basin, it was the Han who were able to meet that demand. Many splendid images of elite women and goddesses adorned in silks have been found on the walls of villas in Pompeii, preserved by the catastrophic eruption of Vesuvius in 79 CE. These gorgeous silk garments are depicted as thin and translucent, vividly colored by the use of the best natural dyes, and often decorated with transverse stripes of gold. Yet most Romans, despite becoming major customers for Chinese silk, had no idea that the fabric derived from the secreted protein from the salivary glands of a small worm. Instead they thought it grew on trees; we know this because of several references to the origins of silk in the works of great Roman authors like Seneca and Virgil.

Conclusion

This chapter has considered the various ways by which large quantities of Han Chinese silk made their way into Central Asia. Most of it was dispatched initially as some form of tribute to various Central Asian nomadic and sedentary powers, but it appears to have been quickly monetized by Chinese envoys and Central Asian elites and merchants. This chapter also traced the geography of the key routes from the Early Han capital of Chang'an into Central Asia via the Tarim Basin, and the role of the Bactrian camel in facilitating the movement of silk and other luxury goods. Finally, we considered the origins and rapid expansion of silk manufacturing in ancient China, made possible by the evolution of the *Bombyx mori* silk moth. In the next chapter, we skip across vast distances to the western end of Eurasia, to pick up the story of the First Silk Roads Era from the perspective of the principal purchasers of Chinese silk, the Romans. In order to make sense of this, we need to first consider the vicissitudes of earlier Roman history that led to the rule of Augustus, who as Princeps or "First Man" in Rome restored peace to a state that had been fractured by more than a century of civil war. It was in this new climate of the *Pax Romana* or Roman Peace, a great age of optimism and cultural achievement, that the demand for silk and many other Asian luxuries increased, leading ultimately to the connection of all the civilizations and people of Afro-Eurasia into a single trans-Eurasian network.

Selected Further Reading

Bertrand, A., "The Hydraulic Systems in Turfan (Xinjiang)," *The Silk Road*, 8 (2010) pp. 27ff.

De la Vaissière, E., *Sogdian Traders. A History*, trans. James Ward, Handbook of Oriental Studies, Vol. 10. Leiden: Brill, 2005.

Hill, J., *Through the Jade Gate to Rome: A Study of the Silk Roads during the Later Han Dynasty, 1st to 2nd Centuries CE*. Charlestown: BookSurge, 2009.

Liu, X., "Exchanges within the Silk Roads World System," in C. Benjamin, ed., *Cambridge History of the World Vol. IV*. Cambridge: Cambridge University Press, 2015, pp. 457–479.

National Geographic: Bactrian Camel at www.nationalgeographic.com/animals/mammals/b/bactrian-camel/.

Torday, L., *Mounted Archers: The Beginnings of Central Asian History*. Seattle: University of Washington Press, 1978.

Vainker, S., *Chinese Silk: A Cultural History*. New Brunswick, NJ: Rutgers University Press, 2004.

Yu, Y.-S., "Han Foreign Relations," in D. Twitchett and M. Loewe eds., *The Cambridge History of China Volume 1: The Ch'in and Han Empires 221 BC – AD 220*. Cambridge: Cambridge University Press, 1986.

5 The Roman Empire and the Western Silk Roads

In 53 BCE, with Han Chinese silk now moving westward across Inner Eurasia through a variety of processes and intermediaries, Roman consul Marcus Licinius Crassus and his legions were defeated by forces of the Parthian Empire under General Surena at the Battle of Carrhae. The battle was fought at a location in the north of modern Iraq, and was one of the worst military disasters suffered by the Romans in their long history. This might also have been one of the first occasions that Romans had encountered Chinese silk. According to two Roman sources, even after waves of heavily armored Parthian cavalry had attacked the legions, the Romans had held their ground until noon, and were even hoping for victory. But then the Parthians charged the Romans again with their drums beating and arrows flying, and as they charged, they opened for the first time in the battle their silk banners to rally their own troops and dazzle and distract the Roman soldiers. The banners were apparently so bright, so brilliant, so shocking to the Roman soldiers that they were completely unnerved, broke ranks and fled, to be mopped up over the next few days by the Parthians.

Greco-Roman historian Cassius Dio (c. 155–235 CE) provides the most detailed account of the Battle of Carrhae, but an earlier Roman historian, Lucius Annaeus Florus (c. 74–130 CE), provides the description of the silk banners: "And so he (Crassus) had scarcely reached Carrhae when the king's generals, Silaces and Surenus, displayed all around him their standards fluttering with gold and silken pennons; then without delay the cavalry, pouring around on all sides, showered their weapons as thick as hail or rain upon them. Thus, the army was destroyed in lamentable slaughter."[1] Of course, the Romans did not lose the Battle of Carrhae because of the dazzling brilliance of the Parthian silk banners, but because of a series of poor decisions made by Crassus, and the Parthians' superb military strategy and leadership shown by their generals. Yet this story does provide us with a glimpse into the way silk

[1] Cassius Dio, *Roman History*, Book 30, 22–26; Florus, *Epitome*, Book 3, 11.

was regarded in the Roman world. On the one hand, it was seen as a beautiful, shining and radiant material that quickly became a prized symbol of luxury for the Roman elites. But on the other, some Romans came to regard silk as a symbol of decadence and the pursuit of luxuries that entices people into lives of excess and immorality, and that could lead the state itself into lethargy and corruption.

We ended the previous chapter by noting that most Romans had no idea that silk derived from the spun cocoon of a small worm. Roman authors like Seneca and Virgil confidently asserted that silk grew on trees.[2] But Roman geographer and statesman Pliny the Elder (23–79 CE) apparently knew better, although we have no real idea about the source of his more accurate information. Writing of the "Silk Moth" in his book *Natural History*, Pliny makes the following observation: "The silk moths weave webs, like spiders, that become a luxurious clothing material for women, called silk."[3] The sources show us that by the mid-first century CE, silk had come to be regarded as something mysterious and exotic in the Greco-Roman world, but also potentially dangerous, evoking responses of both wonder and suspicion among Roman elites. In this chapter, we explore the operation and impact of Silk Roads exchanges from the Roman perspective. We approach this by addressing three linked questions. First, what political and social changes in the Roman state were necessary to allow for more intensive Roman military, diplomatic and commercial engagement with Central, South and, indirectly, East Asia? Second, how did overland traders from the Mediterranean organize their end of the exchange network, what challenges did they face and how did they circumvent them? And finally, what impact did silk and other luxury commodities from Asia have on the culture of the Greco-Romans?

Roman Expansion: From City-State to Empire

To our first question, then, the evolving political and social structure that emerged in the Roman world during the Late Republic, which eventually made possible these intensified connections between the Mediterranean Basin and much of the rest of Afro-Eurasia. The active engagement of the Romans in the Silk Roads can be directly attributed to the political circumstances surrounding the advent of a patrician political leader named Octavian, better known to history by his later title Augustus. To understand why the rule of Augustus was critical to Roman engagement in the Silk Roads, we need to take a brief detour into the complicated politics of Republican Rome, which resulted from the way the

[2] See Virgil, *The Georgics*, II. 121; and Seneca *Hippol.* 386. [3] Pliny, NH, XI, 75–78.

Roman state had expanded from a small city-state to a substantial imperial one. The question of whether Republican Rome ever intended to create a huge tributary empire, or whether Roman expansion was a result of sensible responses to security threats, has long divided historians. There is no doubt that the Romans were indeed forced to respond to a series of external threats, and did so in such an effective manner that they came to dominate first the Italian Peninsula and, before long, the entire Mediterranean Basin.

In 309 BCE, the small city-state of Rome, originally settled by Iron Age farmers around seven hills and a ford across the Tiber River in central Italy, was attacked and occupied by a party of marauding Gauls, who agreed to leave only after they were paid off with a large ransom. In an attempt to ensure this debacle would not happen again, the Romans built a new and formidable professional military force that was based on maneuverable infantry units of 120 men called *maniples*, armed with javelins and short swords. Dwelling in regions of Italy to the north of Rome were the Etruscan people, who may have ruled Rome for a while early in its history; to the south were Greek colonies that had been built in Sicily and around the mainland coast. By the early third century BCE, Etruscan power had waned, but the Greek colonies were increasingly concerned about the threat of Rome and called in a Greek mercenary, King Pyrrhus of Epirus, to come and fight the Romans on their behalf.

Pyrrhus brought war elephants and soldiers across the Adriatic to southern Italy, and in battle with the Romans he defeated them twice. But these victories were earned at tremendous cost to his own forces, and Pyrrhus was forced to withdraw. By 270 BCE, Rome had conquered all the city-states of southern Italy, including the Greek colonies. Despite their actions in calling on Pyrrhus, the Romans did not impose harsh sanctions on the Greeks or any of the groups they defeated in the Italian Peninsula. Conquered states were allowed to remain self-governing so long as they provided levies of troops and supported Roman foreign policy. This enlightened form of hegemony would pay enormous dividends when the Republic faced its most serious challenge in a life-and-death struggle with the Carthaginians.

Punic Wars

After 270, Rome's control of the Italian Peninsula, which juts out into the Mediterranean Sea roughly dividing it in half, became particularly alarming to the powerful state of Carthage, a city established centuries earlier as a Phoenician trading colony on the coast of North Africa. Carthage was a wealthy state and possessed a superior navy to the

Romans, and war between the two powerful states for control of the Mediterranean now seemed inevitable. In a series of three Punic Wars that followed (so called because of the Phoenician origin of Carthage), which collectively lasted for more than a century, the Romans eventually crushed the Carthaginians, although it was a hard-won victory. English historian Adrian Goldsworthy points out that the Punic Wars were fought on a scale scarcely rivaled before the modern age.[4] Hundreds of thousands of military personnel were deployed in theaters of conflict spanning the entire Mediterranean Basin, including the Balkans, Greece, Sicily, North Africa, Spain, France, the Alps and the Italian Peninsula. The cost of maintaining these large armies and navies consumed the economic resources of both states, and the human costs were even higher with massive loss of life suffered at several major battles. In addition, as has been the case with all modern wars, casualties were not confined to the military. Huge numbers of civilians were also killed, massacred following the siege of a city, killed in raids on towns, villages and farms by the armies of both sides or starving because of the confiscation of crops and animals to provision the troops.

By the end of this conflict, Carthage was in ruins and its culture extinguished, and this was despite the extraordinary efforts of the Carthaginian general Hannibal, who, during the Second Punic War, undertook one of the rare examples known to history of an invasion of Europe by an essentially African-based power. Had Rome not been able to withstand this assault, her imperial ambitions and even survival as a state would have been severely undermined, and the course of world history dramatically altered. Rome not only survived, but evolved from being a regional Italian power into a position of unrivaled dominance in the Mediterranean world. By 146 BCE, just five years before Wudi came to the throne of the Han Dynasty in far-distant China and launched a series of expansionary campaigns, Rome was well on its way to creating its own enormous empire that would eventually include much of western Eurasia and North Africa. The struggle with Carthage enabled the Romans to conceive of themselves for the first time as a genuine world power, and accustomed them to sending armies over large distances to fight in several international theaters simultaneously, something that the Romans would continue to do successfully for the next 500 years.

The First Punic War broke out in 264 when Carthage landed a force in Sicily; in a series of naval battles that followed, Rome lost 500 ships, but just kept building more, until an exhausted Carthage was forced to sue for peace. Rome immediately annexed the Carthaginian territories of Sicily,

[4] A. Goldsworthy, *The Punic Wars*. London: Cassell and Company, 2000, intro.

Figure 5.1 Illustration of Carthaginian general Hannibal and his forces crossing a high pass in the European Alps
www.gettyimages.co.uk/license/498424755
Credit: nicoolay

Sardinia and Corsica – the beginning of its overseas empire – and installed senatorial governors to rule them. Determined to avenge this humiliating defeat, a young Carthaginian general named Hannibal set out on an audacious military campaign against the Romans. Hannibal arrived in the Carthaginian province in Spain in 225 BCE aged eighteen; a year later he was appointed as commander in chief of the Carthaginian forces in Spain. In the spring of 221, he provoked the Romans into declaring war against him by besieging and capturing the "neutral" city of Saguntum, then boldly marched north up the coast of Spain and into Roman territory. For a while the Romans had no idea where Hannibal had gone; a group of Roman soldiers was astonished when they stumbled across the

Carthaginians near the mouth of the Rhone River in southern Gaul. Before they could assemble a military response Hannibal disappeared again, floating his army and elephants across the Rhone River before heading east into the Alps. The Romans had no expectation that Hannibal would attempt something as ambitious as crossing the Alps with his army and elephants, especially with winter coming on. But that is exactly what Hannibal did, crossing (probably) the 10,000 feet high Col de la Traversette in November 218 before descending into northern Italy and capturing the settlement of the Torini tribe, the modern city of Turin.

News of Hannibal's arrival in Italy sent shock waves through Rome, which hastily assembled an army and sent it north to head off the Carthaginians. Near the junction of the Po and Ticino Rivers Hannibal defeated the Roman cavalry by superior strategy; a week later he defeated a larger Roman force on the banks of the Trebbia River. In the spring of 217, Hannibal headed south, capturing a Roman colony near modern Florence before trapping and destroying a large Roman army on the shores of Lake Trasimene. Fifteen thousand Roman soldiers were ambushed and killed by the Carthaginians, who came charging down the mist-covered slopes and drove the Romans into the lake, where they were cut down or drowned. As Hannibal continued south, the Romans assembled yet another army, which rushed to confront him on flat ground beside the Ofante River, near the village of Cannae. By using a brilliant pincer strategy, Hannibal trapped and utterly defeated two consular armies at the Battle of Cannae, leaving close to 50,000 dead Roman soldiers on the blood-soaked plain.

After Cannae, Hannibal was supreme in Italy and had nothing to fear from any legions. His generals urged him to march on Rome itself, but the cautious Hannibal preferred to remain in the south and spent the next few years trying to convince the Italian city-states to abandon their loyalty to Rome and come over to the Carthaginian side. The Romans had learned their lesson and did not dare to confront Hannibal in open battle again, adopting instead a cautious rear guard policy and reassuring their allies in the south that they were better off remaining loyal to Rome. By 211, the strategy seemed to be working. Roman forces were strong enough to begin besieging those few cities that had gone over to Hannibal.

In an attempt to lift the sieges, Hannibal marched on Rome itself, camping on the banks of the Arno River, six miles from the city center and in full view of the frightened residents. He rode right up to the very walls of the city, but heavy rain forestalled a battle and Hannibal eventually withdrew. This was as close to Rome that Hannibal would ever come; most of Rome's Italian allies remained loyal, and Hannibal was constantly frustrated in being unable to inflict a mortal blow. Eventually, after sixteen years of Carthaginian "occupation," the Romans under General Scipio Africanus launched an attack on the city of Carthage itself, forcing Hannibal to return to North Africa to defend his homeland. At the Battle of Zama in 201 Scipio defeated Hannibal and Carthaginian power was crushed.

Hannibal's audacious exploits and tactical skill have become the stuff of legend; but ultimately it was Roman patience that allowed Rome to defeat a clearly superior commander. And it was also the enlightened Roman foreign policy that paid off here, a policy of treating conquered Italian tribes and cities as allies so that even when Hannibal had destroyed the Roman legions, most of their allies remained loyal to Rome. This is one of the key reasons why it is Roman civilization that went on to become one of the foundations of Western civilization, and not Carthaginian.

Expansion into Asia

With the defeat of Carthage, the Romans turned to other foreign policy matters. King Philip V of Macedon had allied himself with Hannibal, so in 197 BCE Roman legions conquered Macedonia in revenge, "liberating" the Greek city-states from Macedonian control at the same time. The ruler of the Seleucid Empire, which included much of the Middle East and parts of western Central Asia, then used this opportunity to try and become more involved in Greek affairs, but the Romans forced them to retreat and pay a huge indemnity; when the Seleucids tried to invade Egypt in 168, they were crushed by the Romans. Despite being greeted as liberators by the Greeks, in 146 BCE Roman forces put down an uprising in Corinth, and then annexed all of Greece in the aftermath. A brief Carthaginian revival was put down by Rome that same year and the city was destroyed; after the king of Pergamum bequeathed his kingdom to Rome in 133 BCE, the Romans possessed provinces in Europe, Africa and Asia. Declaring the Mediterranean to be *mare nostrum*, or "our sea," the Romans began to create administrative machinery to hold their growing state together through a provincial system ruled by governors, just as empire builders in Mesopotamia and Persia had done before them, and as the Han Dynasty was doing simultaneously at the opposite end of Eurasia.

Political and Social Unrest in Late Republican Rome

As successful as this rapid Roman military and administrative expansion in Europe, Africa and western Eurasia appears in retrospect, it created serious economic and social problems within Rome itself that were destined to completely undermine the political structure of the Roman state. Because of the conflict with Hannibal, many of the small farms of Italy had been destroyed by Carthaginian and Roman armies and many of the farmers recruited as soldiers. After the wars these veterans moved to the city of Rome to join the ranks of the unemployed and discontented. This gave wealthy patrician farmers the opportunity to buy up much of the abandoned land and then use slaves captured in the wars to grow profitable commercial crops like olive trees for olive oil and grapes for wine, instead of much-needed grain.

At the same time, Roman governors sent to administer the new provinces often behaved in a corrupt manner, many viewing their appointments as an opportunity to enrich themselves and provide their patrician friends with lucrative government contracts. The Roman government was still a senatorial oligarchy, and the tribunes who were elected directly by the people to look after the peoples' concerns were often mere puppets of the Senate, the elite governing body of Rome that held supreme political power in the Republic. Government seemed focused on protecting the rights of the rich and powerful; it had no solutions for poverty and no idea how to govern the large imperial state that Rome had become.

As the gulf between rich and poor rapidly widened, the sprawling city of Rome became increasingly chaotic. These political and economic conditions led ultimately to the collapse of the Roman Republic and its replacement by the Roman Empire, but only after a century of bloodshed and civil war. Attempts to introduce much-needed social reforms by well-meaning elected officials such as Tiberius Gracchus in 133 BCE and his younger brother Gaius ten years later were confounded by the Senate and defeated by direct violence. Tiberius was accused by the Senate of acting like a king and he and 300 of his followers were brutally clubbed to death in the Forum by a military force assembled by the Senate. Gaius took up the cause, and in order to protect against fluctuating grain prices, in 123 BCE he legislated for the government to take control of grain distribution to the urban masses at half the market price, the origins of the dole.[5] But Gaius was forced to commit suicide in 121 BCE, and 3,000 of his followers were subsequently arrested and executed. The Senate remained in total control, and the immediate outcome was a series of bloody civil wars as ambitious patrician men and their private armies competed with senatorial forces for ultimate power.

Civil Wars

The first of these civil wars was fought between Gaius Marius, champion of the people, and Lucius Cornelius Sulla, champion of the Senate. Sulla

[5] See P. Garnsey, *Famine and Food Supply in the Greco-Roman World: Response to Rise and Crisis*. Cambridge: Cambridge University Press, 1988.

emerged as victor, then served as "dictator for the making of laws and for the settling of the constitution" for the Senate until he retired in 80 BCE. During his "reign of terror," Sulla may have been responsible for the murder of almost 10,000 political opponents. His success at exercising virtual absolute power fueled the ambitions of other young patrician men. One of these, Gnaeus Pompeius Magnus, better known as Pompey the Great, was elected consul in 70 BCE. Another, Julius Caesar, was elected consul in 59 BCE; he immediately left Rome and spent the next nine years campaigning in Gaul, accumulating a personal fortune and training a highly skilled and loyal personal army.

When Caesar crossed the Rubicon River and returned to Rome, having refused to obey the orders of the Senate and disband his army, Pompey and most of the Senate fled to Greece. Caesar pursued them and routed Pompey and the Senate's army, bringing an end to this second civil war. By 49 BCE, the victorious Julius Caesar was master of the Roman state, and he assumed the title of "dictator for the administration of public affairs," a title that, just one month before his assassination, was extended for life. We have some extraordinary statistics that demonstrate the size of the urban poor in Rome after more than a century of ineffective government. Legislation Caesar passed reduced the number of people on the dole in Rome from 320,000 to 150,000, out of a total population of about 500,000 people; that is, before this legislation, almost 65 percent of the population of Rome was on the dole.

It is easy to see why, during this period of bitter civil war and widespread poverty, conditions were unsuited to extensive transregional trade. The demand for luxury goods was limited to a very small percentage of the population, and the infrastructure and security necessary to support large-scale, long-distance mercantile activity was not yet in place, particularly as the Roman state was often at war with itself during this period. Caesar believed that only a major change in the political structure of Rome could ensure the survival of the Roman state. He argued publicly that the old Republican structure was unsustainable and essentially dead, and some other form of more stable government was needed in its place, probably a form of benevolent dictatorship. After being accused of acting like a tyrant by his rivals, Caesar was assassinated in the Senate on March 15, 44 BCE, by Brutus and other senatorial conservatives, who claimed that they were attempting to restore Roman liberty and the Republic.

Augustus and the Pax Romana

After the assassination of Caesar, his teenage adoptive son Octavian was determined to avenge his father's murder by marching on Rome

Figure 5.2 Bronze statue of Julius Caesar in the Forum, Rome
http://media.gettyimages.com/photos/julius-caesar-statue-in-city-picture-id680869689
Credit: Kobi Vaknin/EyeEm

with his loyal legions. The assassins fled, but Octavian pursued and defeated them in this third civil war, then seized power in Caesar's name. This was the moment, around 27 BCE, when the Republic effectively gave way to an empire, although no one in Rome would have described it that way at the time. This was also the moment when Rome was able to turn from an internal focus on power struggles and civil wars, and begin to expand its outlook, its political interests and its commercial reach deep into Asia, although occasional conflict with the powerful Parthian Empire along the eastern Roman border did sometimes act as a restraint on overland trade, as discussed in what follows. For the next four decades Octavian, who reigned from 27 BCE to 14 CE, governed as a virtual dictator, although he carefully appeared to rule with due deference to the Senate and to observe the old Republican rituals and institutions. The Senate in gratitude named him *Augustus* – the "revered one" – because he had ended the civil war and restored stability to the state. With total control of the army he was also hailed as *imperator* – "victorious general" – from which the more generic term *emperor* would soon evolve.

This forty-year reign of Imperator Augustus as "First Man" in Rome was something of a golden age known as the *Pax Romana* – the Roman Peace. Augustus enlarged the empire, built new roads to consolidate the gains, reduced government corruption (including in the administration of the provinces), created a permanent professional standing army and established colonies for its veterans. Social relations between classes improved and the economy revived, which helped give rise to a new era of peace and optimism that was celebrated in the brilliant literature of poets like Virgil and Horace. With peace reestablished in the empire, and a vibrant, growing economy in place, there was a natural increase in demand for the import of luxury goods. This led Greco-Roman and other Mediterranean merchants and elites to feel confident enough to begin to invest in long-distance trade. With this historical background in mind, and after having sketched in the previous chapter the routes out of Han China followed by diplomats and merchants, we turn now to our second question. How did overland traders from the Mediterranean organize their end of the exchange network? And what challenges did they face and how did they circumvent them, as they attempted to open up Silk Roads routes from the Mediterranean Basin eastward into Asia?

Evidence of Overland Trade Routes from the Mediterranean

In trying to trace the major overland trade routes out of the Mediterranean and into Asia, historians have to make do with only a handful of ancient sources, which even collectively offer only incomplete and ambiguous details about the routes.

Figure 5.3 Statue of Roman ruler Augustus (reigned 27 BCE–14 CE)
www.gettyimages.co.uk/license/105549406
Credit: Andrea Astes

Parthian Stations

One of these sources is an account written by Isidorus of Charax, titled *Parthian Stations*. We know very little about the life of Isidorus, including the dates of his own lifetime. Most scholars believe that Isidorus flourished during the reign of Augustus, and that this work may have even been commissioned by Augustus himself to provide information in preparation for a potential military action in Parthia by Roman legions under the leadership of Augustus' own son.[6] Sometime possibly around the year 1 CE, Isidorus produced a brief Greek-language account of a route from the Syrian city of Antioch through the Parthian Empire and into Bactria, in a text titled *Parthian Stations*. Most of Isidorus' other works survive in fragmentary form only, and although *Parthian Stations* appears to be a complete text, it also reads more like a summary from some larger work perhaps titled *Journey around Parthia*. Roman statesman and geographer Pliny the Elder makes reference in his *Natural History* to a larger work by Isidorus.[7]

Historian Fergus Millar has argued that *Parthian Stations* should not be read as an account of trade routes, but rather as a collection of information potentially useful for political and military decision-making.[8] However, Wilfred Schoff, an early twentieth-century classicist and translator of Isidorus, believed that *Parthian Stations* outlines the itinerary of a caravan route, along with supply stations or caravanserais, from Antioch through the Parthian heartland and into Bactria.[9] Either way, *Parthian Stations* is critically important to scholars of the First Silk Roads Era, because it remains virtually the only reasonably complete primary source account we have of a potential overland trade route between Roman- and Parthian-controlled territory.

Although not presenting as many geographical challenges as those faced by Chinese merchants, the route outlined by Isidorus was certainly no picnic. It commenced at the Greco-Roman metropolis of Antioch in Syria, located a little inland from the Mediterranean coast on the Orontes River, and proceeded to a first crossing of the Euphrates River at a town known as Zeugma (modern Birijik). From Zeugma, the route followed a direct line along the valley of the Balikh River to avoid a long bend in the Euphrates, before crossing the Euphrates a second time at Neapolis, at its junction with the Chabur River. The route then followed the Euphrates to the Kings Canal before traversing across to the city of Seleucia on the Tigris River. From Seleucia, the route climbed up through the rugged Zagros Mountains, then headed east through fertile valleys to the city of Ecbatana, and eventually on to the city of Merv, located beyond the

[6] See F. Millar, "Caravan Cities: The Roman Near East and Long-Distance Trade by Land," *Bulletin of the Institute of Classical Studies. Supplement* No. 71, Modus Operandi: Essay in Honor of Geoffrey Rickman, Wiley, 1998, pp. 119–137; and W. H. Schoff, Translation and Commentary, *Parthian Stations by Isidorus of Charax*, London, 1914. See http://parthia.com/doc/parthian_stations.htm#PARTHIAN_STATIONS.

[7] Pliny NH, VI, 31. [8] Millar 1998, p. 120. [9] Schoff 1914.

Iranian Plateau in modern Turkmenistan. Given our description in the previous chapter of the three major routes that headed out of the Tarim Basin at the edge of Han China, we would have expected Isidorus' route to continue eastward from Merv to the city of Bactra, and then on through the Zerafshan and Ferghana Valleys to the western reaches of the Tarim Basin on the fringes of the Han tributary empire. But instead the route Isidorus describes turned southward through Bactria and ended at Alexandropolis, an ancient city founded by Alexander, probably identified with the modern Afghan city of Kandahar.[10]

As well as outlining the route, the text of *Parthian Stations* also provides information on the Parthian provinces crossed, names the key supply stations and towns and notes the distances between them. These distances are measured not in length, however, but in the time it would take for merchants and envoys to cover them, a unit known as a *schoinoi* that was based on an average speed of 5.5 kilometers (or just over 3 miles) per hour, perhaps an hour's travel by caravan, as Schoff suggests.[11] This is an example of how Isidorus provides his information: "From that place, Chalonitis, 21 schoeni; in which there are 5 villages, in which there are stations, and a Greek city, Chala, 15 schoeni beyond Apolloniatis. Then after 5 schoeni, a mountain which is called Zagrus, which forms the boundary between the district of Chalonitis and that of the Medes."[12]

Despite the explicit references to "stations" (which Schoff interpreted as something akin to caravanserais), Fergus Millar argues that it is impossible to know if any of the towns or cities Isidorus mentions should be regarded as "caravan cities" or caravanserais at all.[13] This leads to the larger question of just how important overland trade actually was to Roman and west Eurasian merchants during this period, in comparison to maritime trade. In Chapter 8 we explore in detail the well-used sea routes that connected Roman ports in Egypt with ports in the Persian Gulf and South Asia, and the invaluable ancient text that provides a great deal of detailed information about maritime trade in the period, the *Periplus of the Eryhtrian Sea*. The text of *Parthian Stations* clearly demonstrates that there were viable land routes from the Mediterranean into Parthian-controlled Central Asia and on to Bactria. But periods of conflict between Rome and Parthia (explored in the next chapter), not to mention the fact that maritime trade was faster and cheaper, must have made the sea routes a more reliable and safer proposition for merchants.

Although arguing against the existence of genuine caravan cities along the itinerary described by Isidorus of Charax, Fergus Millar agrees that

[10] Millar 1998, pp. 120–121. [11] Schoff 1914. [12] Schoff 1914.
[13] Millar 1998, p. 121.

there were major overland routes from the Mediterranean into western Eurasia.[14] In the Arabian Peninsula, one route connected ports in Yemen with the Mediterranean coast at Gaza. Other routes from the coast may have passed through the agricultural town of Petra, and then north through Gerasa and on to the Mediterranean and ports like Tyre. Most probably trade caravans would have followed at least the first part of the route outlined by Isidorus, from Antioch or other towns on the coast to the Euphrates or Tigris River Valleys. But from here it would have made much more sense for these caravans to have traveled southeast down the great river valleys toward port cities at the head of the Arabian Gulf, such as Isidorus' apparent hometown of Charax, routes and towns that we return to in the later chapter on maritime trade.

Evidence from Palmyra

Further insight into the operation of western Silk Roads trade routes has been provided by archaeological and epigraphic discoveries made in the ancient Syrian city of Palmyra, a city that clearly meets the criteria of a "caravan city." Palmyra is located in the Syrian desert about 215 kilometers (135 miles) northeast of Damascus, in an oasis environment where favorable environmental conditions facilitated successful agriculture. Settled in the eighth millennium BCE, Palmyra is later mentioned in Assyrian documents, and is also noted in the Judeo-Christian Old Testament as a desert city strengthened by Hebrew king Solomon.[15] Palmyra flourished during the Hellenistic Era because of its loyalty to the rulers of the Seleucid Empire. Even after the Romans established the province of Syria in 64 BCE, Palmyra remained independent and traded with both Rome and Parthia.[16] During the reign of Augustus' successor, Emperor Tiberius, Palmyra was incorporated around 14 CE into the Roman Empire, although the city was allowed to remain self-governing. Palmyra flourished under the Romans, becoming a major trading city, and also establishing Palmyrene merchant colonies in other regional trade cities, including Dura Europos.[17] Roman emperor Hadrian visited the city in 129 CE and confirmed its autonomous status by naming it a "free city."

Epigraphic sources discovered at Palmyra and dated to the Roman imperial period explicitly note the operation of organized caravans complete with "chief merchants" and "caravan leaders." These enterprises

[14] Millar 1998, p. 135. [15] 2 Chronicles 8:4.

[16] H. Elton, *Frontiers of the Roman Empire*. London: Routledge, 2013, p. 90.

[17] See L. Dirven, *The Palmyrenes of Dura Europos: A Study of Religious Interaction in Roman Syria*. Leiden: Brill, 1999, p. 20.

Figure 5.4 Ruins of the major commercial city of Palmyra, which thrived during the First Silk Roads Era, located in modern Syria
www.gettyimages.co.uk/license/639630850
Credit: Nick Brundle Photography

were well organized, and caravan leaders used bribes or assembled a quasi-military force to protect themselves against marauding nomads.[18] Discoveries of some 500 pieces of textile in tombs in Palmyra, including 100 or so made of silk and datable to the period of the Later Han Dynasty (first to third centuries CE), have strengthened the claims of Palmyra as a major Silk Roads trading city.[19] In addition, this makes Palmyra, in the words of Marta Zuchowska, "one of the rare places where archaeological finds of silks of Chinese origin are abundant enough to be studied as intentionally imported merchandise rather than curiosa brought accidentally by wandering travelers."[20]

Palmyra had several different connections to Silk Roads trade routes via the Persian Gulf and Indian Ocean ports, and also with the port city of Isidorus' home, Charax, which was located somewhere on the coast in the Tigris-Euphrates delta. The *Periplus of the Eryhtrian Sea* also identifies

[18] Millar 1998, p. 137.
[19] See M. Zuchowska, "From China to Palmyra: The Value of Silk," *Swiatowit* 11, No. 52, A (2013), pp. 133ff.
[20] Zuchowska 2013, p. 133.

a port named Apologos, located at the head of the Persian Gulf near Charax, as important for the unloading of exotic goods from vessels that had sailed from Indian Ocean and Arabian Sea ports.[21] From ports at the head of the Persian Gulf, some silk at least went up the Euphrates Valley and across desert routes to Palmyra, and from there was probably resold to merchants who took the silk further west to the Mediterranean coast via Antioch or Tyre.

Palmyra flourished during the first two centuries CE, the very apex of the First Silk Roads Era, precisely because of the trade between South Asian ports and the Mediterranean coast, via the Persian Gulf and Euphrates Valley. The inscriptions make it clear that the Palmyrenes were organizing overland caravans to Charax and other places,[22] and also at least one maritime trading expedition to a port probably located near the mouth of the Indus River in modern Pakistan, most likely the port city of Barbaricum mentioned in the Periplus.[23] Among the exotic goods imported by the Palmyrenes from such enterprises were scents and spices, and pearls and agate.[24] But Chinese silk textiles were also imported by Palmyrene merchants, both to be sold to other merchants and sent on to the Mediterranean, but also to be worn by wealthy Palmyrene citizens, as the tomb discoveries demonstrate.

Archaeologists have discovered many different types of silk in Palmyrene tombs, including finished Han damask and brocade, much of it multicolored and decorated with Chinese characters.[25] Zuchowska points to the discovery of one very special fragment of Chinese silk in funerary tower 65. Clearly a product of Chinese weaving techniques, the fragment is decorated with images including a man collecting grapes from a vine, camels and tigers and tripod jars. The jars and tigers are common motifs on Han Chinese silks, but the other images on the fragment are unique in the context of Han silk from the period, suggesting that this represents an early example of Chinese production being specifically influenced, as Zuchowska puts it, by "western stylistic preferences" and manufactured for the specific purpose of tributary exchange with one of

[21] On Apologos, see J.-F. Sales, "The Periplus of the Erythraean Sea and the Arab-Persian Gulf," *Topoi* 3, No. 2 (1993), p. 510, n. 57.

[22] See M. Gawlikowski, *Palmyra and Its Caravan Trade*, annales archéologiques arabes syriens, XLii: *Palmyra and the Silk Road*, 1996, pp. 139–145.

[23] J. Starcky, *Inventaire des Inscriptions de Palmyre X*, Damas 1949: no. 96; Gawlikowski 1996, p. 143.

[24] Zuchowska 2013; also A. Witecka, *Catalogue of Jewellery Found in the Tower-Tomb of Atenatan at Palmyra*, Studia Palmyrenskie IX, 1994, pp. 71–91.

[25] See also M. Zuchowska, "Roman Textiles in the Hou Han Shu. A 5th Century Chinese Vision versus Roman Reality," *Anabasis: studia classica et orientalia* 6 (2015), pp. 216–242. On p. 233, Zuchowska uses a pie chart to illustrate that silk makes up about 18 percent of all the fabric types discovered at Palmyra.

the states of the western regions.[26] From there, this product that had presumably left Chang'an as part of a tributary payment to an allied town-state in the Tarim Basin, had presumably made its way to Palmyra via one of the overland routes through Central Asia, or maritime routes across the Indian Ocean and up the Persian Gulf.

While some of the Chinese silk textiles, such as the fragment discovered in tower 65, were apparently exported to Central Asia as completely finished products, other textiles appear to have been woven in Syria or other Middle Eastern regions using imported Han silk thread, which as we have seen was also being used in Han tributary payments to allied states and to the Xiongnu.[27] The presence of Western dyes such as cochineal and kermes demonstrates that some raw imported Chinese silks were dyed in Palmyra or workshops nearby. Palmyrene elites clearly appreciated the luxuriousness of silk, unlike some of their Roman counterparts who were disgusted by it, and wore it in public as a sign of their refined taste and status. Palmyra undoubtedly flourished during the First Silk Roads Era because of its specific role as a trading city. At the heart of a city was a large agora or marketplace that functioned more like an Asian caravanserai than a typical Greek meeting place.[28] The agora was built sometime in the second half of the first century CE. This massive caravanserai measured 71 by 84 meters (or 233 by 276 feet) and had eleven different entrances. The later Roman author Appian of Alexandria also explicitly described the Palmyrenes as merchants who imported products from India and Arabia and sold them to Rome.[29]

Silk Roads trade brought considerable wealth to the city of Palmyra and the elites who organized and benefited from it. Merchants are honored with statues and inscriptions on columns along the main street of the city, the 1.1 kilometer-long Great Colonnade.[30] These merchants included men who spent large sums on organizing caravan and maritime commercial expeditions, and others who functioned as sponsors, guides, caravan leaders and so on.[31] Those families that earned great profits from such enterprises then invested in their city, endowing Palmyra with superb public art and architecture, including the Great Colonnade itself, which boasted the tallest columns in the Greco-Roman regions of the Middle East. The sumptuousness of the elite tombs, which depict men and women wearing superb clothing and jewelry, is further evidence of the lucrative nature of the silk trade, which earned those involved, and the city

[26] Zuchowska 2013, p. 146. [27] Zuchowska 2013, p. 147.
[28] See W. Ball, *Rome in the East: Transformation of an Empire*. London: Routledge, 2002, p. 296.
[29] Appian, *Historia Romana*, V.9. [30] Zuchowska 2013, p. 148.
[31] Gawlikowski 1996, pp. 139–145.

as a whole, a fortune. Outside of Rome, Palmyra provides the clearest example we have of the incredible value of the import of Chinese silk and other luxury goods to the merchants and civic authorities of those Greco-Roman cities that coordinated it.

Marinus of Tyre and a Journey to the Stone Tower

It seems clear that the bulk of Silk Roads trade was carried out by sea across the Indian Ocean between ports in South Asia and ports in Roman Egypt, as is discussed in Chapter 8. However, the evidence from Palmyra and some ancient sources also suggests that a certain percentage of the trade to and from the Mediterranean also traveled along land routes down the Tigris and Euphrates Valleys to the Persian Gulf, and thence by sea to South Asia. Yet other evidence seems to support the idea that some overland trade along the more easterly sections of Isidorus' itinerary, and then on from Merv through Bactra and eventually to the western reaches of Han China, also occurred. The use of such extended overland routes might have made sense early in the First Silk Roads Era, before relations between the Romans and Parthians deteriorated. This possibility is hinted at in another important ancient source reference that seems to be describing a genuinely trans-Eurasian land route, written at the height of the First Silk Roads Era by Claudius Ptolemy. Ptolemy (c. 100–c. 168 CE) was a distinguished mathematician, musician, astronomer and geographer who lived in the great cosmopolitan city of Alexandria on the Mediterranean coast of Egypt. Ptolemy wrote several important scientific treatises, including the *Geography*, which appeared in eight books and was probably written between 150 and 160 CE. The treatise provides instructions on how to make two-dimensional maps of the Roman provinces, and indeed of the entire inhabited world known to Ptolemy. The bulk of the *Geography* describes the various regions of the known world through a series of geographical coordinates, and also discusses the sources Ptolemy had available in arriving at these coordinates.[32]

Ptolemy's principal informant for many of the locations contained in his *Geography* (and the associated maps) was a Greek or Hellenized geographer and mapmaker, Marinus of Tyre, who flourished early in the second century CE. Marinus' own geographical works are lost, but Ptolemy's *Geography* makes explicit references to his work and full use of the geographical coordinates Marinus had assigned to many places of the

[32] On Ptolemy's methods, see L. Torday, *Mounted Archers: The Beginnings of Central Asian History*. Seattle: University of Washington Press, 1998, pp. 404–418.

known world. Marinus had in turn gained a great deal of information from a caravan itinerary he had purchased from a "Macedonian" trader named Maes Titianus, whose agents had apparently traveled extensively through Inner Eurasia. The reference to Maes Titianus in the *Geography* is oblique: "Marinus tells us that a certain Macedonian named Maen, who was also called Titian, son of a merchant father, and a merchant himself, noted the length of this journey [to the Stone Tower], although he did not come to Sera (China) in person but sent others there."[33] Although described as a Macedonian, Maes was more probably a Syrian merchant living in the ancient Phoenician city of Tyre, a major Mediterranean center for the dying of silk and other textiles. Some historians, including Igor Piankov, have speculated that the need of Maes' merchant family to import raw Chinese silk for dyeing before being sent on to Rome might have been the catalyst behind dispatching his agents on extensive travels deep into Inner Eurasia.[34] Historian Max Cary has also argued that the expedition to Central Asia was an attempt by Maes' party to acquire Chinese silk directly from the Chinese, and thus eliminate some of the middlemen in the trading network, particularly the Parthians.[35]

A range of dates for the production of Maes' itinerary has been suggested by scholars, from the Augustan era through to the second century CE. Maes' surname of "Titianus" might suggest he was born during the brief reign of Roman emperor Titus (r. 79–81 CE). Piankov argues that Maes probably flourished during the reign of Augustus, a period in which the overland Silk Roads route was still important and had not yet been supplanted by maritime routes, but the evidence for this is scarce.[36] Piankov attempts to support his argument by noting that Roman coins of the late first century BCE and early first century CE have been discovered in regions of Central Asia controlled by the Kushans, although of course these coins could have been transported there under a range of circumstances and by a variety of mechanisms. These Roman coins are discussed in more detail in the chapter on the Kushan Empire, and their discovery might suggest that there were more intensive overland links between Mediterranean and Central Asian merchants during this period than existed in later periods, when the overland route from Mesopotamia had largely been replaced by the maritime routes.

[33] Ptolemy, *Geog.* I.11.6–7.

[34] I. Piankov, "Maes Titianus, Ptolemy and the 'Stone Tower' on the Great Silk Road," *The Silk Road* 13 (2015), pp. 60–74.

[35] M. Cary, "Maes, Qui et Titianus," *The Classical Quarterly*, New Series, 6.3/4 (July–October 1956), pp. 130–134.

[36] Piankov 2015, p. 62.

Marinus of Tyre was apparently suspicious of the possible exaggeration of distances contained in Maes' itinerary, but for Ptolemy, the route to the Stone Tower was through regions of which he had no previous knowledge or experience, and about which there was nothing written in other sources he had available. Ptolemy decided to divide the route into three sections and recounts it both in his itinerary and in a discussion of the maps he created to illustrate it.[37] The first part of the route headed eastward from the ancient Bactrian city of Bactra (the same city Zhang Qian had visited late in the second century BCE), a route that ascended through mountains named the Komedes. Confusingly, Ptolemy also seems to suggest that a different route goes north from Bactra through a region he names Sogdiana.[38] The second part of the itinerary crosses the Komedes Mountains as far as a gorge; the road through the mountains travels in an initially easterly direction and then bends to the south.[39] The third section of the route passes through the Gorge of the Komedes as far as the "Stone Tower."

Maes' itinerary, reported by Marinus and plotted by Ptolemy, has been variously located by modern scholars as proceeding from Bactra northeastward through the Ferghana Valley, or due eastward and eventually through the Pamir Knot.[40] Piankov believes that Ptolemy is inadvertently describing two different routes and muddling them together. According to Piankov, both routes began in Bactra and must have first crossed the Oxus River. One route then proceeded north through a gorge that might be identified with the modern Karategin Gorge in the Hisar Valley in Tajikistan, and thence to the Stone Tower, a settlement located near some sort of stone mountain or stone structure. Some scholars now place the Stone Tower somewhere in the Daraut-Kurghan region of the Alai Valley, and indeed there might be some archaeological evidence to support this.[41] From the Stone Tower the route continues eastward along the Alai/Kyzyl Suu Valley to Irkeshtam, which is a border crossing between modern Kyrgyzstan and Xinjiang Province in China, about 140 miles west of Kashgar. The alternative route, which, according to Piankov, Ptolemy mixes up with the first, probably passed through Samarkand and the Ferghana Valley before crossing the Terek-Davan pass and heading east on to Irkeshtam. However, despite the efforts of Piankov and others, there is little agreement on the specifics of these

[37] Ptolemy, *Geog.* I.12.7–8 and VI.11–13. [38] Ptolemy, *Geog.* 1.12.7.
[39] Ptolemy, *Geog.* I.12.7.
[40] For a discussion, see J. Lerner, "Ptolemy and the Silk Road from Baktra Basileion to Sera Metropolis," *East and West* 48/1–2 (1998), pp. 9–25.
[41] See Piankov 2015, p. 64.

routes, which have remained notoriously difficult to determine for almost 2,000 years.[42]

If there is any accuracy in the itinerary provided by Maes Titianus to Marinus of Tyre, this would suggest that Maes' agents should be credited with traveling farther east along the Silk Roads than any other Western merchants we are aware of. This is highly speculative of course, but perhaps by taking advantage of a period of relative peace between the Romans and Parthians in the decades either side of the BCE/CE divide, or later in the first century CE, they were able to journey at least once, and perhaps several times, through Central Asia to the very edge of Han China. Taken together, both *Parthian Stations* by Isidorus of Charax and the itinerary of Maes Titianus as reported by Ptolemy (via Marinus) seem to describe different sections (and variants) of overland Silk Roads routes from the Mediterranean coast across Mesopotamia, Parthia, Bactria and beyond, providing some sort of sketchy evidence of the existence of such routes, if very little on the frequency of their use. The more westerly parts of the overland route between the Euphrates and Tigris were clearly the most heavily trafficked; the easterly sections apparently were less so, particularly because of the sometimes contentious relationship between the Roman and Parthian states. No Greco-Roman trader would have followed this complete route, of course. Like their Chinese counterparts, the Mediterranean merchants must have passed their goods onto Parthian, Sogdian, South Asian or Kushan middlemen somewhere along the way, perhaps in Merv or Bactra. These middlemen in turn would have transported the goods across the passes and down into the Tarim Basin, where probably in Kashgar they were sold to Chinese merchants or envoys to be transported back to Chang'an and beyond.

In the 1920s, English historian Martin Charlesworth tried to imagine the sort of atmosphere that must have prevailed in the Central Asian trading cities, where merchants from different cultural and linguistic traditions came together at these commercial outposts. As Charlesworth envisioned them: "Here indeed these merchants, though they little knew it, stood at the very heart and center of commerce for the Old World and the most ancient meeting place on the whole earth."[43] Charlesworth notes that along the Yarkand Valley the way ran eastward to China; to the southeast another route lay open to the Indus Valley; westward there was a way to the Mediterranean and Europe by way of Samarkand,

[42] For maps outlining another possible variant of the route of Maes Titianus, see H.-P. Francfort, "Les Nomades Installes dans La Bactriane: Nouvelles Decouvertes," *CRAI* 4 (November–December 2013), pp. 1544–1555.

[43] M. Charlesworth, *Trade Routes and Commerce in the Roman Empire*. Cambridge: Cambridge University Press, 1924, pp. 126–127.

Parthia and Mesopotamia. In these lonely Central Asian outposts three civilizations, those of China, of India and of the Greco-Roman West, met and gave in exchange their products, their wares and their painting and art.[44] Charlesworth makes clear that what was at the heart of these exchanges – and really this is one of the key reasons why the First Silk Roads Era is so significant to world history – was not so much the commodities themselves, but rather the degree of cultural cross-pollination that occurred in this period of multidirectional, transcultural exchange. And this leads us to the third and final question this chapter addresses: what was the impact of the import of silk and other luxury commodities from Asia on Greco-Roman culture?

Cultural Diffusion and Attitudes toward Silk in Rome

We know from comments in the Han sources that, as the Han Dynasty expanded its tributary empire deep into Central Asia, many of China's new neighbors became "Sinotized" (adopted Chinese cultural practices). This resulted directly from the diffusion westward of some of the key technologies and cultural ideas of Chinese administration and culture. Many of the states of Central Asia, particularly those in the Tarim Basin, were now bound to the Han in a diplomatic and military relationship in which Chinese goods (in the form of tribute and commercial products) and Chinese ideas spread out from Chang'an and into the courts and societies of these kingdoms and city-states. At the same time Chinese culture was also being transformed, as new crop species like the grape, new animals like the heavenly horses of Ferghana and the Bactrian camel, different technologies including new farming and irrigation techniques, new musical instruments and harmonies, new diseases and of course new ideas such as the spiritual ideology of Buddhism also diffused eastward from South and Central Asia into China.

By far the most important of these cultural imports for East Asian civilization was Buddhism, a diffusion that began during the Later Han Dynasty, but that really took root in the centuries following the collapse of the Han, as will be discussed in the final chapter. But even during the Later Han Dynasty there was serious concern among Chinese intellectuals at the unwholesome effect all this cultural borrowing was having on the core beliefs of Chinese culture, on the dilution of Confucianism by Buddhism, for example. Daoism proved itself remarkably flexible, and was able to adapt and blend with Buddhism to create a genuinely syncretic religion for the Chinese people. Yet intense debates on how to preserve

[44] Charlesworth 1924, pp. 126–127.

the foundations of Chinese civilization in the wake of this "cultural barbarization" from the West would occupy philosophers, poets, historians and government officials for millennia after the First Silk Roads Era was over.

Similar concerns were expressed by cultural conservatives in Rome, and there are references in literature to the unpleasant shock Roman authors felt at hearing exotic music in the streets of Rome or smelling the cooking of bizarre foreign foods. Yet Roman culture also proved itself adaptable to this diffusion from the East, as the Roman acceptance and adoption of so many foreign gods and belief systems, such as the Central Asian religion of Mithraism demonstrates. Questions about cultural flexibility in Han China and the Roman Empire are somewhat academic, however, because whatever the attitude of cultural conservatives, the demand for luxury goods in both societies was unstoppable. In the Roman world in particular, the demand for silk and other luxury imports was insatiable during the first two centuries CE.

As the textile became increasingly available during the Julio-Claudian Age (27 BCE–68 CE), a veritable mania for silk clothing developed. During the reign of Augustus, poets like Tibullus, Propertius, Horace and Ovid were all adorning their verses with allusions to the sensual and even erotic nature of silk clothing. Most of these references relate to a specific type of silk that, as early as the fourth century BCE, the Greek philosopher Aristotle had noted was produced from worms on the island of Cos, just off the Anatolian coast of modern Turkey. Aristotle makes no mention of the silk being foreign, so presumably this was a locally produced rather than imported silk that was manufactured on Cos to create garments. To quote Aristotle: "And some of the women unravel the cocoons of this animal by combing them out, and then spin them; and they say that Pamphile that daughter of Plateus in Cos was the first to weave [the resulting fiber]."[45]

Four centuries later, Roman statesman and author Pliny the Elder, building on Aristotle's original observation, also gave credit for silk to this same Pamphile of Cos who, he rather condescendingly wrote, "has the undeniable distinction of having devised a plan to reduce women's clothing to nakedness."[46] So when Roman poets wrote about silk, they were specifically writing about *Coa Vestis*, or the Coan cloth, even though it is far more likely that the silk Roman women were wearing was, by the Augustan age, being imported from Han China via trade cities like Palmyra. As Pliny's comment

[45] Aristotle, *Hist. Anim.* V.19. [46] Pliny, *NH* II.76.

Figure 5.5 Roman female deity wearing silk, painted fresco discovered in the ruins of Pompeii
http://media.gettyimages.com/photos/pompei-fresco-in-a-villa-of-pompei-picture-id170425192
Credit: Buena Vista Images

indicates, silk was closely associated with sensuality and female promiscuity among Roman elites. The poet Ovid noted the transparent nature of the fabric: "In her Coan silk you may see the (adulteress) almost as if naked";[47] Sextus Propertius in *The Love Elegies* asked: "What need is there, mea vita, to come with your hair adorned, and slither about in a thin silk dress."[48]

While the poets clearly found the textile sensual and alluring, more conservative Julio-Claudian authors found it offensive. Seneca the Younger displays this sense of moral horror among conservative Romans at the nature of the silk garments Roman women, including married women, were wearing in public in a much-quoted passage: "I can see clothes of silk, if materials that do not hide the body, nor even one's decency, can be called clothes. Wretched flocks of maidens labor so that the adulteress may be visible through her thin dress, so that her husband has no more acquaintance than any outsider or foreigner with his wife's body!"[49] Seneca also congratulated his mother, Helvia, for resisting the wearing of silk garments: "Never have you fancied the kind of dress that exposed no greater nakedness by being removed."[50]

The poets describe silk garments as thin and transparent, often colored by a fine purple dye made from sea mollusks, and sometimes with transverse stripes of gold.[51] For conservatives, the wearing of silk by otherwise upright women was bad enough, but once the obsession spread to men, the Roman Senate felt compelled to issue edicts prohibiting the wearing of silk, on both economic and moral grounds. According to Roman historian Cassius Dio (c. 155–235 CE), these attempts began during the reign of Augustus' successor, Tiberius (r. 14–37 CE): "In the consulship of Statilius Taurus and Lucius Libo, Tiberius forbade any man to wear silk clothing."[52] Whether this edict had any effect is difficult to know, but further attempts would have been seriously undermined when Tiberius' successor, Emperor Caligula, also took to using and even wearing silk!

Cassius Dio describes a ceremony that took place in the Forum, during which Caligula "sat upon the rostra in a chair between the consuls; some add that he used silken awnings."[53] In his *Lives of the Caesars*, the historian Suetonius (c. 69–120 CE) comments upon Caligula's tastes in clothing: "In his clothing, his shoes, and the rest of his attire he did not follow the usage of his country and his fellow-citizens; not always even that of his sex; or in fact, that of any ordinary mortal. He often appeared in public in embroidered cloaks covered with precious stones, with a long-sleeved tunic and bracelets; sometimes in silk or in a woman's robe."[54] The historian Tacitus (c. 56–120 CE) also discusses attempts to regulate the wearing of

[47] Ovid, *Ars Amatoria*, 2.298. [48] Propertius, I.2. [49] Seneca, *Declamations*, I.
[50] Seneca, *Helvia*, 16.4. [51] Tibullus II. 4 and II. 6. [52] Dion Cass, 57, 15.
[53] Dion Cass, 59, 2. [54] Suetonius, *Cal.* 52, 1.

silk by men, and other matters of "national extravagance": "At the next session, the ex-consul, Quintus Haterius, and Octavio Fronto, a former praetor, spoke at length against the national extravagance; and it was resolved that table-plate should not be manufactured in solid gold, and that Oriental silks should no longer degrade the male sex."[55]

Historian Kelly Olsen, in an analysis of Roman attitudes toward silk, wonders whether descriptions of the erotic and sensual nature of silk might apply to Coan silk only, and not Chinese silk. Perhaps, Olsen speculates, Coan silk was produced using a gauze weave, resulting in a particularly sheer fabric, or its transparency might have been exaggerated because its sheerness more clearly showed the outlines of a woman's body. It is also possible that as the fabric was so expensive, women economized by using less fabric to make more form-fitted garments.[56] But silk was dangerous for Roman conservatives beyond the eroticism and moral degradation it may have represented; it also demonstrated the independence and economic power elite women possessed in Rome.

We know that silk was incredibly expensive. Tibullus puts silk in the same category as other valuable luxury goods like pearls and the purple dye produced in Marinus' hometown of Tyre. He also notes that silk could be stripped with gold, making it even more expensive.[57] Further evidence about the cost of silk comes from the third-century reign of Emperor Diocletian, whose Edict of Maximum Prices notes the price of one Roman pound (about 330 grams) of silk was 12,000 *denarii*, the same price of one Roman pound of gold wire.[58] By way of comparison, the price of one pound of the best wool was only 300 *denarii*, and the finest-quality linen 1,200 *denarii*.[59] All this means that, as Olsen puts it, "Silk was doubly dangerous because the fabric was expensive and could therefore display female economic power and status."[60]

As well as silk, during the first two centuries CE the Roman Empire was also importing high-value precious stones such as pearls and emeralds, and luxury spices from India and Arabia, including nutmeg, cloves, cardamom and pepper, prized as condiments, but also as aphrodisiacs, anesthetics and perfumes. The import of these high-value goods apparently cost the Romans a fortune. In 65 CE, Roman senator Pliny the Elder, in something of a tirade against the "excessiveness" of women, provided incidental evidence of the cost of luxury imports for the Roman state in another much-quoted statement:

[55] Tacitus, *Annals*, II, 33.
[56] K. Olsen, *Dress and the Roman Woman: Self-Presentation and Society*. New York: Routledge, 2008, p. 14.
[57] Tibulus, 2–4, 28–29. [58] Edictum Diocletiani, 23.1a.
[59] Edictum Diocletiani, 25.1a and 24.4–4a. [60] Olsen 2008, p. 14.

> [W]e have come now to see . . . journeys made to Seres [China] to obtain cloth, the abysses of the Red Sea explored for pearls, and the depths of the earth scoured for emeralds. They have even taken up the notion of piercing the ears as if it were too small a matter to wear those gems in necklaces and tiaras unless holes were also made in the body into which to insert them . . . at the lowest computation, India and the Seres and the [Arabian] Peninsula together drain our empire of one hundred million sesterces every year. That is the price that our luxuries and our womankind cost us.[61]

The sum of 100 million *sestercii* is equivalent to something like $1 billion USD, so this is the amount that the Roman state, according to Pliny, was spending on luxury imports each year. Pliny may have been exaggerating the dangers of Rome's imports in order to make a point about the extravagance of elite Roman women, although modern economic historians are more inclined to believe Pliny's figure today, given that imports from South Asia alone might have totaled something like 17.64 billion *sesterces* a year, an estimate discussed further in the chapter on maritime trade.[62] Pliny would also have been acutely aware of the substantial volume of Roman exports, including agricultural products, glassware and high-value art objects from various Roman-controlled regions like Egypt. In addition, some historians have argued that the Roman state would have benefited tremendously from these Asian imports by levying customs duties of up to 25 percent on all the various goods that were imported into the empire.[63] Andrew Wilson goes so far as to argue that "the customs revenue on the import trade alone through the Red Sea would have amounted to perhaps between a quarter and a third of the entire military budget for the empire."[64] More on these economic arguments in Chapter 8.

Conclusion

This chapter began by outlining the often-chaotic history of the Roman Republic through to the advent of Augustus, and the Roman Peace he instituted, which made it possible for the Romans to engage in long-distance trade across Eurasia. It considered the evidence for land-based trade routes from the Mediterranean into Central Asia, using

[61] Pliny, *NH* XII.41.

[62] S. E. Sidebotham, *Berenike and the Ancient Maritime Spice Route*. Berkeley and Los Angeles: University of California Press, 2011, p. 218.

[63] See, for example, R. McLaughlin, *The Roman Empire and the Indian Ocean: The Ancient World Economy and the Kingdoms of Africa, Arabia and India*. Yorkshire: Pen and Sword Military, 2014.

[64] A. Wilson, *The Cambridge Companion to the Roman Economy*. Cambridge: Cambridge University Press, 2012, p. 290.

primary sources and the archaeological discoveries of Palmyra. Finally, this chapter discussed the various ways in which the import of silk and other luxury commodities influenced the culture and economy of Rome. Although poets appreciated the sexual allure of the wearing of silk garments by women, conservatives viewed the practice as a moral disgrace and a "national extravagance," particularly after men, even the emperor himself, also started wearing silk clothes. Several attempts were made to regulate and even prohibit the wearing of silk, using moral, economic and gender arguments. Yet the demand for silk and other luxury products proved unstoppable in Imperial Rome, and this was probably also of considerable financial benefit to the empire through the high customs duties the state imposed on these imports, which might even have partly funded the legions themselves. These same legions found themselves tested over several centuries during periods of conflict between Rome and the powerful Parthians to the east, who became the most formidable enemy the Roman Empire had to deal with. The Parthians are the subject of the next chapter in this study of the First Silk Roads Era, and the sedentary and nomadic empires that controlled it.

Selected Further Reading

Ball, W., *Rome in the East: Transformation of an Empire*. London: Routledge, 2002.

Elton, H., *Frontiers of the Roman Empire*. London: Routledge, 2013.

Lerner, J., "Ptolemy and the Silk Road from Baktra Basileion to Sera Metropolis," *East and West* 48, No. 1–2 (1998), pp. 9–25.

McLaughlin, R., *The Roman Empire and the Indian Ocean: The Ancient World Economy and the Kingdoms of Africa, Arabia and India*. Yorkshire: Pen and Sword Military, 2014.

Millar, F., "Caravan Cities: The Roman Near East and Long-Distance Trade by Land," *Bulletin of the Institute of Classical Studies. Supplement* No. 71, Modus Operandi: Essay in Honor of Geoffrey Rickman, Wiley, 1998, pp. 119–137.

Olsen, K., *Dress and the Roman Woman: Self-Presentation and Society*. New York: Routledge, 2008.

Schoff, W. H., Translation and Commentary, *Parthian Stations by Isidorus of Charax*. London, 1914. See http://parthia.com/doc/parthian_stations.htm #PARTHIAN_STATIONS.

Wilson, A., *The Cambridge Companion to the Roman Economy*. Cambridge: Cambridge University Press, 2012.

Zuchowska, M., "From China to Palmyra: The Value of Silk," *Swiatowit* 11, No. 52, A (2013).

6 The Parthian Empire and the Silk Roads

As valuable as Silk Roads trade was to the Romans, and to the merchants and local elites who ensured the functioning of the Western end of the network, the land routes between the Mediterranean and Central Asia were often threatened because of the unstable relationship between the Roman and Parthian Empires. The Parthians were one of four powerful imperial states that controlled much of Eurasia during the First Silk Roads Era, and their effective administration, along with that of the Kushans, of large regions of Inner Eurasia played a crucial role in the operation of both land and maritime routes. As we have seen, it was the Romans that generated the greatest demand for silk and other luxury imports during the period, and the Han who were best able to meet the demand for silk in particular through their advanced sericulture. But it was groups in the center of the Silk Roads network, including the Parthian and Kushan Empires, various nomadic confederations and other regional intermediaries, that effectively connected the eastern and western Eurasian worlds together during this First Silk Roads Era.

With this in mind, the next two chapters are focused on the center of the network, and on the history and role of the Parthian and Kushan Empires, two of the four great powers of the ancient world during the First Silk Roads Era. Providing definitive answers to key questions about the role of these two imperial states is difficult, however, because the evidence for each is scarce and ambiguous. The first question this chapter considers is: how did the earlier history of the regions that the Parthians and Kushans eventually came to dominate pave the way for their success? Second, given the nomadic origins of both the Parthians and Kushans, how were they able to construct and administer large sedentary empires? A third question concerning the Parthians in particular is, why did they so frequently find themselves in conflict with the Roman Empire? Finally, what role did both the Parthians and the Kushans play in the operation of the Silk Roads, particularly during the first two centuries CE? To begin to answer these questions, we turn in this chapter to the Iranian Plateau, the environmental context for the appearance and success of three great

Persian/Iranian empires, including that established by the formidable Parthians.

Achaemenid Persian Empire

Our first question concerns the earlier history of the region that the Parthians came to dominate, and how this might have contributed to their eventual success. The Parthians were regional successors to the Greco-Macedonia Seleucids, who in turn were successors of the Achaemenid Persians, who constructed the first seriously large empire in world history. Each of these imperial states took control of extensive areas of the Iranian Plateau and surrounding territory. The Iranian Plateau is a high and semiarid region located to the east of Mesopotamia, extending as far as Afghanistan. Geographically it is bounded by the Zagros Mountains on the west, the Kopet Dag Mountains and southern shore of the Caspian Sea to the north, the Caucuses Mountains to the northwest, the Persian Gulf to the south, and the Indus River Valley to the east. As a natural crossroads between west and central Eurasia, it is an area through which numerous migrating peoples have passed, virtually since the time humans started moving out of Africa and Southwest Asia. Late in the second millennium BCE two different migrating pastoral nomadic groups, the Indo-European-speaking Medes and Persians, both settled in the region and organized themselves into loose tribal confederations.

In common with many steppe nomadic peoples, the Medes and Persians were highly militarized, and as the Babylonian and Assyrian Empires in Mesopotamia waned, the Persians in particular began to use their military prowess to construct their own imperial state. Under the leadership of King Cyrus II (r. 558–530 BCE) the Medes were crushed. Cyrus then led his forces out of Iran in a series of successful expansionary campaigns to the east and west. By 539 BCE much of western Eurasia had been conquered, and the Achaemenid Empire stretched from Afghanistan to Turkey. The name "Achaemenid Empire" was chosen by one of Cyrus' successors, Darius I (r. 521–486 BCE), to commemorate the semi-legendary ninth-century BCE founder of Cyrus' dynasty, Achaemenes, to whom Darius claimed a somewhat dubious relationship.[1] Cyrus' son Cambyses

[1] Reliable general sources on the political, military and cultural history of the Achaemenid Persian Empire are R. M. Frye, *The Heritage of Persia: The Pre-Islamic History of One of the World's Great Civilizations*. New York: World Publishing Company, 1963 (Reprinted by Mazda Publishers, 2004); M. A. Dandamaev, *A Political History of the Persian Empire*. Leiden: Brill Publishing, 1989; and the collection of essays in J. Curtis and N. Tallis, eds., *Forgotten Empire: The World of Ancient Persia*. Berkeley and Los Angeles: University of California Press, 2005.

(r. 530–522 BCE) added Egypt to the realm, while Darius I, seeking increased tributary resources through expansionary war, enlarged the empire in all directions until it included parts of India in the east and Macedonia and other regions of southeastern Europe in the west. At its maximum size, the Persian Empire stretched more than 3,000 kilometers (1,900 miles) from the Indus to the Mediterranean and almost 1,500 kilometers (1,000 miles) from Armenia to southern Egypt. At close to 11 million square kilometers in area, this was undoubtedly the largest agrarian civilization the world had ever seen to that point in history.

The Achaemenid rulers were faced with the task of administering a huge, multicultural empire in which a range of languages, religions and cultures existed. Realizing that it would be futile and unwise to attempt to standardize these cultural differences, the Persians focused on building an empire that achieved a fine balance between centralized and local administration. Rulers called themselves "Kings of Kings." They claimed absolute power and ruled from royal capitals like Pasargadae and Persepolis with the advice and assistance of an army of bureaucrats, diplomats, scribes and translators. At the same time, imperial administration was decentralized by the appointment of governors (called *satraps*) who presided over twenty-three different provinces or *satrapies*, a system that the Achaemenids probably inherited from the earlier Assyrians. Although the *satraps* were Persian, most other provincial officials were local, which facilitated a degree of regional autonomy. No attempt was made to institute an imperial law code, and local laws remained in place at the regional and even village level. To ensure against ambitious grabs for power by the *satraps*, the government also appointed military and taxation officials to each *satrapy*. In addition, the kings used a network of imperial spies to travel throughout the empire and conduct surprise audits of tax and other records.

To further unify the empire and facilitate the rapid movement of officials and armies, the Achaemenid kings built a network of well-constructed roads, which also benefited trade and commerce within the empire. Particularly impressive was the nearly 2,400 kilometer-long (1,500 miles) "Royal Road" that stretched from Sardis in western Turkey to Susa in Iran, thus connecting the western and eastern regions of the empire. The road was equipped with facilities for a courier service, and teams of well-mounted couriers were able to get messages from the Aegean coast to Persepolis in about two weeks. Road construction and state administration on this scale were expensive, but the Persian elites were able to access vast tributes paid under threat of coercion by the various conquered states that made up the empire. The eastern *satrapies* alone may have supplied as much as 2,530 talents of silver tribute to the

Figure 6.1 Ruins of Persepolis, one of the capitals of the Achaemenid Persian Empire, now a UNESCO World Heritage Site, Iran
http://media.gettyimages.com/photos/persepolis-iran-picture-id641349420?s=170667a
Credit: Ekkachai Pholrojpanya

Persian government. The maintenance of this vast tributary empire demanded the constant vigilance of kings and elites, and any revolt had to be quickly and ruthlessly suppressed before it could jeopardize the sustainability of the entire imperial structure. By the measures they adopted to deal with the question of state viability, the Persians learned to administer the largest empire ever seen, and at the same time established a model for subsequent Afro-Eurasian imperial governments, including their regional successors, the Seleucids and the Parthians, and their eventual successors, the Sasanians.

Alexander of Macedon and the Hellenistic Era

In a constant quest to expand their already enormous empire, however, the Persians eventually overreached themselves. In the end it was Achaemenid expansion into the Eastern Mediterranean, and their incorporation of numerous Greek colonies along the coast of modern Turkey, that led to the demise of this first Persian Empire. Greek civilization had first emerged on the mainland and islands of the Aegean Sea in the ninth century BCE, during a period of widespread unrest in the Eastern Mediterranean, and early Greek communities had been constructed around a series of fortified citadels called *poleis*. During the eighth century, many of the *poleis* became bustling city-states, and with arable land in short supply because of the geography of the Greek mainland, the cities had established hundreds of colonies around the coastline of the Mediterranean and Black Seas to settle excess populations. These colonies had also flourished, becoming important centers of commercial, political and intellectual endeavor during the centuries that followed.

It is hardly surprising that the sophisticated Greek colonies of the Ionian coast of modern Turkey resented Persian hegemony, and in 499 BCE they rebelled, supported by some mainland Greek city-states including Athens. The Persians responded by crushing the rebellion, then launching an attack on the Greek peninsula to punish the mainland city-states for interfering. Despite having vastly superior forces, a Persian army sent by Darius in 490 BCE was defeated on the plains of Marathon. Ten years later, Darius' successor, Xerxes, invaded Greece with an enormous army, but the Spartans famously forestalled the Persians at Thermopylae, and the Athenians destroyed the Persian fleet at Salamis. The following year (in the summer of 479 BCE) a large Greek army crushed the remaining Persian forces at the Battle of Plataea, bringing to a decisive end the attempted Persian invasion of Greece.[2]

Although the Persians had been driven out of Greece, they still controlled many of the Greek colonies along the Ionian coast. The Athenians assumed the mantle of leadership of the Greek world, and used the ongoing tension with the Persians to justify the establishment of a defensive alliance known as the Delian League. The Athenians demanded that member states pay a substantial amount of cash to Athens so that they could maintain their navy, which would be well equipped to protect members of the League should war with the Persians break out again. But as the years went by with no resumption of hostilities, and after the Persians were driven out of the Ionian colonies in 468, League members became increasingly resentful of having to make these cash donations to Athens, particularly as the money was now being spent on extravagant and expensive building projects in that city such as the Parthenon. The rival *polis* of Sparta formed its own league and argued that Athens was acting like a tyrant city. Tensions reached a boiling point, and in 431 BCE Sparta declared war on Athens.

[2] Two reliable general sources on the wars between the Persians and Greeks are P. Green, *The Greco-Persian Wars*. Berkeley and Los Angeles: University of California Press, 1998; and P. Souza, *The Greek and Persian Wars 499–386 BC*. London: Osprey Publishing, 2003.

The ensuing Peloponnesian War, brilliantly catalogued by the Greek historian Thucydides who was an eyewitness to the events, dragged on for twenty-seven years, despite the outbreak of plague and the signing of an initial peace treaty, which held for six years.[3] The bitter civil war was fought on the Greek mainland, on the island of Sicily, which was home to many Greek colonies, and at sea where the war was finally concluded in 405 BCE with the sinking of 168 Athenian ships by a fleet under Spartan commander Lysander. The war was so bloody, bruising and long that it poisoned the hope of any further unity among the Greek *poleis*, and although civic life did revive during the fourth century, lack of unity among the Greeks led to their eventual conquest by their northern neighbors the Macedonians, under the inspired leadership of King Philip II (r. 359–336 BCE).

When Philip was assassinated, leadership of the Macedonians, and de facto of the entire Greek world, fell to his twenty-year-old son, Alexander, who set out in 334 BCE on an audacious campaign to invade the Persian Empire. Alexander was highly educated, a gifted horseman and athlete, and had inherited his father's skills of charismatic leadership and superb strategic thinking. Despite being vastly outnumbered, the Macedonian/Greek forces routed the Persians in three separate battles, including most decisively at the Battle of Gaugamela in 331 BCE, where Alexander not only defeated Persian ruler Darius II, but also captured a huge fortune. Alexander now became the new "emperor" of Persia and then continued his victorious march into Central Asia and as far as the Indus River, founding some seventy cities and marrying a Central Asian princess before eventually returning to Babylon and an early death in 323 BCE, at age thirty-three.[4]

Over the ensuing half century, Alexander's empire was divided up among his generals, and from 275 BCE Greek culture spread, mostly through commercial expansion rather than conquest, throughout much of western Eurasia during the so-called Hellenistic ("Greek-like") Era. In the same way that earlier Greek commercial activity and colonization had facilitated cultural exchange and integration in the Mediterranean and Black Sea basins, Greek traders, diplomats, scholars and administrators facilitated exchange and integration from India to Europe. Greece

[3] Thucydides, *The Peloponnesian War*, Intro., ed. and trans. M. I. Finley, London: Penguin Classics, 1954.

[4] Reliable accounts of the life and campaigns of Alexander and of the Hellenistic Era that followed include A. B. Bosworth, *Conquest and Empire: The Reign of Alexander the Great*. New York: Cambridge University Press, 1988; P. Green, *Alexander the Great and the Hellenistic Age*. London: Phoenix, 2007; and F. Chamoux, *Hellenistic Civilization*. Oxford: Wiley/Blackwell, 2002.

Figure 6.2 Artist's rendering of Alexander of Macedon during the Battle of Gaugamela, drawn from a mosaic discovered in the ruins of Pompeii
http://media.gettyimages.com/photos/alexander-the-great-picture-id94368693?s=170667a
Credit: tunart

and Macedonia came under the control of the Antigonids, descendants of the general Antigonus, and despite Greek resentment at outside rule, commerce flourished. Egypt was transformed into the wealthy Ptolemaic Empire, and the city of Alexandria (founded by Alexander) became the great metropolis of the region, renowned for its commercial activity, multicultural tolerance and intellectual synergy focused upon the state-sponsored library.

Large regions of southwestern and central Eurasia, including much of the former Achaemenid Empire, were controlled, with difficulty, by the Seleucids, descendants of Alexander's general Seleucus Nicator. Greek colonists and merchants flooded the region, recreating transplanted Hellenistic society in regions like Afghanistan and Pakistan. Greek language became so widespread that the Indian Mauryan Dynasty emperor Ashoka (r. 268–232 BCE) found it necessary to put up multilingual inscriptions that included the major Eastern

Mediterranean languages of Greek and Aramaic. Part of the Seleucid realm included Bactria, where a series of Hellenistic kings ruled independent Greco-Bactrian and Indo-Greek kingdoms from about 250 BCE until, as we have already seen, the arrival of militarized nomads including the Yuezhi a century later destroyed the Greek kingdoms there. Through these various regional polities, the vast empire of the Persians, now recreated as a looser Hellenistic commercial and cultural "civilization," acted as a spatial bridge between Europe and Asia, and a temporal bridge between the Achaemenid Empire and the arrival of the Romans and the Parthians.

Constructing and Administering the Parthian Empire

The defeat of the Achaemenids by Alexander, and the subsequent dismemberment of the Persian Empire by his successors, was not the end of Persian imperial history. Although the Seleucids were able to hold on to some remnants of their diminishing realm until the arrival of the Romans in the early second century, a new power had emerged in Iran in the third century BCE that by then had already created its own vast Parthian Empire. The Parthians were descended from the Parni, another Central Asian pastoral nomadic confederation that spoke an eastern Indo-Iranian branch language. The Parni eventually conquered a large region of northern Iran, including the province of Parthia, after which they adopted the northern Indo-Iranian language of Parthian as the official language of the court.[5] The region conquered by the Parni in northeastern Iran was a *satrapy* of the Seleucid Empire, which now rebelled against the Seleucids. The founder of the Parthian Empire, Arsaces, chose the year 247 as the official start of the Arsacid Dynasty, a date that might mark the year Arsaces was made chief of the Parni, or the year that Arsaces completed the conquest of Parthia and expelled the Seleucids from the region.[6]

Part of the answer to our second question about how the Parthians were able to transform their nomadic confederation into a sedentary imperial state is that the early Parthian kings were influenced by the success of the prevailing Achaemenid and Hellenistic political and economic culture of

[5] See M. J. Olbrycht, "Parthia and Nomads of Central Asia. Elements of Steppe Origin in the Social and Military Developments of Arsacid Iran," in Schneider, I, ed., Mitteilungen des SFB "Differenz und Integration" 5, Halle: Orientwissenchaft, 2003, pp. 69–109.

[6] See V. S. Curtis, "The Iranian Revival in the Parthian Period," in V. S. Curtis and S. Stewart, *The Age of the Parthians: The Ideas of Iran*, 2. London and New York: I. B. Taurus and Co. Ltd., 2007, p. 7; and G. R. Garthwaite, *The Persians*. Oxford and Carlton: Blackwell Publishing Ltd., 2005, p. 67.

the region. For a while the Parthians even agreed to recognize Hellenistic kings as their nominal rulers. During the second century BCE, however, Parthian rulers dramatically expanded the size of their territory, and also began to emphasize the Iranian cultural influences of their Achaemenid predecessors. Under King Mithridates I (r. c. 171–138 BCE) the Parthians used their considerable military skill to build a substantial state that extended from the eastern edge of the Iranian Plateau down into the flat lands of Mesopotamia. Mithridates I built his royal residences in Seleucia and Ctesiphon on the Tigris River, and Ecbatana on the Iranian Plateau to the east of the Zagros Mountains. Mithridates also founded the fortress city of Nisa (or "Mithridatkirk") at the foot of the Kopet Dag Mountains in modern Turkmenistan, which became the burial place of Parthian kings. Rulers modeled their administration on that of the Achaemenids, and also adopted the Achaemenid title of "King of Kings."[7] Mithridates was succeeded by his son Phraates II, who ruled until 128 BCE. Phraates suffered some early defeats in Mesopotamia (including the loss of Babylonia), before restoring Parthian fortunes with a devastating victory over the Seleucid king Antiochus VII.[8]

In administering the empire constructed by the early kings, the Parthians adopted some elements of the political techniques of the Achaemenid Persians, although the Parthian Empire was more decentralized. The empire was divided into eighteen provinces ruled by *shahrdars* or governors, but it also contained several semiautonomous kingdoms. The nobility owned landed estates called *dastkirt* and relied upon lower nobility called *azats* to provide troops when the empire needed a fighting force, which they often did after conflict with the expansionist Romans increased. In their religious beliefs the Arsacid Parthians worshipped the cult of Mithra, a cult that eventually spread widely throughout the Roman Empire as the religion of Mithraism. Parthian elites were also probably adherents of the religion of Zoroastrianism, although they demonstrated a degree of religious tolerance that was a marker of many Central Asian empires, including the Kushans. One example of this: when Jews and Christians were persecuted by the Romans during the first two centuries CE, many of them moved to Mesopotamia, now the heartland of the Parthian realm. The ancient cities of Mesopotamia became even more cosmopolitan under the Parthians, with Zoroastrians, Jews, Christians and pagans coexisting in apparent harmony. Eventually it was Jewish communities dwelling in the Parthian Empire that later codified Jewish

[7] M. Rahim Shayegan, *Arsacids and Sasanians: Political Ideology in Post-Hellenistic and Late Antique Persia*. Cambridge: Cambridge University Press, 2011, pp. 40–41.

[8] See Justin XLII.1,1. Diodorus Vol. XXXV, 16–17 for details.

law under the Babylonian Talmud. We also know of one second-century CE Parthian nobleman who became a Buddhist. According to the Chinese *Hou Han Shu* (*Annals of the Later Han Dynasty*), An Shigao (An from Anxi, the Chinese name for Parthia) traveled to Luoyang, capital of the Later Han Dynasty, and worked as a Buddhist missionary there, translating Buddhist scripture into Chinese.[9] We have much more to say about the diffusion of religions within the Parthian Empire, and across Eurasia more widely, in the final chapter of this book.

Parthian Expansion to the East and Conflict with the Saka

In maintaining the vast territory of their empire, even after the Parthian rulers had defeated the remnants of the Seleucid state in the west they were faced with constant problems in the east of their realm, caused by militarized nomadic confederations of Saka (known as Sai to Han Chinese authors, and Scythians to Greco-Roman authors). The original ethnic identity of the Saka is uncertain, although they were most probably Indo-European-speaking migrants who had intermingled with other sedentary and nomadic groups as they migrated eastward, during the waves of Bronze Age pastoral migration we discussed in the first chapter. As we have already noted in our previous discussion of nomadic confederations, when we use a term like *Saka* or *Xiongnu* or *Yuezhi*, we are using it to describe confederations that shared a common culture, such as the use of composite bows or common artistic motifs. Rather than thinking of the Saka realm as an empire, we think of it as a tribal confederation in which the Saka were the dominant elite.

The ancient Greek historian Herodotus, writing in the fifth century BCE, distinguished several groups within the Saka/Scythian confederation, and he named the core group the "Royal Scythians." The confederation known to Herodotus and the Greeks contained large contingents of fast-moving horse archers highly skilled with the composite bow and arrow, but it also included a range of semisedentary and sedentary cultures who dwelt along the northern coast of the Black Sea. In order to protect these sedentary subjects, the Saka built massive hill fortresses in Ukraine; one near Poltava had defensive walls 34 kilometers in length, enclosing an area of 4,000 hectares.[10]

In the seventh century BCE, the Saka evicted the rival nomadic confederation of the Cimmerians from the Black Sea steppes and down into

[9] For more on this reference and the story of An Shigao, see R. E. Buswell Jr. and D. S. Lopez Jr., eds., "An Shigao," *The Princeton Dictionary of Buddhism*. Princeton, NJ: Princeton University Press, 2014, p. 49.

[10] On the Poltava fortress, see T. May, "Pastoral Nomads," in C. Benjamin, ed., *The Cambridge World History Vol. IV*. Cambridge: Cambridge University Press, 2015, p. 238.

Figure 6.3 Bronze statuette of a mounted Scythian warrior
http://images.metmuseum.org/CRDImages/gr/web-large/DP250462.jpg
Credit: Gift of Norbert Schimmel Trust, 1989

northern Mesopotamia. Sakan pursuit of the Cimmerians brought them into conflict with the powerful sedentary state of the Assyrians, who seemed to have no idea of how to deal with this first wave of militarized nomads to seriously contest with a sedentary civilization. Herodotus wrote that Saka/Scythian cavalry contingents remained in the region for twenty-eight years before returning to the steppes, leaving behind a weakened Assyrian Empire.[11] After the Achaemenid Persians took control of their huge empire, rulers such as Cyrus II and Darius I spent much of the sixth and fifth centuries attempting to subdue the Saka. But these campaigns generally failed because the Saka, like all nomadic armies, used their mobility to retreat back into the steppe, dragging their opponents into unfamiliar terrain and using their strongholds there to send contingents of troops out to harass their less mobile opponents. Darius once famously complained that they would not stand and fight![12]

[11] Herodotus, i. 102–106; iv.1.

[12] On Darius' campaign, see J. Boardman, ed., *The Cambridge Ancient History 10: Persia, Greece and the Western Mediterranean.* Cambridge: Cambridge University Press, 1982, pp. 239–243.

During the fourth century BCE, the political structure of the Sakan confederation was centralized until all the tribes were united under King Atheas into another of the great Empires of the Steppe that, along with those constructed by the Yuezhi and Xiongnu, feature so significantly in the history of ancient Eurasia. Trade and agriculture now became more important components of the Sakan economy, and this, along with closer contact with Greek colonies, increased the sedentization of the nomads. By the second century BCE, Sakan dominance in the Black Sea region was waning after invasions by Celts and Sarmatians, although they still possessed sufficient military power to conquer Greek Black Sea colonies such as Cherson to maintain their dominance in regional trade. Even as Sakans' power waned in the West, they had spread extensively eastward across much of Inner Eurasia so that later Greco-Roman and Han Chinese sources were able to identify three distinct groups of Saka/Sai dwelling across wide regions of Inner Eurasia.

These included the *Saka Tayaiparadraya* of the Black Sea region (probably descendants of the same groups known to Herodotus three centuries earlier); the *Amyrgian Saka*, who were dwelling in the Ysyk Kul region and the Ferghana Valley in modern Uzbekistan; and the *Saka Tigraxauda*, located by the Greek historian Ptolemy in the second century CE as living south of the Jaxartes River, the modern Syr Darya, also in Uzbekistan. It was these more easterly groups, descendants of the original Black Sea Saka who had moved deep into Central Asia, that caused problems for the Parthians.[13] After having defeated the Seleucid king Antiochus VII in 129 BCE, the Parthian king Phraates II (r. c. 132–126 BCE) was forced to immediately return eastward to deal with a Saka invasion in the vicinity of the important trading city of Merv. In the fighting that followed Phraates II was killed; his successor, Artabanos II (r. 126–122 BCE), also died a few years later fighting the Saka, probably by a wound he received from a poisoned arrow.[14] Groups of Saka may then have penetrated the Parthian Empire as far west as Mesopotamia, but continuing Parthian operations against them ensured that they never progressed any further to the west.

[13] For more extensive discussion of evidence for these various groups of Saka, see C. Benjamin, *The Yuezhi: Origins, Migration and the Conquest of Northern Bactria*. Turnhout: Brepols, 2007, p. 181.

[14] N. C. Debevoise, *A Political History of Parthia. Chicago*, 1938, p. 58; and A. D. H. Bivar, "The Political History of Iran under the Arsacids," in E. Yarshater, ed., *Cambridge History of Iran*, 3.1, Cambridge: Cambridge University Press, 1983, pp. 36–39.

Parthian Expansion to the West and Early Conflict with the Romans

Artabanos II was succeeded by Mithridates II (r. c. 121–91 CE), perhaps the greatest of all Parthian kings. Naming himself "King of Kings," Mithridates II moved his capital westward to Ecbatana and recovered some of the eastern provinces that had been lost to the Saka by his predecessors, including driving the Saka back out of the city of Merv. Eventually Mithridates II, whose reign corresponds with that of Han Wudi and the period of social unrest and civil war in Rome, was able to establish Parthian control over a huge imperial state that stretched from the Caspian Sea in the northeast to the Euphrates Valley in the west. Mithridates also took control over the important trading city of Charax Spasinau, at the head of the Persian Gulf, which had been lost to Babylonian rulers while his predecessors were busy fighting the Saka. By 120 BCE, coins of the former ruler of Charax had been overstruck with the titles and portrait of Mithridates II, indicating that the city and region had been reconquered by the Parthians.[15] This gave the Parthians control over one of the key commercial centers and ports of the Persian Gulf, allowing them to play a key role in maritime Silk Roads trade, as discussed in greater detail in Chapter 8.

Figure 6.4 Parthian silver *drachm* of Parthian king Mithridates II (r. c. 121–91 CE)
http://images.metmuseum.org/CRDImages/an/web-large/DP-1114-001.jpg
Credit: Bequest of Joseph H. Durkee, 1898

[15] Debevoise 1938, p. 40.

Mithridates also became increasingly involved with the kingdom of Armenia to the north of the Parthian realm, campaigning in c. 110 BCE against Armenian king Artavasdes, and keeping his eldest son, Tigranes, as a hostage of the Parthians for several years.[16] This Parthian interest in Armenia provides part of the answer to our third question about why the Parthians found themselves in frequent conflict with the Roman Empire. The Parthians and Romans came into direct diplomatic contact for the first time in 96 BCE, when Parthian ambassador Orobazus and Roman proconsul for the province of Cilicia, Lucius Cornelius Sulla (who would later win the First Civil War and rule Rome as virtual dictator), concluded a treaty that established the Euphrates River as the boundary between the two imperial states' respective spheres of interest. This diplomatic agreement was breached by the Parthians in the decade that followed, when Parthian forces twice crossed the Euphrates to campaign against Seleucid forces in Syria.[17] Despite this breach, it was involvement by the Parthians, and increasingly also the Romans, in the affairs of the Kingdom of Armenia that inevitably drew the two empires into conflict. Tensions between them, and their constant meddling in each other's internal problems, culminated with Crassus' invasion into Parthia and subsequent disastrous loss to the Parthians at the Battle of Carrhae in 53 BCE.

A particularly devastating military tactic developed by the superb light Parthian cavalry, and used to great effect at Carrhae and in most other major battles, was the Parthian Shot. While feigning retreat at full gallop, Parthian horsemen suddenly turned their bodies back to unleash a deadly volley of arrows at the army. This demanded superb equestrian skills, including the ability to control their horses just with knee pressure while both hands were employed in firing behind the body with deadly accuracy. But as we have seen repeatedly, all militarized nomads were superb horsemen and deadly accurate with a variety of bows. By the end of the Battle of Carrhae tens of thousands of Roman soldiers were dead, and another 10,000 had been taken prisoner. Many of the latter were settled in Merv, now firmly under Parthian control, where they married local women. Some were later pressed into military service by the Parthians, but their loyalties were always viewed as unreliable by Parthian commanders, and many were returned to Rome more than thirty years later as part of a negotiated deal with Augustus.[18]

[16] Debevoise 1938, pp. 41–42, n. 55.

[17] D. Kennedy, "Parthia and Rome: Eastern Perspectives," *in* The Roman Army in the East. Ann Arbor, MI: Cushing Malloy Inc., Journal of Roman Archaeology: Supplementary Series Number 18, 1996, pp. 77–78.

[18] Horace, Odes iii, 5.5; Debevoise 1938, p. 92.

As a result of their decisive victory at Carrhae, Parthian troops were now regarded as superior to Romans over a vast swath of Eurasia, stretching from the Mediterranean to the Indus. All the lands east of the Euphrates were now unequivocally Parthian, and the Euphrates remained an uneasy border between the Parthian and Roman Empires. Ten years later the Parthians were emboldened enough to involve themselves in the Second Roman Civil War between Julius Caesar and Pompey by sending troops to support anti-Caesar forces at the Battle of Philippi in 42 BCE. In response Caesar began preparing for a major campaign against the Parthians in 45 BCE, including assembling sixteen legions and 10,000 cavalrymen, plus shipping large quantities of weapons and gold to Asia Minor, but his assassination put these plans on hold. With Roman politics in great ferment, Parthian forces took the opportunity to occupy the Roman province of Syria, and subsequently also occupied many Roman cities along the coast of the Eastern Mediterranean. However, by 38 BCE, even in the midst of their Third Civil War, Roman forces had struck back, defeating the Parthians in several battles and driving them back out of Syria.

Once Octavian came to power in Rome and assumed the title of Augustus in 27 BCE, he was also, somewhat reluctantly, forced into further diplomatic and military relations with the Parthians. As we discussed in the previous chapter, it was in this context that Augustus may have commissioned Isidorus of Charax to produce *Parthian Stations*, in order to provide information in preparation for a potential military action in Parthia by Roman legions under the leadership of Augustus' own son. Another period of contested kingship in Parthia allowed the Romans to negotiate a deal whereby the legionary standards that had been captured by the Parthians at the Battle of Carrhae were returned to Rome, which Augustus hailed as a great victory. Indeed, Augustus turned many of his negotiations with the Parthians into propaganda, and celebrated them in art and literature.[19]

Parthian–Roman Relationship in the First and Second Centuries CE

Following the death of Augustus in 14 CE, his Julio-Claudian family provided a series of successors for the next half century, some decidedly more effective than others. Two of Augustus' successors, Tiberius and Claudius, were able administrators, but Caligula was delusional and saw

[19] M. Brossius, *The Persians: An Introduction*. London and New York: Routledge, 2006, pp. 96–99.

himself as divine, also insisting that his horse be made a senator, and Nero murdered his own wife and mother and persecuted Jews and Christians. The year 69 CE was chaotic. Following Nero's death, four emperors contested the throne, but order was restored by the shrewd soldier Vespasian and his sons, who ruled as the Flavian Dynasty for the next thirty years. They were effective but autocratic rulers who stabilized Roman government after the eccentricities and political violence of the Julio-Claudian Dynasty, although the Flavian emperor Titus was responsible for the destruction of much of Judah, including the city of Jerusalem, and the death of many Jews.

For much of the period of Julio-Claudian rule, the Parthian Empire was plagued by near-continuous succession crises, which meant that relations with Rome were relatively peaceful, even as the Romans continued to meddle in the affairs of Armenia. During these decades of constant struggle between rival contenders for the Parthian crown, some of the commercial cities of the Parthian Empire, such as Seleucia, declared their independence in order to continue to function as Silk Roads caravan cities.[20] By the mid-first century CE, however, Parthian king Vologases I (r. c. 51–c. 80 CE) had regained firm control over the empire and over Armenia, and this de facto hegemony would continue, with the occasional brief interruption, through to the end of the Parthian Empire nearly 200 years later. During this period of renewed Parthian unity Silk Roads trade increased, particularly after Vologases I founded a new commercial city named Vologasia near Babylon, perhaps to counter the autonomy of Seleucia. Vologasia is often mentioned in inscriptions in the trading city of Palmyra, whose important role in maritime and land-based trade was discussed in the previous chapter. During the reign of Nero war broke out between Rome and Parthia again in 58 CE, but eventually a peace treaty was concluded in 63 CE. Parthian king Titidates I actually traveled to Italy, where Emperor Nero himself ceremoniously crowned the Parthian ruler "King of Armenia."[21]

Following the thirty-year rule of the Flavian emperors in Rome, a group of five emperors of the Nerva-Antonine Dynasty provided competent leadership of the Roman Empire for the next eighty-four years, between 96 and 180 CE. Under the Antonines Rome reached the height of its prosperity and power, an apogee celebrated some 1,600 years later by English historian Edward Gibbon, who in his epic, *The History of the Decline and Fall of the Roman Empire*, lauded the Antonine Age as "a happy period of more than fourscore years," during which "the public administration was conducted by the virtue and abilities of Nerva, Trajan,

[20] Debevoise 1938, p. 164. [21] Brossius 2006, pp. 99–100.

Hadrian, and the two Antonines."[22] Trajan was born in 53 CE and 98 CE in the city of Italica in Spain; he was a superb soldier and rose quickly through the ranks of the Roman army, serving on some of the most contested of the empire's frontiers, notably against the Germanic tribes. By the time the last Flavian emperor, Domitian, was killed in 96 CE, Trajan was recognized as one of the foremost military commanders of the empire, and this reputation served him well under Domitian's successor, Nerva, the first of the Antonines, who was unpopular with the army and needed to do something to gain its support. He accomplished this by naming Trajan as his adoptive son, a practice that several subsequent Roman emperors also adopted as a way of appointing their successors.

When Nerva died in January 98 BCE, after a reign of less than two years, Trajan succeeded him without incident, becoming the first non-Italian Roman emperor. Trajan's two-decade reign (r. 98–117 CE) was distinguished by the expansion of the empire to its greatest extent. But his successor, Hadrian (r. 117–138 CE), realized that some of these new provinces were indefensible, and when Hadrian came to power, he stabilized the empire by restoring some of these regions to autonomous rule, and also by founding new cities and erecting key defensive walls in Germany and Britain. Hadrian was succeeded by Antoninus Pius and Lucius Verus, and then by the vigorous and competent Marcus Aurelius, who reigned for almost twenty years from 161 until 180. Marcus was forced to spend much of his reign as a soldier fighting on the front lines, mostly against various Germanic tribes; but in his "spare time" he wrote superb Stoic philosophy, collected and published as *The Meditations*. Marcus Aurelius was the last of Gibbon's "Five Good Emperors." By the end of his reign, the Roman Empire stretched from Scotland to Iraq, and was home to at least 65 million people. At its heart was the extraordinary megalopolis of Rome, a sprawling combination of magnificence and squalor with a population of more than 1 million.

Relations between Rome and Parthia were relatively stable during the period of Flavian rule in Rome, and also during the first few decades of Antonine rule. In 109 CE, however, Parthian king Oroses I (r. 109–128 CE) once again began to meddle in the affairs of Armenia, without consulting the Romans. Roman emperor Trajan responded by sending troops into Armenia, and also by capturing the strategically important Parthian city of Nisibis.[23] In 115 CE Trajan personally led Roman forces in an invasion of Mesopotamia. After spending the winter of 115–116 in

[22] E. Gibbon, *The History of the Decline and Fall of the Roman Empire*, 1782, vol. 1, chapter 1, part 1, intro.
[23] On this campaign, see Bivar 1983, pp. 90–91.

Map 6.1 Map of the Roman Empire during the reign of Trajan (r. 98–117 CE)
https://upload.wikimedia.org/wikipedia/commons/0/00/Roman_Empire_Trajan_117AD.png

Figure 6.5 Bronze sestertius depicting Emperor Trajan (r. 98–117 CE)
http://images.metmuseum.org/CRDImages/gr/web-large/DP104782a.jpg
Credit: Rogers Fund, 1908

Antioch, Trajan resumed the campaign in the spring. Marching down the Euphrates Valley he captured key Parthian cities one after the other, including the commercial city of Dura-Europus and two of the Parthian capitals, Ctesiphon and Seleucia. From the Persian Gulf port city of Charax, Trajan famously watched ships departing on voyages down the Persian Gulf for India, and wished wistfully that he was young enough to sail with them.[24] The following year the Roman Empire reached the most easterly point it would ever attain after Trajan captured the Parthian city of Susa. But this was also as far as Trajan would march. After completing what he expected would be a temporary retreat from Mesopotamia in the spring of 117 CE, Trajan suddenly died in August of that year.

Trajan's successor, the more pragmatic Hadrian, reaffirmed the now 200-year-old agreement with the Parthians that the Euphrates River should mark the border between their two respective spheres of interest. Relations between the two powers remained relatively peaceful for the next half century, until Parthian king Vologases IV (r. 147–191) invaded Armenia and Syria. Roman emperor Marcus Aurelius responded by invading both Syria and Mesopotamia in 163 CE. After capturing and

[24] Cassius Dio, 68.29.1.

burning Seleucia and Ctesiphon, the Romans were forced to withdraw after their soldiers contracted a deadly disease, probably smallpox, which was destined to devastate the Roman Empire in the years that followed.[25] In a later chapter we consider the devastating impact of disease epidemics in both the Roman and Han Empires, epidemics partly facilitated by the movement of peoples and animals along the Silk Roads.

This smallpox epidemic was just the first of a series of problems that beset the Romans during the final years of Marcus Aurelius' reign and the decades that followed. The economy began to stagnate as small-scale farmers were forced off their farms by large landowners. Some of the larger farms, known as *latifundia* or "spacious estates," gradually evolved into fortified semi-independent villages. The payment of taxes to the Roman state dried up, and inflation was rampant. As we see in the final chapter, the constitutional monarchy established by Augustus, and largely maintained by the Julio-Claudian, Flavian and Antonine dynasties, was transformed in the first half of the third century by a succession of largely military emperors, twenty-five of whom reigned in just fifty years. The rule of Marcus Aurelius' son Commodus (180–192) foreshadowed this through its incompetence and cruelty.

The succeeding Severan dynasty (193–235) attempted to restore order, but was intimidated and thwarted by the military and by ongoing confrontations with the Parthians. During the reign of Parthian king Vologases V (r. 191–208), Roman emperor Septimius Severus (r. 193–211) launched an invasion of Mesopotamia in 197 CE, again capturing Seleucia and Ctesiphon, and his successor, Caracalla (r. 211–217), also marched against the Parthians and captured the ancient city of Erbil, east of the Tigris and deep in Parthian territory. But Caracalla was assassinated by his own soldiers the following year, and his successor, Macrinus (r. 217–218), had no option other than to settle the relationship with Parthia by agreeing to pay the Parthians more than 200 million *denarii*. The relationship between Rome and Parthia in the third century, and the final decades of the Parthian Empire before its demise at the hands of the Sasanians in 224 CE, are considered further in the final chapter of this book. By the time a tough soldier and shrewd administrator named Diocletian (r. 285–305) was able to restore order in Rome by assuming absolute power and diminishing the role of the Senate, the First Silk Roads Era was over, because it was during the same period of crisis in Rome in the first half of the third century that the Han Dynasty in China, and the Kushan and Parthian Empires that had facilitated Silk Roads trade for centuries, all collapsed.

[25] Bivar 1983, pp. 93–94; Brossius 2006, p. 10.

Parthian Role in Silk Roads Exchanges

The final question this chapter addresses concerns the role of the Parthians in Silk Roads trade. Historians do have available a number of sources that shed light on the relationship between the Parthian Empire and the Romans and Han Chinese, but even with this evidence it is not always easy to determine precisely what role Parthian officials and merchants played in the operation of the Silk Roads. To conclude this chapter, we consider in chronological order Greco-Roman and Han Chinese references that touch upon the commercial relationship between these three imperial states between the second century BCE and the third century CE.

Second and First Centuries before the Common Era

The earliest source evidence we have is found in the histories of the Early Han Dynasty, the *Shiji* and *Han Shu*. In Chapter 3 we followed the exploits of Han envoy Zhang Qian, who traveled extensively in Inner Eurasia during the late 130s/early 120s BCE and gathered considerable information about the many states of the region, including Anxi, the Chinese name for Arsacid Parthia. Zhang Qian's report constitutes the first known Chinese account of this major Eurasian power, and is thus of considerable significance. The crucial and reasonably comprehensive information is included in the *Shiji* of Sima Qian:

> Anxi is situated several thousand *li* west of the region of the Great Yuezhi. The people are settled on the land, cultivating the fields and growing rice and wheat. They also make wine out of grapes. They have walled cities like the people of Dayuan, the region containing several hundred cities of various sizes. The kingdom, which borders the Gui River, is very large, measuring several thousand *li* square. Some of the inhabitants are merchants who travel by carts or boats to neighboring countries, sometimes journeying several thousand *li*. The coins of the country are made of silver and bear the face of the king. When the king dies, the currency is immediately changed and new coins issued with the face of his successor.[26]

The *Han Shu*, completed several decades after the Shiji, contains additional and presumably updated information:

> "It is distant by 11,600 *li* from Xian ... it adjoins Kangju in the north, Wuishanli (Alexandria, possibly Heart in modern Afghanistan)[27] in the east and Tiaozhi (Mesopotamia) in the west[28] ... It is situated on the Gui River ... East of Anxi are

[26] SJ 123, Watson 1993, pp. 234–235. [27] HS, Hulsewe and Loewe, p. 112, n 250.
[28] SJ 123, Watson 1993, p. 235; also HS 96A, 13B.

the Da Yuezhi . . . The territory extends for several thousand *li* and it is the largest of the states . . . Its merchants travel by vehicle or ship to the neighboring states . . . the eastern border is several thousand *li* from the king's capital."[29]

In discussing the military and political strength of Anxi/Parthia, we also learn from the *Shiji* that the Parthians had already incorporated a region named Tiaozhi (probably Mesopotamia) into their empire. Tiaozhi is described as an agricultural state bordering the "Western Sea" (perhaps the Persian Gulf) that during the mid-second century BCE was subjugated by the Parthians: "The ruler of Anxi gives orders to the many petty chiefs of Tiaozhi to the west, and regards them as his vassals."[30] The *Han Shu* also makes explicit mention of a meeting between Parthian forces and an ambassadorial party sent by Han Wudi following the initial expedition of Zhang Qian, observing that: "A force of 20,000 Anxi cavalry was sent by their king to meet and escort Emperor Wu's envoys to the capital."[31] Zhang Qian's original visit to Bactria probably occurred a decade or so following the death of Parthian king Mithridates I (r. c. 171–138 BCE), who had been responsible for a substantial expansion in the size of the Parthian realm, including the conquest of Mesopotamia.

The *Han Shu* also discusses the size and urbanized nature of the Parthian realm, and its impressive coinage:

"Several hundred towns, large and small, belong (to Anxi) . . . When in the course of a journey one is about to approach (the capital) one passes through towns which can be numbered by the ten, and where settlements are uninterrupted . . . They use silver to make coin, the obverse being decorated exclusively with the (image) of the king's face and the reverse with that of his consort. Whenever a king dies a change of coinage is cast."[32]

Both of these Early Han Dynasty texts are clearly describing a large and powerful sedentary state to the west of the realm of the Yuezhi (so west of Bactria) with an established silver coinage, extensive fortified urban centers and flourishing agriculture. They note Parthian control of Mesopotamia and (probably) parts of the Persian Gulf, and both sources also explicitly state that considerable long-distance commercial activity by land and sea is occurring under the control of merchants, who sometimes journey several thousand *li* to conduct their business. Zhang Qian's original diplomatic mission to Bactria was followed up by the dispatching of numerous subsequent embassies to many of the states of Inner Eurasia. This included Anxi/Parthia, and the first Chinese diplomatic caravan to Parthia probably arrived in 106 BCE via Bactria, to be met by

[29] HS 96A 14A, 14B. [30] SJ 123, Watson 1993, p 235. [31] HS 96A 14A.
[32] HS 96A 14A.

a contingent of 20,000 Parthian cavalry, as noted earlier. This might even have been the first time the Parthians encountered Chinese silk, which would have certainly been included among the tributary goods carried by the envoys and their caravan. So here again, Parthian interest in silk and their eventual involvement in Silk Roads trade was probably sparked through Han diplomatic activity.

Along with this evidence of the relationship between the Han and Parthians, a handful of references in Greco-Roman sources suggest the possibility of direct contact between Rome and various other peoples engaged in Silk Roads trade, including the Parthians, Kushans, Indians and even the Han, during the early Roman imperial period. Chronologically the first of these references is found in the work of Roman historian Lucius Annaeus Florus (c. 74–130 CE), who was born in Africa and was active during the reigns of Trajan and Hadrian. Using material from Livy, he compiled a brief history of Rome from its foundation until 25 BCE, known as the *Epitome de T. Livio Bellorum.*

Writing about the early art that was created during the reign of Augustus (r. 27 BCE–14 CE), Florus makes the following statement: "Now that all the races of the west and south were subjugated, and also the races of the north . . . the Scythians and the Sarmatians sent ambassadors seeking friendship; the Seres too and the Indians, who live immediately beneath the sun, though they brought elephants amongst their gifts as well as precious stones and pearls, regarded their long journey, in the accomplishment of which they had spent four years, as the greatest tribute which they rendered, and indeed their complexion proved that they came from beneath another sky."[33] Of course we have no way of knowing precisely where these envoys had come from, but Florus includes sufficient detail for us to speculate that groups of Indian, Central Asian and possibly even Chinese merchants might have made direct contact with Roman officials during this crucial early period of the First Silk Roads Era.

First and Second Centuries of the Common Era

Perhaps completed around the year 1 CE, also during the reign of Augustus, Isidore of Charax's account in *Parthian Stations* of an overland route through the Parthian realm suggests that Parthian officials were controlling the activities of merchants and restricting them to government-controlled routes and infrastructure. Considerable profit was probably being generated for merchants and officials through acting as

[33] Florus, Epitomae II, 34.

middlemen or charging tariffs in Silk Roads trade between Han China and the Mediterranean; and also because of the value of Parthian manufactured goods and art objects that probably also passed in various directions along the routes. We know that trade was tightly controlled at the towns bordering the Roman and Parthian empires in Armenia and Mesopotamia, and merchants were forbidden from crossing over to the other side. However, almost nothing concrete is known about road tolls or taxes exacted from merchants active within Parthia, nor whether merchants received protection from Parthian authorities in exchange for any taxes paid.

As well as their interest in the kingdom of Armenia, located to the north of their empire, the Parthians also expanded southward into the Arabian Peninsula, both for military and for commercial purposes, even taking control of some of the ports on the Persian Gulf. *Parthian Stations* describes not only the overland routes through the Parthian Empire, but also the flourishing ports of the Persian Gulf, which connected Mesopotamia with the Indian Ocean networks. Inland, commercial oasis towns such as Palmyra, Hatra, Babylon, Seleucia and Spasinau Charax became increasingly important trade centers. We have much more to say about the role of the Parthians in Indian Ocean maritime trade in Chapter 8, including evidence that harbor fees were paid by merchants in ports controlled by the Parthians. By the first century CE the Parthians were in control of many such commercial towns and ports, and Parthian administrators often lived in them. We even have some details about the administration of these centers under Parthian control in the form of records kept by one Manesus, the *arabarch* and tax collector of Mesopotamia, and the son of Parthian king Phraates.[34]

During the first century CE the Parthians appear to have further developed their role as middlemen in Silk Roads trade with the Han. Parthian merchants and officials preferred to trade directly with the Han, especially for silk, and were apparently determined to ensure that the Romans were never able to directly gain access Chinese merchants, and circumvent the *no doubt* lucrative Parthian control of sections of the land and maritime routes. From the perspective of the Han government, Anxi was probably never considered as a possible tributary state, being far too distant and powerful. But the diplomatic and commercial relationship between the Han and Persians established late in the second century BCE, based surely on mutual strategic and commercial interests, was maintained through the first two centuries CE. The Han sources inform

[34] M. A. R. Colledge, *The Parthians*. New York: Frederick A. Praeger, 1967, pp. 62–63, 78–79.

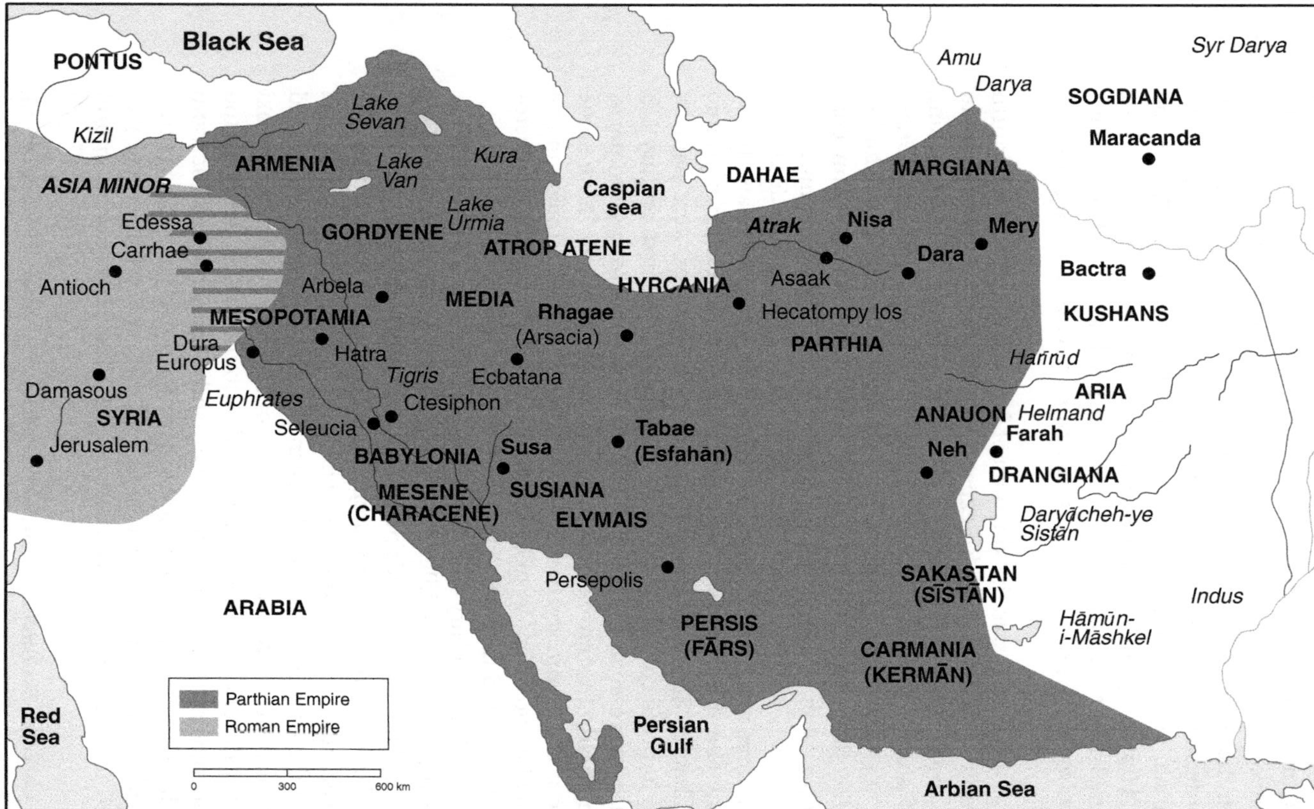

Map 6.2 Parthian Empire in the second century CE
www.iranchamber.com/history/parthians/images/parthian_empire_map.gif
www.iranpoliticsclub.net/maps/images/070%2520Roman-Parthian%2520Wars%252066%2520BC-217%2520AD%25204%2520Map.jpg

us, for example, that in the year 87 CE, during the reign of Later Han Dynasty emperor Zhang (r. 75–85 CE), Parthian king Pacorus II sent a gift of lions and Iranian gazelles to the Han court.[35]

A story recounted in the *Hou Han Shu* (*Annals of the Later Han Dynasty*) also reveals striking Han awareness of the Parthians and of their crucial role as middlemen in Silk Roads trade. The story also demonstrates just how determined the Parthians were to ensure that Roman and Chinese merchants would never be able to meet directly and disrupt the Parthians' lucrative role as intermediaries. In the year 97 CE, Ban Chao, Protector General of the Western Regions, tried to send Han military official Gan Ying on a mission to Rome (known as *Da Qin*, or "Great China" to the Han). According to the reference, Gan Ying reached Tiaozhi (possibly the trading city of Characene) near "the great sea" (the Parthian coast of the Persian Gulf), but was dissuaded by Parthian officials or merchants from going farther. He was informed that the journey to Rome would take many months and even years, so Gan Ying turned back. Here's how the *Hou Han Shu* records the conversation: "'The ocean is huge. Those making the round trip can do it in three months if the winds are favorable. However, if you encounter winds that delay you, it can take two years. That is why all the men who go by sea take stores for three years. The vast ocean urges men to think of their country, and get homesick, and some of them die. When [Gan] Ying heard this, he discontinued (his trip)."[36]

Gan Ying did manage to acquire some additional intelligence about Rome, which provides crucial evidence of the active and lucrative role the Parthians were taking in controlling Silk Roads trade between Roman and Chinese merchants: "They (the Romans) trade with Anxi [Parthia] and Tianzhu [Northwest India] by sea. The profit margin is ten to one ... The king of this country always wanted to send envoys to Han, but Anxi, wishing to control the trade in multi-colored Chinese silks, blocked the route to prevent [the Romans] getting through [to China]."[37] We have no specific reference to any other Han official who ever came this close to directly interacting with Roman traders throughout most of the First Silk Roads Era, and thus the control of the middle of the great exchange network by Parthians (and Kushans, as will be shown in the next chapter) was maintained until the end.

[35] Tao Wang, "Parthia in China: A Re-examination of the Historical Records," in V. S. Curtis and S. Stewart, *The Age of the Parthians: The Ideas of Iran*, 2, London and New York: I. B. Tauris & Co. Ltd., in association with the London Middle East Institute at SOAS and the British Museum, 2007, pp. 100–101.

[36] HHS, see Hill 2009, p. 23 who argues for identifying Taizhou with Characene instead of the previous identification with Ctesiphon.

[37] HHS, see Hill 2009, pp. 25, 27.

There is one final reference in the *Hou Han Shu*, dated to late in the second century CE, that supports the argument that the Parthians and Kushans were successful in keeping Roman and Han officials and merchants from meeting directly throughout most of the First Silk Roads Era. The source notes that an embassy of "Roman officials" (perhaps merchants from the Eastern Mediterranean) had undertaken an extraordinary journey to the Later Han capital of Luoyang in 166 CE. The reference states that the "embassy" arrived during the reign of Han emperor Huan (r. 146–168 CE) and had been sent by Emperor Antoninus Pius, "King of Rome." But as Antoninus died in 161, it is more likely that it was dispatched by one of Pius' successors, probably Marcus Aurelius (r. 161–180 CE), who was also of the Antonine family. The *Hou Han Shu* notes that the embassy came from the south (presumably by sea) and entered China from Jiaozhi (Vietnam), bringing gifts it had acquired in Southeast Asia, including ivory and tortoise shells. The reference also specifically notes that this was the first time there had been any direct contact between China and Rome.[38]

Conclusion

All the literary, numismatic and archaeological evidence we have available indicates that, from 247 BCE, when Arsaces came to power, to the overthrow of the last Parthian king by their regional successors the Sasanians in 224 CE, the Parthians maintained one of the great imperial states in ancient world history for some 470 years. Despite periods of sporadic conflict with the Romans and numerous bloody internal succession crises, the Parthian Empire, along with that of the Kushans, functioned as an effective bridge between western and eastern Eurasia, and flourished because of the strength of its military, the organization of its empire and the political recognition by Parthian elites of the crucial importance of a steady flow of commercial profit generated by Silk Roads exchanges. There is no evidence of any significant conflict between the Han Chinese and the Parthians, and only a vague suggestion of any conflict between Parthia and the Kushan Empire; the commercial relationship between the three was apparently just too important. And even though relations between Rome and Parthia were often tense, in the end the maintenance of commercial ties, and their regulation by the state, was also recognized by elites of both Eurasian powers as being vital to their mutual success. Early in the third century CE Roman emperor Caracalla (r. 211–217) sent a letter to Parthian ruler Vologases IV (r. 181–228)

[38] Hill 2009, p. 27.

proposing an alliance based on their common interest in the trade in textiles and spices.[39] Despite almost three centuries of sporadic warfare between Rome and Parthia, then, in the end the flow of commerce remained a significant consideration in the relationship between all of the great powers of ancient Eurasia during the First Silk Roads Era.

Selected Further Reading

Bivar, A. D. H., "The Political History of Iran under the Arsacids," in E. Yarshater, ed., *Cambridge History of Iran*, 3.1. Cambridge: Cambridge University Press, 1983.

Curtis, J. and N. Tallis, eds., *Forgotten Empire: The World of Ancient Persia*. Berkeley and Los Angeles: University of California Press, 2005.

Curtis, V. S. and S. Stewart, *The Age of the Parthians: The Ideas of Iran*, 2. London and New York: I. B. Tauris & Co. Ltd., in association with the London Middle East Institute at SOAS and the British Museum, 2007.

Dandamaev, M. A., *A Political History of the Persian Empire*. Leiden: Brill Publishing, 1989.

Daryae, T., "Western and Central Eurasia," in C. Benjamin, ed., *The Cambridge World History Vol IV*. Cambridge: Cambridge University Press, 2015.

Debevoise, N. C., *A Political History of Parthia*. Chicago, 1938.

Frye, R. M., *The Heritage of Persia: The Pre-Islamic History of One of the World's Great Civilizations*. New York: World Publishing Company, 1963 (Reprinted by Mazda Publishers, 2004).

Green, P., *Alexander the Great and the Hellenistic Age*. London: Phoenix, 2007.

May, T., "Pastoral Nomads," in C. Benjamin, ed., *The Cambridge World History Vol. IV*. Cambridge: Cambridge University Press, 2015.

Olbrycht, M. J., "Parthia and Nomads of Central Asia. Elements of Steppe Origin in the Social and Military Developments of Arsacid Iran," in Schneider, I, ed., Mitteilungen des SFB "Differenz und Integration" 5, Halle: Orientwissenchaft, 2003, pp. 69–109.

Shayegan, M. R., *Arsacids and Sasanians: Political Ideology in Post-Hellenistic and Late Antique Persia*. Cambridge: Cambridge University Press, 2011.

[39] Herodian of Antioch, 4.10. See E. H. Seland, "Ancient Afghanistan and the Indian Ocean: Maritime Links of the Kushan Empire ca 50–200 CE," in *Journal of Indian Ocean Archaeology*, No. 9, 2013, pp. 66ff., at p. 72.

7 The Kushan Empire

At the Crossroads of Ancient Eurasia

After considering the critical roles played in the First Silk Roads Era by pastoral nomadic steppe empires, and by the Han, Roman and, most recently, Parthian Empires, in this chapter we turn to another key player in the history of ancient Eurasia, the Kushan Empire. The Kushans were one of the major facilitators of Silk Roads exchanges because, not only did most of the key crossroads of the major trans-Eurasian land routes end up being under their direct political control but Kushan elites appear to have been very favorably disposed toward trade and cultural exchange. Like their Sogdian, Parthian and South Asian counterparts, Kushan merchants and officials functioned as important intermediaries in the movement of goods and ideas across Eurasia.

In this chapter we address key questions about the Kushans, probably the least known of the four sedentary Eurasian empires of the First Silk Roads Era. These questions are similar to those we asked about the Parthians: how did the ancestors of the Kushans transition from nomadic pastoralists into sedentary imperial rulers? How did the early Kushan kings construct what became a vast empire? What evidence do we have about the relationship between the Kushans and the other nomadic and sedentary powers of Eurasia? And finally, what was the role of the Kushans in facilitating Silk Roads exchanges? Before we can attempt to answer any of these questions, however, we must first consider the types of evidence that historians have available to help them construct a tentative history of the Kushan Empire, and of their important role in the history of ancient Eurasia.

Evidence for the Kushans

The evidence discussed in what follows indicates that, from the early first century to the early third century CE, the Kushan kings and their courts controlled a large and stable political entity at the heart of Inner Eurasia, which included extensive regions of the modern states of Uzbekistan, Tajikistan and Turkmenistan; the western fringes of modern Xinjiang

Province in China; most of the territory of Afghanistan and Pakistan; and large regions of northern and central India, including the Ganges Basin. It was this political, economic and social stability that helped make possible the smooth flow of material and nonmaterial commodities along the trade routes, particularly as the bulk of land-based trade out of Han China passed directly through their territory, before linking to ports on the coast of South Asia and maritime routes across the Indian Ocean. Internal political stability was reinforced by cordial foreign relations. Most of the evidence suggests that the Kushans maintained relatively peaceful relations with neighboring states, including the Han, Sogdians and Parthians, as well as various contiguous pastoral nomadic confederations like the Saka. This is an additional reason why the Kushans deserve their reputation as one of the key facilitators of the First Silk Roads Era. Kushan-generated regional conflict would have had the potential to disrupt the network the same way that occasional periods of conflict between the Parthians and Romans disrupted land routes further west. The Kushans were thus not only one of the great powers of an era in which much of Afro-Eurasia was controlled by just four imperial dynasties, but their success as a state was crucial to the success of the Silk Roads network. And because of the long-term historical legacy of the First Silk Roads Era, the Kushans not only exerted cultural and economic influence on their contemporaries, but also on their regional successors, the Sasanians, Guptas, Kidarites and Hephthalites, through to the emergence of Islam early in the seventh century CE.

Yet, despite the importance of the Kushans, they remain the most mysterious of all the ancient Eurasian empires. Like the Sasanians and a handful of other states, the Kushans produced no significant body of literature; or, if they did, no examples of this have yet been discovered. The Kushans were of pastoral nomadic origin, and nomads on the whole did not generate a great deal of written material. The only samples of Kushan-generated writing we possess are coin legends and a small number of inscriptions, mostly fragmentary, that have been discovered at sites such as Surkh Kotal and Rabatak, both in modern Afghanistan. But the good news for historians is that the Kushans were reasonably well known to several of their neighbors, and the literature of these contemporary states does contain occasional references to both the Yuezhi (the ancestors of the Kushans, who we met in the early chapters of this book) and to the Kushan Empire itself. Han Dynasty histories are particularly useful, including the three we have already drawn upon so frequently: the *Shiji*, *Han Shu* and *Hou Han Shu*. There are also oblique references in other South and Central Asian sources; in a few fragmentary Greco-Roman

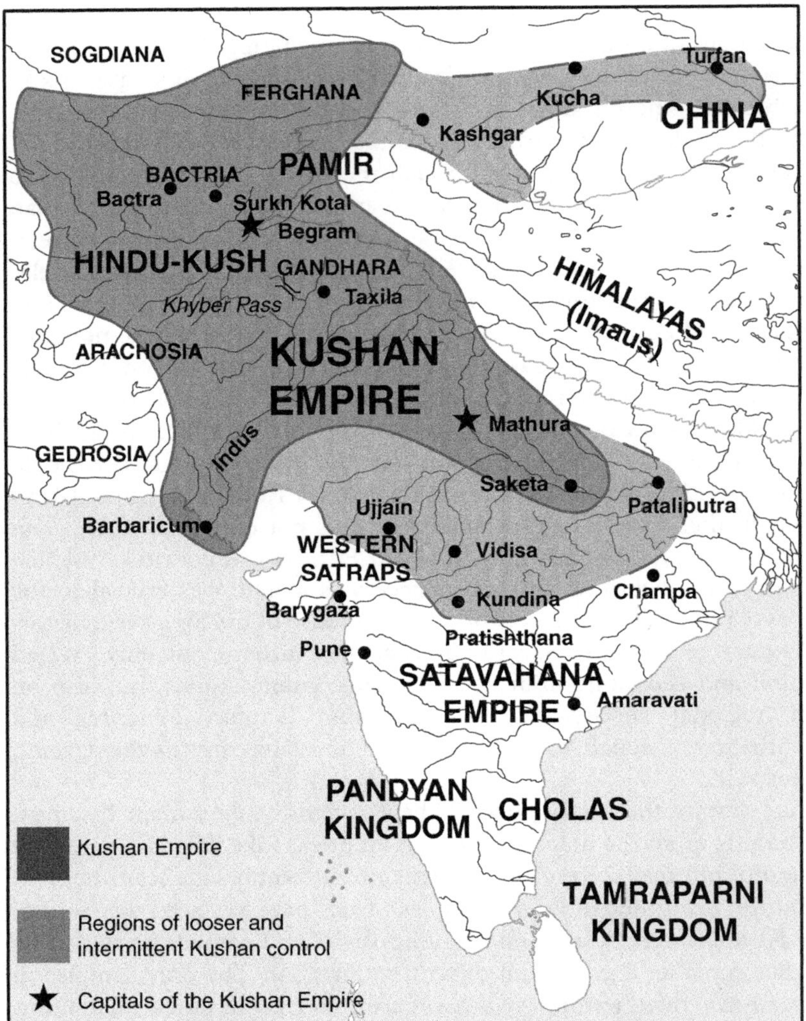

Map 7.1 Kushan Empire in the second century CE

sources; in the invaluable first-century CE mariners' handbook, the *Periplus of the Erythraean Sea* (considered in detail in the next chapter); and even in a handful of Islamic histories written following the conquest of Central Asia by Muslims, centuries after the Kushans had disappeared. These often-incidental references, particularly those in the Han histories, have been invaluable in helping historians piece together the history and legacy of the Kushan Empire.

Archaeology has also added considerably to our knowledge of the Kushans, although few examples of Kushan monumental building have survived. References in post-Han Chinese literary sources, written in the centuries following the collapse of the First Silk Roads network, make occasional reference to palaces, Buddhist stupas, monasteries and dynastic sanctuaries built by the Kushan kings. One example comes from fifth century CE Chinese Buddhist pilgrim Faxien, who traveled through former Kushan territory on a pilgrimage to India. He noted that the Kushan monarch Kanishka I (r. c. 127–153 CE[1]) had "raised a stupa ... more than forty chang (400 feet) high and adorned with all precious metals. Of all the stupas and temples ever seen ... there was none that could be compared with this one for beauty and majesty. It is said that of all the stupas in Jambudvipa, this is the highest one."[2] According to a later Chinese source, the record of the travels of Tang Dynasty pilgrim Xuanzang, Kanishka's stupa was still standing 200 years later when Xuanzang passed through the same region: "At the side of the Pippala tree there is also a stupa built by king Kanishka. Its height is 400 feet; its base measures one li and a half in circumference and is 150 feet high. On top of it he has erected (a shaft with) twenty-five discs of gilded copper one above another, and inside the stupa there is one hu (measure) of relics of the Tathagata" (Buddha).[3]

Between the 1920s and 1960s, archaeologists from the Soviet Union, France and Britain attempted to systematically unlock some of the secrets of the history of ancient Central Asia, including the role of the Kushans. Pioneering pre–World War II Soviet expeditions uncovered and stratigraphically dated the remains of a number of ancient settlements, burial sites and artifacts, although the place of the Kushans in the history of Central Asia was far from clear. After the war, Soviet and Central Asian archaeologists worked on sites at Toprak-Kala in Khorezm, Afrasiab (the town site of ancient Samarkand), and at

[1] Establishing a precise chronology for Kanishka (or any of the Kushan monarchs) has been one of the most challenging questions in ancient Central Asian history for more than a century. This author (in line with most specialists in the field) accepts the conclusion of Harry Falk, which dates the first year of Kanishka's reign to 127 CE. See H. Falk, "The Yuga of Sphujiddhvaja and the Era of the Kusanas," *Silk Roads Art and Archaeology* 7 (2001), pp. 121–130.

[2] E. Zurcher, "The Yueh-chih and Kanishka in the Chinese Sources," in A. L. Basham, ed., *Papers on the Date of Kanishka. Leiden: Brill*, 1968. T 2087 II p. 879.3.15, pp. 278–279.

[3] T 2053 II 230.1.28. See Zurcher 1968, pp. 383–384.

Varaksha in the Bukharan oasis. Through the late 1940s and early 1950s, investigations continued in parts of Tajikistan, Uzbekistan and Turkmenistan, which led to the discovery of the remains of Kushan monumental structures such as stone column bases, and also other material artifacts including pottery, terracotta figures and Kushan and Roman coins.

Between 1959 and 1963, Soviet archaeologist G. A. Pugachenkova excavated the remains of what was probably an early Yuezhi dynastic sanctuary at Khalchayan, in the Surkhan Darya Valley of southern Uzbekistan. The superb wall frescoes and terracotta figures Pugachenkova uncovered have been interpreted as depicting some sort of battle between resident Saka forces and the invading Yuezhi for control of the Greco-Bactrian kingdom further to the south. Inscriptions using the "Bactrian" script, which was adopted by the Kushans (and is explored further in what follows), were discovered in the 1960s at the site of Kara-Tepe in Termez on the Amu Darya, also in Uzbekistan.[4] At the same time, and further south again, French archaeologists working at the site of Surkh Kotal in Afghanistan were excavating what they eventually concluded was an important Kushan dynastic sanctuary. They uncovered monumental structures including Zoroastrian fire temples, along with statues of the Kushan kings and a twenty-five-line inscription using the same Bactrian script discovered at Kara-Tepe.

In Pakistan meanwhile, British and South Asian archaeologists worked for decades on what was later deemed to be a Kushan royal palace at Taxila, near Islamabad, an urban complex that was later declared a UNESCO World Heritage Site in 1980. French archaeologists excavated a second Kushan palace complex at Kapisa near Begram in central Afghanistan in the late 1930s. In a storage room within the complex they discovered a collection of valuable luxury art objects that were at first interpreted as comprising part of some Kushan royal "art museum," but are now thought to be a cache of luxury trade goods that were being shipped along the Silk Roads during the Kushan Era. Among the discoveries were Roman bronze sculptures, Han lacquer boxes, superbly painted Roman and Egyptian glass vessels depicting scenes such as the lighthouse at Alexandria and an African leopard hunt and more than 1,000 pieces of Indian carved ivory and bone sculptures of placidly smiling women and mythical river creatures. We have more to say about

[4] For an overview of the work of pioneering Soviet archaeologists in Central Asia, see G. M. Bongard-Levin and B. Y. Stavisky, "Central Asia in the Kushan Period," *Kushan Studies in the USSR (1968 Dushanbe Conference Proceedings)*, pp. 29–52.

the significance of this discovery later in this chapter. We also explore in greater detail the historical importance of large numbers of sculptures and other art objects that were produced, apparently under Kushan patronage, at workshops in the regions of Gandhara in northern Pakistan and Mathura in northern India. The diffusion along the Silk Roads of the distinctive styles of religious and secular sculpture produced in Gandhara and Mathura has helped historians trace the spread of Buddhism out of India and through Central Asia into East Asia, a process of crucial historical significance discussed in the final chapter of this book.

All these early and more recent archaeological discoveries, reinforced by source references in ancient annals and histories, have certainly helped specialists construct an outline history of the Kushan Empire. But the most important evidence for the Kushans remains numismatic; thousands of Kushan copper, silver and gold coins have been discovered throughout the extent of their territory and further afield. Their interpretation by skilled numismatists has been fundamental to the fleshing out of a more coherent and comprehensive Kushan political, economic and cultural history. Much of the story of the Kushans that follows is only made possible by numismatic evidence, supplemented by source references, a handful of inscriptions and the discoveries of archaeologists. We have already outlined in earlier chapters the prelude to Kushan history in the story of the thirty-year migration of the pastoral nomadic Yuezhi confederation, who were evicted from their homelands on the northwestern borders of Han China in c. 166 BCE by the Xiongnu.[5] Now we pick up the story with the Yuezhi settled in northern Bactria, then go on to explore the reigns of the Early and Great Kushan kings, who collectively played such an important role in the First Silk Roads Era. In the final chapter of this book we conclude the story with an account of the Late Kushan monarchs and their role in the collapse not only of their own empire but of the entire Silk Roads network.

Yuezhi in Northern Bactria

Following their lengthy migration from the borders of western Han China, by roughly 130 BCE the Yuezhi were comfortably settled on the northern fringe of Bactria. As we saw noted earlier in this book, the Yuezhi were so well situated that they refused to go back to China with

[5] For a recent account of the history of the Yuezhi, see C. Benjamin, "The Yuezhi," in *The Oxford Research Encyclopedia of Asian History*. New York: Oxford University Press, 2017, at: http://asianhistory.oxfordre.com/view/10.1093/acrefore/9780190277727.001.0001/acrefore-9780190277727-e-49.

Zhang Qian and join a Han alliance against the Xiongnu confederation. The Han sources imply that the group that went on to found the Kushan Empire was directly descended from one of the tribal components of the Yuezhi confederation. You will remember that, although Zhang Qian was unsuccessful in convincing the resettled Yuezhi to return with him, the information he brought back to the Han court helped persuade Emperor Wudi to adopt an expansionist policy that led eventually to the creation of the huge Han tributary empire by the early first century BCE. This brought the Han into direct diplomatic, military and commercial relations with the elites and merchants of many of the states of Inner Eurasia for the first time.

Yuezhi/Kushan history then enters a kind of evidentiary "dark ages" late in the second century BCE, although their affairs are illuminated briefly again between c. 50 and 25 BCE. In what looks like a later revision to the text of the *Han Shu* we learn that the Yuezhi confederation had now divided into five "princedoms" (called *yabghu* or *xihou* in Chinese) that had apparently settled in various locations throughout Bactria. This updated information might have been obtained from the Office of the Protector General of the Western Regions, which was established in 60/59 BCE, but it might also have been provided as late as 75 CE to *Han Shu* author Ban Gu by his relative Ban Chao, who served as a protector general of the western regions during the first century CE. What we can glean from the revision is that sometime between the early and mid-first century BCE, the Yuezhi had made a decision to split their confederation and settle in five different princedoms in various parts of their realm. We have no real idea why this split occurred: perhaps the death of a unifying ruler led to the reemergence of older tribal, ethnic or political divisions within the confederation. We simply don't know, but whatever its cause, the division lasted for more than a century.

The "dark ages" descended again around 25 BCE, with the Yuezhi living in their five *xihou* scattered across Bactria. The exact location of each of these princedoms within modern Afghanistan has long been debated by specialists, with still no consensus. The *xihou* of the Xuimi might have been located in the Upper Wakhan Darya Valley; that of the Shuangmi north of Khalchayan in the Upper Surkhan Darya Valley; the Guishuang (which would give its name to the Kushan Empire) might have been based at Waksh; and the fourth *xihuo* of the Xitun was perhaps situated between Hutsao and Gaofu. Locating the final *xihou* is even more challenging than locating the other four. The *Han Shu* suggests it might have been based in Kabul, after which it was apparently named, but the later *Hou Han Shu* disputes this, and most scholars agree that the Kabul region was under the control of Indo-Parthians at this time, not the

Yuezhi.[6] Wherever the princedoms were located, the Yuezhi were collectively still in apparent control of Bactria, which they ruled from their "walled cities."[7] The Han sources suggest that the Yuezhi princedoms had adopted a semisedentary, urbanized lifeway and that some of them were even issuing coinage in imitation of preexisting Greco-Bactrian issues. By the time the Han chronicles took notice of the Yuezhi again in the first century CE, they had become a reunited and powerful confederation once more, this time under the leadership of a single prince of the Guishuang dynasty, Kujula Kadphises.

The Early Kushans: Kujula Kadphises Constructs an Empire (c. 25–c. 85 CE)

As we consider our first question – how the ancestors of the Kushans transitioned from nomadic pastoralists to sedentary imperial rulers – we note that numismatic evidence demonstrates, not surprisingly, that the previous sedentary Greek rulers of Bactria exerted economic and cultural influence over the early Kushans. An independent Greek kingdom had been established in Bactria in c. 250 BCE, following the revolt of a Greek *satrap* named Diodotus against his Seleucid masters. Over the next 100 years a series of successful Greco-Bactrian kings had extended their control southward across the Hindu Kush into northern India, establishing an Indo-Greek kingdom there. Beginning in the mid-second century BCE, however, the Greco-Bactrians had come under attack by militarized nomads including the Saka. The arrival of the Yuezhi in c. 130 BCE led to the partial collapse of the Greco-Bactrian kingdom, but the superb coinage issued by its kings strongly influenced the development of early Kushan coins, which are essentially copies of the *tetradrachms* of late Greco-Bactrian kings such as Eucratides, Euthydemus, Heliocles and Hermaeus. Archaeological evidence suggests a period of intensified architectural and irrigational development during the Early Kushan period, as control of the region shifted from the Greeks to the Yuezhi, and as the Yuezhi elites in turn became more skilled at ruling a sedentary state. Urban sites such as Kampyr Tepe on the northern bank of the Amu Darya, Payonkurgan near the road from Termez to Samarkand and the palace at Khalchayan discussed earlier all provide evidence of the construction of fortified Yuezhi settlements, and of

[6] For an extensive discussion of the location of the *xihou*, and particularly the "problem" of Gaofu/Kabul, see H. Falk, ed., *Kushan Histories: Literary Sources and Selected Papers from a Symposium at Berlin, December 5 to 7*, 2013. Bremen: Hempen Verlag, pp. 71ff.

[7] HS 96A 15A, 15B and 14B.

their subjugation of the region.[8] By the mid-first century CE, these transitional Yuezhi settlements in southern Uzbekistan had been incorporated into a rapidly expanding Kushan Empire.

According to the *Hou Han Shu*, sometime in the mid-first century CE a ruler of one of the five princedoms, Kujula Kadphises of the Guishuang *xihou*, successfully reunified the Yuezhi confederation under his sole leadership. The circumstances behind the reunification are unclear, but the conquest of the Kabul Valley in the midst of Yuezhi territory by an Indo-Parthian ruler named Gondophares (r. c. 20–46 CE) must have played a role.[9] Kujula Kadphises is actually named as a prince at the court of Gondophares in an inscription found at Takht-i Bahi, dated to 45 CE.[10] This implies that Yuezhi elites were already significant players in regional politics, an impression possibly supported by the 1978 discovery by archaeologist Victor Sarianidi of burial mounds at Tilya-tepe ("Golden Hill"), near Shibergan in Afghanistan. Tilya-tepe might have been part of the Xidun princedom of the Yuezhi. Sarianidi dated the graves to the early first century CE (the same period that Kujula Kadphises was a prince in Gondophares' court), and the deceased may have been Yuezhi princes, although the identification of the interred remains a contentious problem among specialists. Seven graves were excavated, and collectively they yielded some 20,000 artifacts, including superb gold jewelry (including an Indian gold medallion depicting the Buddha) and objects made of iron and bronze, semiprecious stones and silk. The artistic styles represented demonstrate a wide syncretic range of cultural influences, including Chinese, Greek and Roman, Bactrian, Indian and nomadic. A *terminus post quem* (a Latin term that means "earliest possible date") for the mound is provided by the discovery of a *denarius* of the Roman emperor Tiberius (r. 14–37 CE) among the hoard.[11]

[8] See, for example, K. Abdullaev, "Nomadism in Central Asia. The Archaeological Evidence (2nd–1st Centuries B.C.)," in A. Invernizzi, ed., *In the Land of the Gryphons. Papers on Central Asian Archaeology in Antiquity*. Firenze, 1995, pp. 151ff.; E. V. Rtveladze, "Kampyr-tepe: Structures, Written Documents and Coins," *Bulletin of the Asia Institute* No. 8 (Boston, MA, 1994/5), pp. 141ff.; K. Abdullaev, "Payonkurgan: New Archaeological Discoveries in Northern Bactria," *CIAA Newsletter No 10* (November 1999), pp. 7–9; L. Nehru, "Khalchayan Revisited," in *Silk Roads Art and Archaeology* 6 (1999/2000), pp. 216ff.

[9] On evidence for Gondophares, see, for example, E. Errington, J. Cribb, and M. Claringbull, eds., *The Crossroads of Asia: Transformation in Image and Symbol in the Art of Ancient Afghanistan and Pakistan*. London: The Ancient India and Iran Trust, 1992.

[10] See B. Puri, "The Kushans," in J. Harmatta, ed., *History of Civilizations of Central Asia*, vol. II. Paris: UNESCO, 1994, p. 248.

[11] See M. J. Olbrycht, "Archaeological Discoveries at Tillya-Tepe and Parthia's Relationship with Bactria," in F. Serra ed., *Parthica. Incontri di Culture nel Mondo Antico*, 18, 2016; also Hill 2009, pp. 336ff.; and report of lecture by A. Bivar, *CIAA Newsletter No. 3* (July 1996), p. 10.

Along with this numismatic and archaeological evidence, the *Hou Han Shu* explicitly describes the rise to power of Kujula and the Kushans, and thus helps answer our second question about how the early Kushan kings constructed what became a vast empire. The *Hou Han Shu* was not compiled until centuries after the events it describes, but its author, Fan Ye, had access to many Han Dynasty documents, and his account is generally regarded as accurate. Perhaps in response to the occupation of the Kabul Valley by Gondophares, Kujula moved decisively to unite the five Yuezhi princedoms under the name of the Guishuang before commencing a series of expansionary campaigns of his own, apparently in an attempt to create a Kushan empire. Kujula led united Yuezhi/Kushan forces across the Hindu Kush Mountains and down into the Kabul Valley, which he conquered, evicting Gondophares before continuing south into Kashmir and the Swat Valley of modern Pakistan. Kujula issued coins that were essentially copies of the preexisting regional denominations and types already circulating in each of the areas he brought under his control. But the first Kushan monarch did adopt the innovation, using Indian Kharosthi script, of naming himself *Maharaja Rajarajasa Devaputra Kujula Kara Kadphises*, or "Great King of Kings. Son of a Divine Being. King Kujula Kadphises." According to the *Hou Han Shu*, Kujula was "more than eighty years old when he died."[12] He was succeeded by his equally competent son Vima Kadphises, who continued the process of military expansion by conquering large regions of northwestern India, where he installed "generals" to administer the new territories of what was now very much a Kushan empire.[13]

Relations between the Early Kushans and the Roman and Han Empires

Kujula Kadphises' reign can be dated from c. 25 to 85 CE, although a precise chronology of the Kushans remains uncertain. If these dates are correct, Kujula was a contemporary of several Roman emperors from both the Julio-Claudian and Flavian Dynasties. In considering our third question about the possible relationship between the Kushans and other Eurasian states, we noted in the previous chapter that Roman historians such as Florus described ambassadors from the land of the Seres (China) and India traveling to Rome during this same period, although whether these were independent merchants or some kind of official delegation from Central and South Asian states is

[12] Hill 2009, p. 29. [13] *Hou Han Shu* 118.pa (Zurcher 1968, p. 367).

impossible to determine.[14] Numismatic evidence does indicate some sort of indirect Roman influence on the early Kushan kings. One series of copper *tetradrachms* issued by Kujula depicts a bust closely modeled on that of Roman ruler Augustus on the obverse side, and a curule chair – a symbolic seat upon which Roman magistrates who held imperium were entitled to sit – on the reverse. This depiction of Roman motifs on early Kushan coins is surely further evidence of increasing Roman involvement in transregional Silk Roads trade following the advent of Augustus.

As the Kushan realm expanded under the early kings, it grew into a huge empire that eventually straddled most of the major east–west and north–south trade routes of Central Asia, including routes that gave access to the seaports of northwestern India via the Indus Valley. This meant that the Kushans were ideally positioned to both facilitate and benefit from Silk Roads trade. We have already noted that, in 77 CE the Roman senator Pliny the Elder had provided striking evidence of the volume and value of that trade by noting that it was costing the Romans "100 million sesterces every year."[15] How the Kushans might have benefited from this Roman expenditure can only be surmised, however. As is the case with the Parthians, we have little direct evidence about how trade was conducted in the Kushan Empire, nor of what tolls or fees were probably extracted from merchants. Yet given the undoubted wealth of the Kushans, as demonstrated particularly through their coinage, it is a reasonable assumption that at least part of that wealth was generated through tolls or other fees charged to merchants who were actively engaged in moving Han exports out of the Tarim Basin and either west or south through Kushan territory, as well as importing high-value goods from the West back into Central Asian and on to Han China.

Kujula and his successors were soon powerful enough to exert some sort of Kushan political influence on the western fringes of the huge Han tributary empire. In a 1984 study of the coins of the ancient city-state of Khotan, numismatist Joe Cribb provided convincing evidence of direct Kushan political and economic control of Khotan and Kashgar, two of the major Silk Roads centers in the Tarim Basin, at various times during the first century CE.[16] This political involvement with the fringes of the Han Empire also brought the Kushans into

[14] See Puri 1994, p. 256, for examples of these various references to Asian embassies in Roman sources including Dio Cassius, Florus, Pliny the Elder and Pliny the Younger.

[15] Pliny, *NH* XII.84.

[16] J. Cribb, "The Sino-Kharosthi Coins of Khotan," *Numismatic Chronicle* (7th Series 1984), 144, pp. 128–152.

a closer relationship, sometimes cordial, sometimes conflicted, with Han officials, including General Ban Chao, who was sent to the western regions during the first century CE to help protect Chinese interests there, mostly from the Xiongnu. There is some evidence in the "Biography of Ban Chao" (in the *Hou Han Shu*) that a loose alliance was sometimes in place between Han and Kushan military forces against their common foe the Xiongnu.[17] Ban Chao may have sought Kushan assistance toward the end of Kujula's reign, and then permitted the Kushans to exercise some economic control over Khotan, Kashgar and other Tarim Basin states in return for their support. Any Kushan political and economic control over the key town-states of the western regions would have further facilitated the movement of Han export commodities out of the Tarim Basin and on into Bactria.

In the year 88 CE an incident occurred between the Kushans and Ban Chao that suggests the Kushans may have overstepped the bounds of their relationship with the Han. According to the *Hou Han Shu*, the Kushan court informed Ban Chao that they would like to enter into some sort of a marriage alliance with the Han court, an initiative apparently proposed by Kujula Kadphises' successor, Vima Takh(tu), who had succeeded his father a few years earlier. For whatever reason, Ban Chao decided to oppose the idea and refused to allow the Kushan diplomatic party safe passage through the Tarim Basin and on to Chang'an. In response, two years later in 90 CE, the Kushans dispatched a formidable cavalry contingent of 70,000 mounted archers under the leadership of a viceroy named Xie to confront Ban Chao. Ban Chao was convinced that a force this large could not remain in the arid region of the western Tarim Basin for long, particularly after the difficulties of crossing the passes through the Pamirs and down into the arid basin. He captured and executed a group of Kushan envoys who had been sent to a nearby city-state for assistance, and did all he could to deny the Kushan forces any possibility of obtaining supplies of food and water. The Kushan forces were eventually exhausted by Ban Chao's "scorched earth" policy, and in the end agreed to apologize to the general, who then allowed them to withdraw without offering battle.[18] The following year, Ban Chao's success in pacifying the Tarim Basin states was rewarded when he was appointed protector general of the western regions.

[17] HHS 776.b and 77.7a; Zurcher 1968, pp. 369–370.
[18] HHS 776.b and 77.7a; Zurcher 1968, pp. 369–370.

The Early Kushans: Kings Vima Takh(tu) and Vima Kadphises (c. 85–c. 126 CE)

Kujula was succeeded by his son Vima Takh(tu) (r. c. 85–100 CE) and grandson Vima Kadphises (r. c. 100–126). The *Hou Han Shu* mentions only Vima Kadphises as Kujula's successor, but the existence of a third early Kushan monarch had long been suspected because of inscriptional and numismatic references to a mysterious ruler known only by his title, "Soter Megas" or Great King. The identification of Vima Takh(tu) as the second king of the Kushans (and probably also as Soter Megas) is the result of an important discovery made in 1995 of a stone inscription in Bactrian script, in the name of King Kanishka, the successor of Vima Kadphises and thus the fourth king of the dynasty. This "Rabatak Inscription" (so named because of the location in Afghanistan where it was discovered) refers to the first year of a new "Kanishkan Era" in Kushan history. The new era might have been named to commemorate Kanishka's conquest of the Ganges Valley,[19] but the real value of the inscription is that it explicitly lists the previous kings of the Kushans as Kujula Kadphises (great grandfather), Vima Takh(tu) (grandfather) and Vima Kadphises (father).[20]

The inscription seems to confirm numismatic evidence in the form of a double-busted coin discovered in the nineteenth century that depicts two different Kushan rulers, the left face bearded with the *tamgah* (personal symbol) of Vima Kadphises in the rear, the right face smooth with the *tamgah* of Soter Megas (presumably Vima Takh[tu]) in front.[21] According to the *Hou Han Shu*, Kujula was more than eighty years old when he died, so his son and successor, Vima Takh(tu), must also have been an elderly man, making a short period of joint rule with his son Vima Kadphises (as depicted on the coin) eminently sensible. Kujula's coin issues had been eclectic and had varied in weight, design and denomination throughout the different territories of the early empire that Kujula had brought under Kushan control. But his immediate successors standardized the Kushan copper coinage and then minted the first ever gold Kushan coins, which adopted the practice of engraving an image of the king on the obverse and a deity on the reverse. The discovery of coins issued by the two Vimas over a wide geographic area, stretching from

[19] Hill 2009, p. 595.

[20] J. Cribb, "The Early Kushan Kings: New Evidence for Chronology. Evidence from the Rabatak Inscription of Kanishka I," in M. Alram and D. Klimburg-Salter, eds., *Coins, Art and Chronology: Essays on the Pre-Islamic History of the Indo-Iranian Borderlands*. Vienna, 1999, pp. 177–205.

[21] A. Cunningham, "Coins of the Kushans, or Great Yue-Ti," *Numismatic Chronicle* 3rd ser. 12 (1893), p. 56.

Benares and Mathura in the south, through the Punjab in Pakistan, Kabul and Balkh in Afghanistan, and as far north as Samarkand in Uzbekistan, is evidence both of the size of the Kushan Empire and of its significant regional economic influence.

Earlier in this chapter we mentioned the discovery of a number of inscriptions throughout Kushan territory, many of them, like that found at Rabatak, using the so-called Bactrian script. Bactrian is an extinct eastern Iranian language that must have been spoken in Bactria and that became the official language of both the Kushans and later the Hephthalites or "White Huns" (more on them in the final chapter of this book). We know that the ancestors of the Kushans, the Yuezhi, probably spoke the Indo-European branch language of Tocharian, so their adoption of Bactrian (which the Kushans called the "Aryan Language") must have been part of an intentional policy change by the Kushan leadership. Bactrian was closely related to other Middle Iranian languages spoken in the region, including Parthian, Khwarazmian and Sogdian, so the adoption of Bactrian might simply represent a sensible decision to improve communication with the population over which the Kushans now ruled. But it might also represent a commercial decision, in that the use of Bactrian would facilitate communication between the Kushans and other key intermediaries in Silk Roads trade, particularly their neighbors the Sogdians and Parthians.

The use of Bactrian script also allowed the Kushan royalty to use coins and inscriptions to proclaim their power throughout the region in a language that was widely understood. After Kanishka promulgated the Rabatak Inscription, Bactrian became the exclusive official language of the Kushans, inscribed on all their coins using Greek letters. The adoption of Bactrian is a quintessential example of the cultural syncretism that so characterizes the First Silk Roads Era. The Kushans, whose ancestors spoke the Indo-European language of Tocharian, adopted an Iranian dialect widely spoken in the region they now controlled, but inscribed this in Greek characters, representing the long period of Hellenistic influence in the region following the advent of Alexander of Macedon more than 400 years earlier.[22]

The adoption of Greek-rendered Bactrian script is dated to the reign of the two Vimas. This is implied by the discovery in 1967 of five rock inscriptions at Dasht-i Nawar, near Ghazni in southern Afghanistan. The inscriptions are in different languages: Bactrian using Greek

[22] See J. Harmatta, "Languages and Literature in the Kushan Empire," in J. Harmatta, ed., *History of Civilizations of Central Asia*, vol. II. Paris, 1994, pp. 417ff.; and N. Sims-Williams, "New Light on Ancient Afghanistan. The Decipherment of Bactrian," SOAS, 1997.

characters, Middle Indian using Kharosthi script, an unknown (perhaps Sakan?) script and Greek and Kharosthi (both unfortunately illegible). The script refers to Vima, but whether to Vima Kadphises or to his father, Vima Takh(tu), it is impossible to know. An even more important Bactrian inscription had been discovered a decade earlier by the French at the dynastic sanctuary at Surkh Kotal. This twenty-five-line inscription commemorates the construction of a well inside the sanctuary, undertaken by a Kushan official named Nokonzoko. The inscription is dated to the year 31 of (presumably) the Kanishkan Era, and names Kanishka as "The Lord, the King of Kings, the Mighty Kanishka."[23]

The Great Kushans: King Kanishka (c. 127–153 CE)

Once Kanishka came to power Kushan history entered its most significant phase, which some scholars have termed the "Great Kushans." Indeed, A. K. Narain has argued that the era of the Great Kushans was so important that it deserves to be counted "as one of the great periods of world history";[24] while Janos Harmatta describes the era as "the Golden Age of ancient Central Asia."[25] Kanishka, who probably reigned from 127 to 153 CE, introduced a new regnal dating system and had his coins engraved from the "Year 1" of a new "Kanishkan Era." For decades scholars had assumed that this mean Kanishka had founded a new dynasty of Kushan kings, but the Rabatak inscription demonstrates that his reign was a continuation of the line of succession begun by his great-great grandfather, Kujula Kadphises. This hereditary link seems to continue, as far as we can tell, from Kanishka onward, perhaps as far as the mid-third century CE. This line of unbroken succession of more than two centuries' duration is another obvious reason for the stability and success of the Kushan Empire and its crucial role in facilitating Silk Roads exchanges.

Textual evidence suggests that Kanishka continued to expand the size of the Kushan Empire, which probably reached its greatest extent during his reign. The declaration of a new "Kanishkan Era" might have been made to reflect a successful campaign of conquest in the Ganges Basin of northern India. Certainly the *Hou Han Shu* mentions a new "Eastern Division of the Kushan Empire" (*Dongli*), which it differentiates from the Bactrian heartland of the Kushan Empire.[26] The capital of Dongli is

[23] See D. Schlumberger, "The Excavations at Surkh Kotal and the Problem of Hellenism in Bactria and India." Paris: Albert Reckitt Archaeological Lecture, 1961.

[24] A. K. Narain, "Indo-Europeans in Inner Asia," in D. Sinor, ed., *The Cambridge History of Inner Asia*. Cambridge: Cambridge University Press, 1990, reprinted 1994, p. 164.

[25] Harmatta 1994, p. 489. [26] See Hill 2009, p. 368, for discussion; also ref. on p. 33.

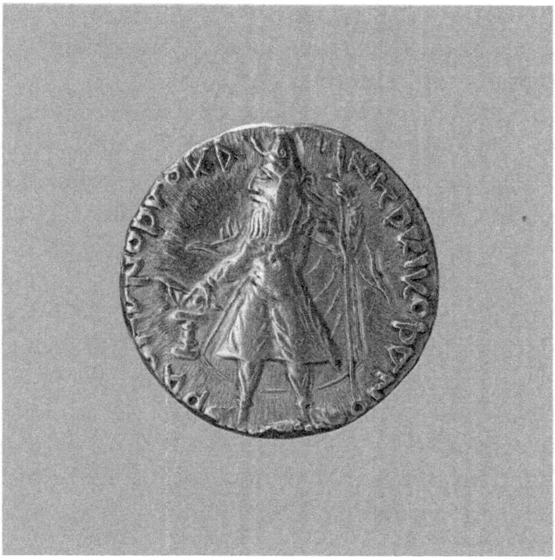

Figure 7.1 Gold coin of Kushan king Kanishka I (r. 127–153 CE), showing the king sacrificing at a fire altar
http://www.metmuseum.org/art/collection/search/39385?sortBy=Relevance&ft=kushan+coins&offset=0&rpp=20&pos=4
Credit: Bequest of Joseph H. Durkee, 1898

identified as Saketa in eastern India. Later Chinese Buddhist accounts also mention Kanishka's "punitive expedition" against India, noting that "when (that country) had been pacified, his majestic power made the world tremble and his success was complete."[27] Other Chinese sources discuss Kanishka's defeat of the city of Pataliputra in India, the capital of the Mauryan Empire three centuries earlier, which would become the capital again under the Guptas some three centuries later.

These same Chinese Buddhists sources, whose reliability needs to be handled carefully, also contain an exaggerated reference to a bloody campaign against the Parthians: "At that time the king of Anxi (Parthia) was cruel and obstinate, and having marshalled his four (classes of) soldiers he attacked Kanishka. King Kanishka immediately chastised him severely. The two armies joined battle, and the daggers and swords were raised incessantly. Thereupon King Kanishka gained his victory, and he killed altogether 900,000 Parthians."[28] Despite this account, there is no other evidence of any conflict between the Parthians and Kushans,

[27] Hill 2009, p. 369. [28] T 2058 *Fufacang Yinyuan Zhuan*. See Zurcher 1968, p. 387.

the two great powers of Central Asia, and two of the major beneficiaries of Silk Roads trade, who seem to have maintained genuinely cordial relations with each other for two centuries.

Perhaps as a result of increased Silk Roads trade through Kushan territory, Kanishka instituted a further modification of Kushan coinage during this reign. Thousands of the king's gold and copper coins have been found across Inner Eurasia, from India in the south to Uzbekistan in the north to Xinjiang in the west. On the obverse of all his coins Kanishka is always depicted standing and sacrificing at a small fire altar. Kanishka also features a range of gods from different cultural traditions on the reverse of his coins, although the great majority are Zoroastrian deities. An additional change was to also include the name of the god on the reverse.[29] Kanishka's most significant innovation was to abandon the Greek coin inscriptions used by his predecessors (and by Kanishka in his earliest issues) and replace them with inscriptions using the Bactrian language, written with Greek letters. What did not change, either during the reign of Kanishka the Great or his successors Huvishka and Vasudeva, was the standard range of copper and gold coins that Vima Kadphises had established. Indeed, the remarkable weight consistency maintained in their gold coinage by the Kushans during much of the period of their empire is yet another reason for the stability they created during the First Silk Roads Era. Immediately following the reign of Kanishka, however, there was a substantial (and unexplained) devaluation of Kushan copper coins during the reign of his successor, Huvishka.

Kanishka and Religion

It is difficult to know how to interpret the meaning of the range of different deities from several cultural traditions depicted on the coinage of the Kushan kings. Does the depiction of Greek, Indian and Zoroastrian gods reflect a tolerant and broadminded approach to religion, or a remarkably practical one in using religion to unify a huge, multicultural empire? The most common royal portrait shows the king sacrificing over a small Zoroastrian fire altar, which suggests that this was the preferred religion of the "Great Kushan" monarchs, just as it was to some Parthian and most Sasanian kings. Yet Kanishka is also recognized in Chinese sources as a great patron of Buddhism, and the depiction of the Buddha on some of his coins is among the first physical representations of the Buddha ever produced. The Buddha coins are undoubtedly an enigma because the great majority of Kanishka's coins feature Zoroastrian gods.

[29] Errington et al. 1992, p. 68.

Nonetheless, Kanishka was the only Kushan king who also issued copper and gold coins featuring images of the Buddha Sakyamuni and the Bodhisattva Maitreya. Only five examples of the gold Kanishkan Buddhist coins have survived, and the fact that each of them is in near-perfect condition supports Joe Cribb's argument that they must have been produced for a ceremonial or commemorative purpose, not for general circulation.[30]

We have already mentioned that Kanishka is venerated in Chinese Buddhist literature for building impressive stupas and monasteries throughout his realm.[31] The same sources include an account of an important Buddhist "conference" that Kanishka had convened in Kashmir. After considerable discussion of the various competing schools of Buddhism, Kanishka decreed that key Buddhist texts were to be translated from earlier languages that used Gandharan and Prakrit scripts, into the classical language of Sanskrit. Xuanzang, the Tang Dynasty Chinese pilgrim who passed through the old heartland of the Kushan Empire more than 500 years later, reported that Kanishka had the new scriptures transcribed on copper plates, which were housed in stone boxes and deposited inside a tremendous stupa more than 400 feet high.[32] This rewriting of the Buddhist Sutras into a more accessible language might have contributed to the spread of Mahayana (or "Great Vehicle") Buddhism throughout Central and East Asia by merchants and monks using the Silk Roads. We have more to say about this diffusion of Buddhism to the east in the last chapter of this book.

Gandharan and Mathuran Art under the Great Kushans

Earlier in this chapter we mentioned the art workshops that emerged under Kushan patronage in Gandhara in northern Pakistan, and Mathura in northern India. The output of both these schools has long been regarded as a quintessential example of the sort of cultural syncretism that was engendered by Silk Roads exchanges. The sacred and secular sculpture produced in both regions traveled along the trade routes and exerted powerful influences on the subsequent development of South, Central, East and even Southeast Asian art. The superb images of the Buddha and various Bodhisattvas, apparently created by the combined

[30] For depictions of these Buddhist coins, see K. Tanabe, ed., *Silk Road Coins: The Hirayama Collection*. Kamakura: The Institute of Silk Road Studies, 1993, 44, nos. 125, 126 and 127.

[31] See in particular comments by Faxian, in T 2087 II p. 879.3.15. See Zurcher 1968, pp. 278–279.

[32] Narain 1990/94, p. 166; Zurcher 1968, pp. 376, 379.

talents of Bactrian, Gandharan, South Asian and Hellenistic artists, perhaps under the explicit direction of the Kushan monarchs, were among the first ever representations of the Buddha, helping to create an entirely new iconography for the spiritual ideology of Buddhism, which underwent significant evolution during the era of the Great Kushans.

Prior to the emergence of Gandharan and Mathuran art in the late first/early second century CE, the Buddha had never been represented in physical form, but only through symbols such as footprints or an umbrella. But now, perhaps in line with some of the developments the Chinese sources discuss during the reign of Kanishka, the artists of Gandhara and Mathura created a physical representation of the Buddha that was a synthesis of a range of cultural influences. This new physical representation helped the ideology of Buddhism transform itself into a religion and spread along the trade routes as far south as Sri Lanka and as far east as Korea and Japan.[33] This diffusion of Buddhism, facilitated perhaps by the direct support of Kanishka and his successors, might constitute one of the most significant legacies of the Kushan Empire to Eurasian and world history.

Gandharan sculptors worked with a hard, gray schist common in the region, using it to sculpt superb three-dimensional sculptures of the Buddha that were influenced by statues of Greek gods like Apollo, and even Roman rulers like Augustus. Schist is a metamorphic rock that usually forms on the continental side of a convergent plate boundary, after the existing sedimentary rocks have undergone metamorphosis because of the tremendous heat and pressure caused by a tectonic plate convergence. This means that the very material that was eventually used to create the first ever representations of the Buddha was created by one of the most consequential collisions in the history of the planet, that between the Indo-Australian and Eurasian Plates, which commenced some 50 million years ago. Gandharan sculptors also used the schist to create a series of vividly realized stair riser reliefs that realistically depict musicians, dancers and sophisticated Kushan aristocracy, a rare glimpse into the social life enjoyed by Kushan elites. Their extraordinary mixture of Indian symbolism, Romano-Hellenistic architectural details and steppe-

[33] A huge literature exists on Gandharan and Mathuran art. The following examples are chosen from different periods to reflect changing interpretations over time: W. W. Tarn, *The Greeks in Bactria and India*. Cambridge: Cambridge University Press, 1938; 2nd edn., 1951; J. H. Marshall, *The Buddhist Art of Gandhara*. Cambridge: Cambridge University Press, 1960; G. A. Pugachenkova and A. Khakimov, *The Art of Central Asia*. London: Aurora Art Publishers, 1988; W. Zalf, *Catalogue of the Gandharan Sculpture in the British Museum*. London, 1996; and D. Jongeward, *Buddhist Art of Pakistan and Afghanistan: The Royal Ontario Museum Collection of Gandhara Sculpture*. Toronto: University of Toronto, Center for South Asian Studies, 2003.

Figure 7.2 Standing Gandharan Bodhisattva Maitreya (The Future Buddha), second century
www.metmuseum.org/art/collection/search/38474?sortBy=Relevance&ft=gandhara&offset=0&rpp=20&pos=3
Credit: Purchase, Lita Annenberg Hazen Charitable Trust Gift, 1991

nomadic costumes is another superb example of cultural synthesis created by Silk Roads exchanges.

The syncretic sculpture produced in Gandhara is so stylistically identifiable that almost 2,000 years after it was created, British explorer Sir Aurel Stein was able to trace the spread of early Buddhism across the Tarim Basin and into China by recognizing the stylistic similarities he found in Buddhist sculpture unearthed at sites along the old Silk Roads routes around the Taklimakan Desert. At Miran, for example, Stein noted that "[t]he surviving drapery of these colossal seated Buddhas proved how closely the sculptor in faraway Lop Nor had followed the elaborate arrangement of the folds which the Graeco-Buddhist style of Gandhara had derived from classical models."[34]

[34] A. Stein, *On Ancient Central Asian Tracks: Brief Narrative of Three Expeditions in Innermost Asia and North Western China*. Chicago: University of Chicago Press (first published 1933), p. 103.

Mathuran sculptors worked in a white-spotted, reddish sandstone, a sedimentary rock that had not been metamorphosed by the plate tectonic collision. Although there are some similarities, Mathuran depictions of the Buddha differ quite markedly from Gandharan representations. Both standing and seated Mathuran Buddhas have broad shoulders and large chests, and the standing Buddha with his legs apart and feet firmly planted conveys a sense of power and energy, unlike the more fragile and even emaciated representations by Gandharan sculptors. Mathuran artists also produced a series of sculptural portraits of the Kushan kings, although each of these had their heads destroyed during the centuries following the collapse of the Kushan Empire. The headless sculpture of Kanishka is particularly impressive; he wears nomadic dress (boots and

Figure 7.3 Mathuran bust of a crowned Bodhisattva, second century CE
www.metmuseum.org/art/collection/search/38634?sortBy=Relevance&ft=mathura&offset=0&rpp=20&pos=2
Credit: Purchase, The Fred Eychaner Charitable Fund Gift, in honor of John Guy, 2016

trousers for horse riding and a long cloak) and holds a mace and a huge sword, and his feet are planted in a manner conveying assurance and power. In addition to Buddhist sculpture and the Kushan dynastic portraits, Mathuran artists also depicted images of sensual women, musicians and dancers and amorous couples in often erotic poses. This imagery also went on to profoundly influence later developments in South Asian art, particularly during the Gupta period. In various ways, then, the superb sacred and secular sculpture produced in these two regions of the Kushan Empire played a critical role in cultural diffusion in the centuries that followed, and are exquisite examples of the legacy of the Kushans and the First Silk Roads Era.

Last of the Great Kushans: Huvishka and Vasudeva (c. 152–c. 225 CE)

Coins, supplemented by occasional inscriptions, provide the best evidence for the two kings who succeeded Kanishka during the period of the "Great Kushans." Kanishka was followed by King Huvishka, a succession confirmed by a die link between a late coin of Kanishka and an early coin of Huvishka.[35] Huvishka's long reign of almost forty years can be dated from c. 152 to c. 190 CE. Although 90 percent of Huvishka's vast coinage falls into four main types, the range of deities he chose to depict on his coins is astonishingly varied – some twenty-five different gods from multiple religious traditions.

Huvishka's successor, Vasudeva (c. 191 to c. 225?), was presumably the son of Huvishka and possibly a South Asian mother; the deity Vasudeva was named after is recognized in the Hindu pantheon as the father of Krishna. Most of the evidence we have for the reign of Vasudeva is also numismatic, supplemented by some inscriptions found at Mathura. Vasudeva's coins have been discovered in their thousands. Like his grandfather Kanishka, Vasudeva chose to be mostly depicted on his obverses standing beside a small fire altar. But while Kanishka is shown holding a spear, Vasudeva holds a trident, which might be interpreted as indicating that the sacrifice was intended for the Indian god Siva. This is reinforced by the fact that most of Vasudeva's reverses depict Siva, sometimes standing beside his bull Nandi. Intriguingly, although the representation is clearly of the powerful South Asian god Siva, the god's name is often inscribed as the Iranian god Oesho. Should we read this as evidence of the possible "Indianization" of the Kushan monarchy, of a lessening of religious tolerance, or as further evidence of Kushan

[35] Gobl 1984, Nos. 80 and 314.

Figure 7.4 Gold coin depicting Kushan king Huvishka (reigned c. 152–c. 190 CE)
www.metmuseum.org/art/collection/search/39386?sortBy=Relevance&ft=kushan+coins&offset=0&rpp=20&pos=3
Credit: Bequest of Joseph H. Durkee, 1898

religious syncretism, blending the images and names of gods from multiple traditions? We just don't know.

Following the death of Vasudeva in c. 225 CE, Kushan history entered a period of decline, although a series of later kings known through their coinage only held on to some vestiges of power in the region for much of the following century. These "Later Kushan" rulers had to deal with the new and rising power of Inner Eurasia, the Sasanian conqueror Ardashir who, after destroying the Parthians, turned to confront the powerful Kushan Empire. According to one ancient Chinese source, King Vasudeva or an immediate successor sent an embassy to the Chinese Wei court in the year 230, seeking an alliance with the Chinese against the Sasanians, but to no avail.[36] The fate of this embassy, and of the Kushan Empire, is considered further in the final chapter of this book. But it is worth noting the irony here: centuries earlier the Kushans' ancestors the Yuezhi had rejected the pleas of Han envoy Zhang Qian to return to China and help in the fight against the Xiongnu. And now, almost half a millennium later, it was the turn of the Chinese to reject pleas from the descendants of the Yuezhi in their fight against a powerful enemy.

[36] *San Kuo Chih* 3:6a; see Zurcher 1968, p. 371, and Puri 1994, p. 256.

Figure 7.5 Reverse of gold coin of Kushan King Vasudeva (reigned c. 191–c. 225 CE)
www.metmuseum.org/art/collection/search/39387?sortBy=Relevance&ft=kushan+coins&offset=0&rpp=20&pos=1
Credit: Bequest of Joseph H. Durkee, 1898

Kushans and Sogdians

The most important Silk Roads routes from the far western Tarim Basin town-state of Kashgar headed either further west through the Pamirs and on through Bactria, or northwest through the region of Kangju and Dayuan in modern Uzbekistan, or south through the Karakorum and down the Indus River Valley to the coast. For roughly two centuries at the height of the First Silk Roads Era each of these routes passed, at various stages, through Kushan-controlled territory. During their original migration to Bactria the Yuezhi had established a diplomatic relationship with the state of Kangju to the north, a region partly identifiable with the later state known as Sogdia. As Etienne de la Vaissière has pointed out, it was probably Sogdians that Zhang Qian had observed living in Dayuan and Kangju.[37] The occupants of the region are described in the *Shiji* as being skillful at commerce and haggling "over a fraction of a cent,"[38] and there is plenty of evidence of an ongoing commercial relationship between the Sogdians and the Han in the centuries that followed this initial contact.

[37] E. de la Vaissière, *Sogdian Traders. A History*, trans. James Ward, Handbook of Oriental Studies, vol. 10, Leiden: Brill, 2005, chapter 2.
[38] *Shiji* 123, Watson 1993, p. 245.

Given the scarcity of Kushan coin finds in the region later known as Sogdia, it is doubtful the Kushans ever incorporated that region directly into their empire, although relations between the two appear to have been cordial. De la Vaissière has speculated that, given the wealth and stability of the Kushan Empire, Sogdian merchants may have actually migrated into Kushan cities, both in Bactria and northern India, to more effectively continue their roles as commercial middlemen in the trade between Han China, Central Asia and the Mediterranean. As de la Vaissière puts it, "the situation in Sogdiana at that time was very mediocre in comparison with the brilliant civilization of the Kushan Empire."[39] After the collapse of the Kushans following Sasanian expansion, Sogdian merchants may have relocated further south into the Indus Valley. A series of Sogdian inscriptions began to appear carved into stone high above the Indus Valley within a few decades of the disappearance of the Kushan Empire. The Sogdians may thus have played a small but still significant role in transregional trade during the First Silk Roads Era, but in the centuries that followed they would become one of the most important trading peoples in all Eurasia during the Second Silk Roads Era.

The Begram Treasure: Kushans and the Silk Roads

Our fourth and final question concerns evidence for the role of the Kushans in Silk Roads exchanges. Early in this chapter we mentioned the discovery in the 1930s of a large cache of luxury goods made by a French archaeological expedition at the site of Begram, one of the "capitals" of the Kushan Empire.[40] Begram is located in modern Afghanistan about 80 kilometers north of Kabul, near the junction of two important rivers, the Ghurband and Panjshir. The Kushan-era site of Begram, which is preceded stratigraphically by Greco-Bactrian layers, consists of extensive fortified areas made up of two walled enclosures, the Burj-i Abdullah in the north, and the so-called New Royal City in the south. Further south again there is a large, unfortified, purely urban city.

It was in Rooms 10 and 13 of the New Royal City that the French archaeologists discovered the treasure. The two storerooms were packed full with an extraordinary array of luxury goods from all over

[39] De la Vaissière 2005, p. 84.

[40] For an excellent introduction to the discovery of the Begram treasure and its historical implications, see R. Mairs, "Glassware from Roman Egypt at Begram (Afghanistan) and the Red Sea Trade," *British Museum Studies in Ancient Egypt and Sudan* 18 (2012), pp. 61–74.

Eurasia.[41] The goods appear to have been deliberately cached, and the storerooms had thick walls and blocked entrances, suggesting these goods might have been stashed away for safekeeping during a period of political unrest. Dating the discovery has proven problematic, although most scholars now agree that these highly valuable goods were probably stashed away in these secure rooms sometime in the first or early second centuries CE.[42]

Originally it was thought that, if the goods had been stored late in the Kushan period (say in the early third century CE), the collection might represent a sort of royal treasure, hidden away for safekeeping during the latter stages of the fragmenting Kushan Empire. However, the now more widely accepted dates of the first or second centuries CE place this cache firmly in the period of Kushan stability and prosperity, which means it is far more likely that these treasures were part of the commercial stock of merchants awaiting further distribution. As Sanjyot Mehendale puts it: "The fact, if established, that the goods at Begram traveled from diverse places in the same era and were stored together in one place suggests that the site was a point of consumption, of collection for further distribution, of active trading, or a combination thereof."[43]

If this interpretation of the Begram treasure is correct, it offers a singularly illuminating insight into the central role of the Kushan Empire at the height of the First Silk Roads Era. The collection provides striking evidence of the vast size and incredibly diverse nature of the trade in valuable luxury goods that characterizes trans-Eurasian commerce during the first two centuries CE. Among the treasures were magnificent carved ivories from India, molded stucco ornaments that appear to be Greek in origin, superb glassware from Syria and Roman Egypt, bronze objects from Egypt and the Roman Empire and lacquer objects from Han China. Along with bales of Chinese silk, these are examples of the sort of high-value trade goods that were passing back and forth along the Silk Roads during the height of their operation, through major commercial nodes such as Begram and the Kushan Empire. Although we lack many of

[41] For more on the actual discovery, see J. Hackin, *Recherches archéologiques à Begram*. Mémoires de la Délégation Archéologique Française en Afghanistan 9. Paris, 1954. *Nouvelles recherches archéologiques à Begram*. Mémoires de la Délégation Archéologique Française en Afghanistan 11. Paris; and R. Ghirshman, *Bégram: Recherches archéologiques et historiques sur les Kouchans*. Mémoires de la Délégation Archéologique Française en Afghanistan 12, 1946; Mémoires de l'Institut Français d'Archéologie Orientale du Caire 79. Cairo.

[42] D. Whitehouse, "Begram, the *Periplus* and Gandharan Art," *Journal of Roman Archaeology* 2 (1989), pp. 93–100; and S. Mehendale, "Begram: Along Ancient Central Asian and Indian Trade Routes," *Cahiers d'Asia centrale* 1 (1996), pp. 47–64.

[43] Mehendale 1996, p. 51.

Figure 7.6 Circular medallion depicting Aphrodite and Eros, discovered as part of the Begram hoard
www.metmuseum.org/art/collection/search/39605?sortBy=Relevance&ft=begram&offset=0&rpp=20&pos=1
Credit: Gift of Alexander Götz, in honor of Samuel Eilenberg, 1996

the details about how that trade was actually conducted, its astonishing diversity and value, along with the critical role the Kushans played in it, is indisputable.

Conclusion

As this chapter has shown, despite being descended from pastoral nomads, the Kushans evolved into a powerful sedentary empire that controlled vast regions of Inner Eurasia for the first two centuries CE. This corresponds precisely with the high point of the First Silk Roads Era, and it is no exaggeration to suggest that it was the stability created by the Kushans, through their unbroken line of royal succession, their superb coinage, their apparent religious tolerance and the cordial relations they apparently maintained with their neighbors once they had carved out their empire, that helped facilitate the extraordinary material and cultural exchanges that epitomize this key period in ancient world history. Despite the fact that the Kushans constructed an essentially land-based empire, at least two of the major trade routes that passed through their territory headed toward ports along the west coast of South Asia, some of which probably came under their direct control during the Great Kushans period. In the next chapter we turn to the maritime routes of the Indian Ocean and Arabian Sea, which were probably responsible for the great bulk of the commercial goods that were transported during the First Silk Roads Era.

Selected Further Reading

Benjamin, C., "The Yuezhi," in *The Oxford Research Encyclopedia of Asian History*. New York: Oxford University Press, 2017, at: http://asianhistory.oxfordre.com/view/10.1093/acrefore/9780190277727.001.0001/acrefore-9780190277727-e-49.

Cribb, J., "The Early Kushan Kings: New Evidence for Chronology. Evidence from the Rabatak Inscription of Kanishka I," in M. Alram and D. Klimburg-Salter, eds., *Coins, Art and Chronology. Essays on the Pre-Islamic History of the Indo-Iranian Borderlands*. Vienna, 1999.

Errington, E., J. Cribb and M. Claringbull, eds., *The Crossroads of Asia: Transformation in Image and Symbol in the Art of Ancient Afghanistan and Pakistan*. London: The Ancient India and Iran Trust, 1992.

Falk, H., ed., *Kushan Histories: Literary Sources and Selected Papers from a Symposium at Berlin, December 5 to 7, 2013*. Bremen: Hempen Verlag, 2016.

Gobl, R., *System und Chronologie der Münzprägung des Kušānreiches*. Wien: Verlag der Österreichischen Akademie der Wissenschaften, 1984.

Jongeward, D., *Buddhist Art of Pakistan and Afghanistan: The Royal Ontario Museum Collection of Gandhara Sculpture*. Toronto: University of Toronto, Center for South Asian Studies, 2003.

Mairs, R., "Glassware from Roman Egypt at Begram (Afghanistan) and the Red Sea Trade," *British Museum Studies in Ancient Egypt and Sudan* 18 (2012), pp. 61–74.

Mehendale, S., "Begram: Along Ancient Central Asian and Indian Trade Routes," *Cahiers d'Asia centrale* 1 (1996), pp. 47–64.

Whitehouse, D., "Begram, the *Periplus* and Gandharan Art," *Journal of Roman Archaeology* 2 (1989), pp. 93–100.

Zurcher, E., "The Yueh-chih and Kanishka in the Chinese Sources," in A. L. Basham, ed., *Papers on the Date of Kanishka*. Leiden: Brill, 1968, pp. 346ff.

8 Maritime Routes of the First Silk Roads Era

So far in this book we have mostly been focused on the overland diplomatic and commercial routes that connected eastern, central and western Eurasia, and most of the imperial states, nomadic confederations and diverse cultures that occupied that vast geopolitical space. In this chapter we turn to the other great conduits of trade during the First Silk Roads Era, maritime routes that connected Roman Egypt, the Arabian Peninsula and the Persian Gulf with South Asian ports and Central Asian land routes. One persistent argument concerning trade by sea has been that maritime routes became increasingly attractive to Silk Roads merchants during periods in which the political relationship between the Roman and the Parthian Empires was tense, and this remains a valid point. However, it is also true that trade by sea always made a lot of sense for ancient merchants, whether conflicts between key states were occurring or not. Maritime trade was cheaper and faster, and was often conducted at levels that seemed largely unaffected by the political relationship within and between states.

There are many sources of evidence for maritime trade during the First Silk Roads Era, including textual, archaeological, inscriptional and numismatic. There are numerous references to maritime commercial activity in ancient Greco-Roman literature, and also a few references in the Chinese Han Dynasty sources, although in terms of Silk Roads trade with the West, long-distance maritime trade appears to have been far less important to Chinese merchants and administrators than land-based trade during the Han Dynasty. The most important textual source for maritime trade during the First Silk Roads Era is the *Periplus of the Erythraean Sea*, a sailors' handbook written in the first century CE by an anonymous author.[1] The *Periplus* shows us that sometime during the preceding centuries or millennia, sailors had learned how to effectively use the monsoon winds that blow in different directions across the

[1] W. H. Schoff, *The Periplus of the Erythrian Sea: Travel and Trade in the Indian Ocean by a Merchant of the First Century*. New York: Longmans, Green and Co., 1912.

Arabian Sea, and it was this discovery, along with an increasing demand for luxury goods in the Roman Empire, that led to a substantial increase in the volume of maritime trade between Roman Egypt and South Asia during the first two centuries CE. Mariners had learned, whether by accident or by trial and error we will never know, that they could use these shifting seasonal wind patterns to move away from the coast-hugging routes that sailors had been following for thousands of years, and instead chart a course across the deep waters of the Arabian Sea, confident that the monsoon winds would blow them eastward on to the coast of India in one season, then westward back to Africa a few months later.

Before long, a network of sea routes linked the ports of the western and southern coasts of Arabia, the east coast of Africa, the Persian Gulf, the west coast of India and Roman ports on the Egyptian coast of the Red Sea into a vast maritime world system. Wherever these ports were located they were linked to preexisting land routes along which valuable merchandise would be transported to the key providers and consumers of these luxury exports and imports. Ports such as Myos Hormos and Berenike on the African Red Sea coast, Charax Spasinau near the head of the Persian Gulf and Barbaricum, Barygaza and Muziris on the west coast of the Indian subcontinent became major centers of seaborne trade, thriving emporiums and clearinghouses for the astonishing diversity of goods that were now crisscrossing the greater Indian Ocean Basin. These goods included bales of Chinese silk, of course, but also precious stones, cotton, wine, metals, pepper, glass and large quantities of Roman gold and silver coins.

In this chapter, then, we turn to maritime trade in the Indian Ocean Basin during the First Silk Roads Era and attempt to answer several pertinent questions. First, how did the geography and environment of the Indian Ocean Basin make it uniquely suited to playing a central role in Silk Roads exchanges? Second, how did early civilizations make use of the Indian Ocean in the millennia that preceded the First Silk Roads Era? And finally, what does the literary, archaeological and numismatic evidence tell us about the infrastructure, commodities and financial arrangements whereby large quantities of trade goods were moved enormous distances around Eurasia by sea during the first two centuries CE?

Geography of the Indian Ocean Basin

The Indian Ocean is a massive body of water that washes upon the shores of the continents of Africa, Asia and Australia. Until recently the Southern Ocean that lies to the north of Antarctica was also considered part of the Indian Ocean, but in the year 2000 the International

Hydrographic Organization (IHA) "removed" all waters south of latitude 60 degrees south from the Indian Ocean. The IHA does still consider a number of northern bodies of water part of the greater Indian Ocean, including the Arabian Sea, the Bay of Bengal, the Persian Gulf and the Red Sea. Collectively the Indian Ocean covers a total area of more than 70 million square kilometers, making it the third largest ocean on the planet after the Pacific and Atlantic.[2]

The climate of the Indian Ocean Basin and the regions contiguous to it is governed by monsoon wind patterns that have profoundly influenced human activity in the region for thousands of years, both on land and at sea. The impact of the monsoon winds on the land and peoples of South Asia is particularly pronounced. The southwest summer monsoon, which blows up from the Indian Ocean and Arabian Sea and deposits substantial amounts of water on the continent, is the most productive wet season on the planet, responsible for 80 percent of all the rainfall in India. Most of this rain falls in the summer and autumn, often torrentially, brought in by winds from the Arabian Sea. The Western Ghats mountain range that runs parallel to the southwest coast of the Indian subcontinent receives particularly heavy summer rains, making it one of the wettest places on earth. Because the Western Ghats capture virtually all of the moisture carried by these monsoon cloud systems, the enormous Deccan Plateau, which lies in the rain shadow behind them, is dry. This monsoon process is essentially reversed in winter, because during the winter months the air over the land has higher pressure than the air over the sea, so that much dryer northeast monsoon winds now blow down from the arid heart of Central Asia, creating an extensive dry season over much of the subcontinent.

These monsoon wind systems have had huge ramifications for South Asian history, affecting not only patterns of agriculture and settlement, but also the regions' long and vital role in trans-Indian Ocean maritime trade. But their impact extends beyond India to much of the Indian Ocean Basin, including the Persian Gulf, Arabian Peninsula and East Africa, and this fact is part of the answer to our first question about how the environment of the Indian Ocean facilitated trade. The word *monsoon* is actually derived from the Arabic word *mawsim*, meaning "season." The monsoons determined precisely when it was safe for Arab dhows and Roman and Indian ships to sail; and because the wind patterns changed over long periods of time, it meant that voyages also had to be planned to last for many months and even years. One estimate of the schedule of voyages connecting the Persian Gulf and ports of southern China during the later Abbasid Period

[2] For more on these data and these decisions, visit the website of the International Hydrographic Organization at www.iho.int/srv1/index.php?lang=en.

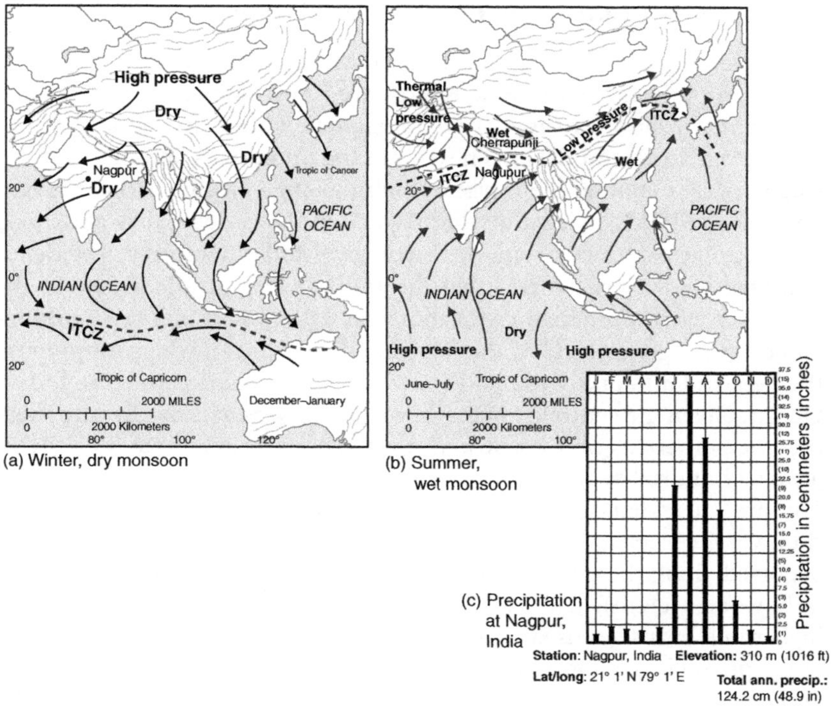

Map 8.1 Indian Ocean monsoon patterns
www.bing.com/images/search?view=detailV2&ccid=dvIQgPSQ&id=240D8E45E9A1B624A45D9AF807F73B1344AB19D6&thid=OIP.dvIQgPSQ9ohXN1PY41pQ_gEsDh&q=indian+ocean+monsoons+map&simid=608039921988668980&selectedIndex=15&ajaxhist=0

(750–1258 CE) indicates that the round trip would take around eighteen months.[3] The long layovers in the various ports of the Indian Ocean Basin necessitated by the monsoons facilitated business (and marriage) connections that, as Lawrence Potter puts it, "helped create a 'brotherhood of the sea' that tied together the Indian Ocean basin."[4]

[3] G. F. Hourani, *Arab Seafaring in the Indian Ocean in Ancient and Early Medieval Times*. Princeton, NJ: Princeton University Press, 1995; discussed in L. G. Potter, *The Persian Gulf in History*. London: Palgrave Macmillan, 2009, p. 8.

[4] Potter 2009, p. 9.

Early Trade in the Indian Ocean Basin

In considering our second question about trade in the Indian Ocean Basin before the advent of the Silk Roads, we know that three of the first agrarian civilizations to appear on the planet emerged in regions bordering the Indian Ocean Basin. These were the Sumerians and their successors in Mesopotamia, the Egyptians with a long coastline along the Red Sea and the Indus civilization that formed in the Indus Valley and along the coast of modern Pakistan. Archaeological and other forms of evidence demonstrate the crucial role that the Indian Ocean trade played in the history of each. Sumerian civilization was established in a region dominated by the great rivers of the Tigris and Euphrates, which empty into the Persian Gulf, one of the bodies of water considered part of the Indian Ocean. Given the centrality of these two great rivers, it is hardly surprising that the Sumerians were constructing water craft by as early as 3500 BCE. Twelve hundred years later Sumerian mariners were sailing their boats out into the Indian Ocean to trade with merchants of the Indus civilization, via the Persian Gulf and Arabian Sea. The key Sumerian products exported along these maritime routes included various textiles (particularly woolen cloth), jewelry and sesame oil, which they exchanged for high-value Indus goods such as pearls, ivory and precious stones.

Egyptian civilization also formed along the banks of a great river, and around the same time that Sumerians were building boats for use on the Tigris and Euphrates, Egyptians were using the Nile River to move people and goods in boats. By 3000 BCE or soon after, the Egyptians had sailed out into the Mediterranean Sea, and by at least 2000 BCE Egyptian mariners had systematically explored the Red Sea, the Gulf of Oman and parts of the Arabian Sea. During the New Kingdom Period (1550–1070 BCE), Egyptian merchants developed a particularly strong maritime trade relationship with East African coastal states, including the mysterious land of Punt, which probably included parts of modern Somalia and Ethiopia. Key Egyptian exports sent along these Indian Ocean coastal routes included jewelry, weapons and tools, which were exchanged for exotic animal products such as monkeys and panthers.

Much less is known about the organization of trade in the Indus civilization, because unlike the Mesopotamian and Egyptian systems, the Indus writing system has never been deciphered. But archaeological (and Sumerian written) evidence clearly demonstrates an ongoing commercial relationship with the Sumerians and their successors between about 2300 and 1750 BCE. Some of these exchanges occurred overland across the Iranian Plateau and down into Mesopotamia, using donkey caravans, but most took place by sea, using ships that followed the

Figure 8.1 Fragment of scene representing the expedition to the land of Punt organized by Queen Hatshepsut (1507–1458 BC), the Temple of Hatshepsut, western Thebes, Egypt
www.gettyimages.co.uk/license/639049766
Credit: Maciek67

coastline between the mouth of the Indus River and the head of the Persian Gulf.

During the millennia that followed, maritime trade continued to flourish along the varied coasts of the Indian Ocean, particularly after the Achaemenid Persians incorporated many of the areas controlled by these early civilizations into their vast empire in the sixth century BCE. Under the Achaemenids, ports in the Persian Gulf flourished, and maritime trade received a further boost when Persian king Darius I had a canal dug that connected the Red Sea to the Nile River Valley, thus effectively connecting the Indian Ocean to the Mediterranean. From the Indian subcontinent, Persian merchants imported aromatic oils, ivory and gold. During the second half of the first millennium BCE in South Asia, urbanization, trade and commerce were also flourishing, particularly during and after the period of the Mauryan Empire (322–185 BCE). New cities appeared on the Ganges Plain, within which tremendous growth in craft production occurred. This in turn led to the appearance of craft and merchant guilds that tended to function independently of political structures, even issuing their own coins and providing banking services for their members.[5]

The post-Mauryan period in India also experienced an expansion of internal and external trade. Cities and regions became specialized in particular types of trade goods, and these were moved by overland and river routes throughout the subcontinent. Maritime trade was also flourishing in India well before the First Silk Roads Era. Indian texts dateable to the fourth century BCE include new terms that were applied to maritime merchants, such as *dvinavadhana* (a merchant who sails with just one ship) and *pancanavapriya* (one sailing with five ships).[6] Even after Silk Roads trade began to flow back and forth across the western Indian Ocean, Indian merchants continued to play a critical role in moving goods up and down the coast, as the *Periplus* notes when it states, "Some ships sail principally to these ports, but some follow the coast and take on whatever cargoes came their way."[7] Despite the vibrancy of all of these preexisting maritime trade networks in the Red Sea, in the Persian Gulf and along the coasts of the Indian subcontinent, it was intensified exploitation of the monsoon winds, along with the emergence of the appropriate political and economic "goldilocks" conditions all over Eurasia, that led to a dramatic intensification in transregional maritime trade during the First Silk Roads Era.

Discovery of Monsoon Winds

Most ancient Greco-Roman literature, including the *Periplus*, attributes the discovery of the monsoon winds to Greek mariners, perhaps to a captain named Hippalos. According to the *Periplus*, in a discussion of routes around the Arabian Peninsula, "The whole coastal route ... men used to sail over in smaller vessels, following the curves of the bays. The ship captain Hippalos, by plotting the location of the ports of trade with the configuration of the sea, was the first to discover the route over open water."[8] However, the Roman geographer Strabo credits a different Greek with the discovery, one Eudoxus of Cyzicus who became involved in trade with India during the Hellenistic Era, when Egypt and its Red Sea ports were controlled by the Ptolemies.[9] Other Roman authors such as

[5] S. Kaul, "South Asia," in C. Benjamin ed., *Cambridge History of the World Vol. 4: A World with States, Empires, and Networks, 1200 BCE–900 CE*. Cambridge: Cambridge University Press, 2015, pp. 480ff.

[6] V. S. Agrawala, *India as Known to Panini: A Study of the Cultural Material in the Ashtadhyayi*. Prithvi Prakashan, 1963, p. 155.

[7] *Periplus* 14. [8] *Periplus* 57. [9] Strabo, *Geog*. 2.3.

Diodorus Siculus attribute the discovery to a merchant mariner named Iambulos, who accidentally discovered the winds when he was blown off course from Africa to Sri Lanka.

As numerous Indian scholars have argued, it seems somewhat ridiculous and decidedly Western-centric to assume that after 3,000 years of sailors using the Indian Ocean for trade, no one had discovered the monsoon winds until Greek merchants appeared at the periphery of the Indian Ocean during the Hellenistic Era. Indian historian Himanshu Ray points out that all the regions contiguous to the Indian Ocean, including India, Mesopotamia and Arabia, had long traditions of successful boatbuilding and maritime trade long before Greco-Roman merchants arrived.[10] Indeed, we should also note that in Strabo's story about the discovery of the trade winds by Eudoxus, a shipwrecked Indian sailor plays a critical role.

> Now it so happened … that a certain Indian was brought to the king by the coast-guards of the recess of the Arabian Gulf [Red Sea], who said that they had found him half-dead and alone on a stranded ship, but that they did not know who he was or where he came from, since they did not understand his language; and the king gave the Indian into the charge of men who would teach him Greek; and when the Indian had learned Greek, he related that on his voyage from India he by a strange mischance mistook his course and reached Egypt in safety, but only after having lost all his companions by starvation; and when his story was doubted, he promised to act as guide on the trip to India for the men who had been previously selected by the King; and of this party Eudoxus, also, became a member.[11]

This suggests that Indian mariners, in this case apparently by accident, had already discovered the secrets of the monsoon winds long before the Greeks, and actually taught the Greeks how to use them.

The Greeks might well have discovered the monsoon winds by themselves, but it is more probable that these patterns had been known to Indian Ocean sailors for centuries before. Whoever "discovered" the secrets of the monsoon winds of the western Indian Ocean, there can be no doubt that it was the arrival of large numbers of foreign merchants (who the Indians called *yavanas*) at ports along the Indian coast during the first century CE that led to a tremendous expansion of maritime trade during the First Silk Roads Era, an expansion well documented by the *Periplus of the Erythraean Sea*.

[10] H. P. Ray, *The Archaeology of Seafaring in Ancient South Asia*. Cambridge World Archaeology, Cambridge; New York: Cambridge University Press, 2003, pp. 55–62.

[11] Strabo, *Geog*. 2.3.

The *Periplus of the Erythraean Sea*

The remainder of this chapter is focused on our third question: what does literary, archaeological and numismatic evidence tell us about the infrastructure, commodities and financial arrangements whereby large quantities of trade goods were moved enormous distances around Eurasia by sea during the first two centuries CE? As noted earlier, the most crucial ancient textual source historians today have available for understanding the way in which mercantile trade between Roman Egypt and the coast of India was conducted during this period is the *Periplus of the Erythraean Sea*. Written in Greek, presumably by some unknown merchant captain, the *Periplus* describes navigational challenges and commercial activities at a number of ports around the coasts of the "Erythraean Sea," which was the name the ancient Greeks gave to what they understood to be the "Red Sea," essentially the modern Red Sea, Arabian Sea and Indian Ocean.

The date of authorship of the *Periplus* has been considerably debated by historians, but there is general agreement today that it was written sometime around the middle of the first century CE, perhaps between 40 and 50 CE. Wilfred Schoff, in an early but still reliable critical study of the *Periplus*, argued that the author of the *Periplus* was probably a Greek merchant dwelling in Roman-controlled Egypt during the reign of Emperor Tiberius (r. 14–37 CE). Schoff believed the author might have been living in the Roman Red Sea port of Berenike (more on this in what follows), and that, given his propensity for mixing Greek and Latin words in sometimes clumsy sentence constructions, he was not a particularly well-educated man. Schoff also wondered whether the author had personally written the text based on his own first-hand experience or had perhaps compiled it from reports from other sailors and merchants.[12]

The *Periplus* consists of sixty-six short chapters, each of them roughly a paragraph long. The chapters generally contain three different types of information: the navigational considerations for safely entering and leaving each port, the range of import and export goods available there, and some brief comments about the political circumstances prevailing in each port. Most locations named in the *Periplus* have been identified by historians, but the information provided about some ports is so vague or ambiguous that considerable disagreement remains on their locations. We have more to say about the key export commodities being exchanged at these ports for Roman coin, but according to the *Periplus*, they were of a staggering variety. They included animals such as Indian elephants, rhinoceroses, tigers and even snakes, which were used in public spectacles

[12] Schoff 1912, p. 16.

in the many arenas of the Roman Empire. Luxury South Asian agricultural products were also in great demand in Rome, including spices, pepper, sesame oil, sugar, lime, peach and other fruits. Other types of high-value exports included Chinese silk, Indian pearls, indigo for dyeing textiles, and cotton cloth for clothing, all of which cost the Romans a fortune, as we have seen.[13] Many Roman coins have indeed been discovered by archaeologists at ancient ports along the coasts of India, most dating to the first and second centuries CE. We also have more to say about the role of Roman gold and silver coins in this maritime trade network, but for now we should note that the lack of third-century Roman coins is clear evidence of the substantial decline in Indian Ocean trade that occurred during that century, at the end of the First Silk Roads Era.

Roman Involvement in Indian Ocean Trade during the First Two Centuries CE

Merchants and sailors of the Indian Ocean Basin thus had a long history of involvement in maritime trade well before the advent of the Silk Roads, connecting various ports along the west coast of India with merchants in the Persian Gulf and Red Sea in particular. But with the seizing of power by Augustus in Rome, and the subsequent increase in the demand for luxury goods among Roman elites, a dramatic intensification of Indian Ocean trade occurred. As we have already seen, this was not just a maritime phenomenon. Archaeological and textual evidence attests to a significant expansion of all trade contacts between the Roman, Parthian and Kushan Empires and the Indian subcontinent during the first two centuries CE.

The expansion of Indian Ocean trade between Roman Egypt and the Indian coast was made possible by the replacement of the Hellenistic Ptolemaic pharaohs in Egypt with Roman imperial rule. After the suicide death of the last Ptolemaic ruler, Cleopatra, the Romans incorporated Egypt as a province in 40 BCE. The Ptolemies had worked hard to expand the Egyptian economy, and had developed preexisting ports on the Red Sea coast in an attempt to boost maritime trade. The Romans took over these facilities, and after Augustus came to power, they further developed port facilities to intensify the frequency and volume of maritime trade with Arabia and India.[14] These sea routes allowed Roman merchants to trade directly with their counterparts in India, thus

[13] M. A. Cobb, "Balancing the Trade: Roman Cargo Shipments to India," *Oxford Journal of Archaeology* 34, No. 2 (2015), pp. 193ff.

[14] See D. F. Lach, *Asia in the Making of Europe: The Century of Discovery. Book 1*. Chicago: University of Chicago Press, 1994, p. 13.

eliminating many of the fees and tariffs being charged along the land-based routes by middlemen such as the Parthians.

The ancient Roman geographer Strabo provides compelling evidence of the increase in maritime trade between Red Sea and Indian ports between the Ptolemaic and Augustan periods: "At any rate, when Gallus was prefect of Egypt, I accompanied him and ascended the Nile as far as Syrene and the frontiers of the Kingdom of Aksum, and I learned that as many as 120 vessels were sailing from Myos Hormos to the subcontinent, whereas formerly, under the Ptolomies, only a very few ventured to undertake the voyage and to carry on traffic in Indian merchandise."[15] According to archaeological, pictorial and written evidence, the vessels Roman merchants used to conduct their trade with India were similar to the ships in use in the Mediterranean. Most of these ships had a carrying capacity of between 75 and 300 tons, although as Peter Sidebotham and others have pointed out, the dimensions of the harbor at Berenike, one of the key Roman Red Sea ports, suggest that it might have accommodated even larger ships.[16]

Principal Roman Ports

Strabo identifies one of the key Red Sea ports developed by the Romans as Myos Hormos; two other important ports were Arsinoe and Berenike. Arsinoe was the preferred port early in the first century CE, but as trade intensified the ports of Myos Hormos and Berenike replaced Arsinoe because they were more accessible to ships. Arsinoe, essentially the ancient port of the modern Egyptian city of Suez, had been developed by the Ptolemies to help facilitate Indian Ocean trade. Ptolemaic merchants used the canal that had originally been dug by the Achaemenid Persians in the sixth century to connect the Nile River with the Red Sea at Arsinoe. Once the Romans had incorporated Egypt into their empire, this canal was dredged and improved to help move goods from the Red Sea to the Nile and on to the Mediterranean.

Navigation to the far northern Red Sea port of Arsinoe was always challenging, however, because of the prevailing wind patterns in the Gulf of Suez, at the head of the Red Sea. The Gulf of Suez is long and narrow, measuring some 314 kilometers (185 miles) from mouth to head, and between just 19 and 32 kilometers (12 to 19 miles) in width. It is subject

[15] Strabo, II.5.12.
[16] S. E. Sidebotham, *Berenike and the Ancient Maritime Spice Route*. Berkeley and Los Angeles: University of California Press, 2011, pp. 195–196.

to dramatically shifting undersea currents, numerous shoals of coral and savage winds that would suddenly blow up just as captains were trying to steer their ships through narrow openings between the shoals.[17] Because of these hazards, the Romans decided to develop two other ports much further south on the coast of the Red Sea, Myos Hormos and Berenike. Both these ports had also been used by the Ptolemies, but now they became increasingly important for the Romans.

Berenike was located at the head of a small inlet sheltered by the peninsula of Ras Banas, some 825 kilometers (roughly 500 miles) south of Arsinoe. It had been founded in 275 BCE by Ptolemy II, who named the port after his mother, Berenike I. The port was well known to ancient geographers, including the author of the *Periplus* and Pliny the Elder, and also to Strabo, who noted that the harbor at Berenike was protected from the prevailing northeast wind by an island named Ophiodes.[18] The Romans eventually built a road, the Via Hadriana, to connect Berenike with the Nile River Valley, to facilitate the passage of commercial goods that were being shipped to the port via the Indian Ocean network.

The ruins of ancient Berenike were originally discovered by Italian archaeologist Giovanni Belzoni in 1818. More recent archaeological investigations that commenced in 1994 and are still ongoing have uncovered extraordinary evidence of the close connections that developed between Roman Egypt and merchants and mariners from the south coast of India in particular. Tamil sailors and merchants from the modern Indian state of Kerala appear to have developed a community in Berenike, based on the evidence of inscriptions written in Tamil-Brahmi script discovered on an amphora fragment at Berenike, and dated probably to the first century CE.[19] Tamil inscriptions have also been found at other Roman Egyptian ports, and also in Thailand, indicating the extraordinary range and critical importance of Tamil sailors and merchants to maritime trade during the First Silk Roads Era.[20] As well as inscriptions, a wide range of South Asian export goods have also been found by archaeologists working at Berenike. These include large quantities of black peppercorns, coconuts, teak wood, precious and semiprecious stones (often in necklaces) and various high-quality manufactured goods including cooking utensils and

[17] For more on the maritime hazards of the Red Sea, see A. Wick, *The Red Sea: In Search of Lost Space*. Los Angeles: University of California Press, 2016, pp. 25–27.
[18] Strabo, *Geog.*, xvi, p. 770.
[19] "Tamil-Brahmi Script in Egypt," *The Hindu*, Chennai, India, November 21, 2007.
[20] "Tamil-Brahmi Inscription on Pottery Found in Thailand," *The Hindu*, Chennai, India, July 16, 2006.

pots. Some teak wood (which is native to South Asia) was discovered being used in houses in Berenike, which suggests that old South Asian ships may have been dismantled there and their timbers reused as building materials.[21]

The precise location of the third major Roman-Egyptian port noted in literary sources, Myos Hormos, is disputed by archaeologists, but recent work suggests it was most probably located at Quseir al-Quadim, some 8 kilometers (5 miles) from the modern Egyptian town of Al-Qusayr. Myos Hormos was also originally built by the Ptolemies, but maritime traffic from the port increased enormously under the Romans. As we saw earlier, Roman geographer Strabo stated that some 120 vessels a year were setting sail from Myos Hormos, bound for India.[22] The Romans built another road to connect Myos Hormos with the Nile Valley. The fact that the road was built in the first century CE is further evidence of the intensification of maritime trade during the First Silk Roads Era, while the abandonment of the port during the fourth century illustrates the decline in transregional trade more generally that occurred at the end of the era.

Principal Roman Exports

Although the Greco-Roman merchants involved in maritime trade in the Indian Ocean apparently paid for the majority of India imports with gold and silver coin, both written and archaeological evidence also attests to a great variety of goods being carried by ships from the Red Sea to be exported to South Asia. These exports included different foods and wines, various drugs and dyes and handcrafted objects in stone, metal and glass, the latter clearly evident in the Begram hoard discussed in the previous chapter. Historian Matthew Adam Cobb provides an illuminating analysis of the role of three of these key types of Roman exports, wine, glassware and metal objects, noting the convincing archaeological evidence of just how valued these Roman exports were in the Indian subcontinent.[23]

Numerous sources attest to the popularity of wine in India, particularly Italian wine, including the *Periplus*, Tamil Sangam poems and business records in the form of ostraca found at Myos Hormos and Berenike. One Roman shipwreck found near the harbor of Berenike contained thirty-four amphorae, at least twenty of which have been

[21] See R. Krishnakumar, "South Indians in Roman Egypt?" *Frontline* 27, No. 8 (April 2010).

[22] Strabo, *Geog.* II.5.12.

[23] Cobb 2015, pp. 193ff.

identified as probably carrying Italian wine. Another shipwreck found south of Berenike also carried a cargo of amphorae used in the wine trade, some of Italian origin and some of Egyptian, while one amphora contained Spanish olive oil.[24] Cobb notes that Roman amphorae have been discovered at more than fifty sites all over India, dated to between 25 BCE and the early second century CE, at the peak of the First Silk Roads Era.[25] The majority of the amphorae have been found in northwestern India, reflecting perhaps the persisting influence of Greek culture in the region following the period of rule by Greco-Bactrian and Indo-Greek kingdoms, which as we saw in the previous chapter controlled much of northwest India and Bactria in the centuries prior to the First Silk Roads Era.[26]

Superb Roman glassware has also been found at a number of archaeological sites in South Asia, including deep in the Kushan Empire at Begram, probably after having been shipped to Barygaza and transported up the Indus River into Bactria. Roman glass beads and bangles have also been found in central and south India, including at the far southern ports of Muziris and Arikamedu.[27] Roman metalwares have also been discovered at numerous sites across India, particularly bronzeware, including plaques, statuettes, a sieve for straining wine, mirrors and even a chair with the legend ROMAE inscribed on its pedestal.[28] These discoveries are clear evidence that, although most Indian exports were probably paid for in Roman gold and silver coinage, there was still significant demand in India for high-quality Greco-Roman imported goods such as wine, glassware and metalware. The Roman ships that set out from the Red Sea ports for the coast of India thus carried a significant mix of export commodities in their holds, as well as quantities of gold and silver coins (more on the coins in what follows).

Principal South Asian Ports

The *Periplus* is the most important textual source we have for understanding the maritime routes that connected Roman Egypt with ports along the coasts of the Indian subcontinent. Chapters in the text contain

[24] L. Blue et al., "New Light on the Nature of Indo-Roman Trade: Roman Period Shipwrecks in the Northern Red Sea," in D. A. Agius et al., eds., *Navigated Spaces, Connected Places*. Oxford: Oxford University Press, 2012, pp. 94–96.
[25] Cobb 2015, p. 195.
[26] See M. G. Raschke, "New Studies in Roman Commerce with the East," *Aufstieg und Niedergang der Römischen Welt* 9, No. 2 (1978), pp. 604–1378, p. 632 for example.
[27] Cobb 2015, p. 196. [28] Cobb 2015, pp. 196–197.

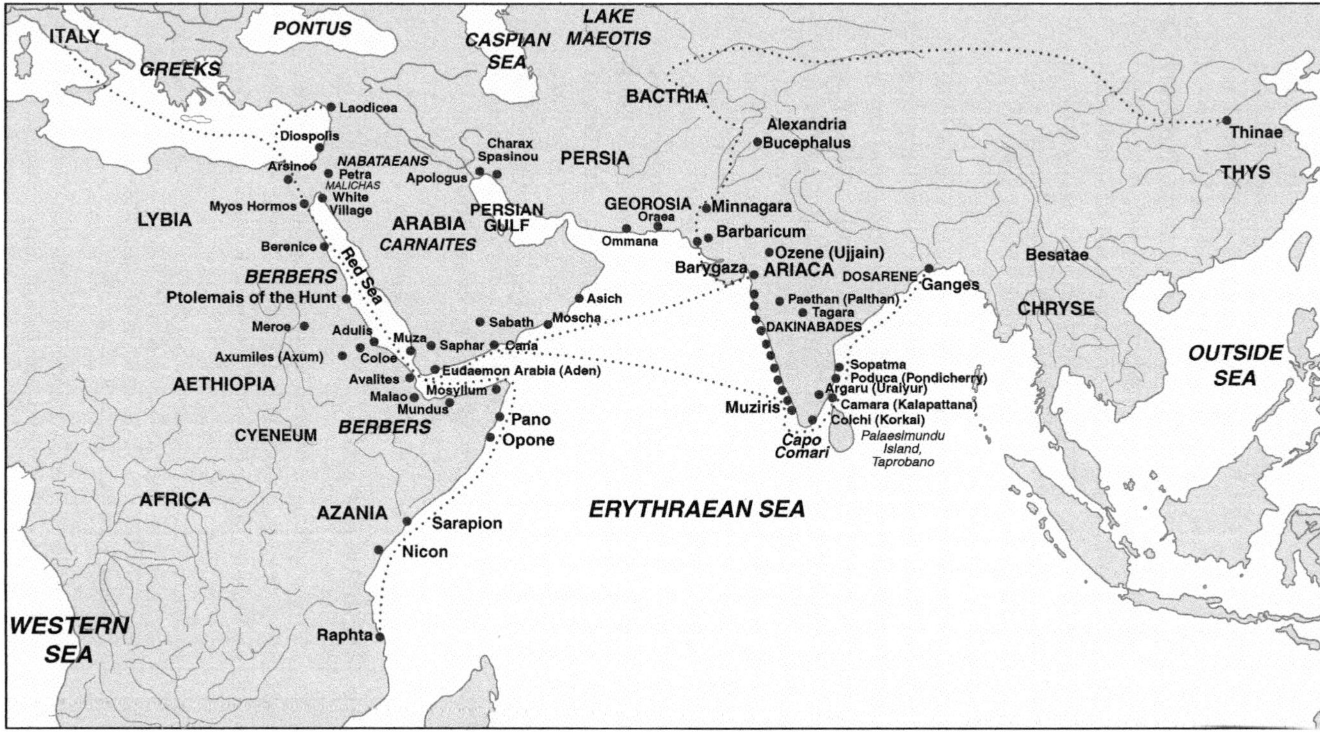

Map 8.2 Map of the Indian Ocean Basin during the First Silk Roads Era
www.columbia.edu/itc/mealac/pritchett/00maplinks/early/periplus/periplusmax.jpg

a great deal of practical information for ship captains and their crews. This includes detailed information on the navigational challenges involved in accessing harbors and ports along the northwest coast of India in particular, because the gulfs and bays of the region were subject to difficult tidal patterns and storms. Archaeological evidence of the challenges ancient mariners faced in the region has been discovered in the form of more than forty stone and lead anchors buried in sediment, all dated to the first and second centuries CE, in the vicinity of Bet Dwarka, an island located in the Gulf of Kutch in the Gujurat Province of India, which is notorious for its huge daily tides.[29] Also discovered in the seas surrounding Bet Dwarka are a number of thick pottery amphorae of different sizes, which were probably used for transporting wine from Egypt to India. The *Periplus* discusses many ports along the west coast of India, and the work of archaeologists such as those active at Bet Dwarka has helped confirm the crucial role played by the most important of these ports in Silk Roads maritime trade, particularly the northwest coastal ports of Barbaricum, Barygaza, the southwest port of Muziris, and, to a lesser extent, Arikamedu on the southern tip of India.

The ancient port of Barbaricum was located near the modern Pakistani city of Karachi, and is described in the *Periplus* as a market town heavily involved in maritime trade during the first century CE. The *Periplus* lists a diverse range of commercial goods that were bought and sold there, including cotton textiles, topaz, coral, frankincense, glass vessels, silver and gold plate, wine, lapis lazuli, turquoise, wheat and rice. The *Periplus* also discusses the import of silk cloth, and of quantities of "thin clothing," possibly a further reference to silk textiles that had traveled overland from China, and then been moved south through the Kushan Empire to Barbaricum (which probably came under direct Kushan political control during the "Great Kushans" period), ready to be shipped on to Rome.[30] The *Periplus* notes that merchant ships and their crews would take some risks in transporting their goods on to Egypt as quickly as possible. The ships would set sail from Barbaricum in the month of July to catch the winds, even though the *Periplus* states that "it is more dangerous then, but through these winds the voyage is more direct, and sooner completed."[31]

Further south, the major port of Barygaza, located near the modern Indian city of Bharuch, was also flourishing during the first two centuries CE. According to the *Periplus*, the ruler of Barygaza was Nahapana, an Indo-Scythian (or Indo-Parthian) king of the western satraps. The region

[29] See S. R. Rao and A. S. Gaur, "Excavations at Bet Dwarka," *Marine Archaeology*, Marine Archaeological Venter, Goa, 3, July 1992, pp. 42ff.

[30] *Periplus* 38 and 39. [31] *Periplus* 39.

surrounding the port is described as fertile, where farmers grow wheat, rice, sesame and cotton, and graze "very many cattle."[32] The *Periplus* also lists a wide range of export and import goods that passed through Barygaza. Among the imports into India are wine (Italian was preferred), copper, tin, lead, coral, topaz, flint glass, and gold and silver coin. Exports that left Barygaza on ships returning to Egypt included ivory, agate, cotton cloth, silk cloth, pepper, lapis lazuli and turquoise. Ships returning to the Red Sea from Barygaza would also set sail in the month of July to catch the winds.

The *Periplus* also makes several claims about the activity and influence of Greeks in Barygaza, noting that in the port and surrounding region Greek-style "ancient shrines, walls of forts and great wells can still be found."[33] The author attributes the construction of these buildings to Alexander, but as Alexander never campaigned this far south in India, and as we know that this whole region eventually came under the control of Indo-Greek kings during the Hellenistic Era, it is the Indo-Greeks who were responsible for continuing Greek influence in the region, including, as the *Periplus* notes, the apparent continued use of Indo-Greek coinage in Barygaza in the mid-first century CE.[34]

Much further south again, somewhere on the coast of the modern Indian state of Kerala, was the port of Muziris. The *Periplus* describes Muziris as a thriving port, abounding "in ships sent there with cargoes from Arabia and by the Greeks."[35] Muziris and its hinterland, including a nearby market town named Damirica or Limyrike, was a major center for the export of black pepper, various other spices, finished metal goods, pearls, semiprecious stones and Chinese silk to the Roman Empire. The Greco-Roman merchants engaged in this export business paid for Indian goods in Roman gold coins, many of which have been found in the region. Muziris is also depicted as a bustling port in certain ancient bardic poems written in the Tamil language spoken in the region. In one example Muziris is described as "the city where the beautiful vessels, the masterpieces of the Yavanas (Westerners), stir white foam of the Culli, river of the Chera, arriving with gold and departing with pepper . . . brimming with prosperity."[36]

The actual location of Muziris has been lost for centuries, but recent archaeological discoveries at Pattanam near the modern town of Cranganore in central Kerala have led some archaeologists to argue that they might have discovered Muziris. These discoveries include Roman coins, fragments of amphorae, shards of Roman glass and Roman gaming counters, all dated from the first to the third centuries CE. Other

[32] *Periplus* 41. [33] *Periplus* 41. [34] *Periplus* 47. [35] *Periplus* 53–54.
[36] See H. Kulke, *A History of India*. London: Routledge, 2004; poem No. 149, 7–11.

materials of Arabian and Mesopotamian origin have also been discovered, such as turquoise glazed pottery and crumbs of frankincense. The presence of the remains of ancient wharfs and warehouses further demonstrates Pattanam's long history of maritime engagement with the Greco-Roman world and West Asia, but whether this is sufficient to firmly identify it with Muziris is currently hotly debated by historians and archaeologists.[37]

Another South Indian port mentioned in the *Periplus* is Poduke, which most archaeologists identify with the archaeological site of Arikamedu, located in the modern Indian state of Tamil Nadu, close to the city of Pondicherry.[38] Excavations, which were first conducted there between 1945 and 1950, unearthed amphorae and Roman lamps, glassware and glass beads, leading British and French archaeologists to publicize the probable role of Arikamedu in Indian Ocean Silk Roads trade. Archaeological work at the site resumed in the 1980s under Vimala Begley, who concluded that Arikamedu had indeed been a trading hub for many centuries (between roughly the second century BCE to the seventh or eighth century CE), but that the most important networks it was involved in operated up and down the eastern seaboard of India, although merchants at Arikamedu were also "trading with the Mediterranean directly."[39]

Barygaza and Connections with the Kushan Empire

During the mid-first century CE, the period discussed by the author of the *Periplus*, the Kushan Empire was in a state of near constant expansion, which might explain the passing reference in the *Periplus*' discussion of regions beyond the northwestern Indian port of Barygaza to "the very warlike people of the Bactrians, under a king."[40] If the *Periplus* was indeed written between 40 and 50 CE, the king referred to must have been Kujula Kadphises (r. c. 25–c. 85 CE), who is described in Han Chinese sources as conquering all of Bactria (ancient Afghanistan) before moving with his forces further south to conquer Kashmir and the Swat Valley of modern Pakistan.[41] This meant that, although the Kushans had no coastal regions under their control during the period described by the *Periplus*, their growing empire was in reasonable proximity to the port of

[37] See *The Seventh Season Pattanam Excavation – 2013*, Kerala Council for Historical Research.
[38] *Periplus* 60.
[39] V. Begley, "Arikamedu Reconsidered," *American Journal of Archaeology* 87, No. 4 (1983), pp. 479–481.
[40] *Periplus* 47. [41] *Hou Han Shu*, Hill 2009, p. 29.

Barygaza via the Indus Valley. The superb glassware found among the high-value luxury goods discovered in the Kushan royal city of Begram was clearly of Roman-Egyptian origin. The stashing of the glassware and other treasures into secure storerooms at Begram has been dated to the first or early second centuries CE. It is most probable that the glassware was carried by sea from one of the Red Sea ports to Barygaza, before being transported by merchants some 2,000 kilometers (1,200 miles) northward into the Kushan Empire via the Indus Valley and Khyber Pass.[42]

Further evidence of connections between the Kushans and Indian Ocean networks via Barygaza can be found in the list of exports taken from Barygaza back to the Red Sea, as described in the *Periplus*. One of these was lapis lazuli, a semiprecious stone that was mined at Shortugai in Badakshan, a region of northwestern Afghanistan then under the control of the Kushan Empire. Another was turquoise, which probably would have come from Nishapur in Iran, then part of the Parthian Empire. Both these valuable commodities would have been transported down the Indus Valley by merchants working within these two great Central Asian empires. And of course, the Chinese silk being shipped out of Barygaza would most probably have traveled overland from Chang'an before being transported through the Kushan Empire and down the Indus to the coast. Through these various routes the great Silk Roads network connected the silk weavers of Han China with the patrician women of Rome via the Tarim Basin, the Kushan Empire, the Indus River Valley and the ships and mariners of the Arabian and Red Seas, further striking evidence of the extraordinary connectedness of the Afro-Eurasian world zone during the First Silk Roads Era.

As we noted earlier, a traditional argument as to why Central Asian merchants preferred to transport their goods down the Indus Valley from Bactria, rather than continue on overland through the Parthian Empire, has been that periods of conflict between Rome and Parthia made the western land routes unstable. However, given that there were long periods of peace between the Roman and Parthian Empires, and also little to no evidence of conflict between the Han, Kushans and Parthians, a more probable reason was that it was simply cheaper to move goods down to the northwest Indian seaports than to continue on overland. A considerable saving would have been made by simply eliminating the many fees and taxes that intermediaries were charging along the route. Both Pliny and Strabo noted that rulers charged merchants fees at every opportunity

[42] See E. H. Seland, "Ancient Afghanistan and the Indian Ocean: Maritime Links of the Kushan Empire ca 50–200 CE," *Journal of Indian Ocean Archaeology* No. 9 (2013), pp. 66ff.

along the overland routes through the Euphrates Valley and through Arabia.[43] As Eivind Heldaas Seland has pointed out, at the time the *Periplus* was written the Indus Valley was not part of the Kushan realm, which meant that Kushan merchants must have had cordial relations with their Indo-Parthian counterparts and rulers like Nahapana in order to conduct their mutually beneficial trade. Later, when all of the Indus Valley as far as the coast had become part of the Kushan Empire, the savings in terms of a reduction in tariffs and fees would have been even more substantial.[44]

The other huge benefit in diverting goods south from the land routes through Bactria, then on to the Indus Valley, would have been a reduction in the actual cost of transport. As Erdkamp has pointed out, sea transport was cheaper than river transport, which was cheaper again than overland transport.[45] This means that, once Kushan or Sogdian merchants had moved their goods across the Karakorum or Hindu Kush Mountains (no easy task, of course), they could easily and comparatively cheaply be

Figure 8.2 The Indus River flowing through Sind Province in modern Pakistan
http://media.gettyimages.com/photos/indus-river-picture-id539071796
Credit: commoner28th

[43] Strabo, *Geog.* 16.1.27; Pliny, *NH* 12.63–65. [44] Seland 2013, p. 72.
[45] P. Erdkamp, "Agriculture, Unemployment and the Cost of Rural Labor in the Roman World," *Classical Quarterly* 49, No. 2 (1999), p. 565.

moved down the Indus River to Barygaza, and on to Roman Egypt by sea. Seland points to the memoires of nineteenth-century traveler Alex Burns, who in the 1830s had counted 700 different riverboats involved in Indus navigation between Lahore and the coast. It took these boats two months using sails to travel all the way upriver to Lahore, but only fifteen days to sail back down again, surely evidence of the feasibility and undoubted cost benefit for merchants using these same forms of river transport nearly 2,000 years earlier.[46]

The *Muziris Papyrus* and the Value of Roman Trade with India

An extraordinary insight into the conduct of maritime Silk Roads trade between India and the Roman Empire is provided by the *Muziris Papyrus*, a second-century CE document that discusses a contract between a Greek merchant importer living in the Egyptian city of Alexandria and a financier.[47] The arrangement between them concerns the export of a high-value cargo of luxury goods from Muziris, and the details reveal the staggering amounts of money involved in these commercial transactions. The papyrus notes that a single cargo of ivory, cloth and nard that is to be shipped from Muziris to Egypt onboard a Roman ship called the *Hermapollon* is valued at almost 7 million *sesterces*!

As we have considered several times, in a statement made in the century before the *Muziris Papyrus* was written, Roman statesman Pliny the Elder had commented that trade with Asia was costing the Romans 100 million *sesterces* a year. The papyrus provides evidence that Pliny was probably not exaggerating to make a moral point, given that a single cargo consignment from one Indian port back to the Red Sea would have accounted for 7 percent of Pliny's total. The *Muziris Papyrus* also documents the weight of this valuable cargo, around 3.18 metric tons.[48] Peter Sidebotham has used this value and weight data, along with Strabo's observation that 120 ships sailed out of Myos Hormos each year for India, to conclude that imports from South Asia alone might have totaled something like 17.64 billion *sesterces*.[49]

[46] A. R. Burns, *Travels into Bokhara*. London: John Murray, 1834, pp. 200–201. See Seland 2013, p. 72.
[47] On the *Muziris Papyrus*, see R. McLaughlin, *Rome and the Distant East: Trade Routes to the Ancient Lands of Arabia, India and China*. London: Continuum, 2010, pp. 40ff.
[48] D. Rathbone, "The Muziris Papyrus: Financing Roman Trade with India," in S. Abd-el-Ghani and W. A. Farag, *Alexandrian Studies in Honor of Mostafa el Abbadi*. Alexandria, 2000, pp. 39–50.
[49] Sidebotham 2011, p. 218.

Most of the textual evidence implies that Romans and other Mediterranean merchants involved in Indian Ocean trade mostly paid for these luxury imports with gold and silver coins. To date, some 6,000 Roman silver *denarii* and more than 1,000 gold *aurei* have been discovered at various sites on the Indian subcontinent.[50] These coins have been found scattered all over India, in hoards, archaeological digs and occasional stray finds. But the largest concentrations have been discovered in the Coimbatore district of southern India, and in the vicinity of the Krishna River in the eastern part of central India.[51] Most of the coins date to the Julio-Claudian dynastic era, but their date of actual export to India is much debated by numismatists.[52] Clearly, though, these coins provide strong supporting evidence of the role of money in facilitating vigorous maritime trade between the Roman Empire and the Indian subcontinent during the First Silk Roads Era.

The source of the enormous sums of money, including the coins, needed to finance Roman trade with the East has also been debated by historians. Christopher Howgego has argued that ultimately the only group in Rome with the financial wherewithal to transfer large sums such as this was wealthy members of the Roman Senate, who could mobilize networks of associates across the empire to finance trade on this scale.[53] However, Peter Temin has noted that genuine banks did exist in the Roman world, such as that operated by the Sulpicii of Puteoli. Wealthy Romans (including senators) would deposit money with the Sulpicii for a fixed interest rate. The bankers earned their profits by lending the deposited money to Greco-Roman merchants, who would use it to finance large-scale imports such as the cargo discussed in the *Muziris Papyrus.*[54]

Because so much senatorial wealth was tied up in trade, this meant that many Roman foreign policy decisions were taken explicitly to safeguard their financial interest in transregional commerce. Matthew Fitzpatrick has shown that many such policy initiatives, including Augustus' takeover of independent Egypt, and numerous campaigns against the Parthians and Nabataeans, were consistent with "a policy that sought to both facilitate trade and investment in these regions for Roman subjects and to incrementally take possession of those trading centers that were within

[50] Cobb 2015, p. 187.

[51] S. Suresh, *Symbols of Trade: Roman and Pseudo-Roman Objects Found in India*. Delhi, 2004.

[52] See Cobb 2015, p. 188, for more on this.

[53] C. Howgego, "The Supply and Use of Money in the Roman World, 200 BC–AD 300," *Journal of Roman Studies* 82 (1992), pp. 28–29.

[54] P. Temin, "Financial Intermediaries in the Early Roman Empire," *Journal of Economic History* 64 (2004), p. 728.

reach."[55] The Indian Ocean network was clearly central to all this, to the movement of shiploads of luxury goods, the large-scale finance involved in doing so and even the foreign policy decisions made by imperial states to facilitate the smooth flow of commerce. As Fergus Millar concludes, sending goods by ship was much safer, faster and cheaper than sending them all the way from Chang'an to the Mediterranean coast by the more dangerous, expensive and much slower land routes.[56] There can be no doubt, then, that the majority of "Eastern" exports that made their way to Rome did so on board ships rather than on the backs of camels or donkeys.

The Arabian Peninsula and Indian Ocean Trade

The *Periplus* is incredibly useful and detailed in its discussions of trade between Roman Egypt and the coast of India, but it has less to say about the other key hubs of Indian Ocean trade, the East African Coast, the Arabian Peninsula and the Persian Gulf. However, the *Periplus* does discuss the relationship between East African ports such as Rhapta and trade towns in Arabia, including Muza. Muza was located on the Red Sea coast of Arabia, and was well known to Pliny, who named it the third port of Arabia.[57] By the time the *Periplus* was written in the mid-first century CE, these East African ports were actually under the hegemony of Arab commercial cities such as Muza. Given that Muza was also commercially linked to Rome via the Red Sea ports, it is hardly surprising that the *Periplus* describes Muza as "teeming with Arabs, ship owners and sailors (and) alive with commercial activity."[58] Like many of the other coastal ports (including Barygaza), Muza was the maritime outlet for an interior commercial city, in this case Saphar.

As well as connections between Arabian Red Sea ports and the east coast of Africa, ancient authors also comment upon overland connections between ports along the Arabian Peninsula and ports on the coast of the Mediterranean. Pliny describes one such route involved in the frankincense trade from present-day Yemen to Gaza, a distance of some 2,200 kilometers (1,300 miles).[59] Strabo, writing during the reigns of Augustus and Tiberius, describes a regularly used route connecting the Jordanian trade city of Petra with the port of Leuke Kome at the mouth of the Gulf

[55] M. P. Fitzpatrick, "Provincializing Rome: The Indian Ocean Trade Network and Roman Imperialism," *Journal of World History* 22, No. 1 (March 2011), p. 42.
[56] F. Millar, "Looking East from the Classical World: Colonialism, Culture, and Trade from Alexander the Great to Shapur I," *International History Review* 20, No. 3 (1998), 507–531.
[57] Pliny, *NH* 6.23. [58] *Periplus* 21. [59] Pliny, *NH* XII.32/63–5.

Figure 8.3 Dhow sailing near the East African island of Madagascar
http://media.gettyimages.com/photos/dhow-floating-picture-id
824624844
Credit: Pierre-Yves Babelon

of Aqaba, the other long and narrow waterway, along with the Gulf of Suez, at the head of the Red Sea.[60] The *Periplus* also mentions Leuke Kome, and notes that, like the ports in the Persian Gulf discussed later, geographic conditions meant that only small craft could dock there: "This harbor also serves in a way the function of a port of trade for the craft, none large, that come to it loaded with freight from Arabia."[61] From Leuke Kome goods were most probably transported by camel across the desert to Gaza, or else inland as far as Petra.

Roman rulers were clearly very well aware of all this commercial activity occurring in the Arabian Peninsula, and a number of policy initiatives were aimed at bringing this activity and wealth under Roman control, including Augustus' attempted conquest of Arabia in 24/25 BCE. As Strabo put it: "He was also influenced by the very longstanding reputation that they (the Arabs) were very wealthy, and exchanged their aromatics and precious stones for silver and gold, but never spent with foreigners any part of what they received in exchange."[62] As Fitzpatrick notes, Strabo is clearly pointing to a large trade surplus the Arabs were

[60] Strabo, *Geog*. XVI.4.23. [61] *Periplus* 19. [62] Strabo, *Geog*. 4.22.

enjoying through their trade in incense and other aromatics to Rome, export goods that were in demand for funerary practices and other religious rituals in the Roman Empire.[63]

Arab involvement in Indian Ocean trade intensified during the first century CE, despite Roman military campaigns against groups like the Nabataeans and others active in the Arabian Peninsula, which Sidebotham described as "blatant Roman economic imperialism."[64] But Roman dreams of conquering Arabian commercial centers and thus gaining control of their lucrative incense markets were constantly frustrated. Key Arabian commercial towns like Adulis (also on the Red Sea coast) were able to retain their independence despite repeated Roman campaigns against them. Ultimately the Romans were never able to gain direct political control of the ports in Arabia, nor indeed of most of the other regions in Africa and Asia connected by Indian Ocean maritime routes. Roman elites had to settle for enriching themselves and the state by taxing the lucrative trade in luxury goods such as African ivory, Arabian incense, Indian pepper and other spices and of course Chinese silk.[65]

The Persian Gulf and Indian Ocean Trade

Ports located in the Red Sea, and along the coasts of East Africa and India, were not the only regional centers of maritime trade operating in the Indian Ocean Basin in the first two centuries CE. In an earlier chapter we saw how the Parthians expanded their empire down to the head of the Persian Gulf, in order to gain control of some of the regional kingdoms that controlled trade at the head of the Gulf, such as Characene. We also saw how the Parthians effectively dissuaded Later Han Dynasty official Gan Ying, who had traveled from China to the Persian Gulf, from continuing on further to Rome, presumably to ensure that the Parthians' lucrative role as middlemen in trans-Eurasian trade was maintained.[66] We also discussed in the chapter on Roman involvement in overland trade the major commercial city of Palmyra, where inscriptional finds demonstrate just how deeply Palmyrene merchants were involved in both land-based trade and maritime trade between the Persian Gulf and India. The *Periplus* includes a discussion of a commercial expedition from Palmyra to a port located near the mouth of the Indus River, probably Barbaricum, so that Palmyrene merchants could acquire spices,

[63] Fitzpatrick 2011, p. 51. [64] Sidebotham, *Roman Economic Policy*, p. 140.
[65] Fitzpatrick 2011, p. 53.
[66] HHS, see Hill 2009, p. 23 who argues for identifying Taizhou with Characene instead of the previous identification with Ctesiphon.

pearls and agates.[67] All of this is evidence that ports at the head of the Persian Gulf were also active in Indian Ocean trade during the first two centuries CE.

Most Persian Gulf ports were small; their role was to unload goods and move them inland for further distribution. Because the environment of the Persian Gulf has constantly changed throughout history, many ports have risen and fallen, including during the First Silk Roads Era. Most of the ports at the head of the Gulf were located on inland rivers many miles inland from the shifting coast. Even today, the Iraqi port of Basra is located on the Shatt al-Arab River, 70 miles in from the river's mouth. The Shatt al-Arab is very prone to silting, and its mouth has dangerous currents that have led to many shipwrecks over the centuries. Because of this, goods are often unloaded into smaller craft to make the journey upriver. This was undoubtedly the same situation merchants faced almost two millennia ago.

Despite these environmental challenges, historically there has always been at least one major port at the head of the Persian Gulf, because this was the closest access point to the Tigris and Euphrates River Valleys, and other regional overland routes toward the Iranian Plateau in the east and the Mediterranean coast to the west. During the First Silk Roads Era, the major Persian Gulf commercial center was Charax Spasinou, the same town that Isidorus of Charax, author of *Parthian Stations*, probably resided in. Like modern Basra, Charax Spasinou was not located right on the coast but further inland along a river. It was connected to the Gulf sea lanes by a small port named Apologos, which might have been the location of the original port that evolved into Basra in medieval times.[68]

Both Charax Spasinou and Apologos were part of the southern Mesopotamian political region of Characene, a region named by both Pliny and Ptolemy. The name *Characene* was derived from the Greek name for the principal city of the region, Charax.[69] Strabo had earlier named the same political region as Mesene late in the first century BCE.[70] The city that became Charax had originally been founded as Alexandria on the Tigris by Alexander of Macedon, presumably to help facilitate trade through the Gulf and on to his new eastern capital of Babylon. According to Pliny, Alexander settled part of the city with invalided Macedonian soldiers, who lived in a special quarter of the port known as Pella.[71] Pliny also informs us that Charax was later destroyed by severe

[67] See Chapter 5.

[68] See J.-F. Sales, "The Periplus of the Erythraean Sea and the Arab-Persian Gulf," *Topoi* 3, No. 2 (1993), p. 510, n. 57.

[69] Pliny *NH*, 6.31.138; Ptolemy *Geog.* 6.5.

[70] Strabo, *Geog.* 16.4.1.

[71] Pliny *NH*, 6.31.138.

flooding in the Tigris Valley. The damage was so severe that Charax could play no role in the developing trade between the Persian Gulf and other regions that took place over the next 150 years.[72] Charax was eventually rebuilt during the reign of Seleucid ruler Antiochus IV, and by 165 BCE it was under the control of a Persian governor named Hyspaosines, who had been appointed by Antiochus.

Charax immediately began to see an increase in trade that was now funneled from the harbor at Apologos through the city and on to the Seleucid capital of Seleucia on the Tigris. Even after Antiochus IV died in 163 BCE, ushering in a period of political instability in the Seleucid realm, Hyspaosines and the city of Charax remained loyal to the Seleucids, presumably to ensure the continuation of mutually beneficial trade. However, the increasing strength of the Parthians who were now contesting with the Seleucids for control of much of Mesopotamia, particularly during the reign of Mithridates I, led Hyspaosines to eventually declare independence from the Seleucids sometime around 140 BCE.[73] By 120 BCE, numismatic evidence in the form of overstrikes with the image of Mithridates II shows that the Parthians had gained complete control over Charax, and Hyspaosines had been relegated to figurehead control of this kingdom at the head of the Persian Gulf.[74]

Soon after this, Charax was again destroyed by flooding, and in the aftermath Hyspaosines had lengthy new embankments constructed to protect the city. Because of these embankments, later Roman writers such as Josephus began to refer to the city as Charax Spasinou, the latter word being derived from "Palisades of Spasines," in turn derived from the name of the city's ruler Hyspaosines.[75] Hyspaosines was eventually succeeded by a series of Parthian vassals as ruler of Charax Spasinou, and of the surrounding political region of Characene/Mesene. Both the city and the region remained an important Persian Gulf commercial center under nominal Parthian control for the next several centuries. When Roman emperor Trajan eventually undertook a punitive expedition against the Parthians in 116 CE, the ruling prince of Characene/Mesene did make temporary submission to the Romans, but otherwise the political region and the town of Charax Spasinou remained solidly part of the Parthian realm for about 350 years.

Throughout most of this period the residents of Charax Spasinou and Characene/Mesene benefited from transregional trade. The *Periplus* notes a special trading relationship between the Characene/Mesenian port of

[72] Pliny *NH*, 6.31, 138.
[73] S. A. Nodleman, "A Preliminary History of Characene," *Berytus* 13 (1960), p. 87.
[74] A. R. Bellinger, "Hyspaosines of Charax," *Yale Classical* Studies 8 (1942), pp. 60–61.
[75] Josephus, *Jewish Antiquities*, 1.6.4.

Apologos and another port named Omana, which might have been located further south in the Gulf, perhaps at el-Dur, as argued by Potts.[76] The two ancient Persian Gulf ports traded frankincense and other commercial products between each other, and many of these same goods were then moved on to the port of Barygaza. As Jean-Francoise Sales describes it,

> "the true picture which emerges from the *Periplus* is a three-station sailing route: Apologos-Omana-Barygaza. We can consider it as a more or less steady and invariable route and trade-unit, with the same ships and agents working regularly along . . . the shipmen of the Apologos-Omana-Barygaza leg of the Indian Ocean trade would have been Indians, [or] more probably Arabs or Persians."[77]

The *Periplus* informs us that Apologos and Omana also exported goods inland, both westward into southern Arabia and north into Mesopotamia and Syria.[78] During the first century CE, new overland trade routes were made to connect Charax Spasinou with the Nabatean city of Petra, in Jordan, and as we noted, other routes connected Charax with the great Syrian trading city of Palmyra. Late in the first century CE a new Characene/Mesenian port was developed 18 kilometers south of Charax at a city on the Tigris River named Forat by Pliny, which was soon frequented by merchants from Petra.[79] Palmyrene inscriptions of the second century also mention trade caravans to Forat as well as Charax. By the early third century CE Charax, Forat and the kingdom of Characene/Mesene had probably become a quasi-independent state within the Parthian Empire. The kingdom and its city and ports then apparently lost much of their importance and relevance during the subsequent reign of the Sasanians, who expanded another small, pre-existing Parthian port city at Siraf, on the northern shores of the Persian Gulf, into a major commercial hub.

What is clear from all this tantalizing evidence is that, while the bulk of Indian Ocean trade was carried on ships between the three major Red Sea ports of Roman-controlled Egypt and a handful of major ports on the west coast of the Indian subcontinent other regions of the greater Indian Ocean Basin were also active participants in this great maritime network. At Persian Gulf ports such as Apologos or Omana, and at ports along the Yemeni and Red Sea coasts and in the Gulf of Aqaba, all manner of valuable commodities that had arrived by sea were being shipped inland to major commercial cities such as Charax Spasinou, Palmyra, Petra or Gaza, to be distributed throughout the Roman Empire, after the appropriate fees and taxes had been levied, of course. In the final section of this

[76] See Potts 1988, pp. 154–155. [77] Sales 1993, pp. 512–513. [78] Sales 1993, p. 512.
[79] Pliny *NH*, 6.32.145.

chapter we turn to evidence of maritime connections between the Indian subcontinent and the other major agrarian civilization deeply engaged in Silk Roads trade, the Chinese Han Dynasty.

Han China and Maritime Trade

Early Chinese dynasties such as the Shang and Zhou were so small and so focused on trying to maintain control over their regional states that there is little evidence of the development of any serious maritime linkages between them, and ports or states in Southeast Asia. Compared to other ancient agrarian civilizations, the first Chinese dynasties developed in relative isolation, engendered both by the forbidding geographical barriers of the arid and mountainous west, and the challenges caused by the sea. However, recent evidence does indicate a few surprising and very ancient connections between early Chinese states and the Indian Ocean. Archaeologists have discovered cowrie shells, both in coastal regions near the mouth of the Huang He, and in inland provinces such as Sichuan and Yunnan that have been dated to as early as the second millennium BCE. The shells had originated in the islands of the Maldives, deep in the Indian Ocean to the south of India, before making their way by ship through the Bay of Bengal, to be eventually exported by land routes through Burma on to various locations in Shang Dynasty China. The cowrie shells were used as personal adornments and in rituals by Shang and other elites, demonstrating just how early in its history China had developed indirect connections to the Indian Ocean Basin, by way of land routes through Southeast Asia.[80]

Following the emergence of the Qin Dynasty in 221 BCE, the first seriously large Chinese imperial state, maritime linkages with other regions, including indirectly the Indian Ocean Basin, intensified. These were a direct product of Qin expansion to the south, and the incorporation of new regions and peoples in what is southern China and northern Vietnam today.[81] As a result of Qin military campaigns, a series of new independent states that the Chinese called *Bai Yue*, or the "Hundred Yue," emerged in southern coastal regions that were populated by non-

[80] H. U. Vogel and S. Hieronymus, "Cowry Trade and Its Role in the Economy of Yunnan from the Ninth to the Mid-Seventeenth Century, Part 1," *Journal of the Economic and Social History of the Orient* 36, No. 3 (1993), pp. 211–252; B. Yang. "Horses, Silver, and Cowries: Yunnan in Global Perspective," *Journal of World History* 15, No. 3 (2004), pp. 281–322.

[81] For an excellent account of the early development of maritime links between Qin and Han China and Southeast Asia and the Indian Ocean, see Tansen Sen, "Early China and the Indian Ocean Network," in P. de Souza and P. Arnaud, eds., *The Sea in History: The Ancient World*. Suffolk: Boydell and Brewer, 2017, pp. 536ff.

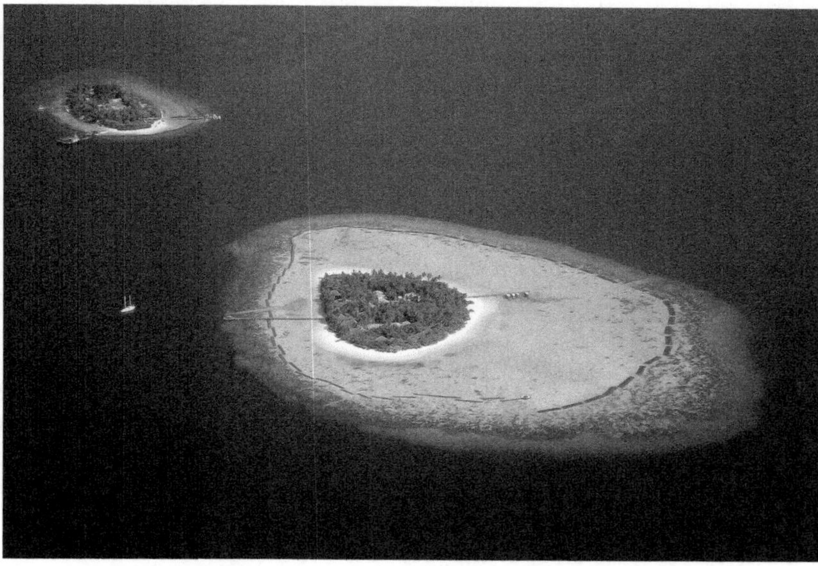

Figure 8.4 Aerial view of two islands in the Maldives, the source of cowrie shells that were traded with the Shang Dynasty in China
http://media.gettyimages.com/photos/maldives-wonder-of-nature-picture-id131963448
Credit: Mohamed Abdulla Shafeeg

Chinese peoples. The best known of these political entities was the Nanyue state, which emerged soon after the collapse of the Qin in 206 BCE. Over the century that followed, the Nanyue state gained control over a large swathe of territory in southern China and Vietnam, including the modern coastal provinces of Yunnan and Guangdong.[82] Once the Early Han Dynasty came to power, and particularly during the reign of Emperor Wudi (140–87 BCE), the Han Chinese empire began to expand in all directions, including south into Vietnam. The Nanyue state was formally annexed by the Han in 111 BCE, in the middle of Wudi's reign.

We can assume that, in part at least, this annexation was driven by the sort of commercial motives that guided much Roman foreign policy during the same period. That is, Wudi and the court wanted to take control of thriving maritime regions and their ports in an attempt to enhance trade contacts with other regions, and thus increase the financial resources available to Han elites and to the state. Commercial

[82] On the Nanyue state, see H. Peters, "Tattooed Faces and Stilt Houses: Who Were the Ancient Yue?," *Sino-Platonic Papers* 17 (April 1990), pp. 1–27.

motivations were also a significant part of the reason for Han expansion into Central Asia, as we have seen. Evidence suggests that, at the time of Han annexation, the Nanyue state had already developed a thriving maritime commercial relationship with various Southeast Asian ports. Merchants used boats sailing close to the shore to connect southern China with ports along the coasts of Southeast Asia, and thus indirectly with the Indian Ocean sea lanes to the west. There is also some evidence to suggest that South Asian merchants and craftsmen settled in some of the Southeast Asian ports, using precious stones imported from South Asia to make jewelry for both local consumption and export by sea into Han China.[83]

Compelling evidence of strong maritime commercial relations between the Early Han Dynasty and Southeast Asia has also been discovered in an extraordinary collection of luxury goods found in elite Han Dynasty tombs, including pearls, glass necklaces, ivory and rhinoceros horn, and crystal and gold ornaments. The most important of these discoveries were made by archaeologists in a very large Han cemetery located at Hepu in southern China, which contains thousands of elite tombs. Indeed, Hepu is probably the best-preserved Han Dynasty period cemetery ever discovered, full of elaborate tombs and exotic luxury artifacts. Many of the imported goods discovered at Hepu are of "foreign" origin, including some of the glassware that was manufactured in South Asia, and crystal and gold ornamental pieces that probably came from the Persian Gulf or Mediterranean region.[84] These discoveries are further evidence of the existence of a vibrant maritime Silk Roads network connecting South, Southeast and East Asia via the eastern Indian Ocean during the First Silk Roads Era. As Tansen Sen concludes: "These artifacts, which primarily date to between 30 BC to 220 AD, are clear indications of coastal China's connections not only to the South China Sea region, but also, through various maritime networks, to the Red Sea area."[85]

Archaeological discoveries are not the only evidence we have of maritime connections between Han China and the Indian Ocean during the First Silk Roads Era. All the major Han sources describe the southern Chinese port of Guangzhou as flourishing, and a place where a great deal of wealth was being generated through transregional maritime trade in

[83] I. C. Glover and B. Bellina, "Ban Don Ta Phet and Khao Sam Kaeo: The Earliest Indian Contacts Re-assessed," in P. Manguin, A. Mani, and G. Wade, eds., *Early Interactions between South and Southeast Asia*. Singapore: Institute of Southeast Asian Studies, 2011, pp. 19–45.

[84] Tansen Sen 2017, p. 540.

[85] Z. Xiong, "The Hepu Han Tombs and the Maritime Silk Road of the Han Dynasty," *Antiquity* 88 (2014), pp. 1229–1243.

luxury goods. Chinese historians have made wider claims for the influence of Guangzhou, arguing that these intense levels of contact with foreign merchants influenced the way agriculture and handicraft manufacturing in the region were carried out, intensifying contacts between the coasts and farming and craft communities inland.[86]

Further evidence of commercial links between Han Chinese merchants and ports along the northwest coast of India, via the Indus Valley and Bactria, or across Karakorum passes, can also be found in the Han sources and in the *Periplus*.[87] The *Han Shu* includes a report by a Han envoy named Du Qin, who discusses an Indian trade delegation that traveled to Gandhara (in northern Pakistan) around 25 BCE: "There are no members of the royal family or noblemen among those who bring the gifts. The latter are all merchants and men of low origins. They wish to exchange their goods and conduct trade, under the pretext of presenting gifts."[88] This delegation occurred at the very beginning of the reign of Kushan king Kujula Kadphises, so before Gandhara had come under Kushan control. Once the Kushans had constructed their vast empire, Silk Roads trade intensified during the two centuries that followed. One result of this, and further evidence of increased commercial contacts between South and East Asia via the Kushan realm, is that Indian merchant delegations now traveled all the way to the great capitals of Han China, where many other foreign merchants were also either visiting or living.[89]

The *Periplus* also clearly attests to connections between China and the Indian ports: "At the northernmost point, where the sea ends somewhere on the outer fringe, there is a very great inland city called Thina [China] from which silk floss, yarn, and cloth are shipped by land via Bactria to Barygaza and via the Ganges River back to Limyrikê. It is not easy to get to this Thina, for rarely do people come from it, and only a few. The area lies right under Ursa Minor and, it is said, is contiguous with the parts of the Pontus [Black Sea] and the Caspian Sea where these parts turn off."[90] The lack of geographical knowledge concerning the actual location of China is hardly surprising, given the great distances between Chang'an and Barygaza, and the fact that the author of the *Periplus* was a merchant

[86] Q. Huang, *Guangdong haishang Sichou zhilu shi* [*The Maritime Silk Road in Guangdong's History*], Guangzhou: Guangdong jingji chubanshe, 2003.

[87] See E. de la Vaissière, *Sogdian Traders. A History*, trans. James Ward, Handbook of Oriental Studies, vol. 10. Leiden: Brill, 2005, chapter 1 on this.

[88] HS 96 A.

[89] For references to various foreign merchants living in Han China, see Yu Ying-Shi, "Han Foreign Relations," in D. Twitchett and M. Loewe, eds., *The Cambridge History of China Volume 1: The Ch'in and Han Empires 221 BC–AD 220*. Cambridge: Cambridge University Press, 1986, pp. 387–397.

[90] *Periplus* 64.

mariner with expertise in coastal trade. Nonetheless this statement certainly demonstrates a remarkably clear understanding of the origins of the silk cloth, yarn and floss that was being exported out of South Asian ports and to the Roman Empire.

It is fair to conclude, however, that, despite all the evidence we have of developing connections between the southern ports of China and those in Southeast Asia (and indirectly South Asia), the bulk of Chinese exports during the First Silk Roads Era was still traveling overland from Chang'an to Bactria, using routes we discussed in earlier chapters, before being transported by merchants down the Indus Valley to Barygaza. This would change dramatically 500 years later during the Second Silk Roads Era (roughly 600–900 CE), when trade between the Tang Dynasty in China and the Sasanian Empire and later Islamic caliphates would mostly take place by sea.

Conclusion

After considering in earlier chapters the development and operation of major Silk Roads land routes, in this chapter we have examined the other great conduit of trade during the era, the maritime routes that connected Roman Egypt, the east coast of Africa, the Arabian Peninsula, and the Persian Gulf with South Asian ports and Central Asian land routes. We have also looked at developing maritime connections between Han China and Southeast Asia, routes that would expand enormously half a millennium later when the Tang Dynasty came to power in China. Political tensions between the Roman and the Parthian Empires might have contributed to the development of the western Indian Ocean maritime connections between ports on the coast of Indian and those in the Red Sea. However, trade by sea was always an attractive option for ancient merchants. Not only was it cheaper and faster, but it could also be conducted by commercial guilds that were often largely unaffected by the geopolitical situation within and between states. In the final chapter of this book we turn to the political, cultural and environmental factors that led to the demise of the vibrant First Silk Roads trading network in the mid-third century CE.

Selected Further Reading

Cobb, M. A., "Balancing the Trade: Roman Cargo Shipments to India," *Oxford Journal of Archaeology* 34, No. 2, 2015, pp. 193ff.

Fitzpatrick, M. P., "Provincializing Rome: The Indian Ocean Trade Network and Roman Imperialism," *Journal of World History* 22, No. 1 (March 2011).

Kaul, S., "South Asia," in C. Benjamin ed., *Cambridge History of the World Vol. 4: A World with States, Empires, and Networks, 1200 BCE–900 CE*. Cambridge: Cambridge University Press, 2015, pp. 480ff.

McLaughlin, R., *Rome and the Distant East: Trade Routes to the Ancient Lands of Arabia, India and China* London: Continuum, 2010.

Millar, F., "Looking East from the Classical World: Colonialism, Culture, and Trade from Alexander the Great to Shapur I," *International History Review* 20, No. 3 (1998), pp. 507–531.

Potter, L. G., *The Persian Gulf in History*. London: Palgrave Macmillan, 2009.

Ray, H. B., *The Archaeology of Seafaring in Ancient South Asia*. Cambridge World Archaeology. Cambridge: Cambridge University Press, 2003.

Sales, J.-F., "The Periplus of the Erythraean Sea and the Arab-Persian Gulf," *Topoi* 1993 3, No. 2 (1993).

Schoff, W. H., *The Periplus of the Erythrian Sea: Travel and Trade in the Indian Ocean by a Merchant of the First Century*. New York: Longmans, Green and Co, 1912.

Seland, E. H., "Ancient Afghanistan and the Indian Ocean: Maritime Links of the Kushan Empire ca 50–200 CE," in *Journal of Indian Ocean Archaeology*, No. 9 (2013), pp. 66ff.

Sidebotham, S. E., Roman Economic Policy in the Erythra Thalassa 30 B.C.–A.D. 217 (Mnemosyne Suppl. XCI). Leiden: E. J. Brill, 1986.

Berenike and the Ancient Maritime Spice Route. Berkeley and Los Angeles: University of California Press, 2011.

Tansen Sen, "Early China and the Indian Ocean Network," in P. de Souza and P. Arnaud, eds., *The Sea in History: The Ancient World*. Suffolk: Boydell and Brewer, 2017, pp. 536ff.

Temin, P., "Financial Intermediaries in the Early Roman Empire," *Journal of Economic History* 64, 2004.

Von Redden, S., "Global Economic History," in C. Benjamin, ed., *Cambridge History of the World Vol. IV*. Cambridge: Cambridge University Press, 2015, pp. 29–54.

9 Collapse of Empires and the Decline of the First Silk Roads Era

During the third century CE, long-distance Silk Roads commercial and cultural exchange diminished significantly as all of the key agrarian civilizations were forced to withdraw from the network. Transregional exchanges late in the First Silk Roads Era may have been partly responsible for this decline, because they contributed to the spread of disease epidemics that had disastrous consequences for populations at the western and eastern ends of the network. These epidemics occurred at the same time as the collapse of three previously stable empires, in what can only be described as a Eurasia-wide cycle of contraction. The Later Han Dynasty officially ended in 220 CE, after warlords had succeeded in taking control of most of China. At about the same time, both the Parthian and Kushan Empires collapsed under a wave of Sasanian invaders led by their dynamic ruler Ardashir. The Roman Empire survived, but experienced a long series of political and military problems during the so-called Crisis of the Third Century, a fifty-year period of instability during which something like twenty-five different emperors reigned, many of them ineffectively, and most dying a violent death.

With political and social chaos occurring across much of Eurasia, particularly in the regions that had generated the supply and demand for silk, it was inevitable that transregional commerce would decrease. Some trade by land and sea did continue in the centuries that followed, particularly between the Sasanian Dynasty, the Byzantines and the Chinese, but at nothing like the levels and intensity that had characterized this First Silk Roads Era. However, with the establishment of the Tang Dynasty in China at the beginning of the seventh century, and the expansion of the *Dar al-Islam* (the Realm of Islam) at about the same time, significant Silk Roads exchanges along both land and maritime routes were revived in the centuries that followed, during what might be called a Second Silk Roads Era.

Our task in the first part of this chapter is to address two questions related to the political context of the First Silk Roads Era. Why did three of the four empires that had made Silk Roads exchanges possible collapse at more or less the same time, while the fourth also went through its own crisis? And what was the geopolitical aftermath of this widespread civilizational contraction? In the second part of this chapter we consider a question related to the ideological context of the First Silk Roads Era. What conditions facilitated the spread of several Eurasian spiritual ideologies, including two that were destined to become genuinely global religions, during the latter First Silk Roads Era and the centuries that followed its demise? In the final part of this chapter we consider a question related to the biological context of the First Silk Roads Era. What evidence is there that connects the outbreak of disease epidemics in ancient Eurasia to the Silk Roads, and what role (if any) did this play in the collapse of the network?

Imperial Disintegration across Eurasia

To our initial pair of questions first concerning the near-simultaneous collapse of formerly stable empires, and the geopolitical aftermath of these processes. We begin by focusing on the circumstances surrounding the collapse of the Han Dynasty in China, then move westward to consider events in the Kushan and Parthian Empires, in South Asia and finally in the Roman Empire.

Collapse of the Later Han Dynasty

In what seems to be a reoccurring pattern in East Asian history, the vigorous and effective Early Han Dynasty emperor Wudi was followed by a succession of less able rulers, and as fiscal problems began to mount, the government was eventually overthrown in the year 9 CE by a Confucian chief minister named Wang Mang, events described in Chapter 2. Wang Mang seized power from an inept Han government in an attempt to redress a series of fiscal and social problems. He abolished debt slavery and attempted to portion the land out to the peasants through an equitable "well-field" system. Then he tried to stabilize the prices of basic commodities by establishing government agencies to buy and stockpile surplus commodities when prices were low, and sell them at a subsidized rate when scarcity forced prices to rise. But Wang Mang's reformist program failed in the end because his policies were resented by powerful landlords, and also because of a series of natural disasters including droughts, locust plagues and massive flooding along the Huang He. Eventually Liu Xiu, a descendant of Han Dynasty founder Liu Bang, assembled a force of rebellious peasants and attacked Wang Mang in the capital of Chang'an. Wang Mang and 1,000 of his followers were killed in battle in October 23 CE in the Wei River Valley. Two years later in 25 CE, Liu Xiu (whose reign name was Guang Wudi) declared the Later Han Dynasty, which went on to rule for almost another two centuries, until 220 CE.

Although the Later Han Dynasty was wealthy and powerful, it never attained the heights of the Early Han. After Chang'an, the capital of the Early Han, had been sacked in the aftermath of Wang Mang's rule, Liu Xiu reestablished the dynasty in a new capital further east at Luoyang, which is why the Later Han is also known as the Eastern Han.[1] Guang Wudi, his son Emperor Ming and his grandson Emperor Zhang are generally considered to have been able emperors whose reigns were the high points of the Later Han Dynasty. But following the reign of Hedi (89–105 CE) the next ten emperors all came to the throne very young, between the ages of three months and sixteen years. With this series of child rulers, the dynasty suffered from corruption and political infighting between three powerful political groups: palace eunuchs, the clans of the empresses and the Confucian scholar-bureaucrats. None of these groups was able to improve the harsh lives of peasants, particularly after 153 CE when China was beset with another series of natural disasters, including massive locust swarms, and more devastating floods along the Huang He. Hundreds of thousands of farmers were forced off the land and took to the roads in a desperate search for food, because the government was incapable of helping them. Confucian students were so disgusted by the conniving and increasing corruption in court that they organized mass protests against the court eunuchs. The eunuchs responded by imprisoning Confucian official Li Ying and the protesting students on the charge of treason. In 166 and again in 169 CE, the eunuchs orchestrated brutal purges of "outer court" officials who were exiled, jailed or killed.

Throughout these decades of crisis Emperor Huan (r. 146–168 CE) largely ignored the economic and political storm by hosting thousands of concubines in his harem. During the reign of Huandi's successor, Lingdi (r. 168–189), Daoist ideals of more equitable land distribution spread throughout the peasantry. A huge peasant uprising known as the Yellow Turban Rebellion swarmed across the North China Plain, the principal agricultural sector of the country. In 184 another massive rebellion, this one led by radical Daoists, resulted in widespread attacks on government officials all over the country. The power once held by the Liu royalty now fell into the hands of local governors and warlords, such as Dong Zhou who attacked and burned the Han capital in 190 CE, and the ruthless and

[1] For a classic account of these events, see H. Bielenstein, *The Restoration of the Han Dynasty*. Stockholm: Elanders Boktryckeri Aktiebolag, 1953, pp. 154–156.

ambitious Cao Cao. Three of these warlords eventually succeeded in taking control of most of China, ushering in the so-called Three Kingdoms Era. Figurehead Han emperor Xian managed to hold on until 220, when Cao Pi (the son of Cao Cao) forced his abdication, bringing to an ignominious end the Han Dynastic Era. The three and a half centuries that followed, sometimes characterized by the label the "Age of Disunity," were marked by political division and a series of smaller regional governments, none of which was able to reunite China.

China during the "Age of Disunity"

It is tempting to draw a comparison between China following the collapse of the Han Dynasty and Europe after the so-called decline and fall of the Roman Empire, particularly as both regions were overrun by militarized nomads at almost exactly the same time. Certainly, with the eventual collapse of Roman power in the fifth century, Western Europe went through many centuries of fragmentation in a period that is sometimes still called the "Dark Ages" (although historians today have largely rejected that term). The "Age of Disunity" in China that followed the fall of the Han was also dominated by weak regional governments that were unable to restore political or social order or stem the tide of militarized nomadic invasions. However, there is one significant difference between western and eastern Eurasia following the collapse of their "classical" imperial structures, and that is, while Europe was never effectively reunified after the decline of Rome, China *was* successfully reunified under a strong central government three and a half centuries after the collapse of the Han.[2]

During the Age of Disunity, many of the ancient political, social, economic and cultural foundations of Chinese civilization were challenged, although most managed to adapt and survive in this new geopolitical reality. Even as long-standing philosophies adapted, new ideologies emerged, particularly Buddhism, that went on to profoundly influence subsequent Chinese and East Asian civilization. It was during the Age of Disunity that Buddhism, which had already diffused out of India and eastward along Silk Roads trade routes during the first two centuries CE, made its strongest gains in China, as we see in what follows.

It was the generals assigned by the Later Han emperors to put down the Yellow Turban uprising that eventually emerged as the new powers of

[2] For an excellent account of the "Age of Disunity" in China, see C. Holcombe, "East Asia," in C. Benjamin, ed., *Cambridge History of the World*. Cambridge: Cambridge University Press, 2015, pp. 418–424.

China. In the north, Cao Cao focused on obtaining resources for his armies by settling landless peasants and captured rebels on huge state farms. Cao Cao also recruited skilled Xiongnu horsemen to be the backbone of his cavalry, and settled many of them in Shaanxi Province (the Romans would do something similar by incorporating skilled Germanic infantry and horseman into the ranks of their military). After his father's death in 220, Cao Pi forced the abdication of the last Han emperor and established a new dynasty in the north, the Wei Dynasty. From his base in the old Eastern Han capital of Luoyang, Cao Pi hoped to reunify China under Wei dynastic control, but his attempt was thwarted by rival warlords. A year after the Wei Dynasty was declared in the north, another warlord named Liu Bei was crowned as emperor of the kingdom of Shu in the west. Eight years later in 229, a third warlord, Sun Quan, declared himself emperor of the kingdom of Wu in the south. This meant that three rival powers had now essentially divided the former Han realm between them, during an era known ever since as the Three Kingdoms, which lasted for fifty years between 230 and 280 CE. In the midst of this period, in 265 a rebel Wei dynasty leader forced the Wei emperor to abdicate, and then declared a new Jin Dynasty. Over the course of the next fifteen years the Jin gradually defeated the Shu and Wu kingdoms, and then attempted to rule a reunified China under its own dynastic name.

The Jin Dynasty is divided into two periods: the Western Jin (265–316 with Luoyang as its capital) and the Eastern Jin (316–420 with the southern and more easterly city of Nanjing as its capital). The Jin did succeed in unifying the country, but only temporarily because they were never able to establish a durable political structure based on the supreme authority of an emperor. Instead, conflict and intrigue between members of the royal family and the civil service debilitated the government, and centralized power was further undermined through the parceling out of enormous tracts of land to imperial princes. As these princes sought to increase their power, civil war broke out and raged in the regions around Luoyang between 281 and 305 CE. This chaotic situation gave the Xiongnu, China's long-standing enemies who had been settled in the north for centuries, the opportunity they had been waiting for. In the year 311 CE, Xiongnu forces sacked the Jin capital at Luoyang; and five years later they sacked the great ancient imperial capital of Chang'an. For much of the following century large regions of northern China were a battleground between Xiongnu and ethnic Han Chinese, during another chaotic period known as the "Era of the Sixteen Kingdoms" (304–439 CE).[3] Millions of refugees fled south across the

[3] See D. A. Graff, *Medieval Chinese Warfare, 300–900.* London: Routledge, 2002, pp. 41–42.

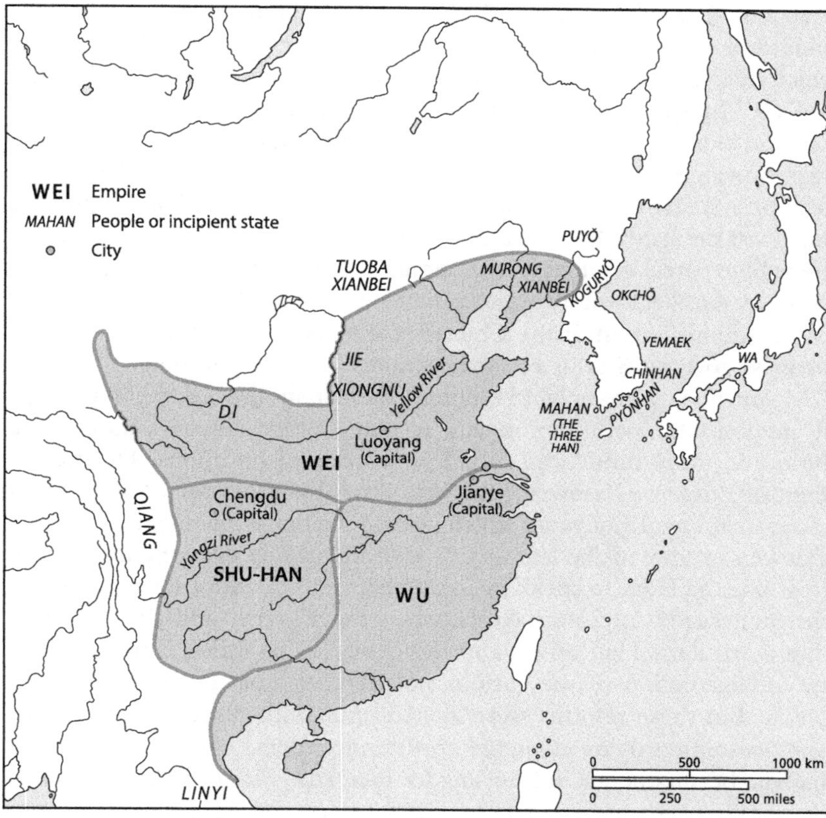

Map 9.1 Three Kingdoms period in post-Han Dynasty China, 230–280 CE
From *Cambridge World History* Vol. 4, Charles Holcombe's chapter, p. 419

Yangtze, and the Chinese economy more or less collapsed. The southern city of Nanjing now became the capital for a series of local power groups collectively known as the Southern Dynasties, which ruled until 589. Each of these southern courts had to deal with powerful hereditary aristocratic families and repeated outbreaks of violence, although the city of Nanjing emerged as a splendid capital and cultural center, a stronghold for Chinese culture.

In the north, meanwhile, rival warlords from all sorts of different ethnic groups continued to contest each other for power. The most successful of these groups was the Xianbei (originally pastoral nomads from southern

Manchuria), who moved out of northern Shaanxi in a series of successful raids until they were strong enough to establish the Northern Wei Dynasty, which ruled much of northern China for almost a century between 439 and 534 CE. Inexperienced in statecraft, the Northern Wei rulers turned to Chinese Confucian bureaucrats to help govern their realm. In 485 CE, these bureaucrats, at the orders of Wei emperor Xiaowendi, overhauled the taxation system by reintroducing an equal field system based on the premise that it was the state that ultimately owned all the land, and thus the state had the right to parcel it out fairly to all families. This equal field system went on to outlast the Wei Dynasty by more than 350 years, becoming a central tenet to the administration of the Chinese Tang Dynasty, and also to various Japanese governments after it was instituted in that island state.

Meanwhile, with only 2 million Xianbei in the midst of perhaps 30 million Chinese, it was inevitable that Xianbei elites would become more and more influenced by Chinese cultural traditions. During the reign of Emperor Xiaowen (471–499) the Wei relocated to the ruined ancient capital of Luoyang, which was now rebuilt as a magnificent city. Xiaowen promoted the learning of Han culture by ordering his men to dress like the Han, to speak their language and to adopt Han surnames. He encouraged intermarriage between the Xianbei and the Han and employed many Han officials in the court, all of which contributed to the amalgamation of the various nationalities now living in northern China. But these reforms were looked upon with disgust by the tough Xianbei soldiers living along the northern frontiers. They came to detest the Xianbei aristocrats in Luoyang for their soft, Sinotized lives, increasingly influenced as they were by Chinese cultural traditions. Civil war broke out again in 524 CE; Luoyang was sacked, and 2,000 of these "soft" officials were slaughtered.[4]

In quick succession, a series of dynasties tried to reestablish control: the Northern Qi in 552 CE, and the Northern Zhou five years later. In 575 CE the Zhou formed an alliance with the southern state of Chen to invade Qi, which was destroyed in 577 CE, but the Zhou were in turn usurped by one of their own generals in 581 CE. It was at that moment that General Yang Jian, who would later be known as Emperor Wen, seized power and declared the foundation of the Sui Dynasty, which finally succeeded in reuniting China, thus paving the way for the successful Tang Dynasty that followed. The Age of Disunity was over, and a new and splendid era in Chinese history, and in trans-Eurasian trade and exchange, was about to

[4] See the series of essays on all aspects of the "Age of Disunity" in S. Pearce, A. Spiro and P. Ebrey, eds., *Culture and Power in the Reconstitution of the Chinese Real 200–600*. Cambridge, MA: Harvard University Press, 2001.

commence.[5] But the history of the Tang Dynasty, and the Second Silk Roads Era they helped institute, belongs to another book.

Collapse of the Kushan Empire

Just five years after the collapse of the Han Dynasty in China, the last of the "Great Kushan" kings, Vasudeva, died in 225 CE. Although a series of lesser kings known exclusively through their coinage did continue to hold on to limited power for some decades afterward, from 225 CE on the Kushan Empire was in decline. These later Kushan rulers were forced to deal with the formidable rising power of Central Asia, the Sasanian conqueror Ardashir who, soon after his coronation in 224 CE, began to lead his forces into Kushan territory. Ardashir died in 242 CE, but his son the equally competent Shapur I (r. 241–272 CE) continued the expansion of the Sasanian realm, and by 262 CE the Kushan royal cities at Begram and Taxila had been destroyed by Sasanian forces. The northwestern areas of the former Kushan Empire were now incorporated into a new Sasanian provincial state named *Kushanshar*.[6]

According to the Chinese source the *Sanguoji*, it was either Kushan king Vasudeva or an immediate successor (perhaps Kanishka II, r. c. 230–242?) who sent an embassy to the Chinese Wei court, which arrived in the year 230 CE. We noted the historical irony of this in Chapter 7. Three hundred and sixty years earlier the ancestors of the Kushans, the Yuezhi, had rejected overtures from Han envoy Zhang Qian to join the Chinese in an alliance against their common enemies the Xiongnu. Now it was the turn of the Kushans to seek an alliance with the Chinese against the Sasanians, but this request was also to no avail.[7] During the long period of Sasanian incorporation of Kushan territories, and the establishment of the new province of Kushanshar, coinage of both imperial powers developed a degree of synchronism. There is evidence of overstrikes by the Kushans on Kushano-Sasanian coins and vice versa, and some Kushano-Sasanian coins copied specific motifs from Kushan coins, particularly images of fire altars and reverses that are derived from the Vasudevan Siva and Nandi types we discussed in an earlier chapter. This is further

[5] On the Tang Dynasty, see S. A. M. Adshead, *T'ang China: The Rise of the East in World History*. New York: Palgrave Macmillan, 2004.

[6] See B. Puri, "The Kushans," in J. Harmatta, ed., *History of Civilizations of Central Asia*, vol. 2. Paris: UNESCO, 1994, p. 255; also J. Brockington, "Imperial India," in A. Cotterall, ed., *The Penguin Encyclopaedia of Classical Civilisations*. London: Penguin, 1993, p. 178.

[7] *San Kuo Chih* 3:6a; see Zurcher 1968, p. 371, and Puri 1994, p. 256.

evidence of the continuing cultural legacy of the Kushans long after their empire had disappeared.[8]

Despite their defeat and subjugation at the hands of the Sasanians, however, other numismatic evidence suggests the continuation of some type of reduced Kushan royal power in the region. Following the reign of Kanishka II, coins of Vasishka, Kanishka III, Vasudeva II, Shaka and Kipunda continue all the way through to the early fifth century.[9] Archaeological evidence from various sites might also indicate that, as B. Puri has argued, "fire and destruction was followed by new activity under the later Kushans."[10] These later Kushan kings might have possessed the status of quasi-independent Sasanian viceroys or similar; perhaps they provided contingents of Kushan cavalry to the formidable Sasanian military when requested. Some of them might even have retained the status of nominally independent monarchs ruling their "kingdoms" under Sasanian suzerainty, perhaps even linked to the Iranian aristocracy by marriage.[11] A. K. Narain has argued that the Kushans of northwestern Bactria never fully submitted to the Sasanians, and that "more than one branch of them was struggling to maintain their independence and enhance their political power during the century-long period of decline."[12]

South of the Hindu Kush, and in the valleys of the Indus and Ganges, new states and kingdoms were also emerging in parts of the former Kushan realm, including those of the Naghas, Maghas and Yaudheyas. Despite this, inscriptional and numismatic evidence suggests that the ancient capital of Mathura might have remained under Kushan control until as late as the year 157 of the Kanishkan Era, which would be 284 CE.[13] The development of these north Indian states was influenced by the Kushan cultural and economic heritage of the region. The Yaudheyas in particular, who were at the zenith of their power in the region between the Ganges and Indus between the third and fourth centuries CE, issued coins that have marked similarities to the copper denominations of Great Kushan king Huvishka. But images of Siva and Nandi that were featured so frequently on Huvishka's coins were now replaced with depictions of either

[8] These overstrikes and other synchronisms were first noted by British numismatists in the nineteenth century, including A. Cunningham, "Coins of the Kushans, or Great Yue-Ti," *Numismatic Chronicle* 3rd ser. 12, 1893, pp. 40–82, 95, 159.

[9] N. Sims-Williams and J. Cribb, "A New Inscription of Kanishka the Great," *Silk Roads Art and Archaeology* 4 (1995/6), pp. 75–142.

[10] B. N. Puri, *India under the Kushans*. Delhi: Bharatiya Bidya Bhavan, 1965, p. 76.

[11] Brockington 1993, p. 201.

[12] A. K. Narain, "Indo-Europeans in Inner Asia," in D. Sinor, ed., *The Cambridge History of Inner Asia*. Cambridge: Cambridge University Press, 1990 (reprint 1994), p. 171.

[13] Puri 1994, p. 258.

Figure 9.1 Gold coin depicting Gupta king Chandragupta II (r. 376–414) as an archer, influenced by Kushan coin design www.metmuseum.org/art/collection/search/39406?sortBy=Relevance&ft=gupta+coins&offset=0&rpp=20&pos=2

the male warrior god Karttikeya or the beautiful female divinity Devasena on the reverse.[14] Similarly, the Western Satraps of northern India, who probably functioned as vassals of the Kushans for much of their history, issued a long series of Kushan- and Indo-Greek-influenced silver coins through to the Gupta conquest of the lower Ganges provinces in the fourth century. Even the early gold coinage of the Guptas seems to have been influenced by Kushan designs, although without the Greek legends.[15]

Early in the fourth century imperial rule returned to much of South Asia under the Guptas, whose empire eventually incorporated most of the former Kushan-controlled regions of India. Using marriage and diplomacy to forge links between regional states, founding ruler Chandragupta created a dynamic kingdom centered in the Ganges Valley that was expanded by his able successors until it approached the territorial size that the Mauryan Empire had attained five centuries earlier. Gupta kings adopted imperial titles such as "supreme lord" and "great king of kings," but rather than establish centralized imperial administration over their realm, they preferred to rule instead through a network of regional

[14] See K. D. Bajpai, *Indian Numismatic Series*, chapter 6, "Yaudheya Coins – A Critical Study," New Delhi: Abhinav Publications, 2004, pp. 26ff.

[15] See M. Price, *Coins: An Illustrated Survey*. London, 1980, p. 285, for an example.

rulers.[16] The superb gold coinage of the Guptas is evidence of Guptan prosperity, wealth that the state used to support and promote Hinduism. But Buddhism also flourished during the Gupta period, notably at the great monastery and university at Nalanda, which attracted scholars and pilgrims from all over the Buddhist world.

Evidence of some form of continuing Kushan power in the Indus Valley well into the fourth century, despite the success of the Guptas, can be found in the history of the Iranian-speaking Kidarites (also known as the Xionites), who began migrating into Bactria in c. 320 CE. The Kidarite king Grumbat engaged in a lengthy and bitter struggle with Sasanian ruler Shapur II (r. 309–379), which only ended when both sides agreed to a peace alliance that saw Grumbat and his forces join the Sasanians in conflict against the Romans. Later Roman historian Ammianus Marcellinus noted that, although Grumbat was "middle aged," "he was endowed with a mind that acted grandly, and he was famous for his many significant victories."[17] Despite this, inscriptional evidence suggests that, until 360 CE the southern branch of the powerful Kidarites, the so-called Red Huns, were apparently forced to accept vassal status to the Kushans of the Indus Valley, until Kidara II was eventually able to lead Kidarite troops from Bactria south across the Hindu Kush to defeat the Kushans of northwestern India once and for all.[18]

The Kidarites were displaced in the last quarter of the fifth century by a new wave of Hunnish invaders, the Hephthalites (or White Huns), who might also have had an intriguing Kushan connection. Chinese chronicles describe the Hephthalites as being descended from one of the five original princedoms (called *yabghu* or *xihun* in Chinese) of the Yuezhi, although this is impossible to substantiate. By the end of the fifth century the Hephthalites had defeated the Sasanians at the Battle of Herat and become the dominant power in Transoxiana. They also placed enormous military pressure on the Gupta kings of India, several of whom were hard-pressed to keep the invaders out. Excavations at Taxila provide evidence of the destructive power of the Hephthalites, yet even these White Huns could not obliterate the rich cultural syncretism that had prevailed in Central Asia for the past half millennium, as demonstrated by

[16] On the administration of the Gupta Empire, see S. Kaul, "South Asia," in C. Benjamin, ed., *Cambridge History of the World*. Cambridge: Cambridge University Press, 2015, pp. 502ff.

[17] Ammianus Marcellinus, 18.6.22.

[18] On the Kidarites, see F. Grenet, "Regional Interaction in Central Asia and North-West India in the Kidarite and Hephthalite Period," in N. Sims-Williams, ed., *Indo-Iranian Languages and Peoples (Proceedings of the British Academy)*. London, 2002, pp. 203–224.

the varied imitative nature of their coins.[19] Most Hephthalite coins copy Sasanian prototypes, but there are also Kushan copies and even Greco-Bactrian imitations, despite the fact that the Greco-Bactrian kingdom had been destroyed by the Yuezhi more than six centuries earlier.

All this suggests that, although central Kushan political administration seems to have collapsed quite quickly, successors to the Great Kushans managed to hold on to some form of regional power in Central and South Asia for at least a century afterward. Having noted this, there is no question that the disintegration of the Kushan Empire brought to an end the so-called Golden Age of ancient Central Asia, even though the cultural, political and economic achievements of the Kushans continued to influence their regional successors for centuries. As we noted at the beginning of Chapter 7, evidence for the Kushans is sparse and ambiguous, yet the story unfolded by archaeology, incidental references in the literature of their contemporaries and most particularly their extensive coinage, is a compelling one. Beginning with Kujula Kadphises, the Kushan monarchs constructed an enormous and powerful empire that dominated much of Central Asia during the first two centuries CE, at the height of the First Silk Roads Era. Because the Kushans played a critical role in facilitating commercial and cultural exchanges across Inner Eurasia, one could plausibly argue that, if there had been no Kushan Empire, perhaps there would have been no Silk Roads. The Kushans played such a critical role in facilitating the extraordinary levels of trans-Eurasian cultural exchange that occurred during the First Silk Roads Era that the period could also be named, with some justification, the "Kushan Era."

Collapse of the Parthian Empire and Rise of the Sasanians

The Parthian Empire also met its demise at the hands of the Sasanians. During the early years of the third century CE, the Parthians had steadily weakened because of seemingly endless wars with the Romans, coupled with internal disunity. Founder of the Sasanian Dynasty, Ardashir I, began his career as a regional ruler controlling the state of Persis (which is Fars Province in modern Iran). Seizing on Parthian indecision, Ardashir began to expand his state by attacking and incorporating surrounding regions, in defiance of Parthian rule. Ardashir then proved his military acumen by defeating and killing Parthian king Artabanus V near

[19] For an excellent online catalog of Hephthalite coinage, see the site maintained by Bob Reis of Raleigh, North Carolina: www.anythinganywhere.com/commerce/coins/coinpics/indi-heph.htm.

Figure 9.2 Drawing of a rock relief at Naqsh-e Rostam, depicting Sasanian king Ardashir I (r. 224–242 CE) receiving the kingship ring from Ahura Mazda. The horses are trampling the last Parthian king, Ardavan, and the evil Zoroastrian spirit Ahriman. Artist: Luft Ali Khan (1797–1869) www.metmuseum.org/art/collection/search/327535?sortBy=Relevance &ft=ardashir&offset=0&rpp=20&pos=1
Credit: Gift of Mr. Sassan Mokhtarzadeh, 1998

Ishfahan on April 28, 224 CE, in the Battle of Hormozdgan, a victory that marked the official end of the Parthian Empire and the establishment of the Sasanian Empire.[20] Ardashir was crowned at Ctesiphon in 224 CE, and took the title *Shahanshah*, or "King of Kings."[21] Ardashir's successors continued to expand the empire, particularly his son Shapur I, who pushed hard against the Romans in Mesopotamia, and also took much of Bactria away from the Kushans. The Sasanian conquest of Central Asia was so complete that by the fifth century Zoroastrianism, the preferred religion of the Sasanians, had become deeply and widely entrenched from Bactria to Mesopotamia. We have more to say later in this chapter about the spread of Zoroastrianism and other religions across Inner Eurasia

[20] K. Farrokh, *Shadows in the Desert: Ancient Persia at War*. Oxford: Osprey Publishing, 2007, p. 180.

[21] R. N. Frye, "The Sassanians," in I. Eiddon and S. Edwards, eds., *The Cambridge Ancient History XII – The Crisis of Empire*. Cambridge: Cambridge University Press, 2005, pp. 466–467.

during the later First Silk Roads Era and the centuries that followed its demise.

As well as destroying the Parthian and Kushan Empires, the Sasanians were formidable foes of the Romans. Just as had been the case with Parthian–Roman conflicts centuries earlier, the Euphrates River became the mutually accepted and often fortified frontier between the Romans and Sasanians. Ongoing wars between the two empires made long-distance trade in the region increasingly untenable, leading to the decline in the third century of some of the most important trading cities of the First Silk Roads Era, including Dura-Europos and Palmyra. Despite ongoing conflict between the Romans and Sasanians, however, some transregional trade did continue to link eastern and western Eurasia during the Sasanian period, both by sea and by land.[22] The discovery of numerous Sasanian artifacts (including many coins) across the Indian Ocean Basin, including at major ports along the Indian and Sri Lankan coasts, is evidence of some revitalization of maritime trade under the Sassanians.[23] Successfully emulating failed Roman foreign policy of centuries before, the Sasanians also conquered southern Arabia in the fourth century, which allowed them to take further control of the trade in luxuries that was passing along land routes through the Arabian Peninsula and on to the Byzantine Empire.[24] Trade in silk and other luxury commodities earned tremendous profits for Sasanian merchants and the state, allowing the Sasanian capital of Ctesiphon to become one of the largest and most cosmopolitan cities of late antiquity. To celebrate his capital and the empire of which he was the twenty-second ruler, Sasanian king Khusro I (r. 531–579) had the Arch of Khusro constructed at a new capital city he built near Ctesiphon; the arch was the tallest structure anywhere in western Eurasia at the time.[25]

It was Sogdian merchants who emerged from the collapse of the Kushan Empire to become vitally important traders in facilitating overland commercial exchanges between China and the Sasanian Empire. A Byzantine text authored by Cosmas Indicopleustes, the *Christian Topography*, provides illuminating details about how cargoes of silk were being transported from China again some three centuries after

[22] T. Daryae, "The Persian Gulf in Late Antiquity," *Journal of World History* 14 (2003), 8–10.
[23] Tomber, "Rome and Mesopotamia – Importers into India in the First Millennium AD," pp. 972–988.
[24] É. de la Vaissière, *Sogdian Traders: A History*. Leiden: Brill, 2005, pp. 228–229.
[25] T. Daryae, "Western and Central Eurasia," in C. Benjamin, ed., *Cambridge History of the World Vol IV*. Cambridge: Cambridge University Press, 2015, p. 292.

Figure 9.3 Illustration of the ruins of the arch built by Sasanian king Khusro I (reigned 531–579 CE), Ctesiphon
www.gettyimages.co.uk/license/699761720
Credit: Nastasic

the decline of the First Silk Roads Era.[26] Written between 547 and 550 CE, Cosmas distinguishes two distinct routes by which silk was being

[26] See Cosmas Indicopleustes, *Christian Topography: The Christian Topography of Cosmas, an Egyptian Monk*, J. W McCrindle, trans. New York: Burt Franklin, 1887.

exported from China to the West: by caravans traveling along land routes through Central Asia, and by sea via ports in Ceylon.[27] Despite Sasanian and Sogdian pro-commerce policies, and the fact that the Sasanians enjoyed close relations with both the Sui and Tang Dynasties in China, *Christian Topography* also provides evidence that the major land route from Central Asia and down the Indus Valley to ports on the northwest coast that had thrived throughout the First Silk Roads Era was no longer in operation. It had been replaced instead by maritime routes from China to South Asian ports via Southeast Asia, and by a land route that stayed well to the north to transport goods through Central Asian cities such as Samarkand and Bukhara, and on to the Sasanian Empire. The Parthian and Kushan empires that had been responsible for the funneling of Chinese goods south from Bactria along the Indus had gone, and now it was Sogdian merchants who had become the key intermediaries in overland silk trade between China and the West, a position they would continue to occupy for centuries afterward, particularly during the Second Silk Roads Era.[28]

Despite the fragmentation of the Roman Empire that occurred in the fifth century, the eastern part of the Roman state went from strength to strength and transformed itself into the Byzantine Empire. By the late sixth century, with Emperor Justinian ruling Byzantium and Khusro I ruling the Sasanian Empire, both these agrarian civilizations had reached their zenith. Despite the chaos caused by the collapse of the Han Dynasty and the Kushan and Parthian Empires, as well as the fragmentation of the Roman Empire, by the end of the sixth century much of Eurasia had been reunited again by the Tang, Sasanians and Byzantines, although the former western Roman Empire remained divided into a series of small, competitive states and kingdoms. Other smaller groups and cultures aligned themselves with the major civilizations, such as the Arabs, who became clients of both the Byzantines and the Sasanians,[29] and the pastoral nomadic Turks, who eventually formed sedentary states that allied themselves with all three of the major powers at different

[27] See de la Vaissière 2005, pp. 85–86, on this.

[28] D. Sinor, "The Establishment and Dissolution of the Türk Empire," in D. Sinor, ed., *The Cambridge History of Inner Asia*. Cambridge: Cambridge University Press, 1994, pp. 299–308.

[29] For the role of the Arabs at this time, see G. Fisher, *Between Empires: Arabs, Romans, and Sasanians in Late Antiquity*. Oxford: Oxford University Press, 2011, pp. 72–127.

periods. As Sasanian specialist Touraj Daryae puts it, "this arrangement constituted the Eurasian world system of late antiquity."[30]

This world system was not to last much longer, however. The end of the Sasanian Empire occurred quickly during the first half of the seventh century. Between 628 CE and the death of its last ruler, Yazdgerd III, in 651 CE, the Sasanian Empire was plunged into crisis. The first raids from Arab forces that had converted to Islam began in 632 CE, and the timing could not have been better. The Sasanian state was on the verge of collapse anyway, weakened by years of war with the Byzantines, serious economic problems, political fragmentation and religious turmoil.[31] The city of Ctesiphon fell to Muslim forces in 637 CE following a long siege, and at the subsequent Battle of Nihawand in 642 CE, Muslim forces crushed a remnant Sasanian army, a victory that ushered in an entirely new chapter in the history of Eurasia.

The ultimate significance of the Sasanians to world history, like the Kushans and the two Persian/Iranian empires that had preceded it, was their role as facilitators of cultural exchange. In the same way that the Achaemenids and Parthians had functioned as geographic bridges between Europe and Central Asia, through their encouragement of trans-Eurasian trade and exchange, the Sasanians also acted as a spatial bridge between China and the West, and as a chronological bridge between the world of late antiquity and the new Islamic empire that went on to control these vast desert lands. Although the Sasanians fell to the expanding world of Islam in the seventh century, the Persian legacy continued to influence the region through Muslim adoption of Persian models of government and administration. For more than 1,000 years during the era of agrarian civilizations, including the entire span of the First Silk Roads Era, it was Persian/Iranian peoples who created some of the most formidable imperial structures in all world history.

Rome and the "Crisis of the Third Century"

Fifteen years after the forced abdication of the last emperor of Han Dynasty China, eleven years after the replacement of the Parthian Empire by the Sasanians, and ten years after the death of the last of the Great Kushan kings, Vasudeva, the Roman Empire also entered a period of political and economic turmoil long characterized by historians as the "Crisis of the Third Century." Between 235 CE, when Emperor Severus Alexander was assassinated by his own troops, and 284 CE, when Diocletian came to the imperial throne and stemmed the crisis, the Roman Empire

[30] Daryae 2015, p. 292. [31] Howard-Johnson 1994, pp. 57–87.

suffered from civil war, invasion and serious economic recession. We know of twenty-six different men who were officially accepted by the Roman Senate as emperors during this forty-nine-year-long period, clear evidence of the instability of the era. The "Crisis" can be divided into three periods. The first dates from the death of Alexander Severus in 235 CE until c. 253, during which the emperors more or less maintained the traditions of the Severan Principate. The crisis reached its peak during the fifteen-year-long second phase, under Emperors Valerian and Gallienus, as internal and external threats multiplied, although both emperors did work hard to rectify the situation. After 268 CE, a significant recovery characterizes the third phase, until eventually emperors from Diocletian to Constantine were able to institute fundamental reforms throughout the empire.[32]

The first phase commenced with the reign of Alexander Severus, who came to the throne in 222 CE. Severus was moderately successful in stemming the expansion of the Sasanians along the eastern frontier, although, according to Herodian, the Roman army suffered severe losses near Ctesiphon, and also during a retreat from Armenia.[33] Some idea of the state of discipline in the Roman army at the time can be seen in the fact that the Syrian legions mutinied in 232 CE and proclaimed a military leader named Taurinus as the new emperor. Alexander suppressed the mutiny, Taurinus drowned in the Euphrates and Alexander returned in triumph to Rome in 233 CE. The following year Alexander was forced to face a new and dangerous enemy after Germanic and Sarmatian tribes launched incursions across the northeastern borders of the empire, crossing both the Rhine and Danube Rivers in large numbers. After attempting to enforce a strict new code of discipline on his troops, Alexander tried to use diplomacy to end the conflict by offering to pay tribute to the Germanic chiefs, a tactic that apparently destroyed his reputation among the Roman troops. Alexander and his mother were stabbed to death by Roman soldiers on March 19, 235 CE, to be replaced by Maximinus I.

The breakdown in discipline within the army that had blighted Alexander's reign continued under his successor, Maximinus I, who ruled for just three years until 238 CE. Conspiracies broke out within the legions, and various groups attempted to promote their own favorites to the position of emperor. Maximinus was forced to defend the frontiers against Germanic tribes while revolts simultaneously broke out in Africa.

[32] For an introduction to the entire period, see D. S. Potter, *The Roman Empire at Bay: AD 180–395*. London: Routledge, 2004.

[33] Herodian 6.5.10 and 6.6.3.

Figure 9.4 Marble bust of Roman emperor Alexander Severus (r. 222–235 CE)
www.metmuseum.org/art/collection/search/258540?sortBy=Relevance&ft=alexander+severus&offset=0&rpp=20&pos=3
Credit: Purchase, Lila Acheson Wallace and Philodoroi Gifts, 2011

The Roman Senate backed several pretenders to the throne, resulting in chaotic scenes of civil unrest in Rome. After Maximinus marched on the city his troops revolted, and in May 238 CE the emperor, his son and his chief advisors were assassinated. The year 238 CE is known as the Year of Six Emperors, but political turmoil continued for decades following the death of Maximinus. Different legions within the now bitterly divided Roman army proposed their own "barracks emperors," while Goths, Vandals and Sasanians continued to mount pressure on the northern and eastern borders of the empire. Climate change might also have contributed to the chaos, causing crop failures in the northwestern provinces of the empire, resulting in forced migrations. Then, in 251 CE, the Plague of Cyprian (which was probably a yellow fever outbreak, more on this later) caused significant population losses throughout the empire.

Following the death of Emperor Valerian in 260 CE, the empire was effectively divided into three separate political entities, during the second phase of the Crisis. The first of these separate states is known as the Gallic Empire, which consisted of the Roman provinces of Britain, Gaul and Hispania. Seven years later, after the death of Emperor Odaenathus in 267 CE, the eastern provinces of Syria, Palestine and Egypt became the independent Palmyrene Empire. This left just the central region of the empire, particularly Italy, as the legitimate Roman Empire, and the entire Roman Empire potentially on the brink of permanent collapse. However, within a year the crisis reached a turning point after a Gothic army was defeated at the Battle of Naissus. The barracks emperors who now assumed power in this third phase of the Crisis, such as Claudius II Gothicus, won further victories over Germanic forces, and also wrested the province of Hispania back from the Gallic Empire. Claudius was taken by a renewed disease epidemic in 270 CE, but his successor, Aurelian, who had led the Roman cavalry at the Battle of Naissus, ruled competently for the next five years and won further Roman victories over Vandals, Visigoths, the Palmyrenian forces and the forces of the Gallic Empire. By the end of 274 CE, the empire was back intact, and troops resumed their positions on the borders of the empire, a restoration of Roman military ascendancy that would last for the next century.

Reinterpreting the "Crisis of the Third Century"

Classical historians have argued for decades that, as a result of this fifty-year-long period of political disunity and military crisis, many Roman cities were depopulated or completely abandoned, and this had a severe impact on the Roman economy.[34] The remaining cities were forced to build serious defensive fortifications for the first time in their history, including Rome itself, which cost these cities a fortune and further weakened their economies. At the same time inflation, a result of decades of devaluation of Roman coinage, led to a dramatic increase in prices throughout the empire and the near collapse of the entire monetary

[34] For a classic example of this assessment, see, for example, H. St. L. B. Moss, *The Birth of the Middle Ages 395–814*. Oxford: Oxford University Press, 1935.

system. Many taxes now had to be collected in kind rather than in cash, and commercial exchanges often occurred without the use of currency.

These problems, the argument continues, contributed to a major disruption of internal and external trade networks. One of the achievements of the *Pax Romana* instigated by Augustus and maintained by his successors had been the facilitation of regular and secure *internal* commerce between Mediterranean port cities and the interior of the empire by means of the extensive road and maritime networks. This allowed for the movement of substantial agricultural products and manufactured goods throughout the empire, as well as the import and distribution of high-value luxury goods from India and Arabia (and indirectly) China, as we have seen. But the disruptions caused by invasion, plague and civil unrest during the Crisis of the Third Century, not to mention the debasement of Roman currency, led to a breakdown of this commercial system and a retreat to a more decentralized and localized commercial system whereby large estates now increasingly took on the role of growing enough food and manufacturing sufficient material goods on the estate, rather than import these from somewhere else. This was the beginning of a trend that would later evolve into the "manorialism" that was to become a defining feature of the Western European economy of the Middle Ages. The trend toward another key feature of the medieval period, feudalism, was fueled by the appearance of a new class of semi-free Roman citizens known as *coloni*, who were forced to give up some of their rights as Roman citizens in order to find employment and security on the large estates.

All these changes – the reduction in size of many cities, the debasement of coinage, the loss of taxation, the breakdown of internal and external trade networks, the appearance of large, quasi-independent estates and the emergence of the *coloni* – were felt more severely in the western part of the Roman Empire, which also suffered from regular invasion. The eastern part remained strong and relatively unified, which allowed it to survive and evolve, for centuries after the eventual fragmentation of the western empire, into the powerful Byzantine Empire. With all this in mind, it is understandable that historians have long argued that the Crisis of the Third Century had significant and long-term historical ramifications and, in retrospect, can be seen as the beginning of the transition from antiquity to the Middle Ages. This was a view shared by ancient historians such as Eutropius, Aurelius Victor and the anonymous author of the *Historia Augusta*, who all viewed the period in an unfailingly negative light.[35]

[35] On these historians, see W. den Boer, *Some Minor Roman Historians*. Leiden: Brill, 1972.

However, modern scholars now offer a significant reinterpretation of this long-standing assessment, particularly that expressed by the ancient Roman historians themselves.[36] Some argue, for example, that the succession of rulers, many of them usurpers, who appeared during the period is actually a common phenomenon during periods of unrest, and the fact that many of them were from the ranks of the military explains why ancient historians, who mostly came from the senatorial classes, would have viewed them so negatively.[37] Several of the barracks emperors were in fact highly successful in defending the empire and restoring order, often against a host of dangerous enemies, laying the groundwork for the later success of Diocletian and Constantine.

The fact that emperors now had to fight campaigns near the borders also meant that the status of the city of Rome itself, though still symbolically important, was downgraded politically, further reason for the negative assessment of the period by ancient historians living in that city.

Scholars also question the notion that the crisis badly damaged the Roman economy, because the effects varied so significantly in different parts of the empire. Even the argument that significant population decline occurred is now called into question. Many regions prospered during the period, notably in Egypt, the African provinces and Hispania. Even in regions that were at the epicenter of military invasions, no general economic decline can be observed. As is often the case during periods of conflict and unrest, the Crisis actually led to significant social and intellectual innovations. For example, the Roman military accepted many men from lower social classes and a wide range of cultural traditions, helping to create a new urban elite that recognized the value of education.

Few Roman scholars today accept the conventional arguments that the period represented a genuine existential threat to the Roman state. There is no doubt that the empire was weakened during the first two phases, but in the end this was only temporary. After 268 CE the emperors gradually restored order, and did this so effectively that the Roman state continued to thrive for centuries afterward. However, all scholars agree that the operation of long-distance trade networks that linked the Roman Empire to the Indian Ocean Basin and Central Asia was severely disrupted, particularly as it was in the midst of the "crisis" that the Han Dynasty in China collapsed, and that both the Parthian and Kushan empires were destroyed by the Sasanians. The Crisis of the Third

[36] See, for example, the interpretation of this period and these events offered by P. Brown, *The World of Late Antiquity AD 150–750*. London: Thames and Hudson, 1971.

[37] For a good summary of Greco-Roman commentaries on the period, see G. Alföldy, "The Crisis of the Third Century as Seen by Contemporaries," *Byzantine Studies* 15 (1974), pp. 89ff.

Century, however it is interpreted, must still be counted as one of the key historical events that marks the end of the First Silk Roads Era.

The Silk Roads and the Diffusion of Religions

To our second topic now: the relationship between the Silk Roads and the diffusion of religions. The spread of various religious beliefs and practices along the land and maritime trade routes provides a striking example of the sort of cross-fertilization of ideas and traditions that occurred across Eurasia during the First Silk Roads Era. The most important of these, in terms of their subsequent impact on world history, were Buddhism and Christianity, although Zoroastrianism, Manichaeism and Hinduism also benefited from the Silk Roads trade routes.

Spread of Buddhism into East Asia

The spiritual ideology of Buddhism first appeared in northern India in the sixth century BCE, partly as a reaction against the rigid caste system of Classical Vedic religion. Eight hundred years later, facilitated partly by the support of Central Asian rulers such as the Kushan king Kanishka, a new version of the faith known as Mahayana (or Great Vehicle) Buddhism began to spread out of South Asia into Central and East Asia along the Silk Roads trade routes. This expansion of Buddhism during the First Silk Roads Era was undoubtedly facilitated by the intensely utilized trade routes from India through the Kushan realm and into Han China, not only because the infrastructure was already in place to support pilgrims and missionaries, but also because it offered the hope of salvation to all regardless of caste or status, and was already popular with South Asian merchants and entrepreneurs.

Han Chinese merchants and diplomats active in the silk trade soon also became attracted to the faith, and returned home to spread the Buddhist message. Chinese edicts of 65 and 70 CE specifically mention the spread of Buddhism and opposition to it from imperial scholars devoted to Confucianism (the dominant ideology of the Han Dynasty, as we have seen).[38] The first Buddhist temple established in China, the White Horse Temple near Luoyang, was built near the Later Han capital of Luoyang during the reign of Later Han emperor Ming (r. 57–75 CE), the beginning of a significant restructuring of the Chinese landscape that would

[38] On tensions between Buddhism and Confucianism during this period, see J. Needham, *Science and Civilization in China: Volume 1, Introductory Orientations*. London: Syndics of the Cambridge University Press, 1972, pp. 112ff.

Figure 9.5 Ruins of the Buddhist monastery complex at Takht-i-Bahi, near Mardan in modern Pakistan. The complex dates to the first century CE.
http://media.gettyimages.com/photos/takht-bhai-takhtibahi-picture-id 173745832
Credit: Nadeem Khawar

result from the diffusion of Buddhism. In 166 CE, the Han emperor Huandi made sacrifices to the Buddha, and the Sutra on the "Perfection of the Gnosis" was translated into Chinese in 179 CE. During the two centuries that followed the collapse of the Han, much of the population of northern China adopted Buddhism, and by the sixth century the ideology had spread widely throughout southern China as well. Buddhism also found ready acceptance in Korea, Japan, Tibet, Mongolia and Southeast Asia in the centuries that followed.[39]

Although Buddhism made its initial foray into China during the First Silk Roads Era, it faced so many linguistic and cultural barriers there that it might have remained just another "exotic cult" had it not been for the chaos we have just been describing, during the Age of Disunity. In this 360-year-long period, many Chinese became increasingly disillusioned about the ability of the ancient philosophies of their civilization or of their political leaders to solve their problems, and so became

[39] On these events, see E. Zurcher, *The Buddhist Conquest of China: The Spread and Adaptation of Buddhism in Early Medieval China*, 3rd edn. Leiden: Brill, 2007, pp. 18–43.

increasingly receptive to Buddhism. With Confucianism, Daoism and Legalism apparently powerless in the face of another bitterly divisive warring states period, Buddhist authorities devoted their energies to winning converts among the disillusioned Chinese at all levels of society. In the north, Buddhist missionaries focused on gaining political patronage among the rival warlords, often using "magical" tricks to convince these tribal leaders that Buddhism was more powerful than traditional Chinese faiths. But the warlords were attracted to Buddhism for another reason; because of its egalitarian creed these foreign and relatively uneducated rulers were not automatically relegated to the lower strata of Chinese culture in the way that Confucianism dismissively did. By the late third century, Confucian elites of the Western Jin also found themselves attracted to Buddhism, and by the early fourth century Buddhist ideas were increasingly being discussed in aristocratic circles.

Elite and aristocratic patronage was just the first step, however. For Buddhism to really gain a hold in China, the faith needed to win converts among the people. The first challenge to this endeavor was translating the Buddhist texts, which were full of foreign ideas and names, into Chinese linguistic and cultural terms. An early solution was to try and adapt as many Buddhist concepts as possible to preexisting Daoist ideas. This meant, for example, that the Buddhist ideal of Nirvana was soon translated as *wuwei*, the Daoist notion of disengagement. And the word *Dao* itself (which means "the way") was now used to translate the Buddhist idea of *Dharma*, or divine law.[40] This meant that for many Chinese, Buddhism was initially presented as a variant of Daoism. More accurate translations of Buddhist literature started to become widely available in China by the late fourth century, partly due to the work of an eminent Central Asian monk named Kumarajiva who lived between c. 344 and 413.[41] During the Sixteen Kingdoms Period, Kumarajiva established a huge translation school in Chang'an that employed several thousand monks to accurately translate many of the major and very lengthy Buddhist texts into Chinese. Chinese pilgrims also began to make the arduous journey to India to more deeply investigate the core beliefs of the faith. The most famous of these was the scholar-pilgrim Faxian, whose fifteen-year journey (including his passage through the

[40] P. Demieville, "Philosophy and Religion from Han to Sui," in D. Twitchett and M. Loewe, eds., *Cambridge History of China: Volume I. The Ch'in and Han Empires, 221 BC–AD 220*. Cambridge: Cambridge University Press, 1986, pp. 821–822.

[41] For more on Kumarajiva and his translation methods see Lu Yang, *Narrative and Historicity in the Buddhist Biographies of Early Medieval China: The Case of Kumarajiva*, Asia Major, Third Series, 17 (2), pp. 1–43.

former Kushan Empire) between 399 and 414 CE is recorded in his own beautifully written account.[42]

But even as these more accurate (and thus culturally distinctive) versions of Buddhism began to appear, the Buddhists continued to work hard to make their faith compatible with the core beliefs of Chinese culture and to play down areas of possible conflict. Numerous attempts were made, for example, to fuse Buddhism with Confucian notions of filial piety; donations to a Buddhist temple and expressions of Buddhist faith were now seen as demonstrations of filial piety. But contentious issues remained that were played up by Daoists and others who resented the wealth and growing influence of Buddhism on Chinese elites and commoners alike. The celibacy of Buddhist monks was decried as an unfilial act, for example, because it failed to provide one's ancestors with an heir. Confucians and Daoists instigated persecutions of Buddhists during the reign of Northern Wei emperor Taiwu (r. 424–452). Orders were issued to close monasteries and to force Buddhist monks and nuns to return to everyday life. A second round of persecutions broke out between 574 and 578 CE, with a concerted effort to destroy the wealthy and increasingly influential Buddhist religious establishment. But neither round of persecutions did permanent harm, and because no attempt was made to suppress private Buddhist beliefs, the faith remained strong. This was particularly so after the Sui emperor Wendi reunited the country and claimed to be a Buddhist king.

The physical landscape of China was also transformed by Buddhism during the Age of Disunity. Records indicate that by the first decades of the sixth century Buddhists had constructed more than 9,000 temples across China, occupied by more than 150,000 monks and nuns.[43] Magnificent Buddhist art and architecture decorated lavish temple and monastic complexes throughout the country, particularly pagoda-style stupas, which now proliferated in the great cities of Chang'an, Luoyang and Nanjing. Luoyang itself was said to have been home to 1,000 Buddhist temples and monasteries. Visitors to that city today can still admire the magnificent Buddhist art carved into the soft limestone cliffs at Longmen. Daoism responded to the growing Buddhist threat by also transforming itself into a religion. Daoist "Celestial Masters" established well-run inns offering travelers free meals, and they became renowned for their ability to heal the sick and for their attempts to achieve immortality. The Daoists also argued a vision of a heavenly bureaucracy that mirrored

[42] Faxian, *A Record of Buddhistic Kingdoms; being an account by the Chinese monk Fa-Hien of his travels in India and Ceylon, AD 399–414, in search of the Buddhist books of discipline*, trans. J. Legge. Oxford: Clarendon Press, 1886.

[43] Ebrey 2000, p. 99.

Figure 9.6 Buddhist sculpture, Longmen Grottoes, near Luoyang, China
www.gettyimages.co.uk/license/149845437
Credit: pius99

the earthly bureaucracy so central to Chinese government. Emperor Taiwu of the Northern Wei, one of the persecutors of Buddhism, received cosmic legitimacy from his Daoist supporters as the head of both the heavenly and earthly hierarchies.[44] Throughout this period, Daoist and Buddhist temples directly competed with each other for political patronage and popular support. The Daoists created their own magnificent religious art, which appeared as sculpture carved into cliffs or as superbly colored images painted onto the walls of caves.

At the end of the Age of Disunity, north and south China were reunited in 581 CE under the short-lived but effective Sui Dynasty. Despite these centuries of political, social, economic and cultural turmoil, many foundational philosophies and ideas of East Asian civilization remained largely intact. Confucianism had been preserved among the conservative aristocratic families, particularly in the south, and notions of filial piety were as strong as ever. Daoism had transformed itself into a religion that competed with the exotic "foreign" faith of Buddhism for political patronage and popular support. The powerful emperors of the Tang Dynasty, which succeeded the Sui and turned China into the strongest, wealthiest and

[44] Ebrey 2000, p. 100.

most powerful state on the planet, also had to deal with these conflicting cultural and spiritual claims for political and popular support, challenges that were a continuing legacy of the collapse of the Han Dynasty at the end of the First Silk Roads Era.

Spread of Christianity in the Eastern Mediterranean and Central Asia

Christianity first emerged in the context of the early Roman Empire, when during the reigns of the Julio-Claudian emperors, certain Jewish sects began to transform their beliefs. Groups like the Essenes worked in secret on a radical new form of Judaism that scholars now recognize as the precursor to Christianity; the famous Dead Sea Scrolls were written by the Essenes. Judea was then part of the Roman Empire, and the Jews were far from happy. Some hoped for a Messiah to rid them of the Romans; others, later, took direct action like the uprising of 66 CE, which was ruthlessly crushed and resulted in the destruction of the Temple in Jerusalem. According to the New Testament of the Christian Bible, prophet Jesus Christ was born in Bethlehem in Judea around the year 2 or 3 BCE. He spent the next thirty years working as a carpenter, but then began to travel all over Judea preaching a message of love. When he reached Jerusalem for the Jewish feast of Passover, he was greeted by huge crowds hoping that he was the Messiah who would lead a revolt against the Romans. When they realized that he had no intention of doing this, the crowds turned against him; he was charged with treason by Roman procurator Pontius Pilate and crucified.

After his death word spread that Jesus had been seen alive, and small communities of Christian believers (a Greek word that means "followers of Christ") began to appear. But Jesus' message of love and compassion might have disappeared like so many other radical ideologies had it not been for the work of Paul of Tarsus, an educated Hellenic Jew, initially strongly opposed to Christianity, who had an epiphany and converted to Christianity. Although Christians were perceived as a dangerous cult by Roman authorities, this didn't prevent Christian missionaries from making full use of the superb Roman road and sea transportation networks during the early centuries CE. Paul of Tarsus was the first and arguably most significant of all early Christian missionaries. It is estimated that he traveled some 8,000 miles throughout the eastern Roman Empire visiting numerous small Christian communities, preaching that Jesus was the Son of God and he had died to atone for the sins of humanity. Paul was executed in Rome in 65 CE, but because of his extensive and active proselytizing large numbers of Christian communities emerged across the eastern Mediterranean.[45] In the third century CE, Christian bishop Gregory Thaumaturgus, or Gregory the Miracle-Worker, also used Roman roads to travel around Anatolia (modern Turkey) to preach, drive out demons and make converts.[46] The efforts of dedicated missionaries like Paul and Gregory meant that, despite official Roman opposition to the faith, by the late third century Christian communities were successfully operating all over the Mediterranean Basin.

During the same period that Gregory was operating, the Roman Empire was divided into two halves to help prevent the sort of problems that had caused the "Crisis of the Third Century." Following the retirement of Emperor Diocletian, the architect of this imperial division, civil war erupted again, and a senior Roman military commander named Constantine fought his way to power. On the eve of the crucial Battle of the Milvian Bridge in 313 CE, Constantine claimed to have a vision of himself raising a Christian cross. He won the battle and declared that Christianity would now be "tolerated" throughout the empire. In 325 CE he convened an important meeting of Christian intellectuals at the Council of Nicaea, which resolved various doctrinal disputes. Then, in 330 CE Constantine moved the capital of the empire to the city of Byzantium (now renamed Constantinople), where he offered financial and political support for the Christian hierarchy, and was personally baptized as a Christian. As a result of this support Christianity gradually became the most important religion in the Roman Empire, and its triumph was complete when in 380 CE the emperor Theodosius (r. 379–395 CE) made Christianity the official religion of the empire.

Further east, beyond the borders of the Roman Empire, missionary activity like that practiced by Paul and Gregory led to the establishment of Christian communities in Mesopotamia and Iran, and even in India. Initially there was close contact between churches in the Mediterranean region and those in Southwest Asia, but after the fifth century significant doctrinal differences developed. In Southwest Asia many Christians adopted the Nestorian version of the faith, named after early fifth-century Greek theologian Nestorius. Nestorians focused on the human nature of Jesus, rather than the divine, an interpretation that was rejected by church authorities in the West. Many Nestorians eventually migrated eastward along the Silk Roads, establishing flourishing communities in

[45] For a comprehensive scholarly account of the travels of Paul, see R. Brenchley, "The Travels of Paul," at www.forumancientcoins.com/Articles/the_travels_of_paul.htm.

[46] On Gregory see C. Herbermann, ed., "St. Gregory of Neocaesarea," *Catholic Encyclopedia 7*. New York: Robert Appletone Company, 1910.

Central Asia and in China.[47] Despite these doctrinal differences, like Buddhism in China, Christianity thrived in the troubled centuries following the end of the First Silk Roads Era. Christianity was a faith that offered something permanent and optimistic to believe in during troubled times, and it was egalitarian in that it maintained that every soul was equally important. Christianity also offered a sense of community based on concern for the welfare of its members, something that the Roman state was increasingly unable to offer in its later stages. Most of all, Christianity held out the hope of something that none of the other religions of the Roman world offered – the possibility of eternal existence in an afterlife.

Spread of Zoroastrianism in Central Asia

The religion that was practiced most commonly throughout the three Persian/Iranian empires was Zoroastrianism, a visionary spirituality conceived of by the prophet Zoroaster who preached in Iran and Central Asia.[48] Traditionally, Zoroaster's life is dated to the sixth century BCE, the century before Cyrus I, the founder of the Achaemenid Empire, came to power, although the prophet might in fact have lived centuries earlier. Zoroastrianism is a monotheistic religion that was influential on both early Christianity and Islam. It conceives of the Great God Ohrmazd, who presides over a world that is a combination of good and evil. Ohrmazd created two twin spirits – Spenta Mainyu (the Holy Spirit) and Angra Mainyu (sometimes called Ahirman, the Destructive Spirit); creation is possible only when these two come together. Zarathustra gave three commandments to his followers urging them to lead perfect lives: *humata* – good thoughts; *hukhta* – good words; and *havarshta* – good deeds.

Zoroastrianism did not become the "official" religion of the Persians until the Parthian and Sasanian Empires, but Achaemenid kings like Darius I and his successor, Xerxes, were probably Zoroastrians, acknowledging their devotion to the faith in the Behistun inscriptions. Parthian royalty also patronized Zoroastrianism (as probably did the Kushan kings). The rulers of the Sasanian state, Ardashir I and his successors, also promoted the religion, as evidenced by depictions on coins and rock reliefs where the kings are shown receiving the symbols of royal power

[47] For a readable account of the spread of Nestorians and other Christian and Jewish communities along the Silk Roads into China, see D. A. Johnson, *Lost Churches on the Silk Roads*. USA: New Sinai Press, 2014.

[48] For a comprehensive introduction to the history of Zoroastrianism, see "Zoroastrianism: Historical Review up to the Arab Conquests," *Iranica Online*, www.iranicaonline.org/articles/zoroastrianism-i-historical-review.

Figure 9.7 Inside an ancient Zoroastrian *dakhma* (Tower of Silence), Yazd, modern Iran
http://media.gettyimages.com/photos/inside-an-ancient-zoroastrian-tower-of-silence-yazd-iran-picture-id700971998
Credit: Jean-Philippe Tournut

from Ohrmazd. The Sasanians used Zoroastrianism as a mechanism for unifying their empire, often building fire temples in captured territory as they expanded along the old Silk Roads trade routes. The Sasanians also expressed interest in the Central Asian universalist religion of Manichaeism but their core adherence was always to Zoroastrianism, to the extent that Jews, Christians, Manicheans and Buddhists were sometimes persecuted while Zoroastrianism was being established.[49] Christianity was viewed with particular suspicion by Sasanian ruler Shapur II, who regarded it as some sort of "fifth column" sent by the Romans. Shapur II singled out Christians for persecution, which led to the writing of several treatises on the martyrdom of Persian Christians.[50] Zoroastrianism achieved its final form during the reign of Sasanian ruler Khusro in the sixth century; the sacred hymns of the *Avesta*, which contains the teachings of the prophet Zoroaster, were written down, and Zoroastrian fire temples were built throughout the

[49] T. Daryae, *Sasanian Persia: The Rise and Fall of an Empire*. London: I. B. Tauris, 2013, pp. 77–78.
[50] Daryae 2015, p. 290.

empire. Zoroastrianism remained the most important religion in Iran and Central Asia until the emergence and rapid expansion of Islam throughout the region in the seventh and eighth centuries CE.

Spread of Manichaeism in Central and East Asia

The religion of Manichaeism also benefited from the Silk Roads after it emerged in Mesopotamia in the third century CE.[51] Its founder, Mani (216–276 CE), was a prophet and devoted missionary who traveled extensively throughout Central Asia and also dispatched disciples. Manichaeism was influenced by Zoroastrianism, Christianity and Buddhism; it was an explicitly syncretic religion that Mani believed was vitally needed in the cosmopolitan world that had emerged in Eurasia, at least partly as a result of intense cultural and commercial exchanges facilitated by the Silk Roads. Like Buddhism, Manichaeism was particularly attractive to merchants, and eventually most of the major Silk Roads trading cities contained Manichaean communities. As we have seen, the powerful Sasanian kings, although initially attracted to some aspects of Manichaeism, preferred Zoroastrianism. Urged on by Zoroastrian priests, Sasanian rulers eventually decided to suppress Manichaeism as a threat to public order, and Mani was imprisoned and then executed in 276 CE by Sasanian king Vahram I.[52] Like Nestorian Christianity, Manichaeism survived by moving further east into Central Asia, where it attracted converts among nomads and merchants.

Spread of Hinduism into Southeast Asia

One final example of the role of the Silk Roads, the maritime routes in this case, in helping in the diffusion of religion is the spread of Hinduism out of India and across the Indian Ocean into Southeast Asia. By as early as the first century CE, Indian cultural influences started appearing in small Southeast Asian states, where rulers adopted the Indian model of kingship and began to call themselves *raja* (kings) in the manner of Indian rulers. Many of the elites in these states also adopted the Indian classical language of Sanskrit as the means for written communication. Because of their proximity to China (and indeed conquest and incorporation into the Han Dynastic empire), Vietnamese rulers had converted to Buddhism, and appointed Buddhist advisors to their courts. Associating with an

[51] For a comprehensive study, see S. N. C. Lieu, *Manichaeism in the Later Roman Empire and Medieval China*, 2nd edn. Tubingen: J. C. B. Mohr (Paul Siebeck), 1992.

[52] P. Brown, "The Diffusion of Manichaeism in the Roman Empire," in *Journal of Roman Studies*. Cambridge: Cambridge University Press, 1969, p. 94.

honored religion like Buddhism and patronizing the Buddhist establishment enhanced the legitimacy of rulers and gave them valuable allies in the monastic hierarchies. But in regions of Southeast Asia less influenced by Chinese culture, elites preferred to embrace the classics of Indian literature, which promoted Hindu values. These rulers were not interested in the caste system, however, and they continued to acknowledge the nature spirits that their people had worshipped for millennia, but they did find Hinduism attractive because the faith supported the principle of monarchical rule, particularly the idea that some were born into a particular class whose destiny it was to rule over others.

Two centuries after the demise of the First Silk Roads Era, a powerful Hindu-influenced state named Funan was established in the Malay Peninsula, which grew wealthy through facilitating trade between India and China. The rulers of Funan called themselves *rajas*, and claimed divine sanction for their rule the way kings in India were doing. They also introduced ceremonies and rituals worshipping Shiva, Vishnu and other Hindu gods. During the sixth century Funan was wracked by a bitter internal power struggle and rapidly collapsed. A new power later emerged based on the island of Sumatra, the kingdom of Srivijaya, which between 670 and 1025 controlled transregional commerce. The elites of Srivijaya were devout Buddhists, and the faith prospered under their patronage. Srivijaya remained a wealthy and powerful trading state for almost 400 years until the eleventh century. In modern Cambodia, meanwhile, the kingdom of Angkor flourished from 889 to 1431. Strongly influenced by Hinduism, the Khmer rulers of Angkor constructed vast temple complexes at Angkor Thom and Angkor Wat. Later Khmer elites gradually embraced Buddhism and added new temples to the complexes to create an extraordinary syncretic mix of two of the most influential religions of South Asia.

For centuries following the end of the First Silk Roads Era, Southeast Asia functioned as a commercial and cultural middle ground between East and South Asia and was heavily influenced by its commercial contact with these regions. Although properly belonging to a separate study of the Second Silk Roads Era, we should briefly note here that from the eighth century on, Arab sailors and merchants also began to filter into the region, bringing their new ideology of Islam into the already religiously diverse region. Merchants and port cities all over Southeast Asia gradually converted to Islam, because this made most sense in facilitating commercial exchanges. This process clearly demonstrates the power of trade as an instrument of conversion – once one of the key cities in a trading network converted, it was in the best interests of the others to follow suit to enhance personal relationships and provide

Figure 9.8 The temple complex at Angkor Wat in modern Cambodia, which blends Buddhist and Hindu architectural styles
www.gettyimages.co.uk/license/657059358
Credit: Cao Wei

a common basis in Muslim law to regulate business deals. Conversion also more tightly tied these port cities to the great trade networks already established by Muslim merchants, linking the Mediterranean, Middle East, Arabia and India with Southeast and East Asia. As this brief account has attempted to demonstrate, most of the religions and spiritual ideologies of ancient Eurasia, notably Buddhism, Christianity, Zoroastrianism, Manichaeism, Hinduism and, later, Islam all flourished and spread far beyond their points of origin by using the network of land and maritime routes established during the First Silk Roads Era.[53]

The Silk Roads and Disease Epidemics in the Second and Third Centuries

Ideas about political legitimacy and religion were not the only nonmaterial products that spread along the trade routes of ancient Eurasia during the First Silk Roads Era; a less welcome fellow traveler that moved with

[53] For further reading on all these early Southeast Asian states, see N. Tarling, ed., *The Cambridge History of Southeast Asia, Vol. 1, From Early Times to c. 1800*. Cambridge: Cambridge University Press, 1993.

the human and animal agents of exchange was disease. Some of these disease pathogens were so contagious that they caused widespread epidemics that devastated populations in regions of Eurasia that had not previously been exposed to these diseases. In the introduction to this chapter we asked: what evidence connects the outbreak of disease epidemics in ancient Eurasia to the Silk Roads, and what role (if any) did these play in the collapse of the network? Unfortunately, historians of the ancient world do not often have access to accurate medical or demographic records, but using what sources are available, it is possible to draw some brief conclusions about the impact of disease epidemics on human populations, particularly in the Roman and Han Empires. This evidence does suggest that Silk Roads exchanges were at least partly responsible for these epidemics, and that epidemics in turn contributed to some of the chaos that afflicted both the Han and Roman Empires in the late second and third centuries.

Antonine Plague (165–180 CE)

Ancient sources provide scattered evidence of disastrous epidemics in both western and eastern Eurasia during the second and third centuries CE, most probably caused either by smallpox or by some form of hemorrhagic fever similar to yellow fever, or even Ebola. Because of their lack of previous exposure to these diseases, populations in the Roman and Han Empires had no resistance to the pathogens, and also no effective medicine against nor even understanding of the illness. The first disastrous plague to strike the Roman Empire occurred at the height of the First Silk Roads Era, the Antonine Plague of 165–180 CE. The plague was probably brought back to Rome by troops returning from the province of Seleucia, where they had engaged in campaigns against the Parthians during the reign of Roman emperor Marcus Aurelius Antoninus (r. 161–180 CE). While stationed in an army camp with his troops, the emperor caught some kind of infection and died. Historians speculate that the emperor's "infection" was caused by the plague, and his family name of Antoninus has long been associated with the epidemic.[54]

There were two distinct outbreaks during this fifteen-year period. Roman historian Dio Cassius (155–235 CE), writing about the second epidemic, reported some 2,000 deaths a day in the city of Rome itself.[55] Other late Roman historians, including Ammianus Marcellinus and

[54] On the possibility that Marcus Aurelius died of the plague, see J. F. Gilliam, "The Plague under Marcus Aurelius," *American Journal of Philology* 82 (1961), p. 249.

[55] Dio Cassius, LXXII 14.3–4 (but note that the book in which Dio Cassius must have discussed the earlier outbreak is missing).

Eutropius, provide evidence of the spread of the epidemic more generally throughout the empire, and of large population losses as a result.[56] Modern demographers have offered estimates of an empire-wide death rate of 7–10 percent, with higher rates of perhaps 15 percent in the urban areas, including Rome.[57] Perhaps the most important ancient source on the Antonine Plague is the ancient Greek physician Galen, who was present when the plague broke out among troops stationed in the northern Italian city of Aquileia in the winter of 168/169. In his classic medical treatise *Methodus Medendi*, Galen describes the symptoms, including fever, diarrhea and the outbreak of pustules on the skin, all symptoms of smallpox.[58]

An "Antonine Plague" in Late Han China? (151–185 CE)

There is also evidence of deadly disease epidemics occurring in Later Han Dynasty China between c. 151 and 185 CE, at the height of the First Silk Roads Era. Historian Rafe de Crespigny has used the writing of late third/early fourth century Chinese author Ge Hong to consider these outbreaks, which were most probably connected to the simultaneous outbreak of the Antonine Plague at the other end of the Silk Roads.[59] This devastating plague added to the concerns and instability that wracked the final decades of Han Dynasty rule, thus directly contributing to its collapse.

Plague of Cyprian (250–270 CE)

A second deadly outbreak of plague devastated the Roman Empire again in the mid-third century, after the decline of the First Silk Roads Era and during the "Crisis of the Third Century." The Plague of Cyprian broke out in Ethiopia in 250 CE and spread into Roman Egypt the following year during the brief reigns of Emperors Decius (249–251) and Gallus (251–253). From Egypt the epidemic spread devastatingly to ravage much of the Roman Empire for at least two decades between 250 and 270 CE. At the height of the epidemic between 250 and 266 CE, up to 5,000 people a day were dying in Rome, depleting the ranks of the Roman army and causing huge labor shortages.[60] The effects of the plague were

[56] See, for example, Eutropius XXXI, 6.24.
[57] R. J. Littman and M. L. Littman, "Galen and the Antonine Plague," *American Journal of Philology* 94, No. (1983), pp. 243–255.
[58] On Galen's descriptions, see Littman and Littman 1983.
[59] R. de Crespigny, *A Biographical Dictionary of Later Han to the Three Kingdoms (23–220 AD)*,. Leiden: Brill, 2007, p. 514.
[60] See Pontius of Carthage, *Life of Cyprian*, trans. E. Wallis, 1885, Online at Christian Classics Ethereal Library.

witnessed by early Christian writer St. Cyprian, the bishop of Carthage, who described its effects, and after whom modern historians have named the plague. Historian Kyle Harper believes that Cyprian's description sounds more like an account of yellow fever or Ebola than smallpox:

> "As the strength of the body is dissolved, the bowels dissipate in a flow; a fire that begins in the innermost depths burns up into wounds in the throat ... The intestines are shaken with continuous vomiting ... the eyes are set on fire from the force of the blood ... as weakness prevails through the failures and losses of the bodies, the gait is crippled or the hearing is blocked or the vision is blinded."[61]

The plague led to scapegoating of Christians, whose faith was blamed for the outbreak, but Cyprian and other Christian authors saw it as a test of faith.[62] Indeed, Harper argues that the psychological impact of the plague was far more devastating on pagan society than it was on the Christians, who responded in a more orderly way, particularly in how they buried their dead.[63] This outbreak also claimed the life of a Roman emperor, when in 270 CE it caused the death of Claudius Gothicus (268–270), further evidence, if followers of Rome's traditional religion needed it, that this plague represented something akin to the end of their world.[64] Assessing the precise demographic impact of these plagues on the populations of western and eastern Eurasia is impossible, despite many such attempts. But it seems reasonable to conclude that these plague outbreaks must have had a devastating impact during the second and third centuries CE, and caused significant political, economic, social and even ideological disruption.

Conclusion

There is no doubt that the extraordinary levels of commercial and cultural exchange that occurred along the land and sea routes of the Silk Roads network had innumerable positive effects on ancient Eurasian societies. The diffusion of new foods, technologies, religions and ideas about art, fashion, geography and so much else rapidly transformed human culture. Yet it was this same interconnectedness during the First Silk Roads Era that also facilitated the rapid diffusion of disease pathogens that had a devastating impact on at least two of the agrarian civilizations that had sustained the

61 Cyprian, *De Mortalitate*, trans. E. Wallis, 1885, Online at Christian Classics Ethereal Library, 14.

62 Cyprian, *De Mort.*, 1885.

63 K. Harper, "Pandemics and Passages to Late Antiquity: Rethinking the Plague of c. 249–70 Described by Cyprian," *Journal of Roman Archaeology* 28 (2015), pp. 223–260.

64 Zosimus, *New History* I, 26, 37 and 46.

network, directly contributing to the collapse of one of those great imperial states, and to the demise of the entire Silk Roads Network. In the conclusion to this book we bring together all the various themes and questions we have addressed in these chapters, and argue once more for the vital importance of the First Silk Roads Era for ancient Eurasian and indeed world history.

Selected Further Reading

Brenchley, R., "The Travels of Paul," at www.forumancientcoins.com/Articles/the_travels_of_paul.htm.

Brown, P., *The World of Late Antiquity AD 150–750*. London: Thames and Hudson, 1971.

Buckley, P. E., *The Cambridge Illustrated History of China*. Cambridge: Cambridge University Press, 1996.

Cyprian, *De Mortalitate*, trans. E. Wallis, 1885, Online at Christian Classics Ethereal Library, 14.

Daryae, T., "Western and Central Eurasia," in C. Benjamin, ed., *Cambridge History of the World Vol IV*. Cambridge: Cambridge University Press, 2015, pp. 271–299.

Daryae, T., *Sasanian Persia: The Rise and Fall of an Empire*. London: I. B. Tauris, 2013

Fisher, G., *Between Empires: Arabs, Romans, and Sasanians in Late Antiquity*. Oxford: Oxford University Press, 2011.

Holcombe, C., "East Asia," in C. Benjamin, ed., *Cambridge History of the World*. Cambridge: Cambridge University Press, 2015, pp. 407–434.

Howard-Johnson, J. "The Official History of Heraclius' Persian Campaign," in *The Roman and Byzantine Army in the East*, ed. E. Dabrowa, Krakow, 1994, pp. 5–87.

Lieu, S. N. C., *Manichaeism in the Later Roman Empire and Medieval China*, 2nd. edn.Tubingen: J.C.B. Mohr (Paul Siebeck), 1992.

Pearce, S., A. Spiro and P. Buckley, eds., Culture and Power in the Reconstitution of the Chinese Realm 200–600. Cambridge, MA: Harvard University Press, 2001.

Potter, D. S., *The Roman Empire at Bay. AD 180–395*. London: Routledge, 2004.

Tomber, R., "Rome and Mesopotamia – Importers into India in the First Millennium AD," *Antiquity* 81/314, (2007), pp. 972–988.

Conclusion

As we noted in the introduction to this book, during a period of roughly three and a half centuries, between the late second century BCE and the mid-third century CE, many of the human communities dwelling across the vast reaches of Eurasia found themselves linked into an interconnected system of exchanges via a network of routes known today as the Silk Roads. This First Silk Roads Era led to the most significant transregional commercial and cultural interactions experienced by humans to that point in history. As we have argued, silk was the most important material commodity that was moved along this network of land and maritime routes, and that fact justifies the continued use of the label coined in the nineteenth century by Ferdinand von Richthofen, the *Silk Roads*. But what ultimately makes this period of ancient history so important is the exchange of nonmaterial "commodities" that occurred in parallel with the commercial interactions. Because of the demand for silk and other luxury goods, a range of different crop species and agricultural technologies, religions and ideologies, languages, artistic styles and epidemic diseases also spread across Eurasia, with profound consequences for subsequent human and environmental history.

It is this extraordinary cultural and biological diffusion that makes the First Silk Roads Era so important. During these centuries, millions of humans became connected in a dynamic and diverse exchange network that allowed many of the core ideas of ancient states and civilizations to diffuse widely for the first time. Perhaps the most significant consequence of this sharing of ideas was the spread of Buddhism into East and Southeast Asia, a process of tremendous consequence to millions of humans ever since. Much of this cultural diffusion was a direct result of the demand by wealthy aristocrats in Rome and other Western Eurasian cities for the sensuous, translucent material called silk that was imported from some exotic place far away across the deserts and oceans. Silk manufacturers in Han China were able to meet this demand by producing the textile on an almost industrial scale, and thousands of diplomats, merchants, mariners and nomads, with their horses, camels and ships, made the movement of silk and other luxury products possible.

Despite the contribution of so many individual traders, animals and regional cultures to the First Silk Roads Era, trade and cultural exchange on this sort of scale was only possible because of the political and economic stability created by the four large imperial states that controlled much of Eurasia during the First Silk Roads Era: the Han Dynasty in China, the Kushan and Parthian Empires in Inner Eurasia, and the Roman Empire. The powerful elites, administrators and armies of these empires established law and order over enormous areas, minted and used coinage and constructed and maintained the transport infrastructure necessary for sustained transregional commerce. It was the successful operation of these four great empires that made commercial and cultural exchanges on such an unprecedented scale possible, so we have also explored the historical processes that led to the establishment and successful maintenance of these vast states. Yet, despite their size and success, these four substantial agrarian civilizations were never able to control the full extent of the Silk Roads network. Communities of pastoral nomads and other more mobile intermediaries also played a critical role in facilitating the exchanges by connecting the imperial states, which is why considerable space has also been devoted to an account of the great pastoral nomadic confederations that formed and thrived during the First Silk Roads Era.

We have explored a range of political, military, economic, social, cultural and environmental themes and consequences of Silk Roads exchanges in the nine chapters of this book. In Chapter 1 we introduced the environment and lifeway of pastoral nomadism, and saw how early pastoralists gradually occupied huge expanses of the Eurasian steppe through a series of Bronze Age migrations. Some of these communities evolved into large and powerful confederations of militarized pastoral nomads such as the Xiongnu and Yuezhi, with their superb horseback-riding archer warriors under the control of often brutal but brilliant military strategists. As a result of Xiongnu aggression, the Yuezhi were forced to undertake a lengthy migration that brought them deep into Central Asia, to a region known as Bactria to Greco-Roman historians and Daxia to the Han Chinese. This migration was destined to have profound consequences for the opening of the Silk Roads. In Chapter 2 we paused to trace the history of early China from the emergence of the first agrarian communities and complex cultures like the Yangshao and Longshan, through to the appearance of the first dynasties of Chinese history: the semi-legendary Xia, the Shang and Zhou, and the great imperial states of the Qin and Han. We also considered the emergence of many of the foundational philosophies of ancient China, including Confucianism, Daoism, Legalism and the Mandate of Heaven, and the way these ideas were used to legitimize government and organize society, up to the so-called Triumph of Confucianism in the Early Han Dynasty, which marked the beginning of Chinese expansion into Central Asia.

In Chapter 3 we picked up the story of the origins of the Silk Roads by following the epic journey of Zhang Qian from the Early Han Dynasty capital of Chang'an deep into Central Asia and back. Zhang Qian gathered considerable intelligence about the geopolitical situation in Inner Eurasia, and his report to Han emperor Wudi led directly to intensified Chinese involvement with sedentary and nomadic states to the west and north. Wudi's decision to end the passive *heqin* policy of his predecessors and adopt a more aggressive military approach to the relationship with the Xiongnu led to a long and bloody war, and by the mid-first century BCE, the Han military had pushed the Xiongnu back to the northern steppe. The Han government then extended fortifications and established a series of military garrisons along its northwestern borders to safeguard its growing tributary empire, and the various diplomatic caravans laden with silk and other tributes that were now making their way into Central Asia.

In Chapter 4 we tried to tease out the various ways by which large quantities of Han Chinese silk might have made their way through Central Asia and on to the West. Contrary to the popular view of Silk Roads commerce, it appears that most of the silk was dispatched as some form of diplomatic tribute to various Central Asian nomadic and sedentary powers, but this tribute was quickly monetized by Chinese envoys and Central Asian nomads, sedentary elites and merchants. We traveled with these diplomatic caravans along the key Eastern Silk Roads routes from Chang'an into Central Asia via the Tarim Basin, noting the crucial role of the Bactrian camel in facilitating their lengthy and often arduous journeys. The manufacture of the enormous quantities of tributary silk that traveled along these often-challenging land routes was made possible by the evolution of the *Bombyx mori* silk moth, and the efficient silk manufacturing industry the Han Chinese constructed. The principal purchasers of this Chinese silk were elite Romans dwelling thousands of miles away at the other end of Eurasia. In order to understand how Rome became such an important market for silk, in Chapter 5 we explored the many twists and turns of Roman history that led eventually to the inspired rule of Augustus and the transition from Republic to Empire. As the "First Man" in Rome, Augustus was able to restore peace to a state that had been fractured by more than a century of civil war. It was in this new climate of the *Pax Romana* or Roman Peace that the demand for silk and other Asian luxuries intensified, leading directly to the connection of most of the civilizations and peoples of Eurasia into a single exchange network.

Chapter 5 also considered the operation of overland trade out of the Eastern Mediterranean into Central Asia. The various primary sources and archaeological evidence historians have available suggest that, although a network of vibrant overland routes undoubtedly connected Mesopotamia, Arabia and Syria with the Mediterranean coast, few routes actually penetrated further east into Iran or Central Asia. However silk made its way to Rome, its impact on the culture and economy of the empire was profound. Poets lauded the sexual allure of the wearing of silk garments by women, but conservatives saw the practice as a moral disgrace and a "national extravagance." Attempts were made to regulate and even prohibit the wearing of silk, using moral, economic and gender arguments, but to little avail. Modern historians now argue that, rather than a national extravagance, the import of silk and other Asian luxuries was probably of considerable financial benefit to the Roman Empire through the high customs duties the state imposed on these imports, profit that might actually have been used to pay the Roman legions upon which the success of the state so depended.

One of the most formidable enemies the legions had to deal with was the neighboring Parthian Empire to the east. Chapter 6 looked at literary, numismatic and archaeological evidence for the Parthians, which shows indisputably that from roughly 247 BCE to 224 CE, the Parthians maintained one of the great imperial states in ancient world history. Despite periods of sporadic conflict with the Romans and numerous internal succession crises, the Parthian Empire, along with that of the Kushans, functioned as an effective bridge between western and eastern Eurasia, and flourished because of its formidable military and its decentralized but effective administration, and because the political elites of Parthia recognized the crucial importance of a steady flow of commercial profit generated by Silk Roads exchanges. These commercial considerations led to generally harmonious relations between Parthia, the Kushans and Han China; and even though relations between Rome and Parthia were sometimes tense, in the end the maintenance of commercial ties and their regulation by the state was recognized by elites of all these Eurasian powers as being vital to their mutual success.

The other great imperial state of ancient Eurasia, along with the Han, Romans and Parthians, were the Kushans, the subject of Chapter 7. Despite being descended from the pastoral nomadic Yuezhi confederation, like the Parthians the Kushans were also able to construct a powerful sedentary empire, which controlled vast regions of Inner Eurasia for the first two centuries CE. These centuries correspond precisely with the high point of the First Silk Roads Era, and it is no exaggeration to suggest that it was the stability created by the Kushans, through their unbroken line of royal succession, their superb coinage, their apparent religious tolerance and the generally cordial relations they maintained with their neighbors once they had created their empire, that helped facilitate the extraordinary material and cultural exchanges that epitomize this key period in ancient world history.

The Kushans constructed an essentially land-based empire, but some of the key trade routes that passed through their territory headed toward ports along the west coast of South Asia. Some of these ports, notably Barbaricum, were probably under Kushan political control during the "Great Kushans" period. In Chapter 8 we turned from land routes to the great maritime network constructed during the First Silk Roads Era, which linked Roman Egypt, the east coast of Africa, the Arabian Peninsula and the Persian Gulf with South Asian ports like Barbaricum and the land routes beyond. Political tensions between the Roman and the Parthian Empires might have contributed to the development of the western Indian Ocean maritime connections between the Red Sea and India, but trade by sea was always an attractive option for ancient merchants, as it had been for thousands of years before the Silk Roads Era. Maritime trade was cheaper and faster, and was generally conducted by commercial consortiums that were often unaffected by the geopolitical situation within and between states, until these reached critical levels. We also noted important maritime connections between Han China and Southeast Asia, connections that would expand enormously half a millennium later when the Tang Dynasty came to power in China and maritime trade flourished again across the vast Indian Ocean Basin.

Finally, in Chapter 9, we considered the demise of the First Silk Roads Era, noting that during the third century CE, transregional Silk Roads commercial and cultural exchange diminished dramatically as all of the key imperial states were forced to withdraw from the network. Silk Roads exchanges may have been partly responsible for this decline, because they unwittingly facilitated the spread of disease epidemics that decimated populations at both the western and eastern ends of the network. But the epidemics were only part of the problem. Three of the previously stable empires of the First Silk Roads era collapsed at more or less the same time, and the fourth went through a simultaneous period of crisis, during what in retrospect looks like a Eurasian-wide cycle of political contraction. The Later Han Dynasty ended in 220 CE, after warlords had taken control of most of China, and during the two decades that followed both the Parthian and Kushan Empires collapsed under a wave of Sasanian military attacks. The Roman Empire survived, but had to deal with a series of political and military problems during the so-called Crisis of the Third Century. With this sort of political and social chaos occurring across much of Eurasia, it was inevitable that levels of transregional commerce declined significantly. Trade did continue, of course, notably between the Byzantines, the Sasanians and various smaller Chinese states, but not with the intensity that had characterized this First Silk Roads Era. Three and a half centuries later the Tang Dynasty came to power in China at the same time that the *Dar al-Islam* (Realm of Islam) was emerging in Southwest Asia, and this restoration of political and economic stability would lead to the revival of high levels of transregional land and maritime trade during what might be called a Second Silk Roads Era.

All of the evidence we have considered in this book, including ancient sources and inscriptions and archaeological and numismatic discoveries, have helped historians construct a reasonably detailed understanding of the major land and maritime routes that operated during the First Silk Roads Era. It was the discovery of monsoon wind patterns in the Indian Ocean Basin, coupled with the appropriate "goldilocks" conditions of a developing demand for "Eastern" luxury goods in the Roman world, and an ability to meet the demand by East and South Asian manufacturers and merchants, that led to the creation of the vibrant Silk Roads network. Cities deep in Central Asia, and ports along the coasts of the Red Sea, the Persian Gulf and the Indian subcontinent, became clearing-houses for the astonishing diversity of goods that crisscrossed the Indian Ocean Basin during the First Silk Roads Era. These goods included Chinese silk, of course, but also expensive precious stones, spices, wine, metals, glass and large quantities of Roman gold and silver coins.

Despite the obvious vibrancy and value of these maritime routes, some economic historians have argued that regional networks of exchange continued to be more important and valuable than transregional networks during the period. Sita von Redden, for example, suggests that it is "almost certain, although it cannot be proved, that the aggregate value of the goods that went on the long journey from Eastern and Central Asia to the Mediterranean and on to Rome was only a fraction of the aggregate value of the same range of goods that continued to circulate in much smaller geographical confines."[1] Von Redden agrees that, as the *Muziris*

[1] S. von Redden, "Global Economic History," in C. Benjamin, ed., *Cambridge History of the World Vol. IV*, Cambridge: Cambridge University Press, 2015, p. 50. See also A. Selbitchka, *Prestigegüter entlang der Seidenstraße? Archäologische Untersuchungen zu Chinas Beziehungen zu Kulturen des Tarimbeckens vom zweiten bis frühen fünften Jahrhundert nach Christus*. Wiesbaden: Harrassowitz, 2012, vol. 1; Di Cosmo, *Ancient China and Its Enemies*, pp. 131–134 and 248; and X. Liu, *Ancient India and Ancient China: Trade and Religious Exchanges AD 1–600* (New Delhi: Vicas, 1988).

papyrus demonstrates, the value of individual commercial journeys was enormous, but these were dependent on, as she puts it, "the consumptive capacities of rather narrow social elites."[2]

Even if it is true that internal trade *within* the Han and Roman Empires was carried on at higher volumes and at greater monetary value than the transregional trade *between* these two vast imperial states, collectively the regional and transregional land and maritime routes of the First Silk Roads Era constituted an enormous, vibrant, interconnected Eurasia-wide globalization that included virtually every single agrarian civilization, city-state, regional culture, pastoral nomadic confederation and hunter-forager band that lived anywhere within this vast world zone. It was trade that brought together so many ideas, religions, germs, artistic techniques, crops, animals, technologies and languages, which collectively constitute the most significant world historical legacy of the First Silk Roads Era. The extraordinary levels of commercial and cultural exchange that occurred along the land and sea routes of the Silk Roads network had innumerable positive effects on ancient Eurasian societies. The diffusion of new foods, technologies, religions and ideas about art, fashion, geography and so much else rapidly transformed human culture. Yet it was this same interconnectedness during the First Silk Roads Era that also facilitated the rapid diffusion of disease pathogens that had a devastating impact on at least two of the agrarian civilizations that had sustained the system, causing serious problems for the Romans and contributing directly to the collapse of the Han, and indeed of the entire Silk Roads Network.

The Silk Roads remain the quintessential example of the interconnectedness of civilizations during the Era of Agrarian Civilizations. Using challenging desert and mountain land routes and lengthy, often stormy maritime routes, merchants and adventurers, diplomats and missionaries, sailors and soldiers and camels, horses and ships carried their commodities, ideas, languages and pathogens enormous distances across the Afro-Eurasian world zone. Each type of exchange was important, but perhaps the most significant consequence of all was the spread of religion, particularly Buddhism, which became one of the key ideological and spiritual beliefs of South and East Asia during the Era. Today, some 2,000 years later, Buddhism remains one of the great cultural bonds shared by billions of people in Asia and beyond, one of the many legacies that the modern world owes to the First Silk Roads Era. As a result of the interactions that occurred, and despite the incredible diversity of cultural participants, the history of Eurasia has preserved a certain underlying

[2] Von Redden 2015, p. 50.

unity to the present day, expressed in common technologies, artistic styles, cultures and religions, even disease and immunity patterns, a unity that had profound implications for subsequent world history. The comingling of so many goods, ideas and diseases around a geographical hub located deep in central Eurasia was the catalyst for an extraordinary increase in the complexity of human relationships and collective learning, a complexity that drove our species inexorably along a path toward modernity.

Bibliography

Primary Sources

Ammianus Marcellinus, *Res Gestae*. See E. A. Thompson, *The Historical Work of Ammianus Marcellinus*. Cambridge: Cambridge University Press, 1947.

Appian of Alexandria, *Historia Romana*. Books XIII–XVII (Civil Wars). Translated by J. Carter. Harmondsworth: Penguin Classics, 1996.

Aristotle, *Historia Animalium*. Translated by D. Eentworth Thompson. At: http://classics.mit.edu/Aristotle/history_anim.html.

Cassius Dio, *Historia Romana*. At: http://penelope.uchicago.edu/Thayer/e/roman/texts/cassius_dio/home.html.

Cyprian, *De Mortalitate*. Translated by E. Wallis, 1885. Online at Christian Classics Ethereal Library. www.ccel.org/ccel/schaff/anf05.i.html.

Diodorus Siculus, *Biblioteca Historica*. At: http://penelope.uchicago.edu/Thayer/e/roman/texts/diodorus_siculus/home.html.

Edictum Diocletiani. See E. R. Graser, "A Text and Translation of the Edict of Diocletian," in T. Frank, ed., *An Economic Survey of Ancient Rome. Volume V: Rome and Italy of the Empire* (1st edn.). Baltimore, MD: Johns Hopkins University Press, 1940.

Eutropius, *Breviarium historiae Romanae*. At: http://reader.digitale-sammlungen.de/de/fs1/object/display/bsb10996065_00002.html.

Faxian, *A Record of Buddhistic Kingdoms; being an account by the Chinese monk Fa-Hien of his travels in India and Ceylon, AD 399–414, in search of the Buddhist books of discipline*. Translated by J. Legge. Oxford: Clarendon Press, 1886.

Florus, Lucius Annaeus, *Epitomae*. At: http://penelope.uchicago.edu/Thayer/e/roman/texts/florus/epitome/home.html.

Han Shu. See A. F. P. Hulsewe and M. A. N. Loewe, trans., *China in Central Asia. The Early Stage: 125 B.C.–A.D. 23. An Annotated Translation of Chapters 61 and 96 of the History of the Former Han Dynasty*. Leiden: Brill, 1979.

Herodian of Antioch, *History of the Empire from the Death of Marcus*. At: www.livius.org/sources/content/herodian-s-roman-history/.

Herodotus, *The Histories*. At: http://classics.mit.edu/Herodotus/history.html.

Horace, *Odes*. The Project Guttenberg EBook of the Works of Horace. At: www.gutenberg.org/files/14020/14020-h/14020-h.htm.

Hou Han Shu. See J. Hill, trans., *Through the Jade Gate to Rome: A Study of the Silk Roads during the Later Han Dynasty, 1st to 2nd Centuries CE. An Annotated*

Translation of the Chronicle on the Western Regions in the Hou Han Shu. Charleston, SC: BookSurge, 2009.

Justin, *Epitome of the Philippic History of Pompeius Trogus.* Translated by J. C. Yardley. New York: American Philological Association Classical Resources, 1994.

Juvaini, Ala Ad Din Ata Malik, *History of the World Conqueror.* Translated by J. A. Boyle. Cambridge, MA: Harvard University Press, 1958.

Ovid, *Ars Amatoria.* At: www.poetryintranslation.com/PITBR/Latin/ArtofLoveBkI.htm.

Parthian Stations by Isidorus of Charax. Translated by W. H. Schoff. London, 1914. See http://parthia.com/doc/parthian_stations.htm#PARTHIAN_STATIONS.

The Periplus of the Erythrian Sea. Travel and Trade in the Indian Ocean by a Merchant of the First Century. Translated by W. H. Schoff. New York: Longmans, Green and Co, 1912.

Pliny the Elder, *Historia Naturalis.* At: http://penelope.uchicago.edu/Thayer/e/roman/texts/pliny_the_elder/home.html.

Pontius of Carthage, *Life of Cyprian.* Translated by E. Wallis, 1885. Online at Christian Classics Ethereal Library.

Ptolemy, Claudius, *Geographia.* At: http://penelope.uchicago.edu/Thayer/e/gazetteer/periods/roman/_texts/ptolemy/home.html.

Seneca, Lucius Annaeus, *Declamations.* Translated by M. Winterbottom. Cambridge, MA: Harvard University Press, 1974.

Helvia. At: https://en.wikisource.org/wiki/Of_Consolation:_To_Helvia.

Sextus Propertius, *Elegies.* At: www.poetryintranslation.com/PITBR/Latin/Prophome.htm.

Shi Ji of Sima Qian. See B. Watson, trans., *Records of the Grand Historian by Sima Qian – Han Dynasty II.* Revised edn. New York: Columbia University Press, 1993.

Strabo, *Geographica.* At: http://penelope.uchicago.edu/Thayer/e/roman/texts/strabo/home.html.

Suetonius, *The Twelve Caesars.* At: http://penelope.uchicago.edu/Thayer/e/roman/texts/suetonius/12caesars/home.html.

Tacitus, Publius Cornelius, *Annals.* At: http://penelope.uchicago.edu/Thayer/E/Roman/Texts/Tacitus/home.html.

Tibullus, Albius, *Elegies.* At: https://archive.org/details/tibullus00bulmgoog.

Virgil, *The Georgics.* At: www.poetryintranslation.com/klineasgeorgics.htm.

Zosimus, *New History.* At: https://en.wikisource.org/wiki/New_History.

Secondary Sources

Abdullaev, K., "Nomadism in Central Asia: The Archaeological Evidence (2nd–1st Centuries B.C.)," in A. Invernizzi, ed., *In the Land of the Gryphons: Papers on Central Asian Archaeology in Antiquity.* Firenze: La Lettres, 1995, pp. 151ff.

"Payonkurgan: New Archaeological Discoveries in Northern Bactria," *CIAA Newsletter,* No. 10 (November 1999), pp. 7ff.

Adshead, S. A. M., *T'ang China: The Rise of the East in World History*. New York: Palgrave Macmillan, 2004.

Agrawala, V. S., *India as Known to Panini: A Study of the Cultural Material in the Ashtadhyayi*. Prithvi Prakashan, 1963.

Alföldy, G., "The Crisis of the Third Century as Seen by Contemporaries," *Byzantine Studies* 15 (1974), pp. 89ff.

Anthony, D. W., *The Horse, the Wheel and Language: How Bronze-Age Riders from the Eurasian Steppes Shaped the Modern World*. Princeton, NJ: Princeton University Press, 2010.

Bagley, R., "Anyang Writing and the Origin of the Chinese Writing System," in S. D. Houston, ed., *The First Writing*. Cambridge: Cambridge University Press, 2004, pp. 190ff.

Bajpai, K. D., Indian Numismatic Series, Chapter 6, "Yaudheya Coins – A Critical Study." Abhinav Publications, 2004, pp. 26ff.

Ball, W., *Rome in the East: Transformation of an Empire*. London: Routledge, 2002.

Beckwith, C., *Empires of the Silk Road: A History of Central Asia from the Bronze Age to the Present*. Princeton, NJ: Princeton University Press, 2009.

Begley, V., "Arikamedu Reconsidered," *American Journal of Archaeology* 87, No. 4 (1983), pp. 479ff.

Bellinger, A. R., "Hyspaosines of Charax," *Yale Classical Studies* 8 (1942).

Benjamin, C., *The Yuezhi: Origins, Migration and the Conquest of Northern Bactria*. Silk Roads Studies 14. Turnhout: Brepols, 2007.

"Collective Learning and the Silk Roads," in L. Grinin and A. Korotayev, eds., *Evolution 2015: From Big Bang to Nanorobots*. Volgograd, Russia: Uchitel, 2015, pp. 101–111.

"The Yuezhi," in *The Oxford Research Encyclopedia of Asian History*. New York: Oxford University Press, 2017, at: http://asianhistory.oxfordre.com/view/10.1093/acrefore/9780190277727.001.0001/acrefore-9780190277727-e-49.

Bersenev, A., A. Epimakhov and D. Zdanovich, "The Sintashta Bow of the Bronze Age of the South Trans-Urals, Russia," in M. Mödlinger, M. Uckelmann and S. Matthews, eds., *Bronze Age Warfare: Manufacture and Use of Weaponry*. Oxford: Archaeopress, 2001, pp. 175ff.

Bertrand, A., "The Hydraulic Systems in Turfan (Xinjiang)," *The Silk Road* 8 (2010), pp. 27ff.

Bielenstein, H., *The Restoration of the Han Dynasty*. Stockholm: Elanders Boktryckeri Aktiebolag, 1953.

Bivar, A. D. H., "The Political History of Iran under the Arsacids," in E. Yarshater, ed., *Cambridge History of Iran*, 3.1. Cambridge: Cambridge University Press, 1983.

Blue, L., et al., "New Light on the Nature of Indo-Roman Trade: Roman Period Shipwrecks in the Northern Red Sea," in D. A. Agius et al., eds., *Navigated Spaces, Connected Places*. Oxford, 2012.

Boardman, J., ed., *The Cambridge Ancient History 10: Persia, Greece and the Western Mediterranean*. Cambridge: Cambridge University Press, 1982.

Bongard-Levin, G. M. and B. Y. Stavisky, "Central Asia in the Kushan Period," *Kushan Studies in the USSR (1968 Dushanbe Conference Proceedings)*, pp. 29ff.

Bosworth, A. B., *Conquest and Empire: The Reign of Alexander the Great*. New York: Cambridge University Press, 1988.

Brenchley, R., "The Travels of Paul," at: www.forumancientcoins.com/Articles/the_travels_of_paul.htm.

Brockington, J., "Imperial India," in A. Cotterall, ed., *The Penguin Encyclopaedia of Classical Civilisations*. London: Penguin, 1993, pp. 193–236.

Brossius, M., *The Persians: An Introduction*. London and New York: Routledge, 2006.

Brown, P., "The Diffusion of Manichaeism in the Roman Empire," *Journal of Roman Studies*. Cambridge: Cambridge University Press, 1969.

The World of Late Antiquity AD 150–750. London: Thames and Hudson,1971.

Buckley, P. E., *The Cambridge Illustrated History of China*. Cambridge: Cambridge University Press, 1996.

Buswell, R. E., Jr. and D. S. Lopez Jr., eds., "An Shigao," *The Princeton Dictionary of Buddhism*. Princeton, NJ: Princeton University Press, 2014.

Cary, M., "Maes, Qui et Titianus," *The Classical Quarterly*, New Series, **6**.3/4 (July–October 1956), pp. 130ff.

Chamoux, F., *Hellenistic Civilization*. Oxford: Wiley/Blackwell, 2002.

Chang, C. S., "War and Peace with the Hsiungnu in Early Han China," in *Essays in Commemoration of the Eightieth Birthday of Professor T'ao Hsi-sheng*. Ann Arbor: University of Michigan Press, 1979, p. 684.

The Rise of the Chinese Empire, Volume 1: Nation, State and Imperialism in Early China ca. 1600 BC–AD 8. Ann Arbor: University of Michigan Press, 2007.

Chang, K. C., *The Archaeology of Ancient China*, 4th edn. New Haven, CT, and London: Yale University Press, 1986.

Chang, K. C. and X. Pingfang, eds., *The Formation of Chinese Civilization: An Archaeological Perspective*. New Haven, CT: Yale University Press, 2005.

Charlesworth, M., *Trade Routes and Commerce in the Roman Empire*. Cambridge: Cambridge University Press, 1924.

Chen, Z., *Juyan Hanjian Yanjiu* [*Study of Documents on Wooden Slips from Juyan Gate*]. Tianjin: Gujichubanshe, 1986.

Christian, D., *A History of Russia, Central Asia and Mongolia vol. I. Inner Eurasia from Prehistory to the Mongol Empire*. Oxford: Blackwell, 1998.

"Silk Roads or Steppe Roads? The Silk Roads in World History," *Journal of World History* 11, No. 1 (2000).

Christian, D., C. Brown and C. Benjamin, *Big History: Between Nothing and Everything*. New York: McGraw Hill, 2014.

Cosmas Indicopleustes, *Christian Topography: The Christian Topography of Cosmas, an Egyptian Monk*. J. W. McCrindle, trans. New York: Burt Franklin, 1887.

Clunas, C. and J. Harrison-Hall, eds., *Ming: 50 Years that Changed China*. London: British Museum Exhibition Catalogue, 2014.

Cobb, M. A., "Balancing the Trade: Roman Cargo Shipments to India," *Oxford Journal of Archaeology* 34, No. 2 (2015), pp. 193ff.

Colledge, M. A. R., *The Parthians*. New York: Frederick A. Praeger, 1967.

Cribb, J., "The Sino-Kharosthi Coins of Khotan," *Numismatic Chronicle* 144 (7th Series 1984), pp. 128–152.

"The Early Kushan Kings: New Evidence for Chronology. Evidence from the Rabatak Inscription of Kanishka I," in M. Alram and D. Klimburg-Salter, eds., *Coins, Art and Chronology: Essays on the Pre-Islamic History of the Indo-Iranian Borderlands*. Vienna: Verlag der österreichischen Akademie der Wissenschaften, 1999, pp. 177ff.

Cunningham, A., "Coins of the Kushans, or Great Yue-Ti," *Numismatic Chronicle* 12 (3rd Series, 1893).

Curtis, J. and N. Tallis, eds., *Forgotten Empire: The World of Ancient Persia*. Berkeley and Los Angeles: University of California Press, 2005.

Curtis, V. S. and S. Stewart, *The Age of the Parthians: The Ideas of Iran*, 2. London and New York: I. B. Tauris & Co. Ltd., in association with the London Middle East Institute at SOAS and the British Museum, 2007.

Cyprian, *De Mortalitate*, trans. E. Wallis, 1885. Online at Christian Classics Ethereal Library.

Dandamaev, M. A., *A Political History of the Persian Empire*. Leiden: Brill Publishing, 1989.

Daryae, T., *Sasanian Persia: The Rise and Fall of an Empire*. London: I. B. Tauris, 2013.

"Western and Central Eurasia," in C. Benjamin, ed., *Cambridge History of the World Vol IV*. Cambridge: Cambridge University Press, 2015, pp. 271–299.

Davis, B., "Timeline of the Development of the Horse," *Sino-Platonic Papers* 177, August 2007.

De Crespigny, R., *A Biographical Dictionary of Later Han to the Three Kingdoms (23–220 AD)*. Leiden: Brill, 2007.

De la Vaissière, E., *Sogdian Traders. A History*. trans. J. Ward, Handbook of Oriental Studies, vol. 10. Leiden: Brill, 2005.

Debevoise, N. C., *A Political History of Parthia*. Chicago: University of Chicago, 1938.

Demieville, P., "Philosophy and Religion from Han to Sui," in D. Twitchett and M. Loewe, eds., *Cambridge History of China: Volume I. The Ch'in and Han Empires, 221 BC–AD 220*. Cambridge: Cambridge University Press, 1986.

Den Boer, W., *Some Minor Roman Historians*. Leiden: Brill, 1972.

Di Cosmo, N., *Ancient China and Its Enemies: The Rise of Nomadic Power in East Asian History*. Cambridge: Cambridge University Press, 2002.

Dirven, L., *The Palmyrenes of Dura Europos: A Study of Religious Interaction in Roman Syria*. Leiden: Brill, 1999.

Drews, R., *Early Riders: The Beginning of Mounted Warriors in Asia and Europe*. New York and London: Routledge, Taylor and Francis Group, 2004.

Ebrey, P. B., *Cambridge Illustrated History of China*. Cambridge: Cambridge University Press, 1996. Reprint 2000.

Elton, H., *Frontiers of the Roman Empire*. London: Routledge 2013.

Erdkamp, P., "Agriculture, Unemployment and the Cost of Rural Labor in the Roman World," *Classical Quarterly* 49, No. 2 (1999), pp. 565ff.

Errington, E., J. Cribb and M. Claringbull, eds., *The Crossroads of Asia: Transformation in Image and Symbol in the Art of Ancient Afghanistan and Pakistan*. London: The Ancient India and Iran Trust, 1992.

Falk, H., "The Yuga of Sphujiddhvaja and the Era of the Kusanas," *Silk Roads Art and Archaeology* VII (2001), pp 121ff.

ed., *Kushan Histories: Literary Sources and Selected Papers from a Symposium at Berlin, December 5 to 7, 2013*. Bremen: Hempen Verlag, 2016.

Farrokh, K., *Shadows in the Desert: Ancient Persia at War*. Oxford: Osprey Publishing, 2007.

Feng, Y., *A Short History of Chinese Philosophy*, trans. Derk Bodde, New York: The Free Press, 1966.

Fisher, G., *Between Empires: Arabs, Romans, and Sasanians in Late Antiquity*. Oxford: Oxford University Press, 2011.

Fitzpatrick, M. P., "Provincializing Rome: The Indian Ocean Trade Network and Roman Imperialism," *Journal of World History* 22, No. 1 (March 2011).

Francfort, H.-P., "Les Nomades Installes dans La Bactriane: Nouvelles Decouvertes," *Comptes rendus de l'Academie des Inscriptions et Belles-Lettres* 4 (November–December 2013), pp. 1544ff.

Frank, A. G. and D. K. Gills, eds., *The World System: Five Hundred Years or Five Thousand?* New York: Routledge, 1992.

Frye, R. N., *The Heritage of Persia: The Pre-Islamic History of One of the World's Great Civilizations*. New York: World Publishing Company, 1963. Reprinted by Mazda Publishers, 2004.

"The Sassanians," in I. Eiddon and S. Edwards, eds., *The Cambridge Ancient History XII – The Crisis of Empire*. Cambridge: Cambridge University Press, 2005.

Gale, M., ed. and trans., *Discourses on Salt and Iron*. Leiden: E. J. Brill, 1931.

Garmsey, P., *Famine and Food Supply in the Greco-Roman World: Response to Rise and Crisis*. Cambridge: Cambridge University Press, 1988.

Garthwaite, G. R., *The Persians*. Oxford and Carlton: Blackwell Publishing Ltd., 2005.

Gawlikowski, M., *Palmyra and Its Caravan Trade*, "annales archéologiques arabes syriens," XLii: *Palmyra and the Silk Road*, 1996, pp. 139ff.

Ghirshman, R., *Bégram: Recherches archéologiques et historiques sur les Kouchans*. Mémoires de la Délégation Archéologique Française en Afghanistan 12. Mémoires de l'Institut Français d'Archéologie Orientale du Caire 79. Cairo, 1946.

Ghosh, A., *A Guide to Nalanda*, 5th edn. New Delhi: The Archaeological Survey of India, 1965.

Gibbon, E., *Decline and Fall of the Roman Empire, Vol. I*, chapter 1, part 1, 1776.

Gimbutas, M., "Proto-Indo-European Culture," in G. Cardona et.al., *Indo-European and Indo-Europeans: Papers Presented at the Third Indo-European Conference at the University of Pennsylvania*. Philadelphia: University of Pennsylvania, 1970, pp. 155ff.

Glover, I. C. and B. Bellina, "Ban Don Ta Phet and Khao Sam Kaeo: The Earliest Indian Contacts Re-assessed," in P. Manguin, A. Mani and G. Wade, eds., *Early Interactions between South and Southeast Asia*. Singapore: Institute of Southeast Asian Studies, 2011, pp. 19ff.

Gobl, R., *System und Chronologie der Münzprägung des Kušānreiches*. Wien: Verlag der Österreichischen Akademie der Wissenschaften, 1984.

Goldsworthy, A., *The Punic Wars*. London: Cassell and Co., 2000.

Graff, D. A., *Medieval Chinese Warfare, 300–900*. London: Routledge, 2002.

Green, P., *The Greco-Persian Wars*. Berkeley and Los Angeles: University of California Press, 1998.

Alexander the Great and the Hellenistic Age. London: Phoenix, 2007.

Grenet, F., "Regional Interaction in Central Asia and North-West India in the Kidarite and Hephthalite Period," in N. Sims-Williams, ed., *Indo-Iranian Languages and Peoples (Proceedings of the British Academy)*. London, 2002, pp. 203ff.

Grousset, R., *The Empire of the Steppes*. New Brunswick, NJ: Rutgers University Press, 1970.

Harmatta, J., "Languages and Literature in the Kushan Empire," in J. Harmatta, ed., *History of Civilizations of Central Asia*, vol. 2. Paris, 1994, pp. 417ff.

Harper, K., "Pandemics and Passages to Late Antiquity: Rethinking the Plague of c.249–70 Described by Cyprian," *Journal of Roman Archaeology* 28 (2015), pp. 223ff.

Herbermann, C., ed., "St. Gregory of Neocaesarea," *Catholic Encyclopedia 7*. New York: Robert Appletone Company, 1910.

Hill, J., *Through the Jade Gate to Rome: A Study of the Silk Roads during the Later Han Dynasty, 1st to 2nd Centuries CE*, Charlestown: BookSurge, 2009.

The Hindu, "Tamil-Brahmi Inscription on Pottery Found in Thailand," Chennai, India, July 16, 2006.

The Hindu, "Tamil-Brahmi Script in Egypt," Chennai, India, November 21, 2007.

Holcombe, C., "East Asia," in C. Benjamin, ed., *Cambridge History of the World*. Cambridge: Cambridge University Press, 2015, pp. 407–434.

Hourani, G. F., *Arab Seafaring in the Indian Ocean in Ancient and Early Medieval Times*. Princeton, NJ: Princeton University Press, 1995.

Howgego, C., "The Supply and Use of Money in the Roman World, 200 BC–AD 300," *Journal of Roman Studies* 82 (1992).

Huang, Q., *Guangdong haishang Sichou zhilu shi* [*The Maritime Silk Road in Guangdong's History*]. Guangzhou: Guangdong jingji chubanshe, 2003.

Hulsewe, A. F. P. and M. A. N. Loewe, *China in Central Asia: The Early Stage: 125 B.C.–A.D. 23*. An Annotated Translation of Chapters 61 and 96 of the History of the Former Han Dynasty. Leiden: Brill, 1979.

International Hydrographic Organization at www.iho.int/srv1/index.php?lang=en.

Ishjamts, N., "Nomads in Eastern Central Asia," in J. Harmatta, ed., *History of Civilizations of Central Asia*, vol. II. Paris: UNESCO, 1994.

Ispahani, M. Z., *Roads and Rivals: The Political Uses of Access in the Borderlands of Asia*. Ithaca, NY: Cornell University Press, 1989.

Jacobsen, E., "Burial Ritual, Gender and Status in South Siberia in the late Bronze–Early Iron Age," *Papers on Inner Asia*, No. 7. Bloomington: Indiana University Press, 1987.

Jarring, G., "The Toponym Takla-makan," *Turkic Languages* 1 (1997), pp. 227ff.

Jennings, J., *Globalizations and the Ancient World*. Cambridge: Cambridge University Press, 2011.

Johnson, D. A., *Lost Churches on the Silk Roads*. USA: New Sinai Press, 2014.

Jongeward, D., *Buddhist Art of Pakistan and Afghanistan: The Royal Ontario Museum Collection of Gandhara Sculpture*. Toronto: University of Toronto, Center for South Asian Studies, 2003.

Kaul, S., "South Asia," in C. Benjamin, ed., *Cambridge History of the World Vol. 4: A World with States, Empires, and Networks, 1200 BCE–900 CE*. Cambridge: Cambridge University Press, 2015, pp. 480ff.

Keightley, D. N., "The Shang: China's First Historical Dynasty," in M. Loewe and E. L. Shaughnessy, eds., *The Cambridge History of Ancient China: From the Origins of Civilization to 221 BC*. Cambridge: Cambridge University Press, 1999.

Kennedy, D., "Parthia and Rome: Eastern Perspectives," in *The Roman Army in the East*. Ann Arbor, MI: Cushing Malloy Inc., *Journal of Roman Archaeology*: Supplementary Series Number 18, 1996.

Krader, L., "The Ecology of Nomadic Pastoralism," *International Social Science Journal* 11 (1959).

Krishnakumar, R., "South Indians in Roman Egypt?" *Frontline* 27, No. 8 (April 2010).

Kulke, H., *A History of India*. London: Routledge, 2004.

Lach, D. F., *Asia in the Making of Europe: The Century of Discovery. Book 1*. Chicago: University of Chicago Press, 1994.

Lerner, J., "Ptolemy and the Silk Road from Baktra Basileion to Sera Metropolis," *East and West* 48, No. 1–2 (1998), pp. 9ff.

"Review of E. V. Rtveladze's The Great Indian Road: India-Central Asia-Transcaucasia," *Anabasis* 5 (2014), pp. 209ff.

Levine, M., "The Origins of Horse Husbandry on the Eurasian Steppe," in M. Levine, Y. Rassamakin, A. Kislenko and N. Tatarintseva, eds., *Late Prehistoric Exploitation of the Eurasian Steppe*. Cambridge: McDonald Institute for Archaeological Research, 1999, pp. 5–58.

Lewis, M. E., *The Early Chinese Empire: Qin and Han*. Cambridge, MA: Belknap Press of Harvard University Press, 2007.

Li, Feng, *Early China: A Social and Cultural History*. Cambridge: Cambridge University Press, 2013.

Li, Liu, *The Chinese Neolithic: Trajectories to Early States*. Cambridge: Cambridge University Press, 2004.

"Academic Freedom, Political Correctness, and Early Civilization in Chinese Archaeology: The Debate on Xia–Erlitou Relations," *Antiquity* 83 (2009), pp. 831ff.

Li, Mian, commentator, *Guan Zhong, Guanzi Jinzhu Jinyi*, 2 vols. Taipei: Taiwan Commercial Press, 1988.

Lieu, S. N. C., *Manichaeism in the Later Roman Empire and Medieval China*, 2nd edn. Tubingen: J. C. B. Mohr (Paul Siebeck), 1992.

Lindner, R., "What Was a Nomadic Tribe?," *Comparative Studies in Society and History* 24 (1982), pp. 689ff.

Linduff, K. M., "Zhukaigou, Steppe Culture and the Rise of Chinese Civilization," *Antiquity* 69 (1995), pp. 133ff.

Littman, R. J. and M. L. Littman, "Galen and the Antonine Plague," *The American Journal of Philology* 94, No. 3 (Autumn 1983), pp. 243ff.

Liu, X., *Ancient India and Ancient China: Trade and Religious Exchanges AD 1–600* (New Delhi: Vicas, 1988).

"Exchanges within the Silk Roads World System," in C. Benjamin, ed., *Cambridge History of the World Vol. IV*. Cambridge: Cambridge University Press, 2015, pp. 457–479.

Liu, Y., *Origins of Chinese Law: Penal and Administrative Law in Its Early Development*. Hong Kong: Oxford University Press, 1998.

Loewe, M., *The Government of the Qin and Han Empires 221 BCE–220 CE*. Indianapolis, IN, and Cambridge: Hackett Publishing Company, Inc., 2006.

Lu, Y., *Narrative and Historicity in the Buddhist Biographies of Early Medieval China: The Case of Kumarajiva*, Asia Major, Third Series, 17, No. 2, pp. 1ff.

MacFadden, B. J., *Fossil Horses: Systematics, Paleobiology, and Evolution of the Family Equidae*. Cambridge: Cambridge University Press, 1994.

Mairs, R., "Glassware from Roman Egypt at Begram (Afghanistan) and the Red Sea Trade," *British Museum Studies in Ancient Egypt and Sudan* 18 (2012), pp. 61–74.

Mallory, J. P., *In Search of the Indo-Europeans*. London: Thames and Hudson, 1989.

"Dereivka," *Encyclopedia of Indo-European Culture*. Chicago: Fitzroy Dearborn, 1997, pp. 156–157.

Mallory, J. P. and V. H. Mair, *The Tarim Mummies: Ancient China and the Mystery of the Earliest Peoples from the West*. London: Thames and Hudson, 2000.

Marshall, J. H., *The Buddhist Art of Gandhara*. Cambridge: Cambridge University Press, 1960.

May, T., "Pastoral Nomads," in C. Benjamin, ed., *The Cambridge World History Vol. IV*. Cambridge: Cambridge University Press, 2015, pp. 235–270.

McLaughlin, R., *Rome and the Distant East: Trade Routes to the Ancient Lands of Arabia, India and China*. London: Continuum, 2010.

The Roman Empire and the Indian Ocean: The Ancient World Economy and the Kingdoms of Africa, Arabia and India. Yorkshire: Pen and Sword Military, 2014.

McNeill, J. and W. McNeill, *The Human Web: A Bird's-Eye View of World History*. New York: W. W. Norton and Company, 2003.

Mehendale, S., "Begram: Along Ancient Central Asian and Indian Trade Routes," *Cahiers d'Asia centrale* 1 (1996), pp. 47ff.

Millar, F., "Caravan Cities: The Roman Near East and Long-Distance Trade by Land," *Bulletin of the Institute of Classical Studies. Supplement* No. 71. Modus Operandi: Essay in Honor of Geoffrey Rickman. Hoboken, NJ: Wiley, 1998a, pp. 119ff.

"Looking East from the Classical World: Colonialism, Culture, and Trade from Alexander the Great to Shapur I," *International History Review* 20, No. 3 (1998b), pp. 507ff.

Moss, H. St. L. B., *The Birth of the Middle Ages 395–814*. Oxford: Oxford University Press, 1935.

Narain, A. K., "Indo-Europeans in Inner Asia," in D. Sinor, ed., *The Cambridge History of Inner Asia*. Cambridge: Cambridge University Press, 1990, reprinted 1994, pp. 151ff.

The Tokharians. Shillong, India: North Eastern Hill University Press, 2000.

National Geographic, "Bactrian Camel," at: www.nationalgeographic.com/animals/mammals/b/bactrian-camel/.

Needham, J., *Science and Civilization in China: Volume 1, Introductory Orientations*. London: Syndics of the Cambridge University Press, 1972.

Nehru, L., "Khalchayan Revisited," in *Silk Roads Art and Archaeology* 6 (1999/2000), pp. 216ff.

Nishijima, S., "The Economic and Social History of Former Han," in D. Twitchett and M. Loewe, eds., *Cambridge History of China: Volume I – The Ch'in and Han Empires, 221 BC–AD 220*. Cambridge: Cambridge University Press, 1986, pp. 545ff.

Nodleman, S. A., "A Preliminary History of Characene," *Berytus* 13, 1960.

Okladnikov, A. P., "Inner Asia at the Dawn of History," in D. Sinor, ed., *The Cambridge History of Early Inner Asia*. Cambridge: Cambridge University Press, 1990, reprint. 1994, pp. 79ff.

Olbrycht, M.J., "Parthia and Nomads of Central Asia: Elements of Steppe Origin in the Social and Military Developments of Arsacid Iran," in I. Schneider, ed., Mitteilungen des SFB "Differenz und Integration," 5, Halle: Orientwissenchaft, 2003, pp. 69–109.

"Archaeological Discoveries at Tillya-Tepe and Parthia's Relationship with Bactria," in F. Serra, ed., *Parthica. Incontri di Culture nel Mondo Antico* 18 (2016).

Olsen, K., *Dress and the Roman Woman: Self-Presentation and Society*. New York: Routledge 2008.

Pankenier, D. W., "The Cosmo-Political Background of Heaven's Mandate," *Early China* 20 (1995), pp. 121–176.

Pearce, S., A. Spiro and P. Buckley, eds., *Culture and Power in the Reconstitution of the Chinese Realm 200–600*. Cambridge, MA: Harvard University Press, 2001.

Peters, H., "Tattooed Faces and Stilt Houses: Who Were the Ancient Yue?" *Sino-Platonic Papers* 17 (April 1990), pp. 1ff.

Piankov, I., "Maes Titianus, Ptolemy and the 'Stone Tower' on the Great Silk Road," *The Silk Road* 13 (2015), pp. 60ff.

Piggott, S., *The Earliest Wheeled Transport*. London: Thames and Hudson, 1983.

Portal, J., ed., *The First Emperor: China's Terracotta Army*. Cambridge, MA: Harvard University Press, 2006.

Pospelov, E. M., *Geograficheskiye nazvaniya mira*. Moscow: Orrialdea, 1998.

Potter, D. S., *The Roman Empire at Bay: AD 180–395*. London: Routledge, 2004.

Potter, L. G., *The Persian Gulf in History*. London: Palgrave Macmillan, 2009.

Price, M., *Coins: An Illustrated Survey*. London: Trustees of the British Museum, 1980.

Puganchenkova, G. A. and A. Khakimov, *The Art of Central Asia*. London: Aurora Art Publishers, 1988.

Pulleyblank, E. G., "The Chinese and Their Neighbours in Prehistoric and Early Historic Times," in D. N., Keightley, ed., *The Origins of Chinese Civilization*. Berkeley and Los Angeles: University of California Press, 1983, pp. 411–466.

Puri, B. N., *India under the Kushans*. Delhi: Bharatiya Bidya Bhavan, 1965.

"The Kushans," in J. Harmatta, ed., *History of Civilizations of Central Asia*, vol. 2. Paris: UNESCO, 1994, pp. 239–255.

Queen, S. H., *From Chronicle to Canon: The Hermeneutics of the Spring and Autumn Annals According to Tung Chung-shu*. Cambridge: Cambridge University Press, 1996.

Rao, S. R. and A. S. Gaur, "Excavations at Bet Dwarka," *Marine Archaeology* 3. Goa: Marine Archaeological Center, July 1992, pp. 42ff.

Raschke, M. G., "New Studies in Roman Commerce with the East," *Aufstieg und Niedergang der Römischen Welt* 9, No. 2 (1978), pp. 604ff.

Rathbone, D., "The Muziris Papyrus: Financing Roman Trade with India," in S. Abd-el-Ghani and W. A. Farag, eds., *Alexandrian Studies in Honor of Mostafa el Abbadi*. Alexandria, 2000, pp. 39ff.

Ray, H. B., *The Archaeology of Seafaring in Ancient South Asia*, Cambridge World Archaeology. Cambridge: Cambridge University Press, 2003.

Rezakhani, K., "The Road That Never Was: The Silk Road and Trans-Eurasian Exchange," *Project Muse* 30, No. 3 (2010), pp. 420ff.

Rossabi, M., "All the Khan's Horses," *Natural History*, October 1994.

Rtveladze, E. V., "Kampyr-tepe: Structures, Written Documents and Coins," *Bulletin of the Asia Institute*, No. 8 (Boston 1994/1995), pp. 141ff.

"The Great Indian Road: India-Central Asia-Transcaucasia," *Anabasis* 1 (2010), pp. 80ff.

Rudenko, D. I. and L. M. Gumilev, "Archaeological Studies of P. K. Kozlov from Standpoint of Historical Geography," *Communications of the All-Union Geographical Society*, No. 3, 1966.

Sales, J-F., "The Periplus of the Erythraean Sea and the Arab-Persian Gulf," *Topoi* 3, No. 2 (1993).

Schinz, A., *The Magic Square: Cities in Ancient China*, Edition Axel Menges, 1996.

Schlumberger, D., "The Excavations at Surkh Kotal and the Problem of Hellenism in Bactria and India." Paris: Albert Reckitt Archaeological Lecture, 1961.

Schoff, W. H., *The Periplus of the Erythrian Sea: Travel and Trade in the Indian Ocean by a Merchant of the First Century*. New York: Longmans, Green and Co., 1912.

Translation and Commentary, *Parthian Stations by Isidorus of Charax*, London, 1914. See http://parthia.com/doc/parthian_stations.htm#PARTHIAN_STATIONS.

Seland, E. H., "Ancient Afghanistan and the Indian Ocean: Maritime Links of the Kushan Empire ca 50–200 CE," *Journal of Indian Ocean Archaeology*, No. 9 (2013), pp. 66ff.

Selbitchka, A., *Prestigegüter entlang der Seidenstraße? Archäologische Untersuchungen zu Chinas Beziehungen zu Kulturen des Tarimbeckens vom zweiten bis frühen fünften Jahrhundert nach Christus*. Wiesbaden: Harrassowitz, 2012, vol. 1.

The Seventh Season Pattanam Excavation – 2013. Kerala Council for Historical Research.

Shayegan, M. R., *Arsacids and Sasanians: Political Ideology in Post-Hellenistic and Late Antique Persia*. Cambridge: Cambridge University Press, 2011.

Sherratt, A., "Plough and Pastoralism: Aspects of the Secondary Products Revolution," in I. Hodder, G. Isaac and N. Hammond, eds., *Patterns of the Past*. Cambridge: Cambridge University Press, 1981, pp. 261ff.

Shilov, V. P., "The Origins of Migration and Animal Husbandry in the Steppes of Eastern Europe," in J. Clutton-Brock, ed., *The Walking Larder: Patterns of Domestication, Pastoralism, and Predation*. London: One World Archaeology, 1989.

Shishlina, N. I., "O slozhnom luke srubnoikul'tury," in S. V. Studzitzkaya, ed., *Problemyarheologii Evrazii. Trudy Gosudarstven-nogo istoricheskogo muzeya*, Vyp. 74. Moscow: Gosudarstvennyi istoricheskii mu-zei, 1990, pp. 23ff.

Sidebotham, S. E., Sidebotham, S. E., Roman Economic Policy in the Erythra Thalassa 30 B.C.–A.D. 217 (Mnemosyne Suppl. XCI). Leiden: E. J. Brill, 1986.

Berenike and the Ancient Maritime Spice Route. Berkeley and Los Angeles: University of California Press, 2011.

Sinor, D., "The Establishment and Dissolution of the Türk Empire," in D. Sinor, ed., *The Cambridge History of Inner Asia*. Cambridge: Cambridge University Press, 1994, pp. 299ff.

Sima Qian, *Shi Ji*, trans. B. Watson. *Records of the Grand Historian by Sima Qian – Han Dynasty II*, revised edn. New York: Columbia University Press, 1993.

Sims-Williams, N., *New Light on Ancient Afghanistan. The Decipherment of Bactrian*. London: School of Oriental and African Studies, 1997.

Sims-Williams, N. and J. Cribb, "A New Inscription of Kanishka the Great," *Silk Roads Art and Archaeology* 4 (1995/1996), pp. 75ff.

Souza, P., *The Greek and Persian Wars 499–386 BC*. Osprey Publishing, 2003.

Stein, A., *On Ancient Central Asian Tracks: Brief Narrative of Three Expeditions in Innermost Asia and North Western China*. Chicago: University of Chicago Press, 1933.

Suresh, S., *Symbols of Trade: Roman and Pseudo-Roman Objects Found in India*. New Delhi: Manohar, 2004.

Tanabe, K., ed., *Silk Road Coins. The Hirayama Collection*. Kamakura: The Institute of Silk Road Studies, 1993, 44, nos. 125, 126 and 127.

Tansen Sen, "Early China and the Indian Ocean Network," in P. de Souza and P. Arnaud, eds., *The Sea in History: The Ancient World*. Suffolk: Boydell and Brewer, 2017, pp. 536ff.

Tarling, N., ed., *The Cambridge History of Southeast Asia, Vol. 1, From Early Times to c. 1800*. Cambridge: Cambridge University Press, 1993.

Tarn, W. W. *The Greeks in Bactria and India*. Cambridge: Cambridge University Press, 1938, 2nd edn., 1951.

Teggart, F. J., *Rome and China: A Study of Correlations in Historical Events*. Berkeley: University of California Press, 1939.

Temin, P., "Financial Intermediaries in the Early Roman Empire," *Journal of Economic History* 64 (2004).

Thorp, R., *China in the Early Bronze Age: Shang Civilization*. Philadelphia: University of Pennsylvania Press, 2006.

Tolstov, S. P. and B. V. Andrianov, "Novie materiali po istorii razvitia Khorezm," *Isnt Ethnografii Kratkiie Soobschenia* 26 (1957).

Torday, L., *Mounted Archers: The Beginnings of Central Asian History*. Seattle: University of Washington Press, 1978.

Tosi, M., "Theoretical Considerations on the Origin of Pastoral Nomadism," in G. Seaman, ed., *Foundations of Empire. Archaeology and Art of the Eurasian Steppes*. Los Angeles, CA, 1992, pp. 27ff.

Vainker, S., *Chinese Silk: A Cultural History*. New York: Rutgers University Press, 2004.

Vogel, H. U. and S. Hieronymus, "Cowry Trade and Its Role in the Economy of Yunnan from the Ninth to the Mid-Seventeenth Century, Part 1," *Journal of the Economic and Social History of the Orient* 36, No. 3 (1993), pp. 211–152.

Von Redden, S., "Global Economic History," in C. Benjamin, ed., *Cambridge History of the World Vol. IV*. Cambridge: Cambridge University Press, 2015, pp. 29–54.

Wang, T., "Parthia in China: A Re-examination of the Historical Records," in V. S. Curtis and S. Stewart, eds., *The Age of the Parthians: The Ideas of Iran*, 2. London and New York: I. B. Tauris & Co. Ltd, in association with the London Middle East Institute at SOAS and the British Museum, 2007, pp. 87–104.

Warmuth, V., et al., "Reconstructing the Origin and Spread of Horse Domestication in the Eurasian Steppe," *Proceedings from the National Academy of Sciences* (PNAS) 109, No. 21 (2012), pp. 8202ff.

Waugh, D., "Richthofen's 'Silk Roads': Towards the Archaeology of a Concept," *The Silk Road* 5, No. 1 (Summer 2007), pp. 1ff.

Whitehouse, D., "Begram, the *Periplus* and Gandharan Art," *Journal of Roman Archaeology* 2 (1989), pp. 93–100.

Wick, A., *The Red Sea: In Search of Lost Space*. Los Angeles: University of California Press, 2016.

Williams, T., *The Silk Roads: An ICOMOS Thematic Study*. Charenton-le-Pont: International Council of Monuments and Sites, 2014.

Wilson, A., *The Cambridge Companion to the Roman Economy*. Cambridge: Cambridge University Press, 2012.

Xinzhong, Y., "Regional Study: Confucianism and the State," in C. Benjamin, ed., *Cambridge History of the World Vol. IV*. Cambridge: Cambridge University Press, 2015, pp. 435ff.

Xiong, Z., "The Hepu Han Tombs and the Maritime Silk Road of the Han Dynasty," *Antiquity* 88 (2014), pp. 1229ff.

Yablonsky, L. T., "Some Ethnogenetical Hypotheses," in J. Davis-Kimball, V. A. Bashilov and L. T. Yablonsky, eds., *Nomads of the Eurasian Steppes in the Early Iron Age*. Berkeley: University of California Press, 1995, pp. 241ff.

Yang, B., "Horses, Silver, and Cowries: Yunnan in Global Perspective," *Journal of World History* 15, No. 3 (2004), pp. 281ff.

Yates, R. D. S., "State Control of Bureaucrats under the Qin: Techniques and Procedures," *Early China* 20 (1995).

Yu, Y.-S., "Han Foreign Relations," in D. Twitchett and M. Loewe, eds., *The Cambridge History of China Volume 1: The Ch'in and Han Empires 221 BC – AD 220*. Cambridge: Cambridge University Press, 1986.

"Zoroastrianism: Historical Review up to the Arab Conquests," *Iranica Online*, www.iranicaonline.org/articles/zoroastrianism-i-historical-review.

Zuchowska, M., "From China to Palmyra: The Value of Silk," *Swiatowit* 11 (52) A (2013).

"Roman Textiles in the Hou Han Shu: A 5th Century Chinese Vision versus Roman Reality," *Anabasis: studia classica et orientalia* 6 (2015), pp. 216ff.

Zurcher, E., "The Yueh-chih and Kanishka in the Chinese Sources," in A. L. Basham, ed., *Papers on the Date of Kanishka*. Leiden: Brill, 1968, pp. 346ff.

The Buddhist Conquest of China: The Spread and Adaptation of Buddhism in Early Medieval China, 3rd edn. Leiden: Brill, 2007.

Zwalf, W., *Catalogue of the Gandharan Sculpture in the British Museum*. London: Trustees of the British Museum, 1996.

Index